Joshua Decter

Art Is a Problem

JRP | RINGIER & LES PRESSES DU RÉEL

Joshua Decter

Art Is a Problem

Selected Criticism, Essays, Interviews, and Curatorial Projects (1986–2012)

Table of Contents

Joshua Decter
Preface as Future Anterior

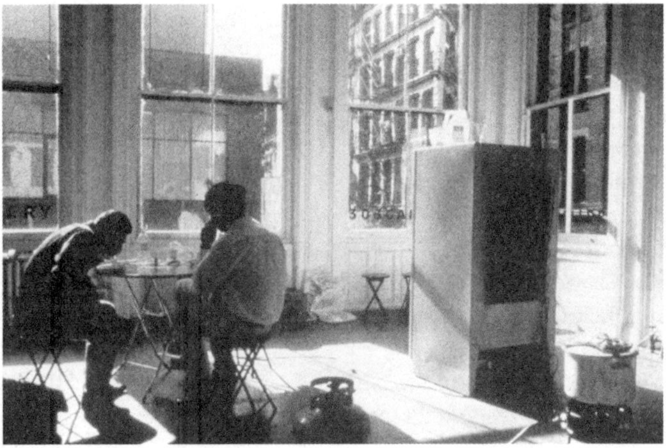

Rirkrit Tiravanija, *untitled 1992 (free)*, 1992

The paradox of sovereignty consists in the fact (that) the sovereign is, at the same time, outside and inside the juridical order.
—Giorgio Agamben, *Homo Sacer: Sovereign Power and Bare Life*, 1998

Oh, make me wanna holler
And throw up both my hands
Yea, it makes me wanna holler
And throw up both my hands
—Marvin Gaye, "Inner City Blues (Make Me Wanna Holler)," 1971, written by Gaye and James Nyx, Jr.

If art is a problem, this book does not claim to be the solution. And if this book creates problems, art may claim to offer remedies. Why title this selection of writings on art, curatorial practice, architecture, cities, and other cultural matters, "Art Is a Problem"? Doesn't this risk marginalizing the book? Or, engendering varying degrees of unease, confusion, fear, and loathing among the very communities and publics that would constitute the readership? Might the title even spur accusations of philistinism? Or, will the title be understood for what it is: a serious yet tongue-in-cheek provocation that invokes the manifold problematics of art? Needless to say, there are bigger problems in the world than art, but one has to start somewhere.

Art may have become a problem only because it is no longer really problematic. Art—however we may choose to define, de-define, re-define, or un-define it—is on the verge of becoming so thoroughly assimilated into or integrated within global social, economic, ideological, and institutional networks that it may no longer be able to pose any problems to those systems. As a result, art seems increasingly insulated from deeply critical questions that would seriously compromise its validity or value. It is also tenable to suggest that this has been art's odd predicament for quite some time. A more difficult question to consider is whether art ever did pose any problems—and what criteria or metric would we use to measure this?

Some would argue that art's assimilation—its distribution into broader networks—allows it to act, so to speak, upon the imaginations of more publics and in increasingly complex, subtle ways than at any other time in recent history. To others, art's ubiquity merely tranquilizes its transformative potential. Sectors of the global contemporary art market may have become economic drivers of employment and wealth, but this does not mitigate the anxiety that comes with acknowledging art's discomfiting paradoxes: it is a creative practice that still can generate meaning beyond itself; a robustly investable class of commodity that reinvents the terms of its own language; and a specialized cultural product that aspires to critical, yet demotic, social and political germaneness.

Yes, there are circumstances in which art has surfaced as a vehicle of dissent, resistance, protest, opposition—seeking to question power and authority, intolerance and repression, and economic and social injustice. The variously termed political, social, critical, interventionist, public, participatory and other "turns" are testimony to ongoing efforts at cultivating a verifiable agency and/or utility for art and artist. Yet, paradoxically, the more tolerant or liberal a society becomes, the more art becomes a naturalized, normative element within an environment of unfettered (and perhaps increasingly undifferentiated) creative production. At the same time, we might say that art embodies these self-same contradictions. Art is an aporia. To express it differently: art can only allegorize its indeterminate relationship to itself, and to everything else. Critical writing may have the capacity to cut through the fog of art's ambiguities and shed light on its contradictory place in the world, but such discourse can do nothing to vitiate these contradictions. To some, this is inspiring; for me, it is occasionally exasperating.

Engaging in critical processes—i.e., questioning, pressuring, and troubling things as they appear to be—may temporarily reduce the psychic pain unleashed by the contradictions of art and its global systems, even though it is in no way ameliorative of these conditions. (For better results, take Ibuprofen.) One's survival in this professional (para-professional) field, however, depends upon sublimating this state of affairs, even though it is quite possible to build and maintain a career (as an academic, an artist, or other cultural producer) by generating endless reams of discourse on all of these contradictions, thereby producing further contradictions. Hypocrisy and the engineering of career are not strange bedfellows. Another way to think about critical activity—whether it is expressed through writing, curatorial practice, journal editing, teaching, or organizing a symposium—is that by engaging in some form of it (as a negative dialectics, for instance), we are at the same time putting the best possible face on the reality that criticality (and criticism) is in the wilderness. In order to be critical, we must convince ourselves that our sovereignty as critical thinkers is meaningful and tangible, even while acknowledging that this very sovereignty is the result of precariously occupying a mental space that is at once inside and outside power. We find creative, even pleasurable, ways to maintain the self-delusion—a suspension of disbelief—that our sovereignty as critical beings is beyond contradiction. It would be hypocrisy not to admit that my criticality is located both outside of and within these contradictions. If anything, this book reflects an ongoing struggle to reconcile the limits of criticality (and criticism) with a continuing desire to imagine that the questioning of things might have some relevance beyond a relatively closed discursive space or community (that is itself constituted both inside and outside power). It is emblematic of the endless circularity of reconciling one's doubt and skepticism with a sense of commitment to art and artists. The kind of thinking that privileges doubt may dwell in a precarious state in relation to various audiences and receptions (academic, non-academic, or other), yet we also understand that skepticism can be fodder for the radical chic mill. Doubt and skepticism are infinitely marketable. It's a truism that criticality and/or criticism is perpetually in crisis, and that dissent can be recuperated for other applications; e.g., dissent as an iPhone app. Yet one may also conceive of doubt as the prerequisite to a commitment to art, artists, and people. Once we work our way through doubt, or at least assuage our skepticism, commitment and engagement may ensue. And so we might consider doubt not as anathema to commitment, but rather as the necessary prerequisite for it. Although this may seem an odd way to commence a book that organizes 25 years of art criticism, writing, curatorial projects, interviews and other activities into seven distinct yet interrelated chapters, I like to think that by acknowledging the limits of criticality (without surrendering to an ethos of post-criticality), an ethical position can still be defended, although this too may be a form of self-delusion. And so one is left in a continuous state of conflict and uncertainty: does any of this activity and production matter? What does "matter" actually mean? Why remain committed? Each time a portal seems to emerge through which to make an exit from this field, I cannot step through it.

Before encountering Baudelaire, Marx, Benjamin, Marcuse, Adorno, Foucault, Greenberg, Steinberg, Krauss, Bürger, or even Barthes, it was the writings of American critic Harold Rosenberg—in particular, his 1972 book, *The De-Definition of Art*—that convinced me to engage with contemporary art. Rosenberg (born 1906, died 1978), is perhaps most associated with the notion of "action painting" in relation to the Abstract Expressionism of the 1950s. Yet it is within his criticism of the late 1960s and early 1970s that we find an effort to scrutinize the contradictions of art and the art world—many of which remain with us today. Rosenberg offered a direct engagement with key issues: the putative death of art, the dematerialization of the art object,

Conceptualism, performance, the art-as-life/life-as-art discourse, participatory art, the relationship of art and politics, the avant-garde and mass culture, art and the academy, among other matters. In "DMZ Vanguardism" Rosenberg argued that although the ideological conditions of negation that were a prerequisite for the making of the historical avant-garde were no longer applicable, the idea of vanguardism (or a "socially reconciled avant-garde," as he puts it) had become a stronger driving force than ever before in the field of contemporary art, because of the need to perpetuate the mythologies of the vanguard's social defiance.[1] He therefore characterized the vanguardism of the late 1960s and early 1970s as a "demilitarized zone": "In sum, while art today is not avant-garde, neither has it been absorbed into the system of mass culture … "[2] He suggested that contemporary art endlessly reconstituted or reproduced an already outmoded logic of crisis that had once belonged to the historical avant-garde period, as a kind of bad faith theatrics. In "Set Out for Clayton" Rosenberg weighed in on the debates concerning art and life, aesthetics and the real, and the democratizing effects of art: "If there is no difference between art and life, there is no difference between the artist and his public. Instead of representing creative mysteries, the artist becomes a group leader. Collective projects, not the cultivation of individuals, are the aim, and it is sufficient that participants are kept cheerfully occupied."[3] For all of the doubts he harbored regarding certain forms of art (as well as certain claims made about art by artists, critics, curators, historians, and others), Rosenberg was more concerned about the deleterious effects of mass culture, having absorbed the lessons of Adorno and Horkheimer's book *The Dialectic of Enlightenment*, and in particular their chapter on the "Culture Industry." And so Rosenberg maintained faith in the notion that art still had the capacity to generate a space for the self-development and self-expression of the individual as a necessary bulwark against broader social homogenization and political repression.

A participant in the quasi-academic milieu of the Whitney Independent Study Program as a Critical and Museum Studies Fellow in the mid-1980s, I endeavored to hone the skills that would enable a critique of art's interrelationship with institutions and power, while at the same time learning how to operate as an institutional curator within those same systems of power; I somewhat naively imagined that it was tenable to construct a discursive space in which new forms of critical interrogation could root out inequities of power, pernicious ideologies, and other societal evils. Yet I harbored doubts.

The transaction wherein a museum offers a platform to an artist for the performance of a critique is not simply an instance of the benevolent institution supporting and protecting artistic expression (the permissions granted by invitation); it also reflects the increasing power of tolerant institutions—and, by extension, the institution's benefactors, constituencies, and publics—to absorb, assimilate, and weather such critiques. During this early period, it was Jean Baudrillard's writings that began to enter my system like a disease (the symptoms of which occasionally return). The alluring pessimism and seductively hypnotic disenfranchisement of art that surfaces in Baudrillard's essay "Gesture and Signature" in the 1972 book *For a Critique of the Political Economy of the Sign*, seemed a powerful antidote to the claims being made about art's transformative capabilities, or its critical powers:

> Modern art wishes to be negative, critical, innovative, and a perpetual surpassing, as well as immediately (or almost) assimilated, accepted, integrated, consumed. One must surrender to the evidence: art no longer contests anything, if it ever did. Revolt is isolated, the malediction "consumed"... Modern art, midway between critical terrorism (ideological) and *de facto* structural integration, is quite exactly an *art of collusion vis*-à-*vis* this contemporary world. It plays with it, and is included in the game. It can parody this world, illustrate it, simulate it, alter it; it never disturbs the order, which is also its own.[4]

At the time, Baudrillard seemed to capture one of art's fundamental problems (or, at the very least, one of my problems with art): that art really did not pose any problems, because as an object of exchange, it embodied and endlessly reproduced the broader economic, social, and cultural logics already embedded in its DNA, so to speak. Contradictorily, however, I endeavored to maintain a sufficient amount of faith that there were art practices capable of problematizing normative social and political conditions—which I often identified with the institutional-critical art of contemporaries and friends such as Mark Dion and Andrea Fraser. My doubts would resurface whenever I observed the increasing compatibility and interdependency between institution and the purveyors of (institutional) critique. I probably expected that when museums invited artists to produce critical interrogations, such commissioned interventions might lead to a fundamental transformation of the power and economic structure of the museum. But it became apparent that institutions were basically outsourcing critique to artists, and though these artists understood the contradictory conditions of their practices, and often played along in sophisticated ways with their so-called complicity, this situation was unnerving.

The first chapter, "Institutional Critique® and its Discontents," reflects this growing ambivalence and anxiety regarding the paradoxes and political double binds generated in relation to institutional critique. Comprised of writings produced from the late 1980s through the mid-1990s, it focuses primarily on the contradictory relations between art, artists, and institutions/museums, examining how authority and power are produced. The chapter commences with an analysis of Michael Asher's 1988 intervention at Artists Space in New York (with a new postscript), and moves to a discussion of Silvia Kolbowski's 1988 interrogation of the Metropolitan Museum of Art in relation to the contextual frame of the art gallery. The 1990 essay, "Decoding the Museum," addresses the practices of Buren, Asher, Broodthaers, Haacke, Dion, Lawler, Fraser, and others, giving them their due, but alluding to the intrinsic contradictions of their practices: "Through historical conventionalization, have the notions and strategies associated with institutional critique blindly perpetuated the fiction of art as socially transformative, or have they replaced that fiction with the necessary double bind of critical complicity and complicit criticality?" In "The Context Has Always Been There" for the 1994 *Kontext Kunst* exhibition in Graz, Austria, I propose that "the challenge to the authority of the cultural institution in this case—and in all others discussed here—remains bound to what I would describe as a *theatrics of resistance*, wherein the museum can be understood as a stage upon which the rites of critical scrutiny are played out before an audience of ... ourselves." A 1990 *Flash Art* magazine interview with the artist Andrea Fraser, and a 1994 discussion with curator Thelma Golden (originally published in *Acme Journal*, which I co-edited/published in the mid-1990s) offer other perspectives on the relationship between art and institutions.

The second chapter, "Aporia (Art as Politics, the Politics of Art)," looks at the endlessly unsolvable contradiction that is art vis-à-vis its broader social and economic contexts. It commences with a 1986 critique of Peter Halley's work in relation to Baudrillard's *For a Critique of the Political Economy of the Sign*. This is followed by "The Administration of Cultural Resistance" (1992), an analysis of notions of art as a mode of political engagement (fairly influenced by Adorno), and examines positions taken by Edward Said, Fredric Jameson, and Hal Foster. I ask,

> How can we begin to evaluate the functional potency of politically engaged art production and art criticism: can these practices transgress the normative institutional boundaries of the cultural vanguard? Inside the frame, all forms of transgression are encouraged and regularly displayed for public scrutiny; high culture is allowed to perennially manufacture its own regime of apparent subversion.

The chapter also includes a version of the 1994 essay, "Stupidity as Destiny: American Idiot Culture as Radical Chic," wherein it is proposed that we reconsider the aesthetics and ethos of stupidity within mainstream culture as a type of vanguard, radical chic in the United States during the 1990s. A more recent analysis entitled "Art and Fictitious Capital" (2009) offers the following speculations:

> the great question of the day: what is the relation between art and fictitious capital? Or, to put it another way, have we reached a point at which, to paraphrase Marx, art ... "is thrown into circulation as capital without any material basis in commodities or productive activity"? Perhaps this has always been

> an element of art's contradictory relationship to value: i.e., it is at once valuable, invaluable, and before and beyond value. It is worthless and worth too much. It is a type of productive, creative labor, yet it is not like any other commodity. It is one type of creative production, commoditized when it enters the system of exchange utilized by the market to establish value, yet already always forged within an ideological system of pecuniary values.

This section of the book also includes reflections on the practices of Emily Jacir, Alfredo Jaar, Yael Bartana, Superflex, Sam Durant, Liam Gillick, and Harun Farocki, wherein I endeavor to scrutinize how these artists attempt to exert symbolic, critical pressures upon various normative systems (history, economy, the political, representation etc.). Overall, these writings reveal traces of Michel Foucault's analysis of institutional power, especially Giorgio Agamben's discussion of Foucault's theory of *political double binds*: "In one of his last writings, Foucault argues that the modern Western state has integrated techniques of subjective individualization with procedures of objective totalization to an unprecedented degree, and he speaks of a real political 'double bind,' constituted by individualization and the simultaneous totalization of structures of modern power (*Dits et écrits*, 4: 229–232)."[5] To me, it seems that art is uniquely capable of expressing this political double bind, and that the "sovereignty" of art is always only partial, contingent upon a structural integration within social orders; this is the aporia of art. In the 2010 essay, "(The) Everywhereness (of Art)," I ask,

> Is art being asked to become more functional (i.e., instrumentalized) by those who expect it to act as an intervention that generates ideologically progressive pressures upon today's political and public spheres so that our societies remain sufficiently democratic, fair, and just? If art disappears into the circuits of the social … if art becomes politics, then everything will truly have become aestheticized. We should be wary of such outcomes. The question is not really which type of art making, per se, is more or less democratic or *freedom-generative* (sometimes the assumption made when

> referring to collective or participatory practices); rather, it is how we analyze culture's interrelationship—on historical terms—with the material and symbolic processes of social, political democratization. For me, this would have to include a reconsideration of Herbert Marcuse's trenchant and disturbing notion of *repressive tolerance*.

The third chapter, "Everything is Social (Platforms, Participations, Publics, Constituencies, Networks, Spaces, Sites, Situations, Collaborations, Cooperations, Conflicts, Interventions ...)," assembles a variety of texts on the social conditions of art—or, art as a social condition. The title itself endeavors to index a discursive space comprised of multiple terms and keywords that have emerged vis-à-vis the ostensibly social turn of art. Commencing with an essay that accompanied Mark Dion's first public art project in 1991—actually, a counter-public art project—sited within the pages of a mainstream newspaper, I examine Walter Benjamin's discussion of the revolutionary potential of the newspaper, and also discuss Dion's *Belize Zoo* project. The 1997 essay, "Elastic Realities: Rirkrit Tiravanija, Lincoln Tobier, Grennan and Sperandio," rethinks the social characteristics of these artists practices. Other texts include an analysis of Gerwald Rockenschaub's meta-architectural remappings of space from 1999, and an account of artist and social activist Rick Lowe's groundbreaking *Project Row Houses* in Houston, Texas, from 2000. "Transitory Agencies and Situational Engagements: The Artist as Public Interlocutor?" from the *Interventions* section of the inSite_05 San Diego/Tijuana *Situational Public* publication in 2006, delves into the framework of this unusual exhibition project, examining how the participating artists responded to the social, political, and economic environment of the US-Mexican border by developing research, project-based works that upended parochial models of site-specificity and public art: "What does it mean for artists, today, to intervene in public, within public space, in relation to distinct publics? *What is public?* And, why should various publics be interested in an exhibition project such as *Interventions*, beyond the relatively insular contingents of cultural intellectuals and producers who have become engaged with the inSite milieu? We enter into these kinds of ruminations, which are not merely rhetorical, to test out the possible reconstitution of the artist's civic role." Related issues also emerge in analyses of recent socially participatory projects by Rirkrit Tiravanija and Paul Ramírez Jonas.

Chapter four, entitled "Convoluted Cities," is comprised of writings on various urban conditions and situations, and addresses art and architectural projects that endeavor to transform our experience and understanding of city-space. A 1990 text discusses Krzysztof Wodiczko's *New York City Tableaux, Tompkins Square*, with a new preface that reframes Wodiczko's project in relation to the broader social-urban context of New York's East Village, and to his *Homeless Vehicle* of that same period. The 1992 "The Fractious Hybrid State (of Things)" offers a self-critical, soul-searching plunge into the contradictions of urban race relations in the United States, in an attempt to understand how economic and social injustices can lead to the kind of extreme discontentment that erupts into the streets. I had just returned from a trip to Los Angeles following the 1992 riots there (triggered by the notorious acquittal of the police officers who brutalized Rodney King), and, drawing upon the writings of Cornel West and Edward Said, I express frustration about the marginal role of art and cultural criticism in relation to these fractious social and economic conditions: "A recent study published in *The New York Times* once again indicates the almost absurd disparity of economic power between the relatively small percentage of wealthy Americans (who continue to control, proportionally, the majority of capital), and the low-income populations (whose opportunity to improve their economic condition has begun to deteriorate); this is a disparity made even more glaring as fortunes and opportunities also decline for the middle class." This section also includes "Communication City," a text produced in 2000 that examines the development of exhibitions that utilize the city as a *cultural laboratory* and *readymade*, in relation to various definitions of public art. "A Strangely *New* New York" from 2002 explores the impact of the 9-11 attacks on lower Manhattan proposes a comparative analysis between the temporary Viewing Platform at Ground Zero and the Rem Koolhaas Prada store in SoHo—with a new 2012 postscript. The chapter concludes with reflections on a recent New Orleans-based project by Marjetica Potrč, as well as a collaborative intervention by Michael Cataldi and Nils Norman that interlaces activism with pedagogy to examine uneven urban development.

The art practices considered in chapter five—"The (Un)De-definition of Art"—embody a desire to rethink the language, definition, identity, and meaning of art in relation to cultures of design, industry, music, and entertainment. The section commences with a critique of Donald Judd's work in 1986, analyzing his practice in relation to philosopher Richard Wollheim's perspective on Minimalism, and Jean Baudrillard's analysis of the structural integration of art (thereby establishing a link to the aforementioned 1980s text on Peter Halley in chapter two). My significant engagement with the work of General Idea during the 1990s is represented by a 1991 interview with AA Bronson, Felix Partz, and Jorge Zontal, and a 1994 essay, "The Theatrics of Dissemination: A General Idea Model." Texts on seminal works by Andrea Zittel, Jorge Pardo, Piotr Uklanski, and Monica Bonvicini from the 1990s and the 2000s reveal what might be characterized as a blending of post-readymade aesthetics with languages of design, architecture, and the codes of popular culture. These practices are emblematic of the paradoxical condition that art finds itself in at the threshold of the symbolic and the real, the pragmatic and the utopian, the accessible and the obscure—and, as artists seek to engineer platforms for the restaging of social relations. Related issues are taken up in the 1997 essay, "Negotiating Convivial Dispersals," which includes a discussion of Lincoln Tobier's limited-range radio stations: "When does an organized social event become analogous to an art activity? When the artist—and the context of the artist's activity—endows the social event with an art condition." A candid and lively discussion with Stephen Prina and Mike Kelley explores interconnections between music, subculture, and art.

"What Do We Want from Exhibitions?" the sixth chapter, begins with a 1992 analysis of documenta IX, "The Desire for documenta," in which I caution—undoubtedly, with Foucault on my mind—that

> it is plausible to suggest that investment in the language and practice of disciplinary expertise

> specialization, particularly in the realm of art history and art criticism, may serve to reproduce the very same relations of power that facilitate the authority of certain dominant cultural institutions and international exhibition platforms (such as documenta, the Whitney Museum's Biennial, The Carnegie International, et al.). To understand critique as a method of developing a framework for the dialogical analysis of specific cultural practices, situations or symptoms (as opposed to mere negation), we must take care not to inadvertently reconfirm the questionable authority granted to us as cultural experts or academic specialists, since this is the same logic of authority exercised by the very individuals and institutions that we seek to not only critically de-construct, but also to challenge the cultural and ideological assumptions of.

This section also includes an analysis of the 1993 *Project Unité* exhibition in Firminy, France; a 2004 statement on the proliferation of curatorial programs and biennials; a playful upbraiding of the biennial model published in the catalogue of the 2008 California Biennial, with a 2012 postscript; and an extensive analysis of the 2008 Prospect.1 exhibition (the inaugural biennial in New Orleans following the devastation of Hurricane Katrina) in relation to the community-based Transforma Projects, entitled "Art and the Cultural Contradictions of Urban Regeneration, Social Justice, and Sustainability: Transforma Projects and Prospect.1 in Post-Katrina New Orleans."

"On the Curatorial Road," the seventh and final chapter, brings together a selection of curatorial projects from 1994 to 2006. What links this sequence of exhibitions is a desire to rethink normative curatorial models, test frameworks of display and exhibition design, propose new interplays between art and other cultural materials, and explore the use of media and interactivity. *Don't Look Now* (1994) at the Thread Waxing Space in New York, featured more than 60 international artists, musicians, and writers who produced works in 35mm slide format regarding the notion of identity as a public *projection*. Within a darkened architectural structure especially designed for the situation, slideworks by participants such as Robert Gober, Liam Gillick,

Renée Green, On Kawara, Martin Kippenberger, Glenn Ligon, Raymond Pettibon, Michelangelo Pistoletto, Stephen Prina, Julia Scher, Sonic Youth, Rirkrit Tiravanija, Lawrence Weiner, and Fred Wilson were projected onto individual screens, generating a frieze of glowing images. *a/drift* (1996), at Bard College's Center for Curatorial Studies Museum, proposed notions of cultural drifting to reflect upon interpenetrations of art, subculture, and popular culture, featuring works (ranging from the 1960s to the 1990s) by more than 90 international artists, filmmakers, and other cultural producers. What was referred to as *non-art* materials gathered from cinema, television, fashion, music, and other sources were displayed within particular zones of the exhibition, and contextualized in relation to arrangements of artworks; an innovative exhibition design amplified the distinctions—and porous interpenetrations—between these various cultural forms. *Screen* at the Friedrich Petzel Gallery (also 1996) proposed interrelationships between painting and television. In addition to works by more than 25 artists, the gallery was equipped with cable TV and a remote control, so that visitors could watch television while also looking at paintings (or vice versa). A video catalogue was produced, comprised of an intermix of images from everyday television and installation shots of the exhibition itself, and a web-specific interactive version of *Screen* was developed with äda web—viewable on the Walker Art Center's website at http://www.adaweb.com/influx/decter/screen.html. That same year, I developed a meta-curatorial project entitled *Cathode Ray Clinic #1* for the alternative space, Apex Art. It featured no artists, just real-time television transmissions. Taking a cue from the fictive Cathode Ray Clinic featured in David Cronenberg's epochal 1983 film *Videodrome*, I conceptualized a television-viewing platform for people suffering from television addiction and/or art fatigue; designed in collaboration with Big Room, the project featured cable television, remote controls, and a seating apparatus. *Transmute*, a 1999 collection-based exhibition at the Museum of Contemporary Art in Chicago, featured interactive programs for the public to manipulate—on virtual terms—the installation of artworks within the museum, and to reconfigure a John Baldessari work from the collection. These virtual curator and virtual artist interactive interfaces (developed with a team of designers and programmers) were made available to the public on kiosks within the museum's bricks-and-mortar space, and on the institution's website, giving visitors and online users an opportunity to intervene with my curatorial authorship—while also opening up the museum to a different sort of public engagement (beyond parochial education programs). *Tele[visions]*, at the Kunsthalle Vienna in 2001, explored the influence of television culture on art, featuring more than 100 artworks contextualized within a special architectural design that transformed the Kunsthalle's space. Expanding upon aspects of all of the aforementioned curatorial projects, *Dark Places* at the Santa Monica Museum of Art in 2006 emerged out of my preoccupation with thinking about cities in terms of psychogeography. This exhibition featured an unusual exhibition design that employed information-based architectural language to generate a display apparatus for the continuous, looped projection of eight distinct visual scripts of digitized works by 76 artists. In this hypermediated environment, viewers encountered a dynamic interpenetration of works that produced a space of simultaneous, collective reception. *Dark Places* was engineered as a riposte to business-as-usual exhibition-making, and—as with the other shows included in this final chapter—a means of problematizing art and curatorial practice.

[1] Harold Rosenberg, "DMZ Vanguardism," *The De-Definition of Art*, The University of Chicago Press, Chicago 1972, p. 219.
[2] Ibid.
[3] Harold Rosenberg, "Set Out for Clayton!," *The De-Definition of Art*, p. 247.
[4] Jean Baudrillard, "Gesture and Signature," *For a Critique of the Political Economy of the Sign*, Telos Press, Ltd., St. Louis 1981, p. 110.
[5] Giorgio Agamben, "Introduction," *Homo Sacer: Sovereign Power and Bare Life*, Stanford University Press, Stanford 1998, p. 5.

John Miller
Introduction

John Miller is an artist, writer, and musician based in New York and Berlin. He is also a Professor of Professional Practice in Barnard College's Art History Department.

This volume of selected essays, interviews, reviews, and curatorial texts, spanning the period 1986–2011, represents a significant part of Joshua Decter's ongoing work as an educator, curator, and critic. The writings form a discourse that engages the interrelationship of these vocations. This discourse is driven largely by a productivist vision of the artwork to the extent that Decter rejects the conventional dichotomy of form and content by which art is presumed to hold meaning like a vessel. Accordingly, he questions contemplative aesthetics and the baggage that goes with it—quality, authorship, connoisseurship, and autonomy. These all reflect the principle of private property. In an age of ever more vigilantly policed intellectual property, for instance, if one owns an art object, does one also own what it signifies? Decter instead sees the artwork from a public perspective and consistently probes its function as a collective representation, its placement in a cultural continuum, and the social relations organized around it.

From fall 1984 through spring 1985, Decter was a Helena Rubenstein Fellow in Museum and Critical Studies in the Whitney Museum of American Art Independent Study Program. In this framework, he pursued a yearlong individual tutorial with Benjamin H.D. Buchloh focused on the work of Theodor Adorno, Louis Althusser, and others. Buchloh's grasp of the political implications of art made a deep impression on him. At the same time, Glenn Ligon, Mark Dion, and Andrea Fraser were enrolled in the ISP's studio section. They entered into an active dialogue with Decter, marking the onset of his engagement with institutional critique. The texts in this book that address this most directly appear in the first section, under the heading "Institutional Critique® and its Discontents." This dialectical formulation registers one of Decter's chief concerns: the omnipresent danger of how what begins as critical inquiry can be reappropriated and reified. He warned of such a prospect in his 1990 essay, "Decoding the Museum":

> institutional critique has itself become a convention among other artistic conventions ... Thus, the double-bind of such work: when the artist incorporates that self-understanding into practice, the possibility of resignation emerges, particularly when the logic of the museum seems always prepared to incorporate difference and criticality within its neutralizing archive of historical information. The critique of the institution is thereby transvalued ... and the fictionalization of history proceeds as usual.

That same year Decter published an interview with Fraser where the artist put forward a notion of site-specificity informed by psychoanalytic transference. Stressing the formation of subjectivity as a component of "site," she characterized transference as "the supposition that another knows what one wants; that another possesses and can restore the lost object that causes that want or desire." Here, transference closely corresponds to what Decter calls "the fictionalization of history." Rejecting transference suggests that the artwork might function as an open-ended process of negotiation, a kind of *porosity.* Indeed, this is a quality that Decter would go on to examine rigorously in his writing and curatorial work. Fraser concludes the interview by taking a defiantly *non-didactic* stance:

> I don't want to provide commentary on commentary, or judgment on judgment—articulating once again the interests of a public for that public, the culture of a public for that public. To me, that's an unethical practice, homologous to the way that museums function.

In some respects, Peter Weibel's term "Kontext Kunst" conveys the artwork's potential porosity—a rethinking of aesthetic autonomy—better than the term "institutional critique." And porosity, in many ways, emerges as Decter's over-arching concern. Hans Haacke's *Shapolsky et al. Manhattan Real Estate Holdings, A Real Time Social System, as of May 1, 1971*, perhaps *the* foundational work of institutional critique, both targeted the legitimation function of the museum and dilated the reach of the artwork as a social practice. Here, Haacke proposed to present photographs and ownership records of tenement properties held by Harry Shapolsky for a solo exhibition at the Guggenheim Museum. In his analysis of this work, Fredric Jameson argues that it offers a comprehensive cognitive mapping of the social space within which it unfolds:

> it is not merely with museum space that we come to rest, but rather the museum itself, as an institution, opens up into its network of trustees, their affiliations with multinational corporations, and finally the global system of late capitalism proper.[1]

This understanding is key for Decter's own inquiry. It presages the dominant themes of his work to follow: mapping, spatialization, globalization, and privatization, as well as the conditions for the dissolution and absorption of the artwork per se. Of all these conditions, perhaps the most vexing, however, is that of the apparatus. Decter alludes to it in his examination of Haacke's *Proposal: Poll of MoMA Visitors* in "The Context Has Always Been There," a text in fact written for Weibel's *Kontext Kunst* exhibition:

> Haacke employed systems of information communication as a way to suggest connections between the context of the cultural institution and the sphere of real-politics. For some, this marked a symbolic point where artists could begin to function, perhaps even inadvertently, as the surrogate political conscience of the museum; in this scenario, museums and sites of official culture import criticism from the institutional non-insider, so that the normative bureaucratic and ideological machineries remain largely intact and unmolested—that is, the preservation of business as usual, a recurring problem which Haacke has often illuminated to great instructive effect.

Given his social systems approach, Haacke used feedback to inform his work. Accordingly, both his *Shapolsky et al*—and *MoMA Visitors*—reveal the apparatus-like mechanism of ideological homeostasis. The form of the apparatus is two-fold: technological and ideological. Typically, these are intertwined. In visual art, they are most immediately apparent in conditions of display. As a curator, Decter has accordingly deployed technology to foreground display itself and its attendant artwork/receiver relation. For example, in *Don't Look Now* (1994, Thread Waxing Space) he built a room-size projection system for a battery of slide projectors. With *Transmute* (1999, Museum of Contemporary Art, Chicago) he augmented his installation of works from the museum's permanent collection with a computer interface where viewers could sketch alternative hangings, and even recompose a special work by John Baldessari. *Dark Places* (2006, Santa Monica Museum of Art) featured a luminescent, architectural system made of compressed plastic designed to function as an image-display for 76 digitized artworks. Each of the structure's eight separate screens projected looped visual "scripts," sequenced through a computer program.

Decter explains his approach to the foregoing exhibitions in the texts that appear under the heading "On the Curatorial Road." Clearly, this methodology is indebted to El Lissitzky's constructivist interventions in exhibition design, especially his demonstration room that incorporated an array of sliding panels to display modular configurations of works. Notably, Lissitzky wrote in 1921 that "if one wants the *illusion* [italics mine] of real life in a closed room, one ... should hang a sheet of glass on the wall and ... attach a periscope which will at each instant reproduce real events in real colors and in real motion."[2] This proposal reads like a description of some sort of proto-television and, indeed, television came to serve as a paradigmatic technology for Decter, not only in the aforementioned exhibits but also in *Screen* (1996, Friedrich Petzel Gallery) and in *Tele[visions]* (2001, Kunsthalle Vienna). Television possesses an unprecedented ability to cut across divisions between public and private, local and global, work and leisure. Yet, as a form of social feedback, it remains an unprecedentedly potent means to impose and maintain ideological norms. Decter puts it quite succinctly: "television, in one way or another, whether we like it or not, touches *everything*." The omnipresence of television has pointed architectural implications, especially for the white cube, that seeming guarantor of the artwork's autonomy. Accordingly, Decter uses this technology to confront, as Lissitzky once did, the dominant political economy of the art world exemplified by the patronage system. Yet, his embrace of television is nuanced and skeptical, a far cry from the techno-euphoria of, say, Videofreex or even Allan Kaprow's sometimes futuristic reveries. Instead, Decter considers television a subtly disruptive social force. In his essay "Tele[visions]" (2001), he observes, well in advance of YouTube and Netflix, that

> Complications arise as more and more people are discovering that leisure time and work time have converged. It is now possible to fold virtually all activities, experiences, forms, and representations into the space of the computer. And, with the rapid development of mobile communication/phone devices, access to everything—including TV transmissions—will be virtually anywhere, all the time.

Decter's invocation of television sidesteps the technological determinism once espoused by Marshall McLuhan. Instead, it offers a glimpse of variability in the relation between artwork and viewer vis-à-vis social conventions embedded in the normative artwork. Changing the artwork's means of display to some extent de-calcifies it. It leaves viewers to consider their own role in this process, namely to consider the extent to which they themselves comprise the public sphere, and how this is mediated. In this sense, TV serves as an allegorical armature for Decter's curatorial work.

Decter's 1996 exhibition *a/drift* took shape as a pointed rejoinder to MoMA's deeply problematic 1990 show *High and Low: Modern Art and Popular Culture*. In lieu of the simplistic dichotomy offered by MoMA, Decter chose to map various zones of a sprawling and playful cultural topography: "elasticity," "a lovely entropy," "TV heads," "almost dumb and apathetic enough," "lifestyles of the ...," "from nihilism to hope and back again," and "carnal matters." These were the categories he used to organize *a/drift*. Instead of erecting a rigid hierarchy, he examined areas of exchange, overlap, and exclusion between these various fields. In each, he exhibited artworks in relation to non-art materials. Furthermore, he worked closely with architect Ken Saylor and artist Judith Barry to produce an exhibition design that underscored the show's mapping logic. To do this, Saylor and Barry cut portals into some of the walls and emblazoned them with supergraphics. These choices contributed to the sense of the exhibit as a staged event. Decter stressed this staging at the outset: "*a/drift* is a multidimensional topography of correspondences—a grammar and syntax of exhibition practice that celebrates the imaginary reality of our social artifices." In so doing, the show in effect enunciated a treatise on curatorial methodology:

> The museum is an alternately real and artificial social environment. Which is to say that it is a theatrical place, one that can be used ... to invent and explore relationships between artworks and all else in the immediate vicinity—elements that might be named non-art.

a/drift brought cognitive mapping into a critical friction with post-minimal theatricality. Its topographic approach correlates to sociologist Pierre Bourdieu's conception of social fields, habitus, and cultural capital. Bourdieu's mapping of social fields did away with the monolithic opposition between the proletariat and bourgeoisie and allowed for a more nuanced articulation of legitimation struggles in contemporary culture. His emphasis on social, symbolic, and cultural capital reworked the presumed empiricism of foregoing economic analysis. As such, it acknowledges the real-life repercussions of these nominally artificial constructs. These are exactly the forms of capital that the museum traffics in. Considered in terms of the proscenium arch, theater initially appears opposed to topography, suggesting as it does a singular focal point, not a spatial mapping. The term "theatricality" originates as a disapprobation in Michael Fried's "Art and Objecthood," designating a "confusion" between the space of the artwork and that of the beholder. Fried went on to argue that art degenerates as it approaches the condition of theater because it suggests "the illusion that the barriers between the arts are in the process of crumbling."[3] In stark contrast to Fried's position, Robert Smithson once quipped that the most interesting thing to be found in a museum is the space between the works. In other words, what exactly is the framework that demarcates the distinction between artifice and reality? And how tenable is it? Moreover, Smithson's comment also suggests that the arrangement of artworks in a museum constitutes an ever-variable representational complex. With the metaphor of drifting, Decter avers that such distinctions are subject to continual renegotiation.

Another implication of the title *a/drift* points toward Decter's next concern: that of the public sphere. Drifting recalls the Situationist International's technique of dérive. Guy Debord described this as a therapeutic process in which individuals and groups would suspend their routine activities and allow themselves to wander in the city, drawn to the attractions of the urban landscape. Underlying this technique is the assumption that everyday life offers a rich yet paradoxically unknown terrain, obscured by habituation to capitalism's obligatory cycles of work and leisure. Ideally, a dérive would awaken its participants to the vitality of the quotidian reality that surrounds them. Another premise is psychogeography. This is an urbanistic concept that posits that a city comprises more than just the physical elements of buildings, thoroughfares, and infrastructure. Rather, its form is linked to social use and cognitive zones of affinity. Debord's psychogeography, in turn, is indebted to Henri

Lefebvre's conception of space as, not an empirically given entity, but instead something that is always socially produced.

In Decter's work, these concerns inform his critique of Yves Aupetitallot's *Project Unité* (1992), co-written with Olivier Zahm in 1993. Here, Aupetitallot chose Le Corbusier's Unité d'Habitation in Firminy, France, as his exhibition site. Decter described this complex as follows:

> Completed in 1967 as part of a larger complex including a youth center, a stadium, and a church, the building was intended as a visionary response to the economic disenfranchisement caused by rapid industrialization. Continuing recession, however, has sharply reduced the local population, and many of those who remain prefer individual residences. Today the *Unité* stands half empty.

He went on to explain the significance of this site as a place to stage a curatorial intervention:

> Aupetitallot's show constituted a considerably more radical attempt to escape institutional limits into the extrinsic social domain, by replacing the art institution with a functioning community—one that already symbolized, within a *living monument* to an unfulfilled utopian pragmatics, a grand, if flawed, integration of art, architecture, design, national culture, economic, politics, and the social. In effect, the participants were asked to assume the role of inhabitants and to reflect upon collective living within the machinery of Corbusier's social architecture.

Given the project's ambition, however, Decter questioned whether many of the artistic projects would have any lasting effect on the place—that after the project participants departed, the residents were "left behind to enjoy the privilege of living in an unquestionably depressing environment with only a dilapidated cultural pride for consolation." This is a recurring question in Decter's analysis of large-scale, context-embedded exhibitions that seek to engage with the social and urban fabric: what criteria do we use to evaluate how such endeavors impact those who inhabit the same space? In "Communication City" (2000) Decter pursues these questions further, writing that the latter half of the 20th-century inaugurates an:

> effort to open up the relative autonomy of vanguard art, to re-distribute the practice, language, and ideologies of art making back into … so-called everyday life. Taking art out of the specialized containers for art—i.e., the studio, the gallery, the museum, the private collection—and returning it to the … ordinary precincts of life: e.g., the street, the home, etc. In one sense, this reflects a … preoccupation with re-injecting the insulated activity of the modernist art world back into the mainstream of cultural activity.

Yet for Decter, again in stark contrast to Kaprow, everyday life is not without artifice, not without institutions, and, accordingly, does not offer any absolute purchase on reality. Instead, Decter roughly paraphrases Oscar Wilde, "Life imitates art, and meanwhile art drifts into the life-condition." "Communication City" also initiates Decter's sense of the city as an adjusted readymade. He brings this up as a proposal to "re-colonize" public space for specialized art activities. Here, it is important to distinguish between the city as readymade and the city as empirically given space. The former accents the social constructedness of urban space and acknowledges the struggles for appropriation and re-appropriation that govern it. The latter merely re-affirms the status quo. Yet, in the aftermath of 9/11, Decter offers a different version of public readymade in "Transitory Agencies and Situational Engagements: The Artist as Public Interlocutor" (2006). He wrote this for the *[Situational] Public* book, the publication documenting the inSite_05 *Interventions* exhibition that commissioned artists to develop projects engaging the San Diego/Tijuana border. In this case, the border appears as a kind of artifice *par excellence*, capable of asserting a severely real force, especially in terms of both immigration and drug trafficking. In this context Decter voices concern for potential dissent vis-à-vis the restructuring of the public sphere in the post-9/11 US, arguing that "public space has become something of a *readymade* domain: over-regulated, patrolled, increasingly securitized and surveilled, a placeholder for the eventual arrival, or appearance, of what might be described as public art." Not surprisingly, he instead advocates for artists who produce platforms and situations that test new possible relations between artwork and receiver. He might just as well include curators and critics in this mandate because this is exactly what his own practice entails. Indeed, in 2010 he went on to found and develop a program uniquely devoted to these issues at the University of Southern California: the MA Art and Curatorial Practices in the Public Sphere. Today, in many respects, the public sphere is a ruin, ravaged by the logic of privatization, manifest in governmental restructuring, financial speculation and cybernetic technologies. The public's widespread embrace of the Occupy Movement that emerged in September 2011 shows that the will to a common community, however, has not been relinquished. It is this struggle that Decter's conception of art vis-à-vis a collective public represents and what makes his critique of these issues more pertinent now than ever.

[1] Fredric Jameson, "Space: Utopianism After the End of Utopia," *Postmodernism, or the Cultural Logic of Late Capitalism*, Duke University Press, Durham, North Carolina 1991, p. 166.

[2] Nancy Lynn Perlhof and Brian Reed (eds.), *Situating El Lissitzky: Vitebsk, Berlin, Moscow*, Getty Publications, Los Angeles 2003, p. 61.

[3] Michael Fried, "Art and Objecthood," *Art and Objecthood: Essays and Reviews* (Chicago: University of Chicago Press, 1998), p. 164.

CHAPTER I
Institutional Critique®
and its Discontents

Michael Asher, *Untitled*

Revised version of a text on Michael Asher's *Untitled*, Artists Space, June 2–July 2, 1988.
Originally published in *Flash Art International*, no. 142, October 1988.

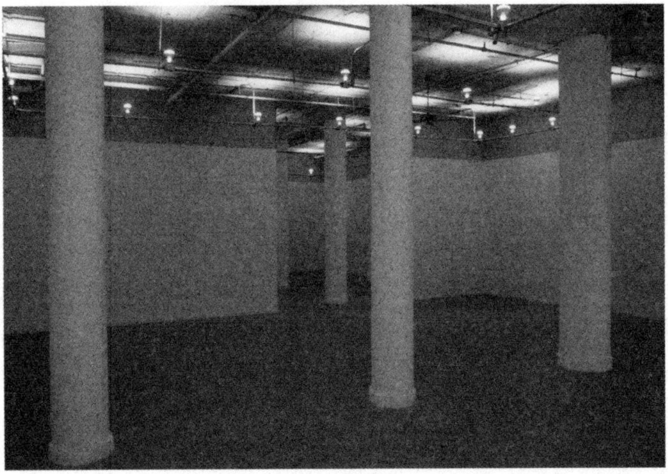

Michael Asher, *Untitled*, 1988

This exhibition marked the much-anticipated return of Michael Asher to the New York contemporary art scene, and his project is something of a *coup*. Asher's intervention is based upon an investigation of the history of the original interior architecture at Artists Space, which had been modified in 1984 with the introduction of partial exhibition walls for expanded display areas. According to the artist, the project is designed to focus upon the arbitrary quality of the wall additions, underscoring the degree to which these structural elements have confounded the architectural characteristics of the original interior. Extending the height of all the partial display walls to the ceiling level, yet leaving these drywall components unpainted, he indexes a mock *completion* of the architecture of the walls, offering a subtle (nearly invisible), wry critique of the structurally awkward character of the original remodeling of this alternative space. As with previous works throughout his career, Asher here is seeking to question our assumptions regarding what constitutes the work of art in relation to a contextual-institutional frame, almost to the point wherein the context, the place itself, becomes the work; i.e., the context or place as adjusted readymade. Asher's architectural-spatial intervention barely calls attention to itself, and it is easy to miss. The project reveals itself merely as dull, beige industrial sheets of drywall in areas of the space where one expects to find white walls extending uninterrupted to the ceiling.

These seemingly unfinished additions-extensions index the usually hidden (sublimated) material substrate or infrastructure of an architectural space, and therefore unsettle the visual codes of a putatively neutral white cube container for the display of art. Visitors to Artists Space might be forgiven for having thought that the show had yet to be installed, or had just been de-installed. In other words, it is easy to miss where the art actually is (and what it is): Asher expects us to do some detective work, to somehow participate in his spatial de-codings and recodings, and to see how the intersection between concept and material execution is made visual as the structural inflection of a given space. Through this procedure—which is at once additive and subtractive—the artist coyly plays at being the architect-interior designer with a not so hidden agenda: to unveil, to lay bare, the intrinsic structural characteristics of place. According to the artist's stipulations, Artists Space has two options at the close of the exhibition: either dismantle the entire installation, or paint over it. If the latter option is selected, the wall additions-extensions will effectively disappear into the architecture of Artists Space. Asher's deceptively uncomplicated gesture succeeds here in revealing the ideology of architectural form that subtends the institutional space of art, and in the process temporarily converts Artists Space (as a contextual platform) into a kind of meta-art: a conflation of (non)architecture, (non)installation, (non)sculpture that facilitates a displacement of place, and a mode of institutional critique.

Postscript, 2012

My initial firsthand encounter with Michael Asher's practice occurred in 1987, at Skulptur Projekte Münster, in the form of the Eriba Familia BS model caravan (a travel trailer), which was driven to a new parking place in the city each Monday of the week (the day museums are closed). Asher had not only developed this project for the initial iteration of the exhibition in 1977, but had conceived of its reappearance every ten years in each successive version of Skulptur Projekte. I had heard reports from people who had seen the vehicle in the first Skulptur Projekte, and it had already become something of an urban art legend: an ingenious conflation of post-Duchampian readymade aesthetics with a playfully rigorous rethinking of site-specificity. The caravan (as acquired utilitarian thing) becomes a mapping device amplifying the concept (and urban materiality) of the city as a site, as visitors would have to navigate the city to locate its new position. It could also be read as a deadpan response to the curatorial framework of this groundbreaking large-scale exhibition of site-specific works. It is as if Asher were retorting to Kasper König (the curator): *as I am being commissioned to produce a site-specific object/work, here's one in the guise of a mobile readymade that changes its site (locational specificity) each week.* Encountering this same work in the 1997 and 2007 versions of the exhibition, I could only laugh quietly to myself: Asher had devised a perfect formula for context-specificity. In 2008, Asher staged another *coup*, executing a major project at the Santa Monica Museum of Art in Los Angeles. The artist researched a particular aspect of the museum's history: the distinct structural configuration of the temporary walls built for all 44 shows organized by the museum (from 1998 through 2008). The plan was to install the infrastructural elements of these walls within the space of the museum. The resultant accumulation of wood and metal studs resulted in an astonishing spatial-historical cartography: a dense, nearly impenetrable, maze-like, meta-installation that colonized the museum's main space, demanding from the visitor a commitment to navigate through an institutional history made tangible. With conceptual rigor and deadpan humor, Asher laid bare the intrinsic logic of the exhibition system: the art space as endlessly adjustable (readymade) platform.

In a separate room, the artist provided an informational coda for the project: a sequence of floor plan diagrams that indexed the formal contours of all the temporary walls (with the corresponding exhibition titles included on the diagrams). Among these was the schematic of an exhibition I had curated for the museum in 2006, *Dark Places*, lingering as a trace among a constellation of other traces.

Silvia Kolbowski, *Enlarged from the Catalogue: The United States of America*

Revised version of a text on Silvia Kolbowski's exhibition at Postmasters Gallery, November 19–December 18, 1988. Originally published in *Arts Magazine*, February 1989, p. 105.

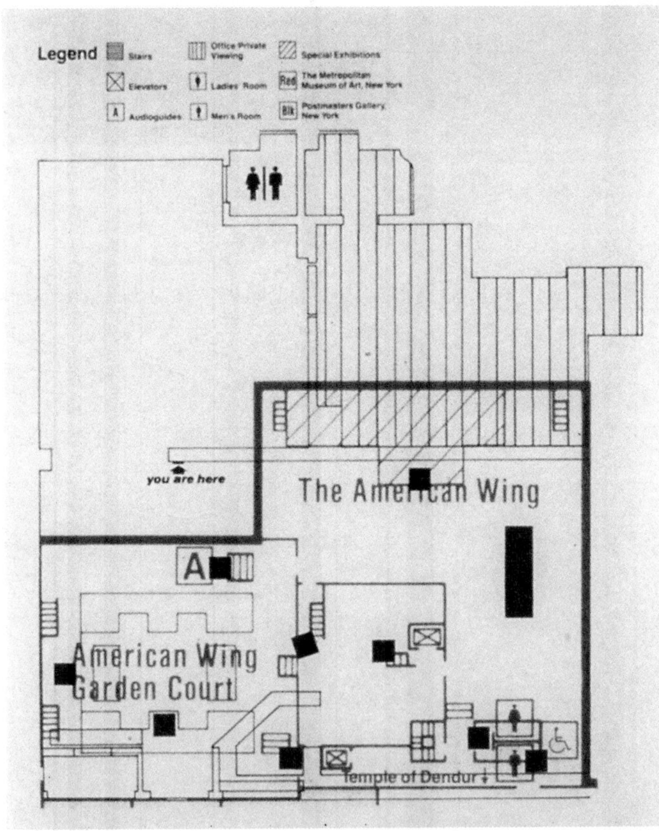

Silvia Kolbowski, *Enlarged from the Catalogue: The United States of America*, 1988

Although the primary focus of Silvia Kolbowski's practice concerns the function of the museum—the site wherein official histories of culture are manufactured and disseminated—her critical methodology constitutes a convergence of pedagogic/informational strategies and intertextual, allegorical procedures.
In other words, Kolbowski's work functions like a cultural palimpsest, examining the ideological permutations of institutions. Kolbowski targets the narrative system of the museum as it manifests itself as a carefully orchestrated interplay of authoritative text (i.e., the catalogue) and exhibition design/display.
In order to reveal the false neutrality or objectivity of such narratives, Kolbowski attempts a critical destabilization of institutional discourse through acts of visual and textual re-narratization. By opening up the seamless historical narratives of the museum to inquiry and scrutiny, Kolbowski illuminates areas of ideological regulation.

Enlarged from the Catalogue: The United States of America represents the artist's most elaborate and ambitious installation to date. Basing her project on an investigation of the Metropolitan Museum of Art's American Wing, Kolbowski focuses on the Met's catalogue representing the entire holdings of the Wing (entitled *The United States of America*), as well as the literal floor plan of the Wing's exhibition areas. The installation consists of a series of display cases, containing silkscreened images produced by an overlapping of the following elements: plates from the original catalogue; a typical corporate couch; a map representing the superimposition of the floor plan of the American Wing over the floor plan of Postmasters Gallery; and an ample supply of Kolbowski's altered American Wing catalogues. The distribution of these elements throughout the gallery space corresponds to a scaled-down and schematic version of the American Wing's exhibition areas, producing a symbolic interface of cultural spaces. The viewer is compelled to use Kolbowski's deconstructed catalogue as a guide through this collision of dislocated signs and indices collated from the actual museum Wing. By interrupting the chronology and narrative logic of the catalogue's original text formatting with her own meta-interpretive narrative, Kolbowski effectively challenges the viewer to unveil, as Fredric Jameson might say, the repressed political unconscious of a normative curatorial method institutionalized by the Met and other museums.

CHAPTER I

The Museological Bind: Desire, Displaced

Revised version of an essay originally published in *Lusitania Journal*, Fall 1990.

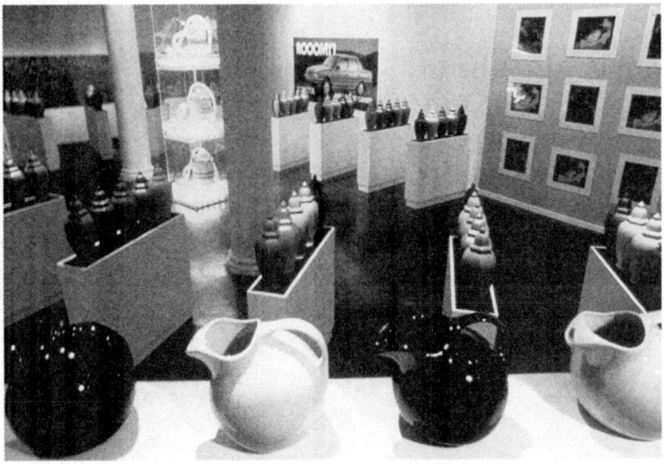

Judith Barry, exhibition design as artist contribution to the exhibition *Damaged Goods: Desire and the Economy of the Object*, New Museum, New York, June 21–August 10, 1986.

When we refer to the critique of cultural institutions, the museum is usually the privileged site of analysis. Artists such as Daniel Buren and Michael Asher have been canonized, or institutionalized, by the very same institutions that they have critiqued, infiltrated, and deconstructed. When museums, art spaces (and even galleries) present exhibitions that thematize institutional critique, this raises some difficult questions about the symbiotic relationship between the institution and those who critique the institution. It seems a bit too easy to default to the usual argument that all artistic avant-gardes, historically, are eventually institutionalized, and that therefore, institutional critique practices are not immune from these normative cultural processes.

An exhibition recently organized for the Whitney Museum, entitled *The Desire of the Museum* (1989), begins to address some of the aforementioned issues. In genealogical terms, the conceptual matrix of *The Desire of the Museum* may be effectively traced back to a show organized by Brian Wallis in 1986 at the New Museum of Contemporary Art, *Damaged Goods: Desire and the Economy of the Object.* The Wallis exhibition should be considered as the first attempt, within the museum/institutional context, at a critical evaluation of certain contemporary art practices–Jeff Koons, Haim Steinbach, Barbara Bloom, Justen Ladda, Gretchen Bender, Ken Lum, Judith Barry, Louise Lawler, Andrea Fraser, and Allan McCollum—which have attempted to programmatically analyze or debunk the economic, political, and psychological conditions under which the high art/mass culture dialectic had become reconfigured in relation to postindustrial consumer society. By reframing these artworks vis-à-vis the various types of critical discourse formulated to address the constituent features of an emergent space of multinational capitalism (to paraphrase Fredric Jameson), Wallis managed to construct a trenchant commentary upon what might be described as the psychopathology of commodity fetishism, as well as related issues concerning mass production/reproduction, the parameters of institutional dominion within contemporary culture, and the influence of mass media/popular culture upon art.

It is possible to identify the ideational core for *The Desire of the Museum* exhibition within the essays produced by Hal Foster and Judith Barry for *Damaged Goods.* In Foster's central argument, the paradigm of the Duchampian readymade—already incorporated into the basic machinery of Pop art, and thus transvalued—functions as an archetype for certain later practices which attempt to underscore (or demonstrate through critical complicity) the "redefinition of the lines between modernism and mass culture,"[1] and examine the fetishistic operations intrinsic to the "late-capitalist economy of the sign."[2] For Barry, who also designed the installation for *Damaged Goods* (i.e., her artistic contribution to the exhibition was comprised of the design of the space, and the configuration of the artworks within that space), it is crucial to understand that the construction of social relations (and, by implication, the formation of ideological hegemonies) is at least partially determined by an intersection of "the discourses that mark, channel, and position the body through and in other perspectives (read as representational systems),"[3] and the literal architectonics (i.e., infrastructure) of built social space. Concluding her essay, Barry observes:

> If architecture embodies our social relations, then presentational forms (including staging and lighting devices from the theater, opera, and Las Vegas, as well as more obvious museological techniques) must refer to ways in which we wish to experience these relations. One confrontational tactic not yet tried is the subversion of the wish for closure, possession, and gratification. One way to do this might be to make threatening the assumed neutrality of the exhibition space itself.[4]

In turn, *The Desire of the Museum* uses Barry's confrontational tactic as a methodological cue. Its exhibition framework not only collates the practices of artists who are currently engaged in various modes of institutional critique, but also attempts to establish a self-reflexive curatorial method through which to analyze (and, ultimately, destabilize) the assumed neutrality of the exhibition space itself, and unveil the normalizing functions of the museum. Using tropes borrowed from psychoanalytic discourse, the curators of this exhibition argue that beyond the economic and political—i.e., ideological—factors which subtend the museum, one can identify a more subliminal dynamic that occurs when the museum-goer and the institutional edifice intersect, as the following curatorial statement enunciates:

> the title of this show, *The Desire of the Museum*, suggests more than special interests and conscious intentions; it imputes an unconscious to the museum—conceives it as a site where different, often disruptive and contradictory desires, beliefs, and needs come into play … it is the play of desires between the viewer and the museum which determines the institutional experience of art.[5]

Utilizing a decidedly anthropomorphic metaphor (e.g., the unconscious of the museum) may seem a rather fanciful employment of neo-Freudian terminology. However, it does manage to suggest that the assumed monolithic structure of the museological enterprise embodies the fundamental contradictions of a bureaucratic apparatus designed to administer art historical knowledge (and therefore determine the value of contemporary forms of art making). This apparatus not only preserves historical canons, but also constructs new ones.

The Desire of the Museum manifests its desire to examine such issues by evidencing (although imposing might be the more appropriate term) an elaborate, gratuitously self-referential/self-indexical, and virtually theatrical (i.e., staged) installation design which operates as a supplementary frame—cleverly inscribed within the pre-determined institutional frame of the Whitney space—for the works of a relatively non-homogeneous group of artists: Richard Artschwager, Ashley Bickerton, Mark Dion, Marcel Duchamp, Andrea Fraser, the Guerrilla Girls, Hans Haacke, Silva Kolbowski, Joseph Kosuth, Barbara Kruger, Liz Larner, Louise Lawler, Sherrie Levine, Allan McCollum, Peter Nagy, Aimee Rankin, Ad Reinhardt, Julia Scher, and Laurie Simmons. Curatorial intervention is signaled through a variety of mechanisms, the most conspicuous (and heavy-handed) of which took the form of two parallel silver bands circumscribing the gallery walls at average eye-level. The majority of artworks are installed along this trajectory, underscoring a system of visual and spatial organization built around the fetishistic gaze of the spectator. This design, however, also seems to reinforce a quite different implication: the intrinsic commodity status of the art objects, strung around the room as if connected to an assembly-line apparatus. The other mode of self-indexical curatorial intervention operates on linguistic terms; phrases such as "institutional taste analysis" or "institutional unconscious" are dispersed throughout the gallery at strategically located points, producing an interplay of institution-critical slogans that seemed almost parodic.

Although this exhibition can be reproached for contextualizing practices within a group show framework that seems to merely institutionalize institutional critique art, it raises important questions regarding the function of the museum. *The Desire of the Museum* reveals, for better or worse, the contradictory and paradoxical condition of the culture industry in general: the fundamental, invisible, and often repressed symbiosis between critical art practice and the targeted domain of the cultural institution. It is a cozy interrelationship often too easily glossed over in the territory of theory, and unmistakably evident in the realm of practice.

[1] Hal Foster, "(Dis)Agreeable Objects," in the exhibition catalogue of *Damaged Goods: Desire and the Economy of the Object*, The New Museum, New York, 1986, p. 17.
[2] Ibid.
[3] Judith Barry, "Dissenting Spaces," in *Damaged Goods*, 1986, p. 49.
[4] Ibid.
[5] Introductory essay by Catsou Roberts and Timothy Landers in the exhibition catalogue of *The Desire of the Museum*, Whitney Museum of American Art, 1989, p. 2.

An Interview with Andrea Fraser

Revised version of an interview with Andrea Fraser, originally published in *Flash Art International*, November/December 1990.

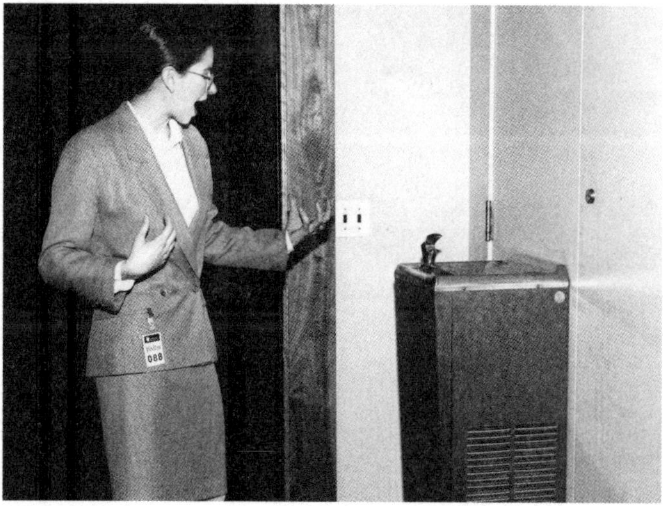

Andrea Fraser, *Museum Highlights: A Gallery Talk*, 1989

JOSHUA DECTER First, I would like to address the history of institutional critique—i.e., practices that take as the site of intervention the museological framework—and to examine your relationship to that trajectory; for example in relation to Louise Lawler's work. How have you developed strategies in relation to the museum context?

ANDREA FRASER I do consider myself to be working within an institutional critique trajectory. The concept of a gallery talk-performance really emerged out of an article I wrote about Louise Lawler's work in 1985, which considered the way her practice involved the taking up of different institutional functions. In 1986, I was invited to participate in the *Damaged Goods* show at the New Museum in New York, so I decided to conduct a tour of the show instead of producing an object for it. I came to institutional critique through site specificity; a sense of an imperative to start where one is standing, a notion of artistic practice also influenced by Lawler's work—an attempt at a functional transformation of the social relations in which one is participating. But, in addition to engaging with social relations in the traditional sense, I wanted to deal with subjective relations. Actually, one of the primary impulses behind my first gallery talk-performance was to try to integrate institutional critique with what could be called a psychoanalytic feminist critique of subjectivity. What I came up with—and am still working with—is something like a psychoanalytic notion of site-specificity that's informed by the concept of transference. What is analyzed in psychoanalysis are the wishes and fantasies made manifest in the analytic situation through the mechanism of transference. Freud writes, "no one can be slain in effigy, in absentia ... " But I'm going off on a tangent ...

JD Well, what does transference mean in this regard?

AF Well, it's ...

JD ... in terms of language ... another approach.

AF I'm nervous.

JD You mean a sort of performative ...

AF Well, I think of transference as the supposition that another knows what one wants; that another possesses and can restore the lost object that causes that want or desire. Only the subject can articulate the particular signifiers, the demands, in which her desire is bound up. Transference is a transference of the power of that articulation in a certain sense, from the subject to another. So, in a way, I began by assuming that people who go to museums, who attend gallery talks, are implicitly addressing to the docent a demand to know ...

JD Information?

AF On an informational level but also on the level of the interests and wants that people might invest in the museum.

JD You're saying that those wants are predicated on the way museums establish cultural values for a public. Right?

AF What I wanted to do in my gallery talk at the Philadelphia Museum was to construct a history of the way that art museums were instituted as the repositories of certain desires, specifically in terms of the museum's status as a public institution. I wanted to consider the establishment of the first museums in the US in the context of the privatization of public provision in bourgeois philanthropy and turn-of-the-century urban reform movements aimed at regulating the poor into a dependent and dependable work force. Museums were, and are, part of an organization of the public sphere aimed at taking hold of and defining the interests, culture, pleasure, daily practices, and highest aspirations of a public. Why do people go to museum? What does the museum promise? In the words of a Philadelphia Museum publication: "happiness," "ideal beauty," "liberation from the struggles imposed by material needs." How can one make good the museum's promise? A docent might know. She's the museum's representative. As a volunteer she represents both the class interests embodied in the museum and its philanthropic purpose: the public good. She's in identification with the board of trustees.

JD Your gallery talks are scripted, and in a subversive way, because you're presenting something that might be mistaken for the institutional language itself—and is in fact largely a collection of quotes from museum publications. If somebody walked into the *Damaged Goods* show, for example, and had not been warned that it was a performance, and if it was not very well advertised …

AF To a purpose.

JD … it could very easily have been identified as a normative institutional discourse. But you're not engaging the audience as the conventional docent does, in an intuitive and interactive capacity. You're not asking questions.

AF Well, I don't ask people what they want. Despite all the references that I've made to what people who go to museums want, I'm finally not dealing with what could only ever be my fantasy of a public. As Jane Castleton, I articulate what the museum wants. But against this museum discourse, I want to introduce what Jane wants, and what I want. Specifically, the point at which my/her desire exceeds what the museum promises, or takes too literally. Or, how the institution takes me/her as its object. The split between her discourse and the museum's is conditioned on her position in the institution; as a woman, as a non-expert, as a volunteer—not a high level patron. This split is a wedge I hope to introduce into the chain of identifications, visitor/docent/bourgeois patron—and what I hope distinguishes my performance from an ironic re-presentation of institutional discourse.

JD So you're allowing a certain normative or conventional discourse to unleash its own inherent contradictions, but not, as with some other institutional critique practitioners, in order to say: this is right and this is wrong, this is the object of critique, and this is the practice of critique.

AF I don't want to provide commentary on commentary, or judgment on judgment—articulating once again the interests of a public for that public, the culture of a public for that public. To me, that's an unethical practice, homologous to the way that museums function.

Decoding the Museum

Revised version of an essay originally published in *Flash Art International*, November/December 1990.

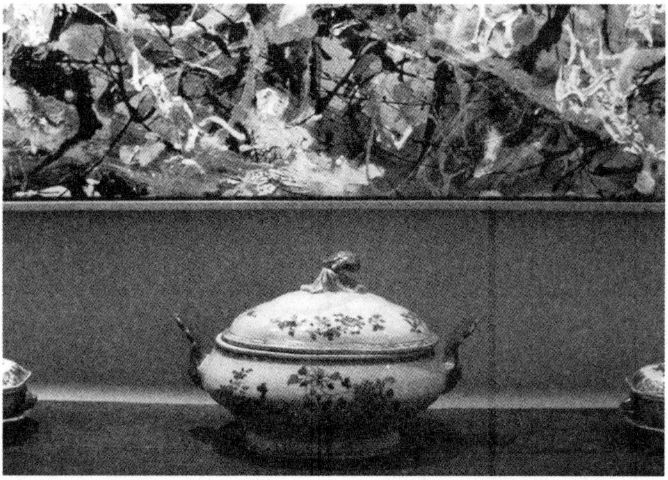

Louise Lawler, *Pollock and Tureen, Arranged by Mr. and Mrs. Burton Tremaine, Connecticut*, 1984

In the 1960s, artists as diverse as Michael Asher, Daniel Buren, Marcel Broodthaers, and Hans Haacke developed various modes of critical reflection upon the cultural, institutional, socio-economic, and political frameworks within which art circulates. These artists revealed a contradiction, a double bind that persists today: namely, that, the critique of the institution is predicated upon a navigation of—if not complicity with—the systems and modes of power under analysis.

It may be problematic to suggest that these precursors to a younger generation of artists who emerged in the late 1980s and early 1990s (and now associated with the term Institutional Critique) were *solely* interested in formulating strategies to examine, analyze, or subvert the hegemonic structures of the institution. Yet they did share an interest in how cultural authority and power was constructed within the site of the museum. And as museums became the locus of critical attention, these institutions became increasingly savvy, adjusting their bureaucracies and curatorial programs to accommodate artists who might question the museum itself. In other words, museums began to understand that by inviting artists to perform a critique, they could also exert more control over these critical interventions.

The museological framework provided artists with a seminal cultural space wherein the valuation and canonization of particular artistic practices was read—on symbolic and material levels—as a system infused with ideological proclivities specific to the perpetuation and maintenance of the traditional function of the institution. Beyond established notions of site-specificity (or, in relation to Smithson's non-site works), artists such as Buren, Asher, Broodthaers, and Haacke understood that museums, galleries, and other types of art spaces constituted a system of artistic production and display, interconnected with economies of public sponsorship and private patronage. Buren would also discuss the function of the artist's studio within this system of production.

The contradictions are clear: as artists desire to construct a strategic framework through which to inscribe or articulate a critical intervention or analytic unveiling, they must become cultural and institutional experts in their own right. And so artists cultivate the imprimatur of expertise regarding the museum (and other sites of artistic production and distribution) in order to re-frame this cultural ecosystem *according to its own rules, structures, and forms*.

In 1968, Marcel Broodthaers opened the *Musée d'art moderne, Départment des Aigles, Section XIXème Siècle* (*Museum of Modern Art, Department of Eagles, 19th-century Section*) in his Brussels apartment. This privatized, pseudo-museum took the form of an arrangement of postcards, crates, and inscriptions that Broodthaers contended was an "invention, a jumble of nothing," invoking the tumultuous political situation in Europe and the US that year. His fictional museum would assume a variety of configurations in different institutional settings. Drawing upon Surrealism, Dada, and aspects of Situationist politics, Broodthaers used self-parody and tongue-in-cheek game playing to mask a rather serious indictment of institutional authority.

In Jürgen Habermas' critique of the revolt against the traditional parameters of modern art in Dada and Surrealism, the sociologist and philosopher asserts that such negativistic programs only unsettled the contents of the autonomous cultural sphere, and had no transformative impact upon other social spheres. Whether or not one chooses to endorse Habermas' privileging of a notion of social communication wherein all the various spheres must interrelate rationally, his claim regarding the failure of the early avant-garde's negation of culture is a significant move toward a deeper understanding of the relationship between the sphere of high culture and other social realms. This is particularly useful when reconsidering the notion that art has the capability of effecting the transformation of hegemonic power structures. In post-1968 art practices, we can observe a significant shift away from negation, toward strategies of institutional analysis and infiltration, exemplified by artists such as Buren, Asher, Haacke, and Broodthaers. No longer are the normative values of high culture sabotaged and destroyed in an anarchistic gesture of nihilistic revolt. Instead, the institutional system is analyzed on ideological, social, symbolic, economic, and political terms. The artist exploits his or her imprimatur of cultural expertise, freely moving from institutional margin to institutional center (and back again), at once complicit and exempt, critical yet invested.

Within the US context, this historical trajectory informs more recent practices that have developed in productive relation to frameworks of institutional critique—locating the museum as the seminal site of analytic rendez-vous. Yet, institutional critique has itself become a convention among other artistic conventions. It is essential to examine the work of artists such as Louise Lawler, Mark Dion, Judith Barry, Andrea Fraser, and Julia Scher with this in mind. These artists run the risk—even if equipped with ample amounts of self-conscious, critical reflexivity—of becoming locked into the same museological system from which they hope to gain the appropriate analytic distance. This is the double-bind of institutional critique, particularly when the logic of the museum incorporates difference and criticality within its neutralizing historical archive. The critique of the institution is thereby transvalued, according to the aforementioned logic, into one more artistic paradigm among others. The recent traveling retrospective of Marcel Broodthaers' museum transformed fictional props into the artifactual remains of a practice that—through an attempt to subvert the museological institution—became inscribed into history. To what extent, then, has the critique of the museum-as-institution become a fiction of itself? How can a temporary intervention by an artist be represented in any other form than a combination of the photographic document coupled with an artifact and critical exegesis? Such archival material might have been re-configured within the museological system to construct a new history when oppositional cultural practices were considered socially transformative. Now, however, the museum exacts its sanctioned bureaucratic revenge.

These questions and issues begin to be addressed in the work of a number of younger contemporary artists, including Mark Dion, whose film project (in collaboration with Jason Simon) entitled *Artful History: A Restoration Comedy*, examines the conditions through which artworks—in particular, paintings—of dubious historical value can become literally and symbolically remade into new works of potential market value through techniques employed by commercial art restoration studios. Dion worked as an art restorer when this installation was first iterated in 1986, drawing upon his own expertise to develop a critique of how, in the wrong hands, art restoration methods can be used and abused to fabricate new market values: e.g., usable sections of otherwise worthless paintings are cropped and then transformed into original works in their own right. (This is distinct from museums that engage in responsible procedures of art restoration in which an attempt is made to reduce the accumulation of dirt, and other wear and tear, in order to return the painting to something closer to its original appearance, although even some of these efforts have also been controversial.) In *Artful History*, Dion installed actual sections of paintings that had been cut into and fragmented so as to provide the material for *fabricating* a restored painting of higher quality, thereby making transparent the process by which marginal old paintings are made anew, and questionable art historical narratives (and art markets) are manufactured. Dion uses a post-documentary method, along with his own imprimatur as an expert in the field of restoration, to reveal how the marketplace of culture and narratives of art history operate in tandem to reconfigure the past according to the logic of current ideological or economic interests. Dion cleverly insinuates just how difficult it has become to distinguish between the real and fictional histories of art, while alluding to the complicity of museum curators, dealers, historians, and restorers who all engage in the game of history-manipulation, and the rewriting of narratives.

Just as the museum establishes its own historical accounts of canonized artworks, playing the central role as the final arbiter of what counts and what doesn't (after all, the museum has been given license to function in this way), it has adopted technologies to facilitate a security system which operates to monitor and ultimately influence the actions of spectators within the architectonics of the museum space. As a relatively surreptitious complement to the design of museum display areas, surveillance systems establish a panoptic logic, inflecting the putatively neutral institutional space with an invisible regime of control. The museum, therefore, can also be understood as a control-space, in the sense that spectatorship takes place under conditions that are thoroughly constructed and monitored. The artists Judith Barry and Julia Scher each address the intrinsic conditions of museological presentation. Barry has written texts regarding the importance of re-examining the assumed neutrality of the exhibition space. She has also designed exhibition displays so as to foreground the vicissitudes of presentational methods and practices. At times, Barry's intervention within a particular space is indexed or signaled by the specific configuration of objects, compelling the viewer to reflect upon the inter-relationship between object and context, and how such a relation inflects the public's experience and understanding. Barry suggests that the exhibition space as determined through display strategies is never neutral, that it connotes certain frameworks of historical knowledge, ideological agenda, aesthetic norm, and cultural politics.

Julia Scher's practice focuses on the technology and utilization of state-of-the-art surveillance and security systems within institutional contexts, revealing these apparatuses to the viewer. The former operator of a private security system company, Scher uses her technical expertise to present elaborate demonstrations of this hardware, while simultaneously manipulating the viewer's relationship to the technology. Furthermore, Scher has produced site-specific installations within museum spaces that do not supplement the pre-established surveillance systems, but rather subvert and complicate them. By demystifying technologies of control, Scher creates situations in which the individual may be in a position to regain a sense of empowerment. Despite their deconstructive logics, little in either Barry's or Scher's practice suggests in some post-idealistic sense, that the hegemonic structures of the museum are easily transgressed, subverted, deconstructed, or dissolved. Rather, both seem to acknowledge that intervention-as-analysis is most productive when it engenders some type of critical knowledge about the conditions of exhibition.

Louise Lawler, in turn, uses the representational system of photography as a post-documentary, conceptual apparatus to produce critical knowledge in relation to the dominant codes of display and presentation within galleries, museums, and private collections. Lawler is a central link between a previous generation of artists engaged in modes of institutional critique and more recent practices. Since the late 1970s, Lawler has engaged in what might be characterized as a mode of complicit criticality and critical complicity in relation to institutional (e.g., museum, gallery) and non-institutional (e.g., private collector, corporate collection) environments wherein art history, aesthetics, taste, and marketplace values are orchestrated and staged through the display of artworks. A perfect example of her practice is the 1984 work entitled *Pollock and Tureen, Arranged by Mr. and Mrs. Burton Tremaine, Connecticut*, in which we observe a decorative tureen with a colorful, flowery motif (perhaps from the 19th-century) placed on a table in front of a colorful Jackson Pollock painting (only a section of the lower half of the Pollock is visible). Lawler had managed to obtain access to the home of these major collectors of 20th-century modern and contemporary art, and she shot a series of pictures that revealed how they arranged/contextualized the acquisitions within their domestic environment, according to their tastes. Indeed, it is almost as if an interior decorator had matched the Pollock with the tureen. Like an agent provocateur/saboteur, Lawler's intervention occurs as she assumes the posture of an observer, imaging the subtle, ambient conditions within which a particular cultural order is preserved and perpetuated—an order which, paradoxically, now includes Lawler herself.

Cultivating the imprimatur as an artist who documents art's contextualization within private and public spaces, she slips into places in order to subtly reframe (i.e., unpack) them. Lawler seeks to reveal how particular constructions of taste, knowledge, history, and financial power are constituted through the display of artworks—that have become the conspicuous signs or souvenirs of an elite culture of accumulation and consumption.

This paradoxical condition of engaging in an artistic vanguard (the successful artist also participating in the construction of that vanguard) while at the same time staging critical removal from it exemplifies both the strengths and weaknesses of Lawler's method. And so it would seem that institutional critique inevitably leads to this kind of double bind for the artist. The Achilles heel of art as critique is its dependence upon the same systems, institutions and constituencies that it wishes to critically target, and from which it also seeks legitimization, if not canonization. (2012 note: Lawler's *Pollock and Tureen …* was acquired by the Metropolitan Museum of Art in 2000, just more evidence that perhaps nothing is immune to institutionalization.)

Andrea Fraser's practice can be characterized as a mode of institutional-specific critique, involving elements of performance, research and writing. Fraser (who has cited Lawler as an influence) decodes the museological enterprise from within. To achieve this, she adopts the theatrical guise of a docent, Jane Castleton; the first instance of this work—entitled *Damaged Goods Gallery Talk Starts Here*—was developed for the context of the New Museum's 1986 exhibition, *Damaged Goods*. This took the form of a performative meta-tour for museum visitors that instead of providing a traditional didactic explanation of the show, offered an analysis of the institutional frame. Fraser's Castleton character delivered a calibrated interplay of interpretational voices, combining theoretical discourse, objective expertise, and the apparent expression of sublimated desire. The research-based, service-oriented methodology that Fraser employed to develop Castleton's rhetorical apparatus involved the intercutting of phrases from the museum's public relations office (concerning the goals and aims of the public cultural institution), readymade docent narratives, and her own subtle linguistic manipulations. Fraser sought to unpack how museums manufacture elaborate images of themselves for public consumption—an image that invariably masks how such institutions actually function as intersections of money, bureaucracy, politics, and cultural production.

What do the aforementioned types of institutional critique offer beyond a relatively circumscribed troubling of the museological framework? Do they deconstruct dominant systems of cultural organization so as to unveil sublimated political, economic, and ideological interests? And if these practices do indeed facilitate a critical knowledge for the viewer (but which viewer?), what is to be done with that knowledge? Should cultural institutions be made to undergo some type of reform? Should museums divest themselves of their necessary interdependence with various economic sources? Once the viewer is made to reflect upon the implicit vicissitudes of the museological system, does this result in something more than temporary institutional demystification? There are no easy answers, yet there is evidence of contradiction: these practices inevitably reproduce the museum's logic even as they engage in a critical interrogation of that logic. Already in the process of being historically codified, have the notions and strategies associated with institutional critique perpetuated the fiction of art as socially transformative, or replaced that fiction with the necessary double bind of critical complicity/complicit criticality?

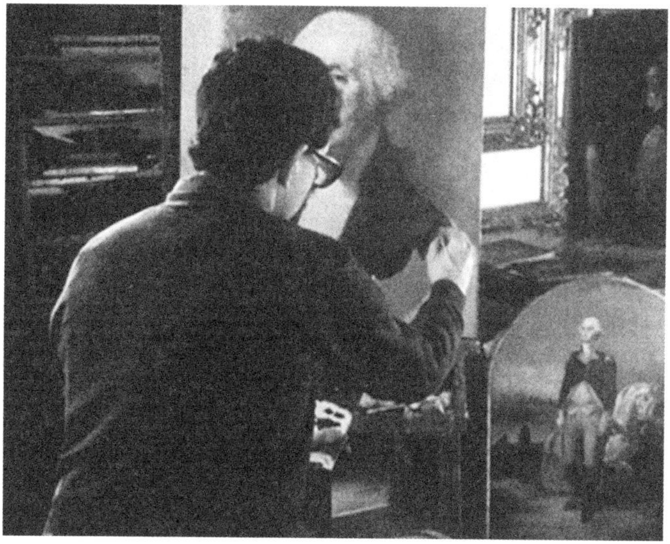

Mark Dion and Jason Simon, *Artful History: A Restoration Comedy*, 1987

Daniel Buren, *To Transform*

Revised version of a text on Daniel Buren, *To Transform*, at John Weber Gallery, November 27–December 21, 1991, originally published in *Arts Magazine*, March 1992, p. 86.

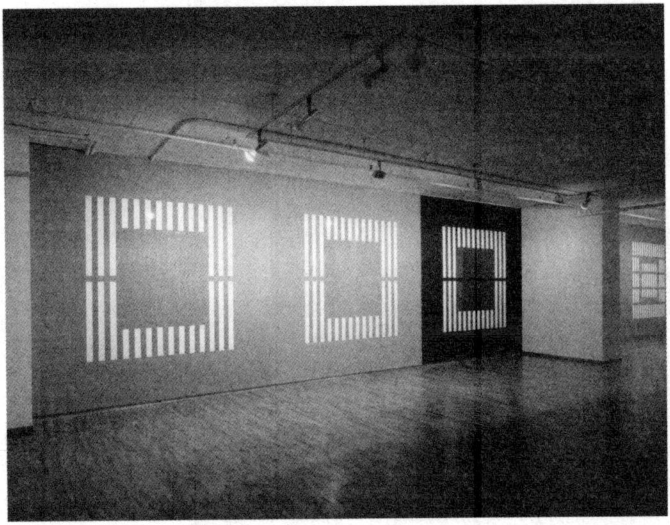

Daniel Buren, *To Transform*, installation view, John Weber Gallery, New York, 1991

It is rather disappointing just how safe Daniel Buren's practice now appears, particularly within the gallery context. Codes of modernist abstraction have always been intrinsic to Buren's visual language, yet his ubiquitous stripe motif now operates merely as a sign for the exhaustion of those same historically determined codes. More troubling, the stripe seems to be deployed as an emblem (aesthetic, corporate) for Buren himself. A strange yet perhaps inevitable logic has emerged here: the already standardized, ready-made version of modernist painting has now undergone a second reification as Buren's signature logo of intervention.

For Buren, the notion of difference-within-repetition is quite apt, since it suggests the tautology of a visual language code that can be redeployed, and essentially recycled, in any context or site. The institutionalized originality of the modernist stripe was already incorporated into Buren's work of the 1960s, which indicates a sustained commentary on the intrinsic bureaucratic patterns of vanguard art. The artist's recent gallery shows have demonstrated the degree to which the stripe as sign/motif/logo now operates as a commodity-sign, ironically, for site-specific intervention. Here the artist installed a series of works entitled *To Transform: Paint on Paint*, and *To Transform*, exemplifying the aforementioned problematic condition. These works may have suggested a critique of the obligation to insert a traditional aesthetic language (i.e., painting) within a decidedly commercial realm, yet this was articulated in a way that merely reinforced the degree to which Buren's practice poses no threat, no problems, to its context. The *Paint on Paint* series comprised regular patterns of white latex stripes on sheets of Plexiglas, overlaid upon the gallery walls, and broken down into large, square, monochromatic quadrants. This double system, wherein the stripe motif is carried on a transparent plane (the invisible canvas support) so as to allow the actuality of the gallery wall to be registered, is a rather obvious way to deconstruct a predetermined architectural space.

Here, the reified conceptual formalism of Buren emerges as a kind of empty design ethic, wherein the site-specific method can now be packaged and sold as individual units of meta-painting, indicating that site-specificity has really become something closer to context-adjustable. In fact, Buren's installation was comprised of a set of individual *To Transform: Paint on Paint* works—each component of the series sold separately, dimensions variable according to the spatial conditions of the next contextual destination (i.e., collection). Well, I suppose this is all too familiar: it's what happens when the demands of the market begin to overshadow other considerations. Disappointing to observe this in an artist whose work and writings, only a couple of decades ago, so cogently analyzed the systems within which art is produced, consumed, and framed.

Renée Green: Re-Mapping Narratives of History and Identity

Revised version of an essay originally published in *Forum International*, January/February 1993.

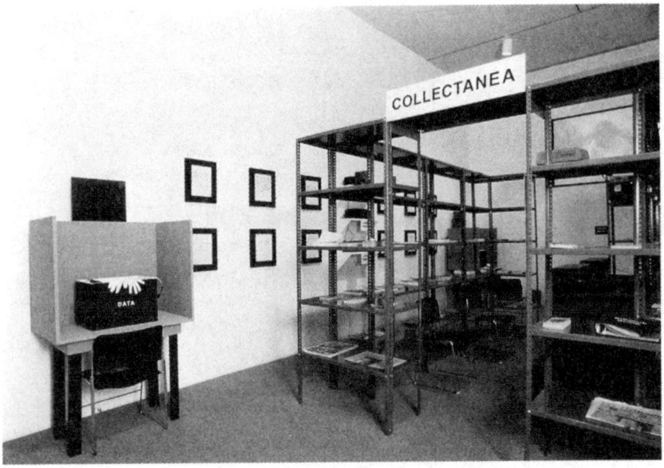

Renée Green, *Import/Export Funk Office*, 1992

(Genealogical Interventions)

Renée Green's practice attempts to come to terms with the corollary processes by which history and identity are constructed through visual and verbal narratives. Although Green always reflects upon her condition as an African-American woman artist, she defers from fixating on it as a self-conscious fetish (or, neurotic preoccupation) within the language of the practice; rather, her "blackness" is unfolded as a territory of intellectual and emotional complexity and contradiction.

Green's installations and objects allude reflexively to a subjectivity in formation, an identity undergoing continuous reconstruction in relation to the genealogical ground of colonial and postcolonial Europe and America as matrices of institutional knowledge and cultural experience.

Reflecting critically upon a legacy of conceptual and institutional critique practices, artists such as

Green, Mark Dion, Fred Wilson, Andrea Fraser, Jon Tower, and Julia Scher (among others) have managed to produce work that articulates new frameworks of engagement with social, ideological, cultural, racial, historical, and political conditions. Their work addresses the institutional site of exhibition (the gallery or museum) and those domains outside—but socially adjacent to—the frame of official vanguard art culture. Green and these other artists productively reformulate techniques of critical infiltration.

Disciplinary models borrowed from archaeology, anthropology, and historiography have become the methodological underpinnings for Green to articulate an investigation of Western systems of representation in relation to the construction of (her) multi-layered identity—itself a product of this contradictory history. In an important sense, Green is remapping the visual and verbal genealogies of Western culture—and its desire to impose a regime of power over other societies. As Green suggests in her work, the legacy of colonialism implicates us all—we (Americans, Europeans, African-Americans, African-Europeans, Africans, etc.) are all caught up in its contradictions. In 1991, Green produced a work-in-progress, ten months in duration, entitled *Sites of Genealogy* for P.S. 1's *Out of Site* exhibition. During this process, the artist traced variously interconnected genealogies: the traditional binary division between "black" and "white" (in terms of racial theories, the moral components of religious narrative, literary traditions, etc.) and other histories, using the architectural hierarchies of the site to guide her installation decisions. For example, selected canonical texts by African-American authors were incorporated into certain rooms depending upon Green's desire for historical and literary allegory; e.g., Richard Wright's *Native Son* was inscribed into the boiler room, while Harriet Jacob's *Incidents in the Life of a Slave Girl* found its way into the building's attic. Here, Green was interested in motivating the viewer to become a participant in the unfolding of these layered narratives—or, constructed histories—of gender, race, art, and culture so as to reveal the coding of subjective experience (and self-identity) in relation to the contradictory fabric of cultural representations.

A project entitled *VistaVision: Landscape of Desire* (1991) explored the ways in which the continent of Africa was—

and to some extent, remains—the subject of a strong desire and fascination for the (colonialist) West. Once again using an architectural environment to generate meaning (as a kind of spatio-temporal construct), Green focuses upon the evocation of the Teddy Roosevelt memorial wing of the American Museum of Natural History—an archetypal and paradigmatic site in which the societies and cultures of the so-called Dark Continent were re-represented through the filter of colonialist ideology. Yet Green is never herself absent from the context of these allegorical mise-en-scènes: her own contradictory relationship to this dominant genealogy of representations becomes part of the narrative underpinning, suggesting a kind of de-objectified, post-anthropological method of self-analysis. Furthermore, Green suggests the extent to which Europe and America have become transformed into *exotic* territories of desire and fascination for some Africans—an ironic, although logical, cultural inversion.

In a 1992 project entitled *Import/Export: Funk Office*, Green employed even more elaborately developed techniques of anthropological and ethnological study to examine the historical and current relationship of imported and exported cultural products between Germany and the United States (specifically, the cultural milieus of Cologne and New York). The artist focused upon the ways in which America's Black hip-hop culture has become a locus of fascination for certain German fans, and the crucial history behind this phenomenon. Invoking the figures of Theodor Adorno (the Frankfurt School social critic who wrote often about American jazz and jazz culture) and Angela Davis (the Black political activist who studied with Adorno in Frankfurt in 1960) as symbolic icons of an historical framework of German-American cultural contradictions, Green proceeds to study the movements of a German music and cultural critic (Diedrich Diederichsen) as he followed the trail of urban-based hip-hop culture as if on a sociological expedition into the indigenous "other." During this period, hip-hop was already in the process of becoming an increasingly commercialized aspect of the popular culture. By interviewing Diederichsen and others about these complex conditions, Green was able to develop a narrative account of how colonialist sensibilities continue to permeate the domain of inter-cultural encounters. And, just as Green implicates herself within this contradictory situation, she compels us to reflect upon our own (un)conscious investments, and ideological and cultural positions.

The Context Has Always Been There

Revised version of an essay originally published (in German translation) in the catalogue of the 1993 exhibition, *Kontext Kunst*, Neue Galerie Graz, Austria (Dumont Buchverlag, Cologne 1994).

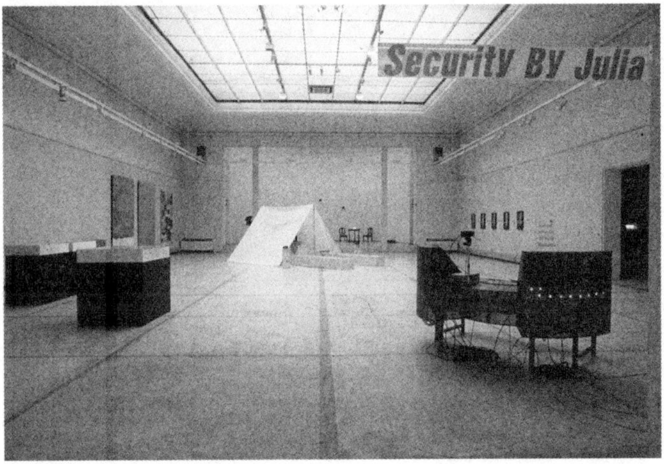

Renée Green, Julia Scher, *Kontext Kunst*, installation view, Neue Galerie Graz, Künstlerhaus, Graz, 1993

The critique of the institution—in its multifarious manifestations—is now invited, if not actively courted, by the cultural institution itself. What do we make of this development? And what are the effects? A kind of self-justifying logic emerges which might make us somewhat uncomfortable: museums produce official cultural meanings and representations, and these institutions are entrusted with the responsibility (for better or worse) of packaging such meanings and representations for diverse publics. When such institutions invite analysis and critique of their outward and intrinsic contextual conditions from artists (institutional outsiders), they are creating, at least to some degree, *insider* artists and practices. This creates the impression for various audiences that the cultural institution has become willing to submit itself to critical scrutiny, and is therefore somehow more progressive. In the United States, context-specific art has become increasingly attractive for museums that seek the imprimatur of cultural expertise that is signaled when an artist undertakes a critical deconstruction of an institutional context. The institution then becomes a benevolent creature that accommodates—if not facilitates—the desires of naughty yet intellectual artists. A new protocol of compromise is established, and the mouth that bites the hand that's feeding it is duly rewarded. Now, please don't misunderstand me: I'm not proposing to cynically dismiss those artists who have chosen to participate in a cultural system that is burdened with paradoxes, contradictions, and conflicts of interest.

In this regard, I believe that it would be instructive to look at the example of Hans Haacke's *Proposal: Poll of MOMA Visitors* produced for the context of The Museum of Modern Art's *Information* show of 1970, wherein the artist's intervention involved a direct form of viewer participation. Fundamentally a sociological model of statistical analysis was imported into the language-methodology of an art practice (and, into the official frame of high culture, again, as an art practice), allowing Haacke to function, albeit fleetingly, as a kind of interlocutor between the institution, the extrinsic sociopolitical environment, and the visiting public. Visitors were asked to respond to questionnaires designed to probe their knowledge of what actually occurs behind the closed doors of the museum (e.g., "To whom should trustees of museums be accountable?"), and their views on topical political issues (e.g., "Would the fact that Governor Rockefeller has not denounced President Nixon's Indochina policy be a reason for you not to vote for him in November?"). Here, functioning as a kind of sanctioned—if not provisionally sanctified—agent of critical infiltration, Haacke employed systems of information communication as a way to suggest connections between the context of the cultural institution and the sphere of real politics. For some, this marked a symbolic point where artists could begin to operate, perhaps even inadvertently, as the surrogate political conscience of the museum; in this scenario, museums and sites of official culture import criticism from the institutional non-insider, so that the normative bureaucratic and ideological machineries remain largely intact and unmolested. This is the preservation of business as usual, a recurring problem which Haacke has often illuminated to great instructive effect.

As Arthur Danto has noted, art only becomes art when it is defined as such by a community of specialists. In other words, art comes into existence—or presence—through its interpretive reception, its discursive contextualization. Clearly, Danto's argument reveals a predisposition for historical validation and institutional legitimation: it is the authority of the disciplinary field of art history, aesthetics, and criticism that sanctions the artist and/or the work of art. What is missing from this analysis, among other things, is the question of taste—its history, and its transformation into opinion and standards of evaluation. But in terms of the issues at stake in the *Kontext Kunst* exhibition, I think what Danto expresses here remains important in relation to a broader understanding of the discursive context within which art gains meaning and cultural grounding. Any notion or practice of context-specific art presupposes some type of conceptual re-affiliation with—or structural re-integration into—everything that constitutes the frame of culture. The context has always been there. How could it be otherwise?

> The more actively all cultural work can be related, either to the whole organization within which it was expressed, or to the contemporary organization within which it is used, the more clearly shall we see its true values. Thus *documentary* analysis will lead out to *social* analysis, whether in a lived culture, a past period, or in the selective tradition which is itself a social organization.
> —Raymond Williams, "The Analysis of Culture," 1961

In any discussion which attempts to analyze art production that "thematizes the social and ideological conditions under which it is produced" (quoting from Peter Weibel's description of his *Kontextualismus* exhibition), it is essential to recognize that models of institutional critique, for instance, emerge from a long tradition of art production that embodies and/or allegorizes its broader social, economic, political, cultural, and ideological frame(s) of possibility.

Joseph Beuys used the institutional frame of pedagogy as a platform to explore alternative strategies of intellectual, social, political, and ideological work that would precipitate emancipatory effects. For Beuys, art was merely one component of an overall process of converting the spiritual life of the individual into the matrix of the social, political, and ideological; the interaction of educational, artistic, cultural, and political/activist tasks to create conditions for social reform, as well as a new aesthetics. The contradictions of his artistic language are still immensely provocative, revealing a struggle between the desire for a sensuous communion with the material world of corporeality, and a commitment to cultural activism.

Robert Smithson adopted the discourses and methods of archaeology, geology, ecology, to assemble an interdisciplinary practice that engaged both the land and cultural space as distinct yet interrelated spheres of action; he is a crucial historical figure for artists such as Mark Dion and Peter Fend, two participants in the *Kontext Kunst* exhibition. When I consider Smithson's ingenious inter-substitutions of cultural context and environmental site, in relation to Beuys' "Save the Woods" from 1973 (a photo offset of Beuys and cohorts engaged in a contextually-specific action in the forest, fighting the good ecological battle), a pathway opens to aspects of Dion's and Fend's practices. Both have made an art of stepping in and out of the prescribed domain of visual art culture, of re-inventing themselves as proto-specialists in other fields, equipped with specific agendas. Dion has taken the ecologist/environmentalist route, emulating, in a sometime ironic manner, the specialized protocol of a research scientist; he now spends most of the year on the road, foraging around South American jungles and rain forests, or the environs of New York, for samples of indigenous fauna and flora, or teaching Chicago school children about their environmental context (as part of a special exhibition project). Dion arranges scavenged materials into tableau-like structures that function like archival workstations, each coalescing into a specific argument about eco-crisis and other social-environmental conditions.

Fend, on the other hand, has transformed himself into a postmodern cartographer, intent upon revealing the nefarious condition of today's geopolitical structures, and offering alternative—if provocatively visionary—models of global mapping and environmental reconfiguration. He has used television and computer technologies to create an alternative communication network designed to unveil the ideology of mainstream media, and to deconstruct misinformation disseminated about the true inter-relationships between state power, nationalism, geographic and political boundaries. Although both Dion and Fend have vigorously tested and contested the boundaries between artistic activity (and its institutional systems of support) and other specialized types of cultural work (and their institutional modes of support), it is tenable to argue that such interdisciplinary or inter-contextual strategies ultimately reveal the profound gap that separates art production from the spheres of politics, activism, science, etc. I believe that such strategies can be placed in the category of the symbolic gesture, wherein a model of revised cultural work and behavior is set forth as a kind of virtual praxis. Sophisticated infiltrators, artists such as Dion and Fend have yet to locate the formula that would allow them to more effectively penetrate the corridors of institutional power *extrinsic* to the art world. Yet I do not believe that such a formula is possible in today's socio-cultural structure, particularly in relation to artists who contest the ideological status quo. Just because cultural institutions grant permissions for artists to critique hegemonies, doesn't mean that the political establishment is listening.

The agenda of the *Kontext Kunst* exhibition is to re-evaluate the specific history of context-specific art practices in direct relation to more recent strategies, thereby constructing a new knowledge. Although this endeavor may be admirable, the logic of this group show requires scrutiny. Any effort to historicize practice is contiguous with an inexorable process of institutionalization. And, ironically, since many of the artists included in this exhibition (e.g., Andrea Fraser, Louise Lawler, Christian Phillip-Muller, Julia Scher, etc.) interrogate the conditions of cultural institutions, their strategies of infiltration are dependent upon a successful negotiation of the requisite protocols that ensure access to the power structure of cultural institutions such as museums, alternative spaces, kunstvereins, kunsthalles, etc. These artists are, in a sense, connoisseurs of institutionalization. One question that arises is what happens in the power relations between artist and cultural institution when that cultural producer is invited to participate in a group show that addresses context-specificity or context-criticality?

My purpose here is not to invoke melancholic nostalgia for the reputed good old days, when an ethos of post-revolutionary politics might have filled the air with hope for an authentic overturning of institutional hegemony. Rather, let us come to terms with the relatively benign character of most forms of institutional critique, and how comfortable these practices have become within the host body of the museum.

These are conditions that an artist such as Andrea Fraser has actually addressed. In *Museum Highlights: A Gallery Talk* (1989), Fraser performed the role of a docent at the Philadelphia Museum, taking unsuspecting visitors on a tour of the site that sought to unveil the historical and ideological unconscious of the museum. For her context-specific project for the 1993 Whitney Biennial, Fraser produced a tape of recorded interviews with the show's organizers which she cut up and reassembled, allowing visitors to peruse the exhibition while listening to a mélange of cleverly sabotaged curatorial voices.

Yet the challenge to the authority of the cultural institution in this case remains bound to what I would describe as a *theatrics of resistance*, wherein the museum is merely a stage upon which the rites of critical scrutiny are played out before an audience of … ourselves.

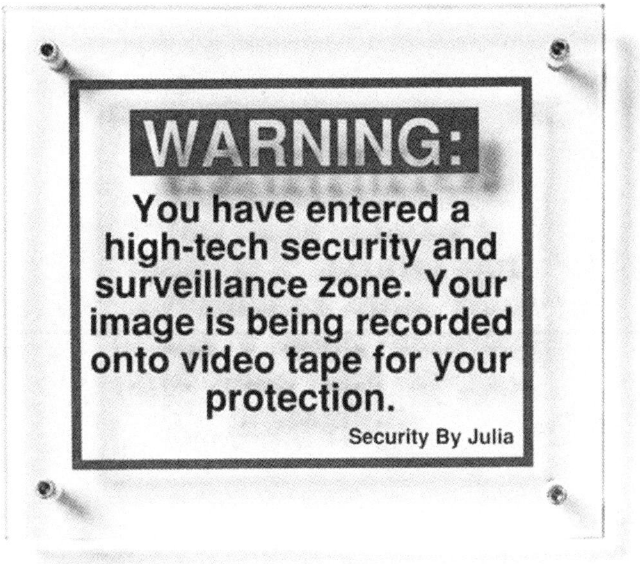

Julia Scher, *Warning Sign*, 1995

Museums, Identity, Race, Permissions, and Other Institutional Questions: Thelma Golden Talks with Joshua Decter

Historical note: in 1994, Thelma Golden was a curator at the Whitney Museum of American Art in New York. She is currently Director and Chief Curator of the Studio Museum in Harlem, New York. Revised version of "Discussion: Thelma Golden talks to Joshua Decter," originally published in *Acme Journal* #3 ("Cultural Permissions" issue), 1994.

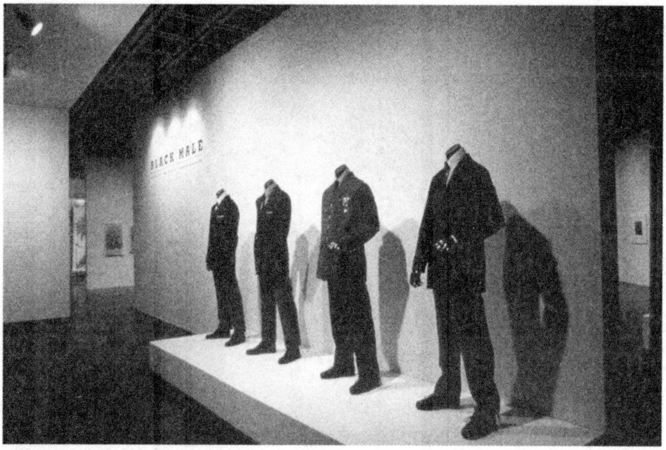

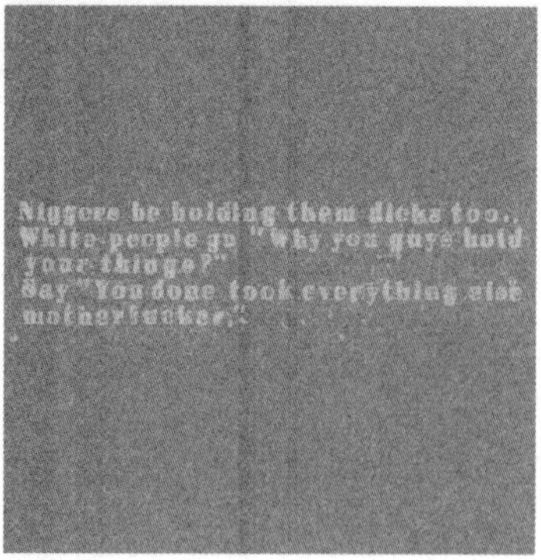

Fred Wilson, *Guarded View*, 1991
Glenn Ligon, *Cocaine (Pimps)*, 1993

JOSHUA DECTER In thinking about issues of cultural representation, I'm interested in discussing the idea of redistribution as it pertains to the museum as an institution with the power and authority to present new art practices to a wider audience. What is the museum's responsibility as an agent for the redistribution of cultural representations?

THELMA GOLDEN Well, I don't think it's so much the responsibility of the institution, per se, as much as it is a question of personal and individual responsibility, in whatever capacity one happens to occupy within an institution.

JD But, to a certain extent, you—as an individual—are invested in the particular institution you work in, and conversely, it's invested in your presence, so these things are not so easily separated. So, do you believe that museums—as institutions taken in particular directions by the people that work in them—are responsible for presenting the work of artists—regardless of race, ethnicity, class, etc.—that has fallen through the cracks of the mainstream art system?

TG Yes, I do, but I would not want to impose a kind of formulaic approach to this challenge. And on a personal level, I would want to re-emphasize the distinction between thinking about this issue in terms of what the museum presents, and the internal institutional structure of the museum. These are two related, yet significantly different conditions, and while I believe that exhibition programs can work to redistribute representation, it is necessary to rethink the internal structures of institutions in order to root out the more fundamental causes of why there have been certain absences and marginalizations, historically and in the present. This is the important groundwork that needs to be done, and the questions regarding how to broaden the museum audience could be built upon this groundwork.

JD Well, this really concerns how the institution goes about representing a subaltern set of cultural practices. But why do you think that people have generally not been able or willing to distinguish between the question of who or what is literally presented in the museum's exhibition program and the intrinsic structural conditions that regulate the power relations of the museum?

TG Maybe. I think part of this had to do, perhaps, with the well-meaning but somewhat misguided dialogues that occurred during the really concentrated push for multiculturalism, which was based upon the idea of a visual presence as an indication of change—for example, the various shows that included the "other people" during that period. So it was about representation that was made visible within certain exhibition contexts, and much less about addressing the fundamental, institutional conditions that allowed such shows to take place. Also, the institutional structure is always somewhat hidden to the public in important ways.

JD Should it remain hidden?

TG No, I don't think so. It should be more public, and open to some kind of public criticism—for example, in the case of a museum, its exhibition program …

JD But why should it be subject to public scrutiny?

TG I'm not saying public scrutiny necessarily, but when you ask how an institution should change, that change should not be based entirely upon the criteria of visual presentation or representation—in other words, who or how many are represented in this or that show.

JD And in terms of cultural permissions?

TG I think cultural permissions are taken. I take them. For me, they're taken. Maybe I never thought anyone would give them. But this has more to do with some of the issues we're talking about regarding how institutions change. In terms of issues of constituency, I think they are far more complex then we tend to think. There's no one-to-one relationship between what the museum presents and the project of building a new constituency. It's not as simple as that. Although fundamental, institutional changes can make an impact upon the building of new audiences. The way the whole constituency dialogue has emerged, particularly around the multiculturalism question in relation to the mainstream institution, is that these "other" communities are considered to be somewhat monolithic.

JD Do you mean that as soon as we name something as occupying a putative outside location, that this outside begins to assume a hegemonic identity?

TG Exactly. So, in order to begin thinking in institutional terms about how to reach out to different and new communities, the idea of monolithic simplicity has to be reconsidered. First the complexity of other communities has to be thoroughly understood.

JD So you do believe that mainstream museums or alternative spaces can really function as effective brokers between different communities within the visual arts culture(s)?

TG Certainly now the push is in the direction of thinking about the museum space as a microcosm for an outside reality, at least in theory. But this is not yet a reality. I think museums can be focused and inclusive, but this requires an understanding of the complexity of the various communities that are out there.

JD This also relates to the museum as a place wherein sometimes competing cultural values are reinforced, redefined, and even newly generated on an ongoing basis. It's a tricky balancing act, particularly in relation to new audiences who have different sets of expectations. For instance, there may or may not be productive dialogues between audiences who love Edward Hopper, and those who love Glenn Ligon.

TG Sometimes those are the same people! But when they are not, the real question is how the museum can bring in the various kinds of viewers who might be interested in Edward Hopper, as well as the different kinds of people that might be interested in Glenn Ligon, and create some kind of interaction between them. And I don't think this has really happened yet.

JD What type of interaction do you mean?

TG Interaction within the same cultural space—on physical terms as well as on symbolic terms. Right now, the cultural community is still rather segregated, in terms of how people interact within institutions and in other less formal social situations. So I'm interested in how the institution can begin to redefine itself so that a wider range of people can be brought in.

JD And you believe that such changes can occur through the implementation of different curatorial programs and new strategies in education?

TG No, I think change happens initially on a structural level within the institution, which then triggers new and broader exhibition approaches, which in turn triggers different public programs.

JD Do you think that a productive way of changing institutions is to appoint individuals to key, decision-making positions who are deemed as being representative of new constituencies—and therefore potentially new audiences?

TG Well, I don't think that people should be brought in specifically to represent particular constituencies. It's just not possible. For example, I cannot represent the black community; I *don't*, quite often.

JD But how could you, alone, represent the black community?

TG It's not possible. But, unfortunately, within recent institutional practice, there have been attempts to do just that. And this is done not only along racial lines, but also gender, geographic, etc. But I do think that it is important that people from different experiences can bring those experiences to the table when decisions are made. It makes the dialogue richer, and perhaps the decisions that are made will suggest something different in nature than a more monolithic cultural position. Although I do not represent the black community, there are things that I can articulate that may find their way into the decision-making processes of the institution, and that may change the character or complexion of the museum. There are ways of diversifying the institutional structure in a non-formulaic way, so that one doesn't simply nominate so-called special interest advocates.

JD But I think this is how things mainly work today.

TG Not exactly. I think it is possible to rethink this approach, although it doesn't seem that the art world as a whole is very receptive to the idea. But, on the other hand, it's difficult to talk about curators of color in mainstream institutions—there are so few of us, which suggests that it might just be too premature to deal with the questions of representation on institutional terms.

JD Do you think that there should be an explicit quota system in the art world?

TG No, there shouldn't. I think there should be a system that calls for some personal responsibility to acknowledge the diversity that exists in the world. Of course, what diversity is changes from situation to situation. I don't think that quotas come with any power attached to them; they seem to exist in order to name something, to make it visible. Beyond that function, they don't really accomplish very much.

JD What do you mean by not accomplishing much? Naming something, or making something or someone visible, still seems to be important.

TG Beyond creating visibility within the institution, nothing much happens.

JD But what's supposed to happen?

TG Well, as I said before, I think that we have to think about fundamental changes at the structural level of institutions—at the central decision-making and programming levels. And in terms of the question of statistics, numbers are important to me now because they remind me of just how much has to be done in a more general cultural sense.

JD Do you endorse some of Cornel West's visionary yet admittedly idealistic proposals regarding the need to create real overlaps and exchanges between individuals and groups within society, so as to foster an environment of intercultural, interracial, interethnic, and cross-economic contacts, and to re-enfranchise all who are marginalized under the auspices of advanced capitalism?

TG Yes, I believe that what West described is completely necessary, but I don't think anything like this can happen in the art world now, since fundamental actions have yet to occur. Fundamental contacts between cultural communities are not really taking place now; those that have taken place have been for public consumption only.

JD But when you start talking about establishing alliances across boundaries of race and class, for instance, such alliances have to be formulated in some way. There has to be some sort of program of action, some methodology employed to achieve this sort of thing. Various communities may not desire these sorts of alliances, for political and other reasons, so artificial measures may have to be taken to construct interactions, and this may be alienating for many.

TG As someone who encounters various sides of this problem, I always have some ambivalence and anxiety about how—or if—to deal with such issues. I think it requires, as problematic as this sounds, an acknowledgement of a mainstream and a margin. Only from this premise can one begin formulating approaches. In the complex territory of today's cultural situation, there may be alliances struck across racial and class lines, but the real challenge is to go beyond such lines, and cease making the type of divisions which have been used to create a kind of power as people begin talking about the idea, quite simply, of integration …

JD Are you invoking a postracial situation?

TG No, but while there have been some changes in the art world, with more diversity, more substantial and daring interactions are not taking place. While certain cultural institutions have become recognized as exemplary representatives of culturally specific practices within a mainstream context, such as the Studio Museum or El Museo del Barrio, are we adequately acknowledging spaces such as Kenkeleba House or the Chinatown History Project? The alienation emerges when you exist outside of the lines drawn up by a certain group of institutions.

JD So you're talking about a kind of comfort zone.

TG Yes.

JD People cross lines only after this process has become institutionalized.

TG Exactly. In order to establish real cross-community dialogues in the culture, we have to interrogate what the community is, where the power lies in that community, and what the interests are in maintaining that power.

JD But why should there be this kind of communication between communities, when at least part of the definition of community involves significant degrees of self-interest. Without self-interest, the community ceases to exist …

TG Well, I think that self-interest can be maintained for political or social reasons, but in terms of cultural issues, self-interest should probably be put aside, and not be a mitigating factor.

JD But I see the political and social self-interest of communities intimately tied up with cultural and representational interests—these things seem to feed off of one another. And this sometimes seems to be a real stumbling block; it's one thing to share cultural practices, but it's quite another thing to address disparities and contradictions in class position, quality of life, opportunity, etc. Things get thornier since these interests are not really aligned; there are competing self-interests. Obviously, discussions of class and race often are repressed and this repression influences the type of value and aesthetic judgments that we make about various kinds of art. But I have a somewhat strange question for you: what is it like to be a black woman in your position working in the art world?

TG I've worked in a couple of different art worlds over the past few years, so I've had different experiences. But in terms of the art community that I work in now, it's a somewhat bizarre experience because I constantly and consistently have to locate community. But it's also exciting, because of the newness of my capacity in an institution.

JD Do you think that it's a stupid question?

TG No, but it's just fraught with a lot of different emotions for me.

JD Have you experienced racism in the art community?

TG Well, I've felt the constraints of being pigeonholed by others concerning my race.

JD Do you think that the various discourses around otherness have a tendency to reinforce whatever potential racist tendencies may exist in parts of the art community? In other words, a situation wherein codifications of difference and otherness may actually reinforce segregation and factionalization? So perhaps we should relinquish this codified language?

TG Yes, that may be one solution to the situation as it exists now. It's interesting to remember the beginning of these discussions regarding difference, since many of these dialogues and languages were brought into the art world from outside academic and cultural places, so this fact created a comfort zone for people in the art world. When the serious theoretical dialogues around difference first began to appear, the first wave, they initially didn't include people from different cultural contexts. This only began to occur during the second wave of these dialogues, at least within the academic arenas. But in the art world, if you notice, the "people of difference" who were brought into these discussions were usually from outside of the art community, and this created a certain level of comfort.

JD In other words, the tendency to invite people from other cultural and disciplinary areas to analyze the prevailing conditions of the art world, rather than finding those individuals within the art community.

TG Right.

JD I've always found this to be troubling.

TG While the theoretical analyses could be important, the pragmatic effect of such writings was—and is—not always clear. And people in the art world seem to be more comfortable talking about otherness in quotations than they are about speaking directly about issues of race and gender in the art world.

Stephen Prina, *Dom-Hotel, Zimmer 101, Köln, 1994*

Revised version of a text on Stephen Prina exhibition, *Dom-Hotel, Zimmer 101, Köln, 1994*, at American Fine Arts, Co., New York, October 22–November 19, 1994. Originally published in *Artforum International*, January 1995.

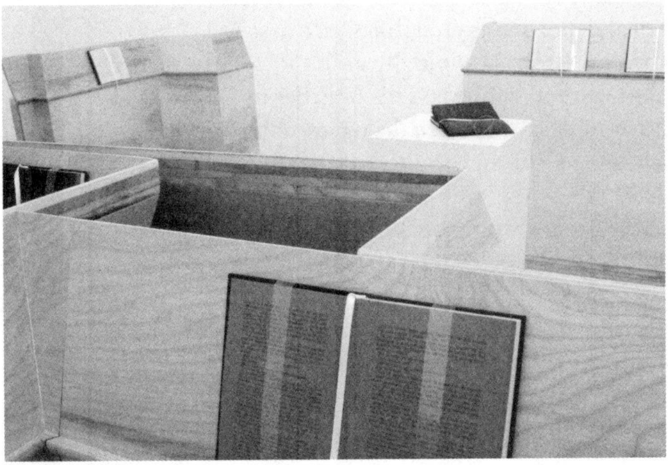

Stephen Prina, *Dom-Hotel, Zimmer 101, Köln, 1994*, 1994

As Stephen Prina's newest project, *Dom-Hotel, Zimmer 101, Köln, 1994*, suggests, analyzing the institutional context of art can be fun. Earlier works such as *Exquisite Corpse: The Complete Oeuvre of Manet* (1988), and *Monochrome Painting* (1988–1989), addressed the way in which our insatiable appetite for constructing elaborate architectures of classification inevitably leads to a privileging of the naming and coding system over the objects themselves, thereby reducing cultural artifacts to the status of pitiable signs to be exchanged like commodities.

Like Sherrie Levine, Prina repudiates the notion that the terms of originality have remained constant, particularly in an era in which speaking through the appropriated voice(s) of history is no longer tantamount to original sin, but, rather, understood as a productive use of the anxiety of influence. For example, Prina has re-presented the history of abstract monochrome painting and the complete painting production of Manet by converting art history's Modernist canon into a generic catalogue of available tropes. In a similar vein, *Stephen Prina: Galerie Max Hetzler* (1991), addressed institutional codes of display. For this project, Prina assembled an honorific history of Hetzler's galleries in Cologne and Stuttgart with photographic documentation of all exhibitions and scaled-down models of the gallery's various architectural transformations. The show became something of a retrospective of the gallery itself, with Prina playing the role of conceptual archivist, both mapping and reconstructing the institutional space's genealogy of self-representations.

In *Dom-Hotel, Zimmer 101, Köln, 1994* we were presented with a project contingent on its own spatio-temporal evolution. Prina designed a continuous series of interconnecting wooden shelves based upon the floor plan of a room in the hotel that functioned as the location for a scene in Jean-Marie Straub and Danièle Huillet's 1965 film *Not Reconciled, or, Only violence helps where violence rules*. A film still of this scene, in which a character identified as Johanna Fähmel recites a long monologue while looking out of her hotel room window, was placed in the gallery with two other related images: a recto-verso picture of the same room during the day, and a second view of it on the evening (September 9, 1994) of the book signing of Prina's limited-edition publication, *Johanna Fähmel's Monologue*. Each day, throughout the duration of the exhibition, three of these books were put on display on the shelving units, with three more pages of the German/English text opened to the readers. By the end of the show, the shelves were filled and the entire book exposed for scrutiny.

The book is the key element here, for it is as much a self-contained conceptual project as it is the source of information for understanding the distinct layers of historical, geographic and cultural reference that have framed Prina's various activities. Moving through the first pages of the publication, the artist provides just enough data for us to form a sense of his purpose; we see that he "read the fifth chapter from Heinrich Boll's novel, *Billiards at Half-Past Nine*, in English translation, on February 13, 1987, at Beyond Baroque Literary Arts Center, Venice, California ..." This appropriated chapter from the Boll novel comprises the main body of text in Prina's publication. Flipping through a number of blank black pages, we run across a reference to the artist's book signing at the Dom-Hotel, then the still from the Straub/Huillet film on facing pages. Finally, the (appropriated) Boll text, printed in English and German on consecutive sections of black, red, and orange paper.

What are we to make of all of this? It seems that Prina is attempting to develop a new language to map the conceptual processes of art by revealing suggestive fragments of his own intellectual and experiential history. By using himself as an example, Prina subtly reminds us that our own cultural desires and fascinations are also subject to the sublimely ridiculous, albeit libidinal, urge for order and rationality.

Unmistakably Art, Anything But Art: Zobernig's Subversive Doubt

Revised version of an essay originally published in the catalogue of Heimo Zobernig's exhibition at the Wiener Secession, Vienna, Austria, July 27–August 27, 1995.

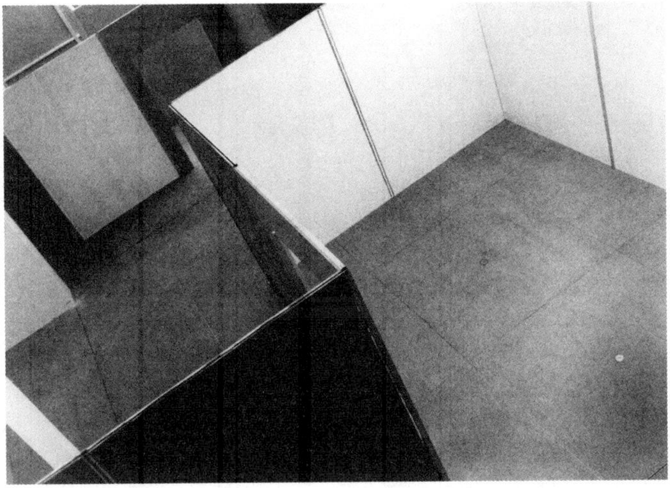

Heimo Zobernig, installation view, Wiener Secession, Vienna, 1995

The Comforts of Uncertainty

Heimo Zobernig is playing it cool, but not safe. Coolly playing an unsafe game of art, that is. As he whispers allegiance to a principle of uncertainty, as he contests meanings that appear stable, Zobernig asks us to reflect seriously upon our preconceptions about the art condition. But what is the "art condition"? Nothing more or less than everything we believe differentiates art from all else—even if we feel that art is really just like anything else. Yes, Zobernig is making art: it just feels and looks too much like art to be anything *but* art.

Art, for Zobernig, has at the very least a double life: it is perhaps a means of articulating a proposition about things that we take for granted—a mischievous proposition that quietly and elegantly upsets the already precarious connections between what we presume to know and what is right there in front of us. Without doubt, it is fair to say that Zobernig has become an expert at using his doubt as an instrument for playful subversion in all the right places, and at the appropriate moments. Take, for instance, his cooperative venture with Albert Oehlen in an exhibition last year at the Kunsthalle Wien entitled *Jetztzeit*: Oehlen installed a large room with a series of paintings, while Zobernig simply replaced the space's existing lighting system with fluorescent lamps. The result? Due to a peculiar optical phenomenon, the Oehlen paintings appeared to be stripped of all color—the eye registering the works in virtual black-and-white. The meaning of this union? First, we must commend Oehlen for submitting his paintings to this kind of seditious treatment, and then praise Zobernig for managing to persuade Oehlen to actually go through with it (or perhaps it was the other way around). Here we have a situation in which the formal integrity of a painter's work is degraded by an artist who himself employs painting as one of a number of language strategies, and we are offered a consensual-conceptual moment wherein the uniqueness of painting, per se, is at once destroyed and re-affirmed. In other words, Oehlen's visual language is both suspended and redefined by Zobernig, and Zobernig's context-specific approach is in turn modified, naturally, by Oehlen's practice. In the end, an exquisite neutralization occurred, made possible through the complicity of an arrangement where both artists have taken advantage of a benevolent form of mutual subversion.

A Precise Ambiguity

Zobernig's monochrome and striped paintings seem, at first, to bear a strong family resemblance to the chilly look of certain varieties of American and European formalist and Minimalist painting, yet at the same time resonate with a grave ambiguity about the project and ideology of painting itself. Irony dwells somewhere along the margins of Zobernig's work, yet it is a light-hearted doubt—a doubt that has haunted artists dealing with the problematic status of painting throughout this century.

While Zobernig could never be truly mistaken for a pure painter (as his collaboration with Oehlen reaffirms), he does prefer to conduct his aesthetic business, so to speak, through a language that we would associate with the now mundane codes of high or late-modernist geometric abstraction. And if Zobernig's work does suggest a philosophical link to Minimalist practice, it is manifest through his deliberately equivocal attitude toward painting. For him, the autonomy of painting is contingent upon its being entrenched within the architectonics of everyday circumstances.

Is Zobernig a conceptual artist? And what does it mean to be named a conceptual artist today? Is he producing meta-statements, or something akin to meta-art? Does anyone really know the difference between art and meta-art, anyway? And what do we make of Zobernig's smooth integration of painting into architecture—or is it the other way around? For his 1994 exhibition at the Kunsthalle Bern, Zobernig deftly set into motion a number of conceptual and material conversions: painting into place, place into painting, painting into object, architecture into painting, painting into object, and architecture into object.

Provisional Similitudes, Provisional Subversions

Zobernig feeds us uncertainty where we would least expect to find it: at the center of what seems to be an utterly rational model of art-language. In a sense he turns the certainty of his own model inside out, so that we might scrutinize all the seams and frayed edges. Is this thing what it appears to be, or is it something else? Is it a painting? Architecture? A sculptural object? None of the above?

Each thing and phenomenon contains its own antithesis, or, in other words, its imminent demise. This suggests a continuous exchange of recognition and misrecognition, a slippage, through which we read and misread signs that stand in for the things and the phenomena themselves. These signs are both supplement and surrogate of the apparently recognizable, coded world of objects and structures: signs facilitate a similitude of things and phenomena in the world, and yet they are those things too. Signs are abstract: they constitute a system, a cultural language; signs are exchanged within economies of communication, yet they also assume a materiality. Signs carry within themselves the seeds of their own annihilation.

Take away the apparent order established through systems of cultural distinction, and things begin to fall apart in the loveliest way imaginable. For instance, when is a café at once a café and not a café? When it is the product of an art activity that creates the similitude of a café. When is architecture both architecture and not architecture? When it is the product of an art activity that creates the similitude of architecture. And when is sculpture at once sculpture and not sculpture? When it is the product of an art activity that creates the similitude of sculpture. Zobernig's contribution to the 1993 *Project Unité* exhibition project in Firminy, France, was all of the above, and probably much more. In curator Yves Aupetitallot's novel approach to the question of site-specificity, a group of artists, designers, and architects were invited to produce works within vacated apartments in a disused wing of the city's Le Corbusier residential building. Zobernig responded by transforming his particular apartment into an actual—i.e., functional—café, thereby re-defining the building's indigenous rules concerning distinctions between private and public space. Visitors and residents frequented the café-as-apartment/apartment-as-café, helping themselves to coffee and other beverages, and the space's social utility seemed to outweigh the issue of whether this was art, non-art, or something in-between. Zobernig produced the similitude of a café, and this similitude was real.

The Philosophical Puddle

As a complex object/art object located within an architectural field of visible and invisible structural relations, a Zobernig painting becomes a material signifier for an intervention—a sign that becomes the index for site. This referencing of context confers upon Zobernig's works a theatricality linked to Michael Fried's coining of that term in "Art and Objecthood," an essay in which Fried offered a negative analysis of Minimalism's literalness. You may recall the argument: Fried claimed that as art approached the condition of theater, as artists focused attention upon the phenomenology of the viewer's (i.e., subject-object) experience and diminished the viewer's ability to be absorbed within the complexity of the art object, the more art became a mere object—a prop upon the stage of everyday life, a surrogate for the human body, a component of the overall situation in which the literal object of art dwelled. Fundamentally, Fried was nervous about the demise of a certain kind of art, and a certain kind of art experience; he saw the work of the Minimalist artists (or literalists, the term he preferred) as a threat to the autonomy of art's specialized language forms.

For Zobernig, painting is camouflage for an art activity or an art condition. Painting is a mask that makes art look more like art. A Zobernig painting is certainly an actual painting, but it is also quite possibly something other than a painting.

When is a painting at once a painting and not a painting? When it is the product of an art activity that creates the similitude of a painting. And when is an art object or art activity at once an art object/art activity and not an art object/art activity? When allegory takes over. The allegorical function of an art object or an art activity brings it into a narrative (or meta-narrative) relation with both everyday life and art. Art cannot be taken for granted. Why? Because it no longer takes itself for granted—if it ever did. More and more, art threatens itself with a kind of majestic extinction, and what we like to call art often seems perilously close to a kind of self-willed dispersion. Dispersal into what? Into that which invariably refutes it: i.e., everything that has yet to become art.

As art begins to distance itself from itself in order to become more like an everyday thing, it moves closer to what it is already. In other words: an extraordinary-everyday thing.

A Happy Crisis of the Art Condition

Zobernig engages in a seriously playful kind of sabotage inside the agreed-upon boundaries of art's conceptual envelope so as to move beyond that fairly insular framework of meanings, yet he also seems prepared for the inevitability that there may be no actual outside, no real beyond: in other words, no truth beyond the artifice of art's language. Zobernig deftly reframes the architectonics of institutional space so as to illuminate the inevitability of art's contextual frame.

CHAPTER II

Aporia (Art as Politics, the Politics of Art)

Peter Halley (vis-à-vis Baudrillard)

Revised version of a text on Peter Halley's exhibition at International with Monument gallery, April 3–May 4, 1986. Originally published in *Arts Magazine*, vol. 60, no. 10, Summer 1986, p. 110.

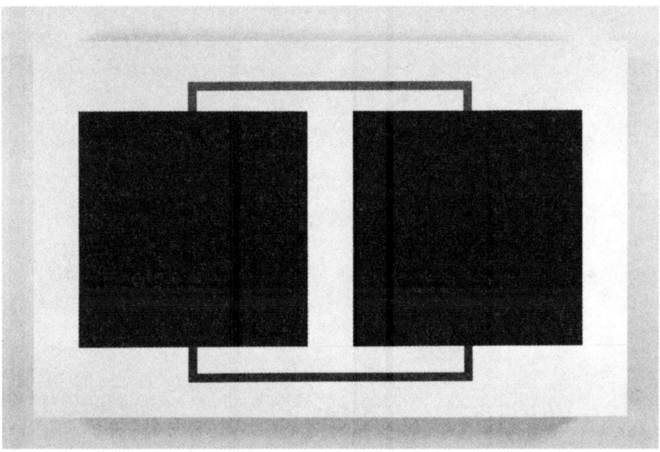

Peter Halley, *Two Cells with Circulating Conduit*, 1986

One may refer to Jean Baudrillard's relatively early essay entitled "Gesture and Signature" from *For a Critique of the Political Economy of the Sign* (1972) to locate an integrated Structuralist-Marxist analysis of the relationship between the paradigm of serial repetition as manifested in certain types of modernist practice, and the corresponding systemization of consumption and circulation of everyday objects. Radically extending the totalizing or one-dimensional conception of industrial (consumer-ist) capitalist society introduced by members of the Frankfurt School, Baudrillard attempts to foreground the new status of the art object as it assumes a homological relationship to the circulating mechanisms of consumption. Absorbed within this structure, the art object asserts its difference from everyday objects, yet paradoxically simulates the immanent structure of commodity-production through an implicit or explicit seriality.

For Baudrillard, this systematized condition removes the possibility of a transformative art practice. Warhol, for instance, developed serial strategies appropriated from mass production, claiming that "reality has no need of an intermediary; it is necessary only to isolate it from the surroundings, to transfer it to the canvas." For Warhol, the transposition of the commodity emblem from the sphere of the social into the realm of the aesthetic was not an act of transgressive, critical terrorism, but a relatively neutral maneuver designed to produce an expedient *sameness*. Baudrillard has noted that "everydayness is difference in repetition," yet he also has located the paradox that characterizes the contradictory nature of the modern (or postmodern?) art object. On the one hand, the art object is a product of a subjective activity which an artist such as Warhol attempts to deny and remove in order to be replaced by a regulated system of dissemination; on the other hand, the art object must simultaneously reference or signify the condition of the everyday. Thus the art object is "always already" differentiated from the everyday object, although on one level it will remain within the domain of the commodity. Art calls attention to itself as it is "caught" attempting to reproduce and conjugate itself according to the principles of exchange and consumption; the "representation" of these mechanisms becomes a latent criticality.

Peter Halley, who has embraced Baudrillard's later writings such as *Simulations*, seems to have welcomed the implicit nihilism contained in these treatments of contemporary society. In the brief theoretical essay issued for his latest exhibition, Halley claims that, among other transformations, "the abstract becomes the real, and the entire environment becomes a model of the environment … Thus there is only the reality of the model, but there is also no other reality other than that of the model." Further on, Halley contends, "Likewise, in this universe, by virtue of psychology and physiology, human beings can be only models of human beings."

It seems evident that, on the level of theory, Halley has taken Baudrillard's already "totalizing" conception of communication society—wherein the system of objects, previously characterized as an assembly of *signs heavy with meaning*, has been dissipated into networks of circulating channels of communication—and has arrived at a discourse on contemporary life which is conspicuously one-dimensional and disingenuously nihilistic. It is significant and troubling that this type of critical method has superseded other Marxian or post-structuralist discourses (such as the work of Jameson, and elements of Foucault) that have not dispensed with the categories of the *defining subject* and struggle on the level of social contradiction and the power relations formed from this disparity. The current availability and seductiveness of this language of pseudo-opposition allows Halley to define himself (and be defined) as a socially critical artist. Yet Halley wants to have his cake and eat it, too.

On the one hand, Halley announces that, "the vocabulary of modernism is retained, but its elements, already made abstract, are finally and completely severed from any reference to any real." On the other hand, Halley views his art practice as a critical (or self-critical) inquiry into geometric structures (the grid, cell, and conduit) which not only reference and deconstruct the history of idealist non-objective art (e.g., Malevich, Mondrian, Newman), but more significantly function as metaphors for the implicit governing social networks of communication, labor, and power. The paintings become emblems of this ideology of geometric signs. According to Halley, "Geometric signs still remain the most ubiquitous and influential in our society."

The contradictory nature of this position is abundantly clear, for Halley wishes to argue simultaneously that the language of neomodernism is incapable of referencing the real, yet his paintings, seemingly exempt from this crisis of signification, function critically as metaphors of an identifiable social referent. According to Halley, this "real" is a simulation or model of itself, and one would conclude that he defends his paintings as symbolic "models" of an archetypical structure located within social life, a structure which is totalizing in its unrelenting consumption, circulation, and neutralization of difference-as-opposition.

The central question provoked by this work becomes an issue of political exigency: is it tenable to endorse the worldview offered by Halley's prison houses of social organization? As Baudrillard has stated, "The world only really becomes mechanical from the moment it can no longer be evoked save mechanically." Halley's project reveals itself to be an uncritical, acquiescent acceptance (and imposition) of a monolithic systemization of social life, within which the still extant social, economic, and cultural contradictions of late capitalism are condoned.

CHAPTER II

The Administration of Cultural Resistance

Revised version of an essay originally published in *Texte zur Kunst*, Spring 1992.

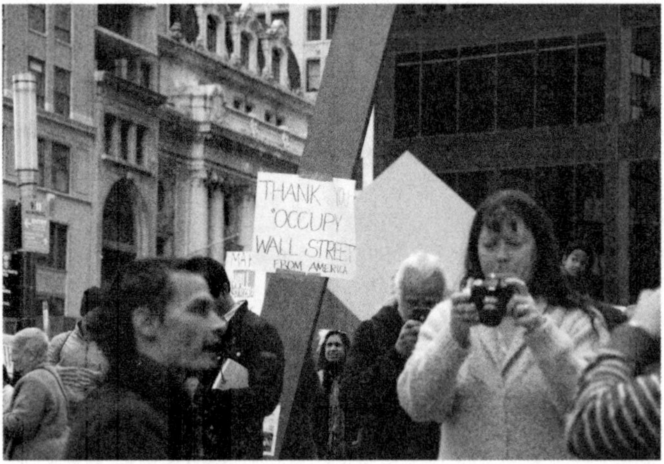

The Occupy Wall Street scene, Zuccotti Park in Lower Manhattan, October 17, 2011.

Works of art, which by their existence take the side of the victim of a rationality that subjugates nature, are even in their protest constitutively implicated in the process of rationalization itself. Were they to try to disown it, they would become aesthetically and socially powerless: mere clay. The organizing, unifying principle of each and every work of art is borrowed from that very rationality whose claim to totality it seeks to defy.
—Theodor Adorno, "Commitment"

How can we begin to evaluate the viability of politically engaged art production and art criticism: Can these practices transgress the normative institutional boundaries of the cultural vanguard? Inside the frame, all forms of transgression are encouraged and regularly displayed for public scrutiny; high culture is allowed to perennially manufacture its own regime of apparent subversion.
But what is the impact of politically engaged vanguard art production

outside the frame of relatively stable, communicative rationality? Do such practices ever migrate beyond the normative parameters of the cultural sphere, puncturing the skin of another social domain, and not merely in the form of artworks adorning the walls of corporate boardrooms? How can we begin to think critically about our own institutional and disciplinary entrapment? Have recent manifestations of cultural activism (such as Act Up), functioned to re-politicize the vanguard, breaking down the prevailing conditions of institutional and disciplinary segregation?

Art criticism remains a largely insular, and insulated, discourse and profession. One struggles to locate a pragmatic connection between the task of art criticism and whatever is meant by political engagement today. Cross-cultural and interdisciplinary projects are designed to maintain their theoretical integrity, intellectual viability, and supposedly iconoclastic appeal according to the logic of academic institutionalization—i.e., the regime of specialization that codifies even cross-disciplinary activities and interdisciplinary discourses. Edward Said has discussed the implications of what might be described as the cult of expertise in relation to literary criticism:

> it is supposed that literature and the humanities exist generally within the culture ("our" culture as it is sometimes known), that the culture is ennobled and validated by them, and yet that in the version of culture inculcated by professional humanists and literary critics, the approved practice of high culture is marginal to the serious political concerns of society. This has given rise to a cult of professional expertise whose effect in general is pernicious. For the intellectual class, expertise has usually been a service rendered, and sold, to the central authority of society.[1]

While it would be inappropriate to draw an exacting analogy between the academic realm of literary criticism and the quasi-academic, quasi-journalistic role of art criticism, Said's comments are nevertheless useful in beginning to understand the degree to which art criticism—as a relatively autonomous discipline—operates as an arbiter of aesthetic taste and value at particular moments in the development of visual art cultures. Somewhat related to the role of art history, art criticism functions as a method of expertise designed to discriminate between what is worthy, and what is unworthy. Art criticism, like art history, has traditionally maintained an ambiguous, complex interconnection with the logic and central authority of the art marketplace, a relationship constructed during the late 19th-century, when the two fields began to assume the characteristics of relatively autonomous disciplines. But as Said suggests, it would be wrong to reduce the relationship of art criticism to the art marketplace. It is crucial to understand that on institutional terms, professional expertise (the maintenance of disciplinary codes, conventions, etc.) can become a channel for the establishment of cultural hegemonies. This is evident not only in relation to dominant trends in the marketplace of visual art, but also within the marketplace of ideas—e.g., the commodification of political theory.

It is difficult to see how art criticism could become a pragmatic instrument of political engagement or activism without relinquishing the conventional language categories, methodological structures, and historical codes that constitute its disciplinary autonomy or integrity. In other words, art criticism would have to become unrecognizable. Yet, it is unclear what type of political function would result if questions of the institutional frame were not actively addressed. Is it pragmatic to expect that evidence of political commitment (indicated by an effort to construct viable intersections between political language and political action) within the precincts of the vanguard, would have an impact upon other social spheres without the presence of a more collective political agenda shared by various institutional zones? When the majority of citizens in a heterogeneous society like the United States do not manifest a deep desire for large-scale economic and ideological transformation (or have not found the means by which to express this desire), then we are confronted by the type of administered segregation of cultural-political activism that a rationalized society produces on a daily basis. Transgression is permitted only to the extent to which it conforms to the conventional logics of subversion and resistance already tolerated within enclaves of society. Said, adopting what might be described as a kind of post-Marxist, neo-humanist position, calls for criticism to "think of itself as life-enhancing and constitutively opposed to every form of tyranny, domination, and abuse; its social goals are non-coercive knowledge produced in the interests of human freedom."[2] Furthermore, he suggests that "criticism belongs in that potential space inside civil society, acting on behalf of those alternative acts and alternative intentions whose advancement is a fundamental human and intellectual obligation."[3] Are we to infer that Said is arguing that criticism should assume an oppositional relationship to those conditions within a society that deter the freedom of the individual? Or is he claiming that criticism should support all that is marginalized within general culture?

We might conclude that when Said refers to a "potential space" within the social fabric, he is alluding to a hypothetical realm or enclave within (or out of) which criticism is endowed with the power to operate on behalf of disenfranchised intellectual and artistic practices. Yet it could be argued that this "potential space" already exists in the form of vanguard culture, wherein marginalization is lamented and railed against until the marginal becomes absorbed into the mainstream—leaving us in a rather uncomfortable, and all-too-familiar double bind, since the mainstream is considered as the alternately repressive and beneficent apparatus of cultural empowerment. The problem with Said's discussion is that even if criticism were to somehow become socially transformative, it's not only that we lack an agreed upon set of criteria to determine what "socially transformative" actually means, but further, a rationalized society has the capability of neutralizing criticism through processes of administrative regulation. Although this might well smack of the kind of pessimism often associated with Adorno and Horkheimer's somber evaluation of the total system of advanced capitalist society in "The Culture Industry: Enlightenment as Mass Deception," I am not attempting to construct an argument that privileges a model of totality wherein society absorbs its own self-produced oppositions, contradictions, and differences in the name of freedom. Nor am I willing to concede, like Baudrillard, that all models of collective social transformation are predicated upon the same systematic logic that underlies the administrative regimes of postindustrial organization, even though it is difficult to think productively beyond such categories. In an introduction to a book featuring the critical debates between Adorno, Lukacs, Brecht, and Benjamin, Fredric Jameson offered some telling observations regarding the notion of a culture industry for our current circumstances:

> More relevant in the present context, however, is the Frankfurt School's premise of a "total system," which expressed Adorno's and Horkheimer's sense of the increasingly closed organization of the world into a seamless web of media technology, multinational corporations, and international bureaucratic control. Whatever the theoretical merits of the idea of the "total system," we may at least agree with Adorno that in the cultural realm, the all-pervasiveness of the system, with its "culture"—or (Enzenberger's variant) its "consciousness-industry"—makes for an unpropitious climate for any of the older, simpler forms of oppositional art, whether it be that proposed by Lukács, that produced by Brecht, or indeed those celebrated in different ways by Benjamin and Bloch. The system has a power to co-opt and defuse even the most potentially dangerous forms of political art by transforming them into cultural commodities.[4]

Jameson would modify his own critical relationship to this notion of the "total system" a number of years later when he attempted to construct a theoretical model of what might constitute a viable type of politicized art practice in the age of late capitalist postmodernism:

> an aesthetic of cognitive mapping—a pedagogical political culture which seeks to endow the individual subject with some new heightened sense of its place in the global system—will necessarily have to respect this now enormously complex representational dialectic and to invent radically new forms in order to do it justice … the new political art—if it is indeed possible at all—will have to hold to the truth of postmodernism, that is to say, to its

> fundamental object—the world space of multinational capital.[5]

Here Jameson, the cultural critic, understands his disciplinary role as more than simply offering another hermeneutic (which would consign this particular piece to an essentially academic use-value), and proceeds to develop a model of aesthetic-political engagement and production. Therefore, he attempts to wrench critical activity away from an exclusive preoccupation with interpretation, and coax it in the direction of a practice that has the potential for broader cultural, social, and political applications. Ironically or not, this particular Jameson essay has had considerable influence within the field of art criticism, where it has been appropriated by some writers as a means of legitimizing examples of contemporary art.

Art historian and critic Hal Foster has used Jameson's notion of "cognitive mapping" in an essay ("Signs Taken For Wonders," *Art in America*, June 1986) that offers a rather trenchant and persuasive critique of the work of a number of quasi-abstract painters and photographers who came to prominence in the 1980s (e.g., Jack Goldstein, Peter Halley, Sherrie Levine, Philip Taaffe). Foster argues that the visual language of such practices—specifically, the aesthetic construct/paradigm of painting—has become outmoded, no longer a viable framework through which to examine (and represent) the emergent conditions of late capitalist society:

> So, too, if we do inhabit a new social space of immanent flows and simulated effects, as Halley suggests, it is not at all clear that it can be painted, let alone represented, by a single image of a cell and a conduit. His painted image, its metaphoric functions, its iconic placement on a Cartesian grid—all of these elements constitute a mode of representation incommensurate with the hypothesis of a new social network of cybernetic interconnection. Such a network demands instead both a new mode of apprehension and a new strategy of intervention (such as the one suggested by certain Keith Sonnier works of the 1970s that hooked directly and diagrammatically into radio, telephone, and television systems).[6]

In the footnotes of his essay, Foster discusses the relevance of Jameson's notion of the aesthetic of "cognitive mapping," and then goes on to fulfill the disciplinary obligations of the art critic by citing an art practice that might demonstrate one practical application of this new aesthetic: "An instance of this aesthetic at work may be Martha Rosler's videotape *Global Taste*, which begins to map out the late-capitalist penetration of both First-World psyches and Third-World markets."[7] Whereas Jameson cautiously retains the theoretical character of his ideas and writing, Foster re-purposes this theoretical construct into the art critical language of evaluation, interpretation, and in certain cases, advocacy.

In this scenario, the precursor theoretical language migrates into the more topical realm of art criticism, where it is essentially transformed into an instrument of cultural commodification—i.e., the endorsement of certain art practices in the name of a political-aesthetic agenda. At the conclusion of an essay entitled "Readings in Cultural Resistance," Foster asserts:

> Here important tasks for criticism and art alike emerge: for criticism to (re)apprehend in the (historical) work of art the revolutionary conflicts (between the sign-systems and ultimately perhaps between classes) that the work of art resolves or otherwise engages; and for art to expose rather than reconcile these contradictions in the present, indeed to intensify them. What I propose is not entirely new: it is basically what Nietzsche termed a "genealogy" and what Foucault called the "insurrection of subjugated knowledges." But what must be stressed is the need to connect the buried (nonsynchronous), the disqualified (the minor), and the yet-to-come (the utopian or, better, the desired) in concerted cultural practice. For finally it is this association which can most fully resist major culture, its semiotic appropriations, normative categories, and official history.[8]

Although we might salute Foster's interest in promoting the notion of a concerted ensemble of disparate cultural practices, his notion that such a constellation would offer some type of resistance to a mainstream or dominant culture that is itself partially comprised of the very ensemble of marginal, emergent, and repressed art practices, seems a bit optimistic, even politically naive. What are the consequences when those practices attain an official position, migrating from the outside or periphery (are these the precincts of the "minor" culture?) into the supposed center of the major culture? Isn't Foster really just calling for the supposedly marginalized to produce and write their own histories? And doesn't a concerted or collective response of heterogeneous cultural practices suggest the emergence of merely another new major culture based upon the empowerment of the peripheral? Isn't Foster implicitly asking for the substitution of an emergent dominant for a residual dominant? And isn't major culture in America already a field of contestation between residual and emergent aesthetic, ideological, political configurations? In calling for a resistance to the "semiotic appropriations, normative categories, and official history" of the major culture, Foster seems to overlook the degree to which his own activity as a critic—for instance, his well-known books on contemporary culture, such as *The Anti-Aesthetic*—facilitates the construction of yet another permutation of the official (which has its own semiotic structures and normative categories).

By neglecting to reflect critically upon the institutional norms and structures of art criticism, Foster's writing reproduces the normative logic it desires to destabilize. One abstraction is simply replaced by another. Foster certainly cannot be singled out for this problem, since it characterizes the dilemma of art criticism on an institutional level. Clearly, this is a situation that must be understood in relation to the market-oriented conditions of our culture, wherein, for example, critical discourse, promotional language and advertising have become increasingly interchangeable within art magazines.

Yet one cannot blame the double binds of art criticism entirely upon the art world's umbilical cords of gold. The failure of politically engaged artists, curators, writers, and others to generate wider cultural resistance is due to a fundamental balkanization of society. The spheres of vanguard culture have been carefully insulated from other public spheres, particularly within the United States. This predicament has been discussed, in historical terms, by

Jürgen Habermas in "Modernity—An Incomplete Project." Some are troubled by his endorsement of a singular cultural tradition functioning as a unifying force for various social spheres in the name of *communicative rationality*, for it suggests the hegemony of one tradition over others. And who would determine the character of that unifying cultural tradition?

Yet he is more persuasive in analyzing how rationalized society atomizes socio-cultural spheres, wherein the rupturing of one sphere (e.g., the sphere of culture) does not necessarily lead to the rupturing of others. Habermas uses the notion of a unifying cultural tradition as code for a type of collective, trans-institutional, cultural resistance that might galvanize links between various domains by exploiting the already established system of rationalized communication for different ideological-political ends. He is practical enough to recognize that the possibilities of such developments are rather limited in the contemporary situation, but nonetheless goes on to cite an example of what he believes is the socially transformative potential of the "re-appropriation of the expert's culture from the standpoint of the lifeworld."[9] (The relationship between this notion and Said's ideas is compelling.) Habermas provides an example of how such "re-appropriations" might function by referring to an account in Peter Weiss' *The Aesthetic of Resistance*, wherein a group of workers (during the late 1930s) attended school in order to educate themselves about a part of high European culture from which they were essentially alienated, and then applied this newly acquired knowledge to their own social context: "These young workers went back and forth between the edifice of European art and their own milieu until they were able to illuminate both."[10] Yet Habermas is careful to re-emphasize that such strategies could only be effective if the economic and ideological structures of the society were steered in a quite different direction by concerted, trans-institutional efforts; the prospects for this, within advanced capitalist society, Habermas suggests, are not good at this point. And we should ask ourselves whether vanguard visual art culture can be used as a launching pad for political resistance if we continue to insist upon preserving normative categories such as art production, art criticism, art history, and so on and so forth.

In the spirit of Walter Benjamin's *The Author as Producer*, Benjamin Buchloh offers a critical discussion of the transformation of Soviet productivist aesthetics (formed out of the language of the early modernist avant-garde) from a collective instrument of emancipatory change to a centralized instrument of repression in "From Faktura to Factography." Buchloh trenchantly cautions against the potential dangers of (re)appropriating demonstrably faulty historical models of cultural resistance for contemporary use. He also argues that a notion of "simultaneous collective reception" offered by Walter Benjamin (on a theoretical level) and Lissitsky (on the level of practice), and used within the context of revolutionary Russia, would subsequently facilitate—as a result of its intrinsic structure—the aesthetic and technological instruments developed within the totalitarian system of the Soviet Union and the fascist systems of Germany and Italy to perpetuate such ideological structures. Furthermore, Buchloh goes on to assert that these ironic and paradoxical historical transformations regarding the conversion of "simultaneous collective reception" from a strategy of social emancipation into a tool of social control would eventually become linked to capitalism's culture industry. If we do not wish to accept the Adorno-inflected "total system" model implicitly endorsed by Buchloh, and we also have difficulty maintaining the conviction that art galvanizes political action beyond the sphere of the art world, what are the alternatives? And what is to be done?

This dilemma cannot necessarily be resolved by claiming that an alternate set of art practices, activist strategies, critical discourses, or theoretical models would somehow be more politically consequential or effective. While such a rhetorical maneuver might be well received within certain precincts of the art world, it would merely feed an apparatus that seeks to monetize and/or institutionalize the next exemplary artist and practice.

[1] Edward Said, "Secular Criticism," *The World, The Text, and The Critic*, Harvard University Press, Cambridge, Massachusetts 1983, p. 2.
[2] Ibid., p. 29.
[3] Ibid., p. 29.
[4] Fredric Jameson, "Reflections in Conclusion," *Aesthetics and Politics*, NLB, London 1977, p. 208.
[5] Fredric Jameson. "Postmodernism, or the Cultural Logic of Late Capitalism," *New Left Review* 146, July–August 1984, p. 92.
[6] Hal Foster, "Signs Taken for Wonders," *Art in America*, June 1986, p. 88.
[7] Ibid., p. 139.
[8] Hal Foster, "Readings in Cultural Resistance," *Recodings*, Bay Press, Seattle 1985, p. 179.
[9] Jürgen Habermas, "Modernity—An Incomplete Project," *The Anti-Aesthetic: Essays on Postmodern Culture*, ed. Hal Foster, Bay Press, Seattle 1983, p. 13.
[10] Ibid.

CHAPTER II

Stupidity as Destiny: American Idiot Culture as Radical Chic

[The *Beavis and Butt-Head* animated television series was originally aired on MTV from 1993 through 1997. A feature-length animated film, entitled *Beavis and Butt-Head Do America*, was released in 1996. In 2011, due to a significant cult following, MTV Networks [Viacom] revived the television series with new episodes.]

Earlier versions of this text appeared as "Stupidity as Destiny: American Idiot Culture," published in *Flash Art* 178, October 1994; and "Radical Chic—American Style: The Idiot Culture Meets Political Correctness," originally published in the *Radical Chic Reader*, Kunstlerhaus Stuttgart, 1994.

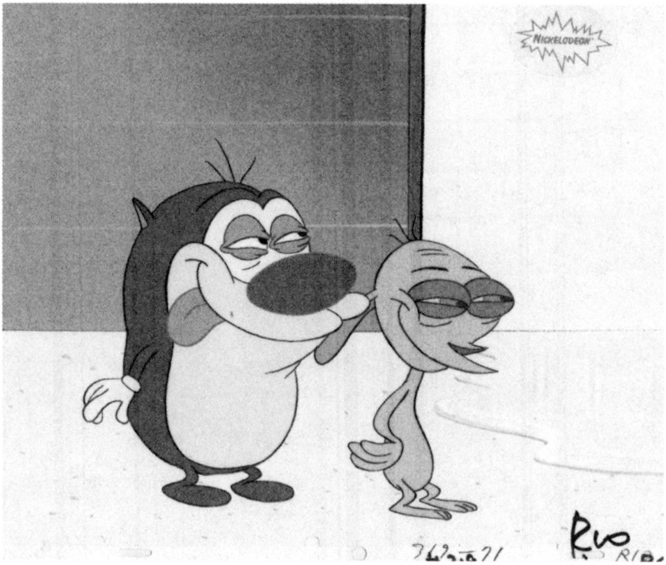

The Ren & Stimpy Show, Nickelodeon Animation Studios

"Happy Happy Joy Joy, Happy Happy Joy Joy."[1]

I wish to offer what could be described as a symptomatic analysis of recent tendencies in American popular culture and the visual arts, focused upon the premise that idiocy and stupidity have become dominant trends in American society. In the United States, we have finally come to terms with the radical will of our own libidinal penchant for stupidity, and we have responded with nuanced apathy. Allegories of hope, promise, and socio-economic upward-mobility that enjoyed prominence in the movies and on television for many decades may now have finally been replaced by allegories wherein every-one—regardless of race, cultural identity, or economic standing—is stuck in the rut of banal existence. Well-trodden models of success are now in some disrepute. Today, we love the endless replaying of banality for the sake of banality:

the objective is to evoke the lowest common denominator of blue-collar, white trash, lower middle-America (e.g., the TV show *Married with Children*) because it is either deemed to be a reflection of lives beyond any sort of social or spiritual redemption, or a vision of what we fear could have been—or might become—our eventual fate, if we had been born in Cleveland or Detroit.

Today, we seek out both inspired and insipid varieties of stupidity. We probably depend more on the entertainment industry (rather than the visual arts) to remind us of just how addicted we have become to the idea that our collective mediocrity is exemplary. Judging by the immense popularity of television situation-dramas such as *Melrose Place* (the spin-off of *Beverly Hills 90210*) and *Bay Watch*, where perfect human—i.e., American—specimens can barely put together a grammatically correct sentence, or contemporary lifestyle-films such as *Singles* and *Reality Bites*, our greatest cultural aspiration at the end of the century might just be to stall, indefinitely, the evolutionary process itself. It seems that the more frequently we are reminded of the threatening depths of mediocre experience, the more fervently we seek out the thrill of using dumbness as a tool for critically accessing our own slide down into enchanted intellectual impoverishment. The pursuit of stupid experience has become our treasured national pastime. Stupidity is a banal sublime that cannot be breached by rationality or common sense, because it has now replaced both of these categories. From its inception, television has managed to build into itself an auto-critique, specifically within the realm of comedy and comedy-oriented programs. The history of television comedy is at the same time the history of a popular vanguardism that reveals mainstream culture's ability to survive regular campaigns of lampooning itself. Here is a regulated system of checks and balances in which mediocrity and its critique exist peacefully alongside each other. It is legitimate to suggest that contemporary television just might be at its best when it can develop shows that smartly and entertainingly take on the convention of the medium itself, indicative of a kind of self-critical formalism that moves the language forward, as in the visual arts.

A number of cultural theorists have sought to rethink the definitions, functions, and meanings of culture in the late 20th-century, so as to challenge the traditionally modernist ideological divisions between high and low, moving beyond the condemnatory, moralizing discourse on mass culture found within the writings of the Frankfurt School (e.g., Adorno and Horkheimer's *The Culture Industry*), and proposing new analytic methods. For example, in a 1984 interview with Stephen Heath, the late Raymond Williams (who wrote extensively on the sociological conditions of television in the 1970s), referenced another notion of popular culture, in which "everyday conversation and exchange," including "jokes and idioms" and "everyday gossip," are somehow converted into the "serial" structures that we find within the language of television.[2] Here, Williams references the shift from notions of "folk culture" to the expanded framework of "popular culture" (preferring this phrase to the totalizing concept of "mass culture") as this unfolds through the platform of television as a shared media experience. John Fiske, a media theorist who wrote extensively on television, focused more on Pierre Bourdieu's emphasis upon how in "the culture of everyday life," people do not make a distinction (or create a distance between) art and life. Fiske endorses Bourdieu's notion of social space as habitus—i.e., distinct spaces inhabited by "dispositions," higher levels of education, specific tastes, wherein cultural capital is constructed (thereby embodying various economic, class, and social positions). Fiske suggests that within the same habitus, theories can be generated amongst those of similar "dispositions," which actually (re)produce, paradoxically, another kind of distancing from the mundane aspects of life.[3] But he also suggests that the overlapping of different habituses—i.e., social habitats—naturally creates a densely textured zone of activities, practices, etc. And it is television, he suggests, which is used by people to increase and enrich the texture of everyday culture. For Fiske, television is always re-appropriated by individuals to enhance the texture of everyday life, partly because television constantly re-presents that texture in manageable units of information. Fiske is endeavoring here to find a way out of the rather familiar quagmire that occurs when academics take on the material of everyday culture; he does not seek to elevate or recuperate television, per se, on aesthetic terms, but rather to understand its social operations.

Both Williams and Fiske were suspicious of totalizing models of everyday culture, and the term "mass culture" was problematic for both. This tendency can be linked to Fredric Jameson's claim that the cultural critic could no longer deploy the older, moralizing, ideological attacks on mass media and or popular culture (i.e., the Frankfurt School approach), because "postmodernist space" had generated "new cultural categories" (e.g., conflations of high and low culture), making those earlier ideological models of critique much less reliable.[4] In this way, Jameson was also taking issue with normative Enlightenment and modernist academic categories of cultural analysis, wherein the refined arts (whether visual, musical, or other) are seen as the highest expression of a society—and everything else is mere dross (or worse, kitsch). A more amplified riposte to modernist models of culture—and in particular, distinctions between high and low—can be observed in AIDS activist and cultural critic Jan Zita Grover's embrace of Williams' admonition that "culture is ordinary," and her outspoken disapproval of the specialized language and elitist assumptions of academic criticism.[5] This is not anti-intellectualism, but rather skepticism regarding the social insularity of academe's ivory towers. Outside these ivory towers, at least in the United States, we have finally come to terms with the radical will of our own libidinal penchant for stupidity. Something has unquestionably changed, and it concerns the way in which popular culture has managed to reinvent the relationship between audience and media within the terms of comedy logic: we celebrate the lowest common denominator. Comedy genre shows on television such as *Seinfeld*, *Ren and Stimpy*, and *Beavis and Butt-Head* are the vanguard of popular entertainment, and each of these shows elevates stupidity to a new sublime.

In the late 1980s, a new cult of stupidity began to emerge that had not been witnessed before in the history of popular culture—a stupidity articulated with an unparalleled sophistication. Witness the emergence of David Letterman's talk show, which featured Stupid Pet Tricks and Stupid Human Tricks: these were self-conscious, parodic, theatrical stagings of obtuse, abject activities. Indeed, the comedy was indistinguishable from the abjectness (and vice versa). Letterman may have only sought to deconstruct the historical conventions of the talk show (as a form of mass-media postmodernism), yet such expositions of sheer stupidity also revealed a desire to subvert the audience's expectations of just how far popular culture would go to transmit unmitigated idiocy. Does it make us stupid for enjoying these programs? Perhaps, on some level, we have found our inner idiocy. Stupidity—i.e., a type of practiced, self-conscious stupidity—also has the potential to be critical, beyond sheer entertainment. The aforementioned TV programs incorporate self-critique—and therefore a critique of the television/entertainment culture in general—within the texture of their programs. *Beavis and Butt-Head* sit on their couch analyzing music videos on MTV, and so become the foremost media critics in America. What could be more radical chic than television that cannibalizes itself in order to critique and parody itself? But where does this leave the cultural critic? In an increasingly precarious—if not imminently obsolete—position.

Stupidity has become its own conceptual paradigm, equally but differently applicable to the realms of popular culture and visual arts culture. Contemporary art offers numerous examples of smartly executed dumb ideas. For example, in Bruce Nauman's *Self-Portrait as a Fountain* (1966-67), Duchamp's urinal-as-fountain readymade is commemorated and parodied—in the form of an admittedly dumb art historical insider's joke. As in many of Nauman's video and holographic works from the 1960s, we are not really meant to be duped into believing that something truly meaningful is happening. Rather, that only something truly meaningful could be happening if we accepted the premise that fundamentally stupid activities create their own kind of meaning; and they do, of course, but only under the spell of a conceptualized stupidity. And what about when Chris Burden crucified himself on a Volkswagen, or when he had himself shot in the arm, or when he took a shot at an airplane flying overhead? These are dumb acts that suggest a kind of cultivated irresponsibility. Nothing is more seductive for the art world than to observe artists testing the limits of obtuseness. Warhol, in his own kind of idiot-savant style, did this all the time; the Brillo boxes were a brilliantly dumb idea that momentarily collapsed the already stupid conceptual-philosophical-institutional distinction between artworks and other cultural things. And what of Vito Acconci's *Step Piece* (1970), wherein the artist stepped up and down from a stool at a rate of 30 steps per minute each morning for the duration of a month? This took redundancy to a new tautological extreme. What might strike us as dumb here is the repetition of a seemingly mindless physical act that forces the body into a ritualistic endgame, suggesting a collapse of meaning. How much more radical—or chic—can you get than this stupid, yet vanguard, human activity?

Back to popular culture: the animated characters *Beavis and Butt-Head* sit at home watching MTV 24-hours a day, making deeply stupid jokes about music videos, occasionally identifying a video as being *cool*—their favorite critical term. These two are the new critics of our idiot culture, the sages of the moment—role models, not only for kids, but also for teenagers and young adults. They represent the vanguard, leading edge of cultural idiocy, and they have become a phenomenal success in the US today. Occupying the center of the popular culture, these two cartoon characters are irredeemably idiotic. Yet they are blissfully ignorant of their condition, and so have no qualms about imposing their model of behavior—which might be adequately described as unconsciously asocial—upon others they encounter. Curiously, we never get to meet the parents, who perhaps abandoned them. But the American public has embraced them. I love them too.

Stupidity is the ultimate escape from responsibility and necessity. Stupidity is a new aesthetic. Stupidity is a new sublime. Stupidity is a new fantasy for the intellectual class. Stupidity is an opiate for the masses. Stupidity is the new model of comedy. Stupidity is now hip, whether it is drug-induced or simply innate. Stupidity has become a designer behavioral mode, the costume we most comfortably fit into after a long day of purposive rationality and goal-oriented labor. Our newfound stupidity has utilitarian value, it is instrumental. It makes everyone laugh—at our own fascination with intellectual regression. This may be the sign of a decadence sprung from our fin-de-siècle era: a steady erosion of literacy and intellectual fluency that bespeaks a willing abandonment of an Enlightenment model of cultural advance or progress, instead favoring a capitulation to the hopelessness of a nation in a state of social and educational degeneration. We love the culture of stupidity because it is our future, and this future is seductive, regardless of its moral or ethical implications. Part-time masochists, we relish the possibility of witnessing our own demise. We love our stupidity; it has become a national treasure.

Today, to participate in the idiot culture—for we all participate, like it or not—is considered not only chic, but also a mode of behavior which might be deployed as a way of transforming intellectual debasement into a form of critical engagement. What an idiotic idea!(?)

[1] Theme song from *The Ren & Stimpy Show*, a Nickelodeon Animation Studios cartoon production. This animation series was originally televised from 1991 through 1996.

[2] "An Interview with Raymond Williams by Stephen Heath and Gillian Skirrow," *Studies in Entertainment*, ed. Tania Modleski, The Regents of the University of Wisconsin System, Madison 1986, p. 5.

[3] John Fiske, "Cultural Studies and the Culture of Everyday Life," *Cultural Studies*, eds. Lawrence Grossberg, Cary Nelson, Paula Treichler, Routlege, London and New York 1992, p. 154–173.

[4] Fredric Jameson "Postmodernism, or The Cultural Logic of Late Capitalism," *New Left Review*, I/146, July–August 1984.

[5] Jan Zita Grover, "AIDS, keywords, and Cultural Work," *Cultural Studies*, ed. Lawrence Grossberg, Cary Nelson, and Paula A. Treichler, Routledge, New York 1992.

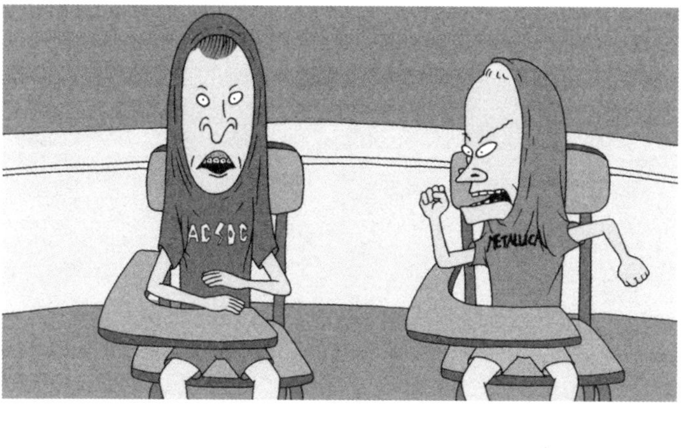

Beavis and Butt-Head, MTV Networks (Viacom)

Liam Gillick, *The State Itself Becomes a Super Whatnot*

Revised version of a text on Liam Gillick's exhibition at Casey Kaplan Gallery, New York, May 8–June 14, 2008. Originally published in *Artforum*, October 2008.

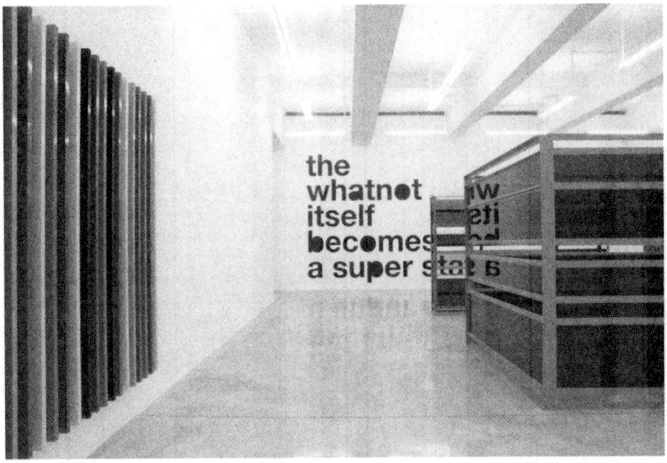

Liam Gillick, *The State Itself Becomes a Super Whatnot*, installation view, Casey Kaplan, New York, 2008

"The state itself becomes a super whatnot"—what*ever*! I so want to believe in Gillick's post-Fordist cosmology of poeticized socio-economic rhetoric. Alas, the elegant array of new works grouped here under the aforementioned title phrase merely reconstitutes Gillick's ongoing project: the re-instrumentalization of codes of Minimalism and Conceptualism, inflected by rather soft, ingratiating contextual/situational tactics. His enterprise engenders a variant of intellectual ventriloquism: decorative object-structures are deployed to give voice to a broader ideational framework—supplemented by an obligatory press release spun in the language of hazy social relevance.

Structured so as to be self-referential, the show proposed a closed binary system of formal and structural relationships. The title, writ large on the entry wall in slick black vinyl letters, is actually a work in and of itself; a neo-conceptualist conceit laced with hip design aesthetics. On the wall of the next room Gillick reordered the title (the whatnot itself becomes a super state), linguistically framing four works: *Between Kalmar and Udevalla* (2008), a wall-based sculpture that, comprising 40 powder-coated-aluminum slat-like elements, resembles a large multicolored radiator unit; *Sometimes They Worked in Groups of Three* (2008), a large, red, freestanding, rectilinear structure made of aluminum and Plexiglas; *Status Following Closure* (2008), a much narrower, freestanding, rectilinear structure composed of the same materials in multiple colors; and a wall-installed ventilation-unit-like work, *Projected Retraction*.

The next room featured two sculptures that appear to remix the structures and colors of the works in the previous space. In addition, the relatively inconspicuous *Prototype Double Mounted Wall Rail* from 1988—a blue-gray object mounted high on the wall—evokes Gillick's ongoing preoccupation with the relations between reductive sculptural aesthetics, architectural design, and art's contextual and spatial frames. Each work here is tightly calibrated in its conception, design, and execution, and the formal conflations are indeed clever. Gillick employs abstraction (aesthetic and social) to signify everything and nothing (the "whatnot" of the title, perhaps?), building reductive structures that transmit meaning as if it were meaningless.

Now, back to the mother of it all: the press release. The works here apparently relate to "Construccion de Uno (Construction of One)," a text around which Gillick has been making work since 2004. We read that this body of work "evolves from Gillick's research of past and present evaluations of the aesthetics of social systems by focusing on modes of production rather than consumption"; that it emerges out of an investigation into "Brazilian research into Scandinavian car production" and how workers have rethought modes of production. The release goes on to indicate that this is ultimately a "scenario," reverberating upon itself in a series of linguistic and structural moves that "mark the site of the exhibition as an extension of the complex processes of democratic deferral and infinite subcontracting that underscore our current processes of exchange." It's hard to determine whether this is trenchant analysis, the masking of obscure rumination behind the discursive smog of low-octane critical inquiry ... or somehow both!

I give credit to Gillick for the way he crafts his semiotic games, but I get the sense we are just meant to be beguiled by his multifaceted practice (and his multitasking presence, redistributed across a network of art world and academic situations), charmed by his intellectual resourcefulness, and seduced by meta-rhetorical operations wherein meaning is always held in suspense. Here, ambiguity is an art form, a variant of late postmodernism. The putatively relational dynamic that Gillick engineers is the mirror image of an insider's game of linguistic, semantic, and social twists and turns, more conservative in ideology than we might want to admit. His is a post-critical discourse, ultimately suggesting that our current social conditions and economic processes are too complicated for us to understand. In this scenario, it may be the public that becomes a *super whatnot.*

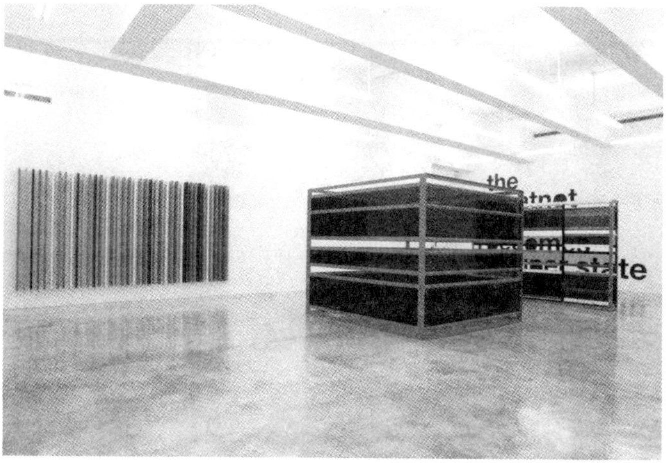

Liam Gillick, *The State Itself Becomes a Super Whatnot*, installation view, Casey Kaplan, New York, 2008

Superflex, *Flooded McDonald's*

Revised version of a text on Superflex, *Flooded McDonald's*, at Peter Blum Gallery, New York, January 22–March 27, 2010. Originally published in *Artforum*, vol. 48, April 2010.

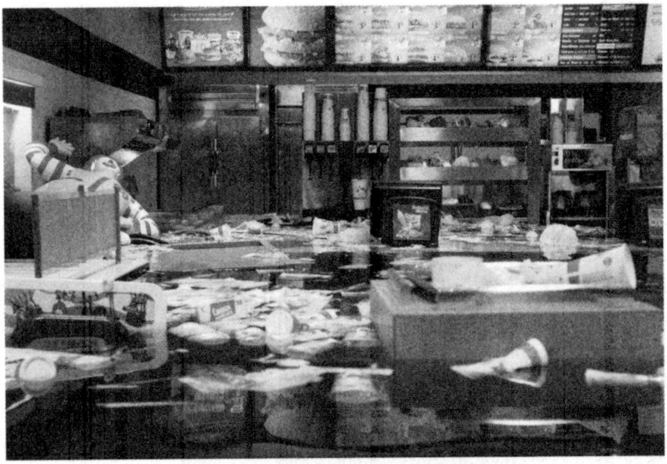

Superflex, *Flooded McDonald's*, 2008

Since 1993, the three-person Danish art collective Superflex has been encouraging locally driven, globally networked forms of self-organized cultural and economic labor in order to counter the abstractive tendencies of post-Fordist global capitalism. A well-known ongoing project is Guarana Power (2003–), an actual soda for sale and consumption, which Superflex has been producing in collaboration with a cooperative of guarana farmers in the Brazilian Amazon. They have also tested the possibility of free economic exchange, for instance with *FREE SHOP* (2003–): real shops temporarily converted into places wherein goods or services can be purchased free of charge.

By contrast, for *Flooded McDonald's*, Superflex's first "solo" show in New York, the collective presented three video works: *Burning Car* (2008), *The Financial Crisis (I–IV)* (2009), and *Flooded McDonald's* (2009). The first is a deadpan, nine-and-a-half-minute-long HD-video documenting a burning Mercedes. The film, shot in a single take, begins with the explosion that sets the car alight. Flames quickly begin leaping high into the air; the car windows explode; the camera slowly circles around the burning object, with occasional close-ups of paint bubbling off the chassis, tires popping, the interior cage smoking madly, resulting in a burnt-out hulk. The fetishistic aesthetic of TV car commercials here serves to generate a post-apocalyptic scene in which a luxury brand is incinerated.

While the video could be read as a celebration of an icon of advanced capitalism undergoing creative destruction—presumably reflecting a desire to drown our seemingly unquenchable commodity-fetishism—it also, perhaps, offers a commentary on the uncomfortable interrelationship between the spectacle of consumerism and the spectacle of anti-consumerist protests. As Debord suggested many decades ago, spectacle consumes contradiction. Seen this way, Superflex's flame-engulfed car functions as an emblem of a post-contradictory world, wherein the spectacular codes of capitalist culture and anticapitalist invective are functionally equivalent. On the level of micropolitics, Superflex does emphasize its commitment to an open-source, postcapitalist model of informational, intellectual, and artistic exchange, having made this video available for free downloading via the Pirate Bay, thereby espousing a copyleft relationship to their own artistic production (even if the piece is, at the same time, an edition of three with one artist's proof).

The Financial Crisis (I–IV) (2009) takes on the recent financial crisis through the unlikely agency of a hypnotist (an actual hypnotist named Bo Groth Christensen), who, as Superflex states on its website, "guides us through our worst nightmares to reveal the crisis without as the psychosis within." Beautifully scripted and elegantly shot, the piece is designed, perhaps ironically, to be therapeutic. Christensen declares, "Close your eyes ... Try to imagine that you lie in a nice house that means a lot to you ... Now you can only watch the system collapsing and there is nothing you can do ... This is a disaster for you. Realize what it means to you ... You have no money, you will lose your house, your pension, and your credit cards." He then intones, "You are losing everything." Whether this results, for the viewer, in a psychically revelatory process, further alienation, or both, remains unknown.

Flooded McDonald's, meanwhile, meticulously documents the gradual flooding of a handmade, to-scale, detailed replica of a McDonald's restaurant. It is shot and edited expertly, generating deadpan hilarity and unlikely dramatic buildup. At the start, water begins to seep in, rather innocuously, from under a door, and for the next 20 minutes it keeps slowly rising, as the iconic site of consumerism turns into a topography of trash, and the store's contents (Ronald McDonald, french fries, soda cups, etc.) become unmoored. Whether the result of a busted sewer line or Nature itself (read: global warming), the simulated space of the hegemonic fast-food economy is eventually swallowed up and transformed into a prehistoric primordial muck.

What is the place of these videos within the Superflex toolset, vis-à-vis their interrogation of global capitalism? Perhaps, deploying hyper-professional codes of commercial TV ads is imagined as a means of detonating critical consciousness. Here, Superflex reproduces the seductive, high-tech codes of television ads in an attempt to intervene—at the level of media language—in the symbolic, visual mechanisms of global capitalism. In the process, the collective re-animates a tradition of critique and political activism in video art.

Emily Jacir, *dispatch*

Revised version of a text on Emily Jacir at Alexander and Bonin, New York, October 28–November 28, 2009. Originally published in *Artforum*, January 2010.

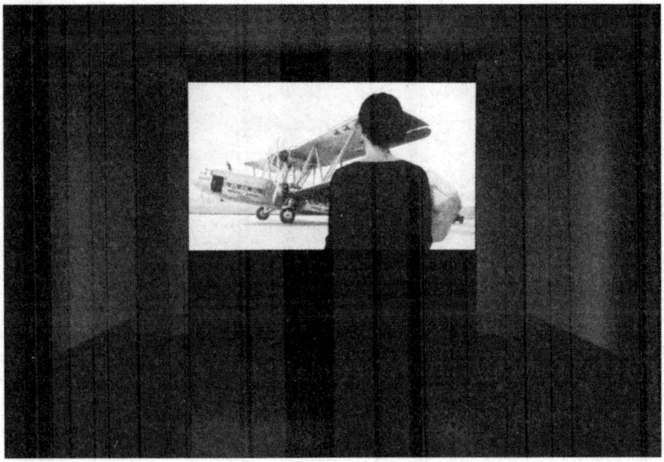

Emily Jacir, *Lydda Airport* 2007–2009

Emily Jacir's exhibition, *dispatch*, is comprised of a new film, *Lydda Airport* (2007–2009), and documentation of an unrealized project entitled *stazione* (2009). Both are emblematic of the artist's construction of subjective and spatial geographies to reimagine identity, history, and place. *stazione* was commissioned as part of Palestine c/o Venice, a collateral event of the 2009 Venice Biennale. The artist had envisaged the temporary inscription of Arabic translations alongside the Italian names of the vaporetto stops on the legendary route #1 along the Grand Canal. A trilingual (Arabic, Italian, and English) brochure was to have been distributed around Venice. In addition to a map, the brochure summarized the historical influence of the Arab world on Venice since the 16th century, not only in terms of trade but also of cultural and scientific exchange—informing us, for example, that the blowpipe technique used by Venice's glassmakers was invented in Palestine, and citing the incorporation of Arabic and Eastern stylistic codes into Venetian architecture.

Yet the project never happened. A brief statement inscribed on the wall of the gallery stated: "*stazione* is a public intervention which was slated to take place at the 53rd Venice Biennale. It was abruptly cancelled by Venetian municipal authorities and remains unrealized." No further explanation was forthcoming, and we can only guess at what rattled the Venetian authorities so much that they put the kibosh on the project. Was it an irrational fear that Jacir's modification would confuse residents and tourists alike? Were they afraid that people would imagine that Venice had suddenly somehow become subject to Arab colonization? And, further, doesn't this apparent act of censorship itself reproduce the very problems that Jacir sought to illuminate?

The other component of the exhibition, *Lydda Airport*, was a short, looped black-and-white film using CGI technology in conjunction with photographs of the airport during its construction offering a poetic meditation on the history of the British Mandate of Palestine in relation to the airport of its title, originally built in 1936 as part of Britain's Empire Route. (The airport was captured by the Israeli Defense Forces in 1948, and in 1973 became Ben Gurion International Airport, as it is known today.) We observe a British plane flying over the airfield, taking off, and landing, intercut with images of a woman waiting in the empty airport. Jacir is here obliquely referencing the story of a Royal Air Force plane that disappeared in 1940 en route to Sharjah, as well as invoking the specter of Edmond Tamari, a transport company employee from Jaffa, who apparently was instructed to await aviator Amelia Earhart's arrival at Lydda Airport and welcome her to Palestine. She never arrived. The young woman digitally inscribed into these scenes is Jacir herself, suggesting a mapping of an uncertain identity and subjectivity onto the airport, re-imagined as a palimpsest of repressed historical trajectories. The airport reappears in a room directly behind the film presentation in the form of an elegant, white architectural model—an apparition of history that reinforces the impression that Jacir would like us to reconstruct the airport as a heterotopic site. In other words, as a non-place/place that dwells between the real and the imaginary, as much a contemporary airport as a phantom indicator of the contested historical, geographical, and spatial narratives of the British, the Palestinians, and the Israelis. Jacir here continues her poignant negotiation of a postcolonial, diasporic condition, invoking qualities of appearance and disappearance, longing and (not) belonging, and displacement and emplacement: “in-betweenness,” as Homi Bhabha has put it. Perhaps it was a recognition of the power inherent in this concept that so unnerved the Venetian authorities.

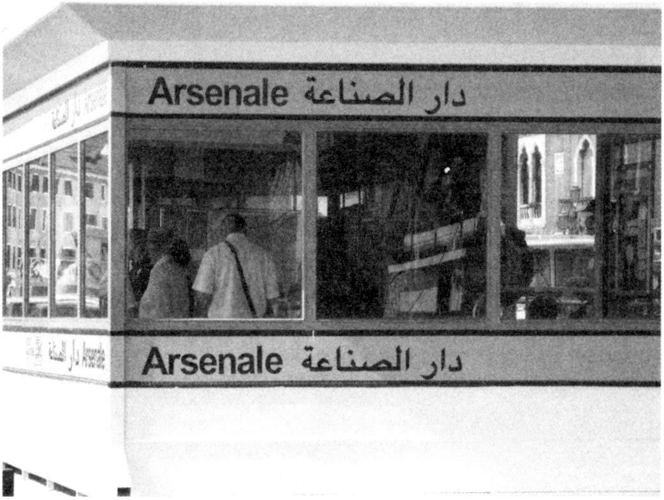

Emily Jacir, *stazione (Arsenale)*, 2009

Yael Bartana: An Aesthetics of Restorative Justice Deployed into the Space of Quotidian Injustice

Revised version of a text on Yael Bartana's survey exhibition at MoMA P.S. 1, New York, October 19, 2008–May 4, 2009. Originally published in *Artforum*, April 2009.

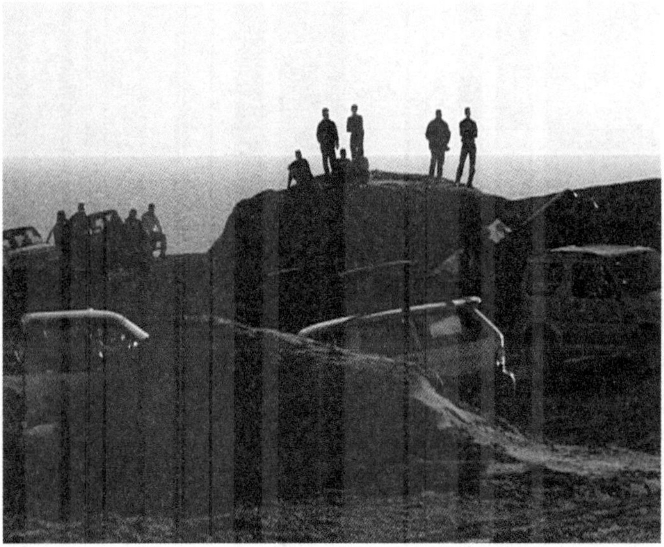

Yael Bartana, *Kings of the Hill*, 2005

Disputatious claims of belonging and emplacement; boundaries and flows; communication and misunderstanding; and historical narratives in contradiction. These are some of the central preoccupations of Yael Bartana's post-documentary, allegorical practice. Born in Israel in 1970, Bartana constructs resonant reflections on the cultural, political, geographic, psychological, and religious irreconcilabilities of the Israeli and Palestinian peoples. Yet Bartana's work cannot be considered as activist in any normative sense. It is best understood within a broader context of artists (e.g., Emily Jacir, the Atlas Group with Walid Raad) who hybridize conceptual structures, documentary codes, and post-representational strategies, deconstructing assumptions of truth and stable ideological systems, while also remaining within the proximity of realpolitik. Artists such as Bartana, Jacir, and Raad might be said to embody postcolonial, post-diasporic transnational identities, inhabiting interstitial geographic spaces (Bartana between Israel and Amsterdam, Jacir between Ramallah and New York, and Raad between New York and his de/reconstructed Lebanon). Their practices reactivate the viewer's relation to—not complicity with—the entanglements of these conflicted worlds and illuminate the interdependencies of artistic and political labor for viewer and producer alike.

Bartana's P.S. 1 show—her first institutional exhibition in the US, originally curated by Sergio Edelsztein for the Center for Contemporary Art in Tel Aviv and organized here by Klaus Biesenbach—features five works produced over the past eight years. The earliest is *Trembling Time* (2001), a deceptively simple video that embodies the contradictions of a society tangled up in secularity and urbanity on the one hand and religiosity and a deep commitment to historical commemoration on the other. From atop the Hashalom Bridge in Tel Aviv, Bartana shot the city's main highway during the event marking the start of Israel's Remembrance Day, which honors fallen soldiers: sirens wail across the country, broadcast on all media outlets; a minute of silence is observed; and the nation briefly grinds to a halt. Initially we observe a rather mundane scene. Cars and trucks pass below at normal speed, but then velocities change and a subtle time lapse of sensuous dissolves and fades makes it appear as if the vehicles are moving through one another, creating ghostly afterimages and displacing real-time modalities. A siren is heard; cars gradually come to a stop; the passengers step onto the asphalt, stand in the middle of the highway, and then return to their vehicles. We are witness to a historically transcendent memorialization that is at once tangible and phantasmic—a momentary break with a normative order of things that has, itself, become normalized. Significantly, Bartana's simultaneously narrative and non-narrative depiction of the episode is looped, alluding to the tautology that is intrinsic to all rituals, including rituals of non-reconciliation. The work is testimony and counter-testimony, at once documentation and a displacement or de-realization of the event into other (i.e., aesthetic) terms—what might be described as a process of social abstraction.

Questions of responsibility, territory and place come to the surface in *Wild Seeds* (2005), a two-screen installation that presents images of a cluster of Israeli teenagers engaged in what is clearly a staged outdoor activity. In fact, they are playing a game devised by Bartana that functions as a social platform for the reenactment of the struggle by Israeli police to evict settlers from illegal outposts. The young actors take on the requisite roles: those playing the settlers seek to establish themselves as an interlocked, horizontally positioned unit of resistance on the ground; those playing the police attempt to pull them apart and eject them from entrenched positions. Yelling and screaming ensue. On the second screen, perpendicular to the first, the rhetorical battle is translated from Hebrew into English: *A Jew does not deport another Jew*; *Where is your conscience?*; *Motherfuckers*, etc. Smiles suggest it is all in good fun, yet there are also moments of uncomfortable laughter and tension, as well as real physical struggle, mirroring the larger existential struggle. We understand that Bartana has enacted a social-symbolic episode that allegorizes the extent to which Israeli society has been torn apart by territorial claims, with the state becoming the hegemonic other, the institutional bad cop, in the eyes of some extremist settlers. It is a powerful indictment of the schizophrenia of a society that may or may not be able to heal its largely self-inflicted wounds. Some viewers might assume that these amateur theatrics are meant to represent Palestinians and Israelis, rather than an internecine Israeli fight. Ultimately, the fundamental issue here remains the irresolution of the overarching conflict. Bartana's work seems to demand that we ask: If the Israeli people cannot even work things out amongst themselves, what hope is there for a sensible rapprochement with the equally factionalized Palestinian people?

In the same room, the beautifully reductive *Low Relief II* (2004), a silent four-channel video, stealthily reveals protesters (whether Israeli or Palestinian is unclear) struggling with either the army or the police. The images, appropriated from media sources, have been formally manipulated to suggest the look of an ancient sculptural relief, generating an oscillation of movement and stasis. Four quadrants of scenes playing on the palimpsest-like screen as inscriptions and erasures, moving in and out of legibility. Here, the collective media unconscious resurfaces as an excavation of a future history, endlessly discordant. This is how

Bartana's practice gains its force, functioning as a response to localized realities while at the same time generating social imaginaries that productively dislocate us into regions of broader political allegory. Potentially, this allegory operates on transnational terms, allowing us to project ourselves into territories beyond normative media representations.

Kings of the Hill (2003), delivers a kind of anthropological abstraction of a particular social rite within contemporary Israeli society: on Friday afternoons, just prior to the start of Sabbath, men drive their SUVs through a hilly landscape, proximate to the sea, engaged in a reckless game of vehicular reterritorialization of the land. Bartana recasts this ritual as a quasi-militaristic spectacle, wherein the barely sublimated violence of macho car culture becomes a cipher for the tautological, absurd, and yet embodied paroxysms of occupation.

Perhaps the most complex yet straightforwardly condemnatory of Bartana's video works is *Summer Camp* (2007), a standout at documenta 12. It commences with shots of rubble and a sequence of images that gradually establish a sense of place: tractors on a road, an eagle flying overhead, an Arab man dressed in white, a group of people who resemble tourists greeting this man, and then soldiers, presumably Israeli, observing the scene. The title of the work appears, and then we see the aforementioned group of people engaged in construction amidst the rubble. Bartana recorded this footage during the reconstruction of a house in the Palestinian village of Anata, near Jerusalem, that was demolished by the Israeli Army in 2005. The rebuilding project was organized by a group called the Israeli Committee Against House Demolitions (ICAHD), composed of people from Israel, the Palestinian territories, and elsewhere who organized in opposition to the Israel Defense Forces' tactic of razing homes suspected of housing militants or their families. We observe these activists engaged in actions that temporarily deconstruct official Israeli policies through material reconstruction, transgressing laws that demand violation.

Moving around to the verso of the double-sided screen, we discover black-and-white images of people of apparently European descent riding camels through an idyllic desert landscape, cacti and palm trees blowing in the wind. A phrase appears: "To the pioneers in Palestine." It turns out that we are looking at a print of the 1935 Zionist film *Awodah*, directed by Helmar Lerski, which, according to Edelsztein, was "commissioned to promote the immigration of European Jews to pre-State Israel, hailing agricultural development as a collectivizing epic." Bartana skillfully edited her ICAHD documentation so as to echo the Zionist-socialist-realist style of the historical film's utopian narrative. With composer Guy Harries, she created a new score based on her previously reedited version of Paul Dessau's original heroic-modernist music for *Awodah*, now incorporating traditional Arab music to suggest the inevitability of cross-cultural hybridization between Israel and Palestine—an ironic consequence of their entwined fates. We cannot help experiencing or reading one film (and one history) through the filter of the other.

We are here invited by Bartana to reflect on the profound contradictions of Israel's settlement policies in the occupied territories in relation to its own history. If the Jewish people cannot be separated from the land of their biblical heritage, why should there be a different standard for Palestinians, who also make their own legitimate claim? This transgenerational dispute is now ultimately a question of equal rights under the law, at least within the current terms of occupation. In its Tel Aviv incarnation, Bartana's exhibition was titled *Short Memory*. One recognizes a wry reminder of just how selective a nation's memory can be, and how we forget that our collective destiny is predicated on the fate of others. Bartana's work eloquently reminds us of the disturbing psychosocial media feedback loop of tit-for-tat violence—the trauma of conflict endlessly reanimated—that taints Israelis and Palestinians alike. By extension, she implicates all viewers, us, within a seemingly hopeless complexity that is calling out for imaginative acts—dare we say cultural and artistic operations—of global responsibility and engagement.

Bartana may not be claiming that art can ameliorate calamity, but she does appear to have just enough faith in the emancipatory potential of allegories of social justice, even as her work functions as an allegorical rendering of social injustice. As an artist, she can only hope to reengineer these social, political, cultural, and religious entanglements into another kind of representation, a conflictual zone of deferred imaginary reconciliation. Within her cartography of trauma, the land is not transfigured into an essentialized condition, but rather is conceived as a post-territorial space that simultaneously precedes and exceeds, includes and excludes, religion, culture, politics, ideology, and perhaps even representation itself. In other words, the land is a space of possibility wherein social imaginaries cross-pollinate with realpolitik. Might her practice be understood as an aesthetics of restorative justice deployed into the space of quotidian injustice?

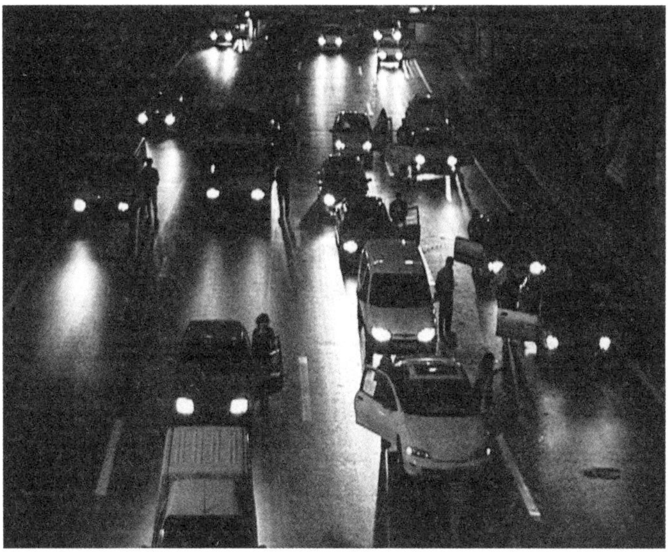

Yael Bartana, *Trembling Time*, 2001.

Art and Fictitious Capital

Revised version of an essay originally published in the catalogue of *ReGift*, an exhibition at the Swiss Institute Contemporary Art, New York, February 18–April 4, 2009.

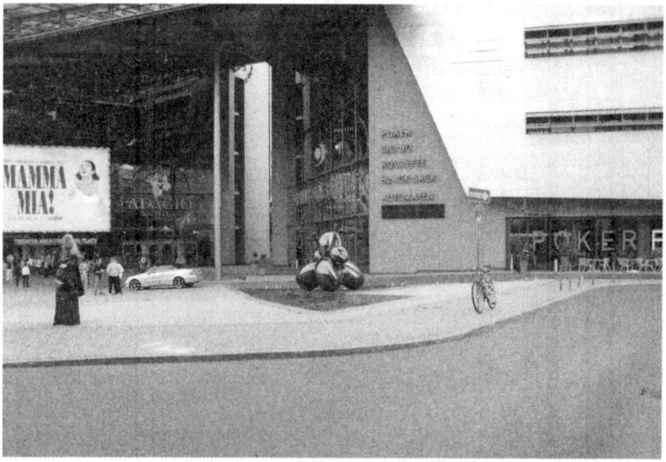

A Jeff Koons balloon flower sculpture in front of the Spielbank Berlin Casino on Marlene-Dietrich-Platz, Berlin, June 18, 2008.

In his introduction to the 1983 book *The Gift*, Lewis Hyde writes: "What is it about a work of art, even when it is bought and sold in the market, that makes us distinguish it from such pure commodities as these? It is the assumption of this book that a work of art is a gift, not a commodity. Or, to state the modern case with more precision, that works of art exist simultaneously in two 'economies,' a market economy and a gift economy. Only one of these is essential, however: a work of art can survive without the market, but where there is no gift there is no art."

The shortcomings and contradictions of Hyde's argument have been thoroughly discussed over the past two decades, even though his warm and fuzzy brand of new-age, popcorn-humanistic cultural thinking remains attractive to people who prefer soft-boiled ideas. Hyde surely misses the point: an artwork is more than just a commodity, but so is a car or a shirt or a toothbrush also more than just a commodity. And, if, as he contends, "a work of art can survive without the market," surely it is not possible for an artist to survive without it. Hyde should have written: where there is no artist there is no art.

The conceptualization of art as a gift is a kind of fiction, a fiction borne of a dream of new social exchange values in a specialized realm of culture. Certainly, one can receive a work of art as a gift, just as one receives a pair of gloves, or a set of knives, and this would be a normative type of gifting—even if one might be especially grateful to receive a work of art, as opposed to a new scarf, but then again everything is relative. Much of this depends upon how one perceives the quality of the artwork, one's taste, and of course whether one is more interested in the utility of the scarf as opposed to the non-utility of the artwork, unless one is principally interested in the investment quality of the artwork, and therefore appreciates that type of use-value (or use-valuation). If the promise of an ever-expanding value for that gifted work of art has enchanted you, it is unlikely this work will be regifted to another, unless we are talking about familial regifting, such as for the establishment of inheritances (for purposes of love and/or taxes).

Art practices that are conceptualized or formatted in relation to cultural and social rituals of gifting (or regifting) are more than likely just mimicking these cultural and social rituals. If one receives a work of art as a gift that has been conceptualized to operate within a system of gift giving, does this social transaction break the spell, so to speak, of art's commodity status? Well, not really. The commodity status of a thing does not accrue simply as the result of a process of exchange: as a produced thing (whether a painting or a scarf), it was already produced as a part of a system of production, and enters into that system ready to be exchanged as both thing and product. Art conceived and produced in relation to the rituals of gifting or regifting is itself a system of exchange that does not fundamentally alter the status of the object or thing as a quasi-commodity, even though gifting and regifting might tend to erode a bit of the unique value—or newness—of the product itself. Most folks would prefer to buy a new BMW, rather than a pre-owned BMW, but finances enter into the equation to determine what is attainable; likewise, one would no doubt prefer to give and receive a new gift as opposed to a regift.

Does the work of art conceived as a gift break with the laws of commodification under the aegis of capital, throwing a monetary system of exchange into some degree of jeopardy? On symbolic terms, perhaps yes; on the level of material culture, it is unlikely, since all of these systems of object exchange also produce systems of value exchange that always remain tethered to the logic of capitalism… unless that logic itself is redefined by a whole new set of economic processes. True, a gifted or regifted work of art is still just a work of art, just as a gifted or regifted set of wine glasses remains just a set of wine glasses. What distinguishes these things as gifts or regifts is a mode of receivership: one recalls such things as gifts, or perhaps senses they are actually *regifts*, in the process of recollecting their origin: i.e., they were received as a present. One pays a price for every gift received, and one passes that price on each time a gift is regifted to another, but, as alluded to earlier in the rules of regifting, this is not a chain of guilt, but rather a chain of associative connections between individuals within a social system, engaging in a particular kind of ritual.

The great question of the day: What is the relation between art and fictitious capital? Or, to put it another way, have we reached a point at which, to paraphrase Marx, art "is thrown into circulation as capital without any material basis in commodities or productive activity"? Perhaps this has always been an element of art's contradictory relationship to value: i.e., it is at once valuable, invaluable, and before and beyond value. It is worthless and worth too much. It is a type of productive, creative labor, yet it is not like any other commodity. Art is always forged within an ideological system of pecuniary values, yet one would be engaging in vulgar economic determinism to suggest that art is merely the reflection of market exchange. For we understand that the relationship of art to its markets is at once highly calibrated (i.e., the cultivation of art as an instrument of investment), and also disturbingly arbitrary. Let's face it: the fiction of artistic value is a growth industry, and there does not seem to be much anxiety even when the curtains are pulled back to reveal the wizards manipulating the strings—such as within the quasi-public scene of the auction. Indeed, one might even suggest that the art auction is a kind of sanctioned cultural pornography, in the sense that nothing is left to the imagination: the transvaluation of art into investment is consummated before our covetous eyes.

And so we might ask whether art is real capital that produces the effects, or residual effects, of fictitious capital? Is it the other way around? Or both?

Do the mechanisms that exist for institutional art gifting—for instance, the notorious and perhaps diminishing practice of fractional gifts from collectors to museums—have the potential to undermine art understood in relation to its pecuniary value? No, these mechanisms of gifting are predicated upon certain understandings about the intrinsic aesthetic values of a particular work of art—understandings that tend to create a mutually reinforcing system of faith in the pecuniary value of a work of art, resulting from a consensus of experts and tastemakers who collectively manage, if you will, the valuation of a work of art.

Art is not a gift; it is a necessity. We seek an art that can submerge into the social ocean and yet swim against the mainstream political currents; we seek an art of relevance, whatever that might mean in a particular time and place. This is not accomplished through gestures of gifting or regifting as an art methodology, per se, because such strategies are based on the faulty and untested assumption that to engage in such acts of generosity and graciousness will engender a political or social panacea. In other words, the conceptualization of art as a gift, or a regift, appears to offer an effective means of restoring a social dimension through non-pecuniary exchanges, or contacts, with the world. While this dream of infinite social contact and putative non-pecuniary exchange may be reassuring for some, it is merely a superficial treatment to a much deeper wound. This is the wound of an enervated public cultural sphere, in which the role of art as a catalyst for social and political re-animation has been largely marginalized by the reign of fictitious (cultural) capital, which, paradoxically, has been generated out of an irrationally exuberant speculative art market. A reactivated public cultural sphere is what we need; this cannot be gifted or regifted, but it might be regenerated.

2012 Postscript

Every once and a while, I receive an email describing and promoting an art project or a curatorial endeavor that claims to offer a lesson on the development of post-monetary systems of economic exchange and value (in the middle of yet another phase of capitalism's endlessly destructive and procreative crises). I infer that such efforts are directed at publics in developed economies (which are becoming hybrid forms of state capitalism anyway), rather than developing societies (many of which have also produced forms of state capitalism). It is all well and good to organize exhibition projects that offer interdisciplinary test cases regarding imagined post-monetary economic formations, as a symbolic resistance to the ills of un- or under-regulated late capitalism (although the Occupy movements have generally done a better job of this than any art projects …). Art may have a peripheral role to play somewhere, but since these art and exhibition projects are supported by networks of either private or public monies (or both), try explaining to people who either have had no access to capital or markets, or have very limited access, that they should forsake a global market economy at this juncture in the development of their societies. One obvious example: anyone who has visited Brazil over the past decade has observed a significant expansion of the middle class—more significantly, perhaps, millions have been lifted out of poverty (with the Bolsa Familia program). Historically, Brazil has experienced glaring economic inequality (the gap between the haves and the have-nots), and so these are welcome developments. Yes, maybe eventually, we will move toward fully developed post-monetary economies of service exchange, or something like this, but for now those urgent issues—such as the global inequities of uneven and unequal economic development and the social injustices this produces—need to be addressed in a way that does not make the situation worse for the have-nots.

Alfredo Jaar, *The Sound of Silence*

Revised version of a text on Alfredo Jaar at Galerie Lelong, New York, February 28–May 2, 2009. Originally published in *Artforum*, Summer 2009.

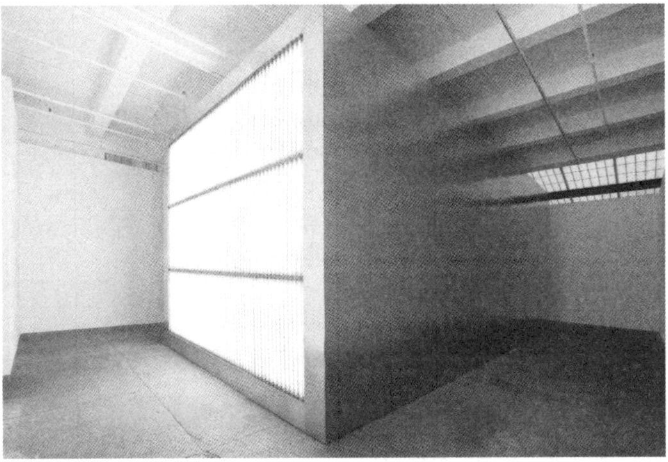

Alfredo Jaar, *The Sound of Silence*, 2006

Alfredo Jaar, an artist who has committed many years to examining the potentialities of art's response (and perhaps responsibility) to those at the extreme margins of life, or in the crosshairs of social, political, and existential crises, produced an unremittingly complex and disturbing installation in 2006, *The Sound of Silence*. Originally presented at DiverseWorks in Houston within the context of FotoFest 2006 (and subsequently in a number of international contexts), the work here makes a long overdue appearance in New York.

Entering a corridor, and passing in front of a vast array of vertically organized fluorescent bulbs—a veritable wall of light on one side of a large aluminum-clad structure—the viewer's eyes are momentarily overloaded. Here, light materializes as space, swiftly dematerializing into an all-consuming luminosity. This is perceptual manipulation of the highest order, certainly strategic on Jaar's part, effectively provoking questions about the visual, cultural, and political conditions (or consequences) of how we allow ourselves to be manipulated. To venture further into this installation might lead one into optical and cognitive obliteration. Yet we desire to continue, to be further manipulated. A wall text indicates the rules of the game: not to enter the enclosure until the red light turns green. Jaar interpellates the viewer as subject and controlled body, thereby reenacting the inscription of power within space—an ironically critical maneuver.

Playing within the darkened enclosure is a soundless film in which a textual sequence appears on a black ground, conveying a narrative about the peculiarly tragic life of freelance South African photojournalist Kevin Carter. We are informed that Carter became known as a risk-taking photojournalist in apartheid South Africa, and eventually traveled to Sudan, shooting an image that would be published in *The New York Times* in 1993: a picture of a starving, emaciated, Sudanese child watched over by a patient vulture. A narrative excerpt: HE POSITIONED HIMSELF FOR THE BEST POSSIBLE IMAGE/HE WAITED 20 MINUTES/ HE WAS HOPING THE VULTURE WOULD SPREAD ITS WINGS/BUT IT DID NOT/HE TOOK HIS PHOTOGRAPHS/ AND CHASED THE BIRD AWAY/HE WATCHED AS THE LITTLE GIRL RESUMED HER STRUGGLE/HE SAT UNDER A TREE AND LIT A CIGARETTE/TALKED TO GOD/AND CRIED/KEVIN/KEVIN. We then read that, in 1994, just a couple of months after receiving a Pulitzer Prize for this very picture, a distraught, haunted, and perhaps guilt-ridden Carter committed suicide, while the fate of the child in the photograph remains unknown. We also learn that the rights to the image are under the auspices of Corbis, owned by Bill Gates. Flashes of light then violently penetrate the space, and we are interpellated once again, becoming the unsuspecting object-victims of a feigned photographic gaze, and Carter's photograph appears furtively onscreen, like an afterimage.

The Sound of Silence triggers some important questions: Do we need such images so that we can be confronted with what we might not want to believe is inextricably connected to our own lives: the suffering of others? Is Jaar here endeavoring to deconstruct the relentless transfiguration of bare human empathy into its banalized cousin: manufactured pity? Does the eliciting of our suffering (a guilty conscience, or the pain of knowledge itself) have a chance of becoming politically transformative or socially restorative? If everything is connected to everything else, how might we understand where our responsibility as alienated observers begins and where it ends? Are we traumatized, incapacitated witnesses, groping about in the gap between passive outrage and mobilized action, perhaps unwitting accomplices in the further objectification of the suffering Other? Jaar may be suggesting that we are perpetrators and victims, objects and subjects, endlessly exchanging roles in the grand feedback loop of the scopic field, at once complicit and exonerated. Is art sufficient to the task of unpacking these contradictions, or should it complicate matters further? Such questions are unanswerable.

Sam Durant, *Dead Labor Day*

Revised version of a text on Sam Durant, *Dead Labor Day*, at Paula Cooper Gallery, New York, March 13–April 17, 2010. Originally published in *Artforum*, Summer 2010.

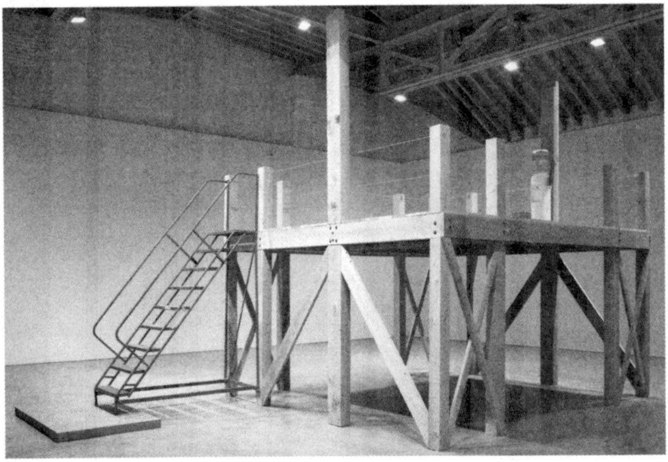

Sam Durant, *Dead Labor Day*, 2010

No one can accuse Sam Durant of restraint when it comes to contesting mainstream, representational narratives of American history. His recent work includes *Proposal for White and Indian Dead Monument Transpositions, Washington D.C.* (2005), which envisages moving all the memorials to Native Americans killed during colonization to the National Mall in Washington, DC; *End White Supremacy* (2008), a sign adapted from a 1963 civil rights protest displayed on the facade of Paula Cooper Gallery during the 2008 presidential election; and a show of former Black Panther Emory Douglas' posters and prints that Durant curated in 2007 for the Los Angeles Museum of Contemporary Art.

As evidenced by the aforementioned *Proposal for* … , Durant's work is most persuasive when it uses the conventional language of public, social memorializing against itself to interrogate how structures that claim to represent collective memory actually mask their own ideological underpinnings. It is refreshing that the artist makes no bones about his ideological, critical tendencies, as evidenced in his deployment in the text accompanying this exhibition of the notion of capital as "dead labor," which, in Marx's words, is "vampire-like, [and] only lives by sucking living labor."

Titled *Dead Labor Day*, Durant offers a platform—literally and figuratively—for us to reconsider the uncomfortable interpenetration between labor relations (in American history and in contemporary terms) and capital punishment. The exhibition is efficiently comprised of three interrelated elements. *Gallows Composite C (Billy Bailey Gallows, Haymarket Gallows, Rainey Bethea Gallows, Saddam Hussein Gallows)* (2008), is a small wood and metal model, mounted on a mirrored pedestal, that represents a hybrid of the four disciplinary structures used for these executions in the US; here, the interpenetration of the architectural forms operates to embed and materialize the interconnection of largely repressed historical narratives. The light-box piece *Break Room with International Mass Meeting* (2010), meanwhile, reproduces the ghostly afterimage of a document from 1916 announcing a meeting in San Francisco commemorating the "29th anniversary of the martyrdom of the Chicago anarchists," superimposed over an upside-down color image of an unidentified mid-20th-century workers' break room. Durant's text for the show recounts the back story of the repressed history to which the work draws our attention: after a rally in Chicago's Haymarket Square in support of the eight-hour workday turned violent, police arrested five anarchist labor activists; four of them were publicly hanged a few months later (one had committed suicide in prison). These events led, 20 years later, to the establishment of the eight-hour workday, and to the founding of International May Day.

The exhibition's largest work, *Dead Labor Day* (2010), is a symbolic and material consolidation of the two other pieces. It operates as an unnerving conflation of worker break room and gallows—an extrapolation of the scaffold used to hang the Haymarket Martyrs, as these anarchists came to be known. Upon signing a release that indemnified the gallery, one can walk up the structure's perforated metal stairs onto a wooden platform, and encounter a functioning office-style water dispenser, along with disposable cups and a trashcan. In a delightfully sinister maneuver, Durant invites the viewer to walk over a subtly embedded trap door (the gallery floor visible through the wooden slats) in order to reach the water cooler. The gallows structure, a public instrument of social discipline designed to invoke the ultimate power of the state, here playfully induces a sense of dread in the viewer-as-subject inhabiting a psychological space that conflates the prototypical site of labor—the factory or office break room—and the apparatus of capital punishment. With resonant black (or even gallows) humor, *Dead Labor Day* asks us to perform the living labor of intervening in our alienated contemporaneity through intertextual re-readings of history. Durant's practice converts the fruits of research processes—made transparent to gallerygoers in the form of books and other historical sources that supplement the works—into forms and structures that operate as materialized sociopolitical allegories, enacting a kind of discursive insurgency.

Jill Magid, *A Reasonable Man in a Box*

Revised version of a text on Jill Magid's *A Reasonable Man in a Box*, Whitney Museum of American Art, July 1–September 12, 2010. Originally published in *Artforum*, November 2010.

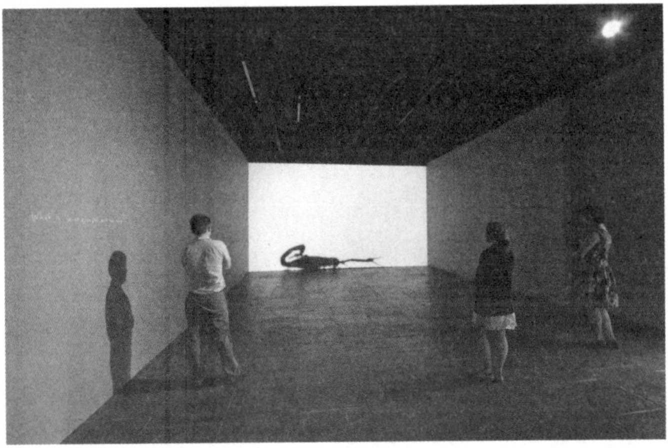

Jill Magid, *A Reasonable Man in a Box*, installation view, Whitney Museum of American Art, New York, 2010

In a 2007 work, *Lincoln Ocean Victor Eddy*, Jill Magid enacted a performative infiltration into a remote world by cultivating an ambiguous, clandestine relationship based on her fascination with a New York City police officer; Magid persuaded him to train her as a cop, shadowing this cop on the night shift. Magid's 2010 *A Reasonable Man in a Box*, a project developed for the Anne and Joel Ehrenkranz Gallery on the Whitney Museum's first floor—composed of a large-scale video projection featuring a scorpion and a wall text with manipulated excerpts from the now infamous Bybee memo (aka the "torture memo")—likewise seeks to perform a critical operation on power, this time in relation to the Bush administration's imperious version of presidential authority that facilitated the infamous war on terror. Elements of the Bybee memo leaked to the press in 2004, and the Bush administration later rescinded it; Barack Obama declassified the entire memo in 2009.

Magid uses the memo—designed to provide legal justification for the administration's covert desire to blur the line between interrogation and torture—to enact an allegory meant to foreground the absurd legal (and linguistic) contradictions of the amoral text, focusing specifically on an excerpt that responded to the CIA's request to place insects in a confinement box as a technique of interrogation of a high-level Al Qaeda operative with a purported fear of bugs. Upon entering the gallery, we initially encounter the question—"What is a reasonable man in a box?"—in enlarged handwritten script. This question leads us to the opposite wall (to the immediate left of the entryway), where Magid has silkscreened a collage of the aforementioned passage. Crafting a kind of concrete poetry, she disassembles and reassembles the text, setting the words off-kilter and making strategic use of black-band redactions by which an already tautological or simply illogical legal argument is rendered all the more perniciously absurd. Magid's deconstruction of the nonsensical legal argument concludes with: "the insects' placement in the box would not constitute a threat of severe physical pain or suffering to a reasonable person in [the operative's] position."

Devised to circumvent torture statutes (i.e., to reframe torture as non-torture), the language is unnervingly oxymoronic, implosively tautological—qualities that Magid amplifies through the use of a typographic style that suggests a breakdown of the signifying chain, and the erosion of rational legal discourse. However, one of the results of Magid's intervention is the recognition that the original Bybee memo does not really need any reconfiguring for us to grasp its dangerously arbitrary relationship to morality, ethics, humanity, reason, and, fundamentally, the law: it is a self-indicting document. And so it is a bit doubtful as to whether Magid's textual de- and re-construction exposes these nutty legalistic convolutions and contradictions, or merely reaffirms them. One imagines that Magid deploys the question—"What is a reasonable man in a box?"—to prick us into realizing the ludicrousness of it all, but most reasonable people already came to this conclusion long ago.

The video projection, occupying the gallery's far right wall, commences with a silhouette of the scorpion being placed into our field of vision by a pair of tweezers.

The specimen scuttles about as if performing a kind of insect shadow theater, although little menace is generated by a scaling-up of the image. One surmises that the video is meant to evoke the psychological terror of sharing a confinement box with a live scorpion, and that by positioning us within a darkened gallery space, we become the *reasonable* victims of the brand of torture masked as interrogation sought by the Bybee memo. Ironically, though, the video comes across as the more didactic element here, converting into literal visual representation that which the memo—either Magid's version or the original itself—so chillingly and perversely evokes through legalese; plus, it is hard to feel like an enemy combatant at the Whitney Museum. While Magid's project is a useful reminder of the Bush administration's pernicious effort to circumvent international law (we are left imagining that intelligence agencies may still be conducting interrogations at the margins of legality), one wonders whether it would have been more fecund and trenchant if the artist had also alluded to the conditions of power that arise within the context of the museum as a stage for art that seeks to engender political praxis.

(The) Everywhereness (of Art)

Revised version of an essay originally published in *The Exhibitionist*, no. 2, June 2010, Archive Books, Berlin/Turin.

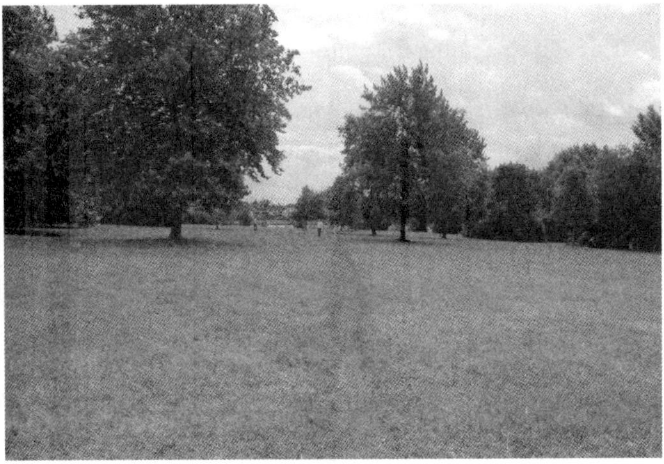

Pawel Althamer, *sciezka (pfad)*, 2007

Art becomes art *in public*, so to speak, as it enters into discursive spaces of ideational, social, and economic exchange. The becoming of art (in public) also unfolds through the communicative platforms of school (academia), the studio/office, the not-for-profit space, the commercial gallery, the museum, and other institutional contexts increasingly based upon public and private partnerships, the virtual realms of the Internet, and other cultural zones.

Since the emergence of bourgeois society, art's *modernity*, so to speak, has become indistinguishable from its publicness: i.e., the emancipation of art into public realms. Art has been situated in places (universal expositions, galleries, museums, biennials, symposia, etc.) wherein public domain encounters can be staged. Such places help to establish the discursive conditions through which art *publicizes* itself (sometimes promiscuously) as art.

Perhaps, art—as thing, as language—activates encounters with individuals, audiences, constituencies, publics, and counter-publics. Art's entry into the world constitutes its potential for the generation of public domain experiences, or the possibility that art might somehow inflect our relationship to the built environment. We seem to desire any and all space—whether public, private, virtual/cybernetic, or something other—as potentially available for penetration by some type of art activity. And it matters little whether this activity is recognized or not, at least initially, as an art activity within a particular situation. Perhaps the scent of art is sufficient today.

Is there any space that has not already been converted into a place (or *non-place*, to invoke Marc Augé)—a location, platform, a territory—that functions as a venue for the instantiation of art today? When I use the term art, I mean art in one form (or non-form) or another—whether it can be characterized as temporary, ephemeral, time-based, performative, or permanent. Within art history, art criticism, curatorial-organizational practices, and discursive platforms (e.g., symposia, meetings, conversations), art as a mode of intervention or as a form of social practice is of course intrinsically linked to various notions of social space and the public realm.

Every act of art—whether by permission, institutionally supported, or guerilla-like—that takes place (and art does seem to be *taking place* just about everywhere these days) and is experienced beyond the literal territory of sanctioned cultural space is at the same time proclaiming an enhanced connectivity to broader constituencies and publics. This has been the traditional claim of public art.

If art disappears into the circuits of the social, if it melts into place, if art becomes politics, merely alluding to a political condition (as some hope for), then everything will truly have become aestheticized. We should be wary of such outcomes. The question is not really which type of artmaking, per se, is more or less democratic or *freedom-generative* (sometimes the assumption made when referring to collective or participatory practices); rather, it is how we analyze art culture's interrelationship—on historical terms—with the material and symbolic processes of social, political democratization. For me, this would have to include a reconsideration of Herbert Marcuse's trenchant and disturbing notion of *repressive tolerance*.

Just as global capitalism, in all of its micro and macro functionalities and dysfunctionalities, is a space of turbulent economic and social *flows* (to invoke Manuel Castells), it is within these flows—the liminal zones that invisibly trace the thresholds, imagined and real, between leftover notions of public and private—that art (whether formulated as autonomous practice, collectivist organization, or something else) may still have a chance to apply certain pressure points. Such pressure may only be a means of generating and or maintaining counter-public enclaves (to evoke Michael Warner) that might also be defined as the constituencies of the subaltern, the sub-cultural, and perhaps even the *extra*-cultural. In this regard, we have to take into consideration the re-surfacing of DIY art production, certain forms of collective and participation-based work, and various modes of art-as-activism—all of which aspire to more authentically open encounters and exchanges with communities, constituencies, and publics.

Certainly this suggests a reanimation of strategies and tactics derived from 1960s and 1970s counterculture and political activism: the perennial manifestation of the critique of autonomous forms of artistic production as a means of countering the more pernicious effects of an unregulated free market, and proposing other ways of social and economic organization (e.g., services bartering, edible estates, etc.).

Today's formula seems to be: the autonomous work of art must be sacrificed to usher in the collectivist or activist work. In reality, however, these modes of cultural production—i.e., the so-called autonomous work of art, and the so-called collectivist work of art—are merely two sides of the same coin within liberal, democratic society. We have no way of knowing which is actually more politically or socially progressive (these words have largely lost their meaning within the discursive space of contemporary art). In other words, we lack the criteria to determine how this or that art practice generates a more or less progressive politics.

Publics and counter-publics seem to swim together in a *politically undifferentiated* soup of utterances, iterations, claims, attacks, whispers, shadowy expressions, shadow movements, and crude ideological eruptions. The street and the domicile have been collapsed together into some ecstatic zone of *interpenetrations.* In his 1985 essay *The Fire Next Time*,

Paul Virilio reflects on how the nebulae of contemporary media space has produced a hyper-temporal condition in which a modernist conception of space as territorial (the bounded, bordered, and material nation-state) had given way to another order. The event becomes indistinguishable from its *temporal space*. And so the world becomes a network of distinct velocities, a *simultaneity of events* at once produced by—and transmitted through—television. Media representations are at once localized and unmoored, cutting through the literal geopolitical territories and borders of nations and states. It is the world as a dislocated mediation of itself. Is there really any space that is more public than the Internet as a cosmos, accommodating hyper-simultaneous states of being there, nowhere, everywhere, or just somewhere? In the beginning, there was nothing; out of nothing, there emerged information. Isn't the space of information our creative commons? What isn't accessible to us, and therefore somehow public?

Private experience is being obliterated within the hyper-public social media networks of Facebook and other platforms. With mapping software such as Google's Street View, we have clearly moved beyond the quaint modernist dichotomies of private/public, and into another dimension of post-private and post-public experience. We already seem to be performing our so-called private lives upon the screens and virtual stages of public cybernetic social space. This might be considered as the hyperbolic expression of what Richard Sennett already lamented in his 1977 *The Fall of Public Man*, wherein those psychological, social, and individual experiences formerly consigned to the private domain, such as sex, have been exteriorized into public domain. And so if life has become a performance (of itself), what is the need for performance art in the gallery, museum, or alternative institutional space? Isn't everyone, and everything, already a performance today? And hasn't every place become a platform for some kind of performative activity—i.e., for the endless re-performance of life?

The proliferation of whatever art happens to be today—intervention, exhibition, discursive act, nothingness, decoration—throughout the *temporal or experiential spaces* (real, virtual, imaginary, or other) of our cities, suggests that society has an agenda for contemporary art: the conversion

of *every* place into a platform, a venue, a frame, *for art*.
So, just maybe, we have reached a threshold, wherein art's promiscuous public*ness*—its *everywhereness*—produces the illusion that art is on the verge of a magical undifferentiation from anything else. If art is everywhere, perhaps it is nowhere.

Harun Farocki, *Images of War (at a Distance)*

Revised version of a text on *Harun Farocki: Images of War (at a Distance)* at The Museum of Modern Art, New York, June 29, 2011–January 2, 2012. Originally published in *Artforum*, November 2011.

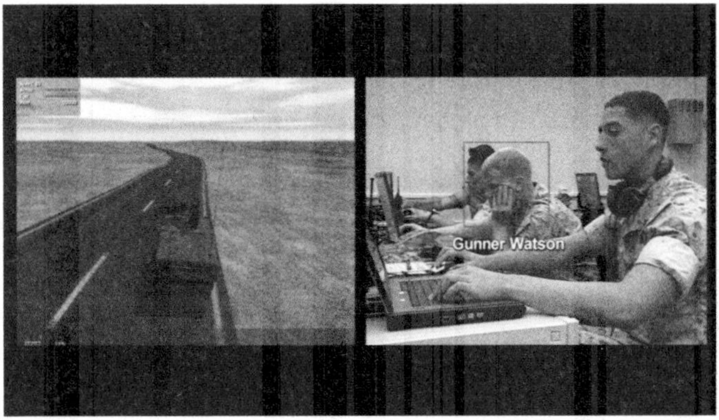

Harun Farocki, *Serious Games I: Watson is Down* (2010), from *Serious Games (I-IV)*, 2010

Harun Farocki: Images of War (at a Distance), the artist's first museum survey in the United States, features 36 films, videos, and installations recently acquired by The Museum of Modern Art. The exhibition offers an illuminating view of Farocki's development, beginning with his emergence in post-1968 West Germany and moving through more than 40 years of filmmaking, writing, editing, and curating. Farocki consistently analyzes the constructed language of film and video, applying critical pressure to traditional structures of narrative cinema, questioning ideologies of cinematic authorship, and contesting documentary's claims to objectivity. Paired with footage procured from institutions in the military-industrial-corporate complexes, Farocki examines the politics of representation within late capitalist scopic regimes. His work at once compresses and delineates interpenetrations of mass media, technology, the body, vision, commerce, gaming, surveillance, discipline and punishment, and militarism and war.

The first room of the MoMA survey includes vitrines displaying a selection of film journals that Farocki has contributed to or edited, in addition to a sequence of single-channel monitors presenting 16-mm films and videos, from *Inextinguishable Fire* (1969), to *Images of the World and the Inscription of War* (1988), to *War at a Distance* (2003). These provide context for the room's main attraction: the multi-screen video projection *Serious Games I–IV* (2009–2010). Composed of four looped parts—each projected onto a separate screen—the work centers on computer-generated combat simulations used by the US military for training exercises, which the artist apparently obtained directly from the military (suggesting that transparency can be a PR strategy). Rather than subject us to heavy-handed ideological critique, Farocki allows the appropriated visual materials to speak for themselves; brief descriptive texts interspersed among the footage provide the only explication. The work's first part, subtitled *Watson is Down*, features soldiers at their computer terminals conversing in military jargon, and clips of the simulated battlefield wherein armored vehicles endeavor to maneuver around IEDs. In *Three Dead*, the second part, a mock town (akin to a movie set) at a military base in the US serves as the site of a training exercise and achieves an uncanny virtual reality. Here, war as simulacrum and reality approach a kind of representational, psychological, and perceptual conflation. The third part, *Immersion*, includes footage of a workshop on using virtual reality to administer therapy to sufferers of post-traumatic stress disorder, while the fourth element incorporates footage from combat simulations. Farocki allows the military to indict itself. By reminding us of the deep economic and techno-cultural synergies between military culture, mass media, and entertainment (e.g., video games) in the United States, he implies that we are all enabling this situation.

Housed in the adjoining room are the earlier installations *I Thought I Was Seeing Convicts* (2000), and *Eye/Machine I–III* (2001–2003). Utilizing prison-surveillance footage of a guard shooting an inmate (and, separately, of a prisoner interacting with a woman during visiting hours), the former work explores the ways in which surveillance technology has become the primary instrument of control within institutions of discipline and punishment—alerting us that these scopic regimes have penetrated deeply into our quotidian social space. The latter piece reflects on connections between the first Gulf War and the mass media, demonstrating that technologies of vision (such as guidance systems for missiles) have become surrogates for human sight in both military and civilian contexts.

Farocki's work archives, indexes, reassembles, and deconstructs the representational systems of late capitalism in order to engender critical knowledge. Avoiding piousness and didacticism, Farocki suggests that we are all caught up in these cultural contradictions. Yet, as we semi-distracted cultural tourists are ported through the institutional environs of MoMA while surveillance cameras silently observe and track our movements, one wonders whether it is truly possible to imagine an experience that is not mediated by the very mechanisms of control that Farocki endeavors to unravel.

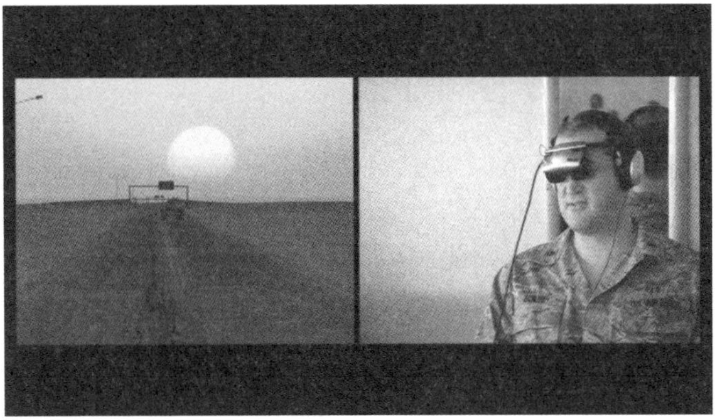

Harun Farocki, *Serious Games III: Immersion* (2009), from *Serious Games (I-IV)*, 2010

CHAPTER III

Everything Is Social (Platforms, Participations, Publics, Constituencies, Networks, Spaces, Situations, Collaborations, Cooperations, Conflicts, Interventions …)

Mark Dion's Critical Interface: The Newspaper and Cultural Production

Revised version of "Critical Interface: The Newspaper and Cultural Production," an essay in the newspaper insert for Mark Dion's newspaper project *Art… Not News*, in *The Hartford Courant*, organized by Real Art Ways, Hartford, Connecticut, 1991.

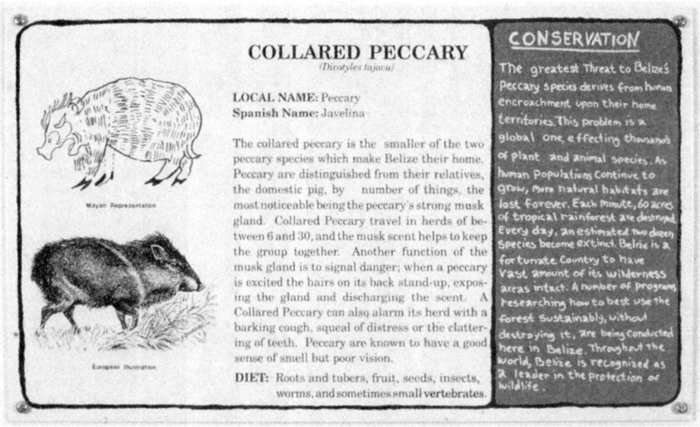

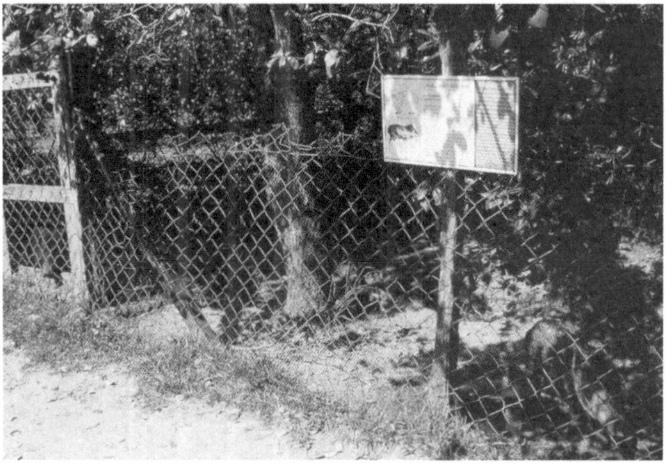

Mark Dion, *Project for the Belize Zoo (Collard Peccary)*, 1990

A political tendency is the necessary, never the sufficient condition of the organizing function of a work. This further requires the directing, instructing stance on the part of the writer. And today this is to be demanded more than ever before. An author who teaches writers nothing, teaches no one. What matters, therefore, is the exemplary character of a production, which is able first to induce other producers to produce, and second to put an improved apparatus at their disposal. And this apparatus is better the more consumers it is able to turn into producers—that is, readers or spectators into collaborators.
—Walter Benjamin, "The Author as Producer" (1934)

In his seminal 1934 essay, "The Author as Producer," Benjamin discusses the function of the newspaper in terms of its potential to operate as an apparatus of social and ideological transformation, i.e., as a tool for the enabling of revolution. For Benjamin (who was no doubt familiar with Lenin's utilization of the newspaper system within Russia to foster and disseminate the ideological, political, and cultural goals of the Revolution), it was crucial to understand that there could be no authentic social transformation and transformation of *consciousness* if only the repressive attributes of a particular political structure were to be disposed of, merely to be replaced by an equally authoritarian system. It would be necessary for the specific type of production (e.g., newspaper journalism) to facilitate a reflexive and critical shift in the apparatus of production itself, thereby reconfiguring the relationship between author as cultural producer and the reader/spectator. According to Benjamin, a form of political collaboration could then emerge from the negation of institutional and disciplinary segregation. Taking a cue from Lenin, Benjamin suggested that artists should employ their formal and technical skills within the framework of a collective endeavor designed for mass reception—such as the newspaper.

This introduces a notion of how artists and their production might operate politically in a more material, instrumental manner—beyond symbolism and allegory—in relation to hegemonic ideological, social, and economic formations. Benjamin's ideas, of course, have resurfaced throughout the 20th-century, and have been retooled and instrumentalized at various moments as artists have sought to develop new models of political or activist practice. Perhaps it is dubious to suggest that one can adopt a model of viable interface between art production and whatever we mean by political engagement, since a model always needs to undergo permutation in response to the specific conditions of the historical period, the contextual situation on the ground, etc. But if the specific, unique conditions of the social landscape at a particular time are critically taken into account, a method may emerge that can facilitate productive investigations of—or interventions within—the dominant system of sociopolitical representations. As long as we can agree that art is, ultimately, just one more representation within this broader system of representations.

The project conceived and implemented by New York artist Mark Dion, for the Hartford, Connecticut-based alternative art organization Real Art Ways, is an attempt to offer a critical examination of the political, ideological, ethnic, economic, ecological, and cultural histories of Connecticut as viewed by a group of diverse artists from that state who were selected by Dion. He asked each participant to submit a design for a full newspaper page that would appear in *The Hartford Courant* (the oldest continuously-published newspaper in the United States, and the largest daily paper in the state of Connecticut). Each of the seven projects, including Dion's, appeared for one of seven consecutive days on the back cover of Section A, a significant commitment of space for a major newspaper. In Dion's statement describing the project, he refers to the current problematic conditions of public art:

> The major problem with public art projects is that they rarely respond to the issues of the communities in which they appear, and often they exclude artistic representations from these communities. This project is an attempt to rethink and restructure such methods of presenting public art works, as well as to emphasize the diversity and talent within the region. Utilizing Connecticut's rich history as a field of investigation, each artist's page is stylistically and conceptually unique.

For Dion, then, this project expands the parameters of public art; i.e., art produced for a site, location, or place outside the normative boundaries of museums and galleries. Dion is also endeavoring to examine the possibility of art production as a mode of broader cultural, even sociological, investigation, while at the same time recognizing that art is not the same thing as sociology (or politics for that matter). When Benjamin asserted that it was necessary for the institutional apparatus to undergo transformation so as to catalyze a shift in the relationship between the author and the techniques of his/her discipline (and, by extension, to redefine the relationship between author and reader as a productive collaboration), he was most likely proposing that such changes would be predicated upon a more fundamental, collective goal: the political transformation of a society. While Dion's project is not actually calling for revolution, per se, it is conceived and designed to at least see what might happen when an artist operates in relation to (and within) a different cultural and social domain—for instance, the discursive space of the newspaper, a central component of the modernist public sphere, according to Jürgen Habermas—while also exploring a model of art practice that blends together aspects of curation, editing, collaboration, and participation. Habermas has written extensively about the function of communication with respect to the *rationalization of everyday life* in terms of the development of "specialized knowledge complexes" that tend to be segregated from one another within advanced capitalist societies; he has called into question the ability of avant-garde art practices, which inhabit the cultural sphere, to somehow penetrate the insulated boundaries of other spheres (the political, the legal, etc.). The issue of communication is central to Dion's project, since the newspaper functions as a ubiquitous yet disposable source of communicating information, reportage, and analysis, as well as the dissemination of various ideological perspectives. Here, the newspaper is being re-purposed as a public forum for the wider dissemination of art production to various readers and constituencies.

Challenging the atomization of distinct fields and disciplines codified within Enlightenment philosophy, Dion has developed a method of borrowing certain procedures, rituals, and habits of thought from areas of specialization generally considered to be outside the realm of art making, at least according to the modern doxa. These include the natural sciences, ecology in particular. For example, his recent *Belize Zoo Project* saw the artist working with the zoo's experts in that small Central American nation to develop the visual and discursive elements for signs to represent the various species of endangered animals in the zoo. The resulting designs incorporated three different naming and representational systems: the scientific language of Western zoology, the ancient Brazilian Indian pictographic lexicon, and text elements that, rather than providing generic, didactic descriptions of the animals, instead featured narratives that analyzed the conditions leading to the endangered status of the species, and measures that could be taken to rectify their endangered status.

In a gesture that fused meta-anthropology, meta-zoology, and meta-ecology, Dion engineered a juxtaposition of normative Western modes of scientific discourse and representation and the codified sign systems of indigenous peoples, and provided visitors to the zoo with instruments, so to speak, to de-code the function of the zoo itself (as a kind of institutional space), and the various cultural significations of the animals. That Dion conceived and designed a of signage that functions, on a practical, day to day basis, as a primary educational-informational component of the zoo, while at the same time existing as a commissioned work of art, indicates that he pushed notions of site-specificity and institutional critique in a daring direction. Taking a cue from Robert Smithson's non-site methodology, the artist also displayed the Belize zoo signs within the context of a New York gallery, a symbolic displacement suggesting that Dion sought to enable a process of interlocution between distinct cultural sites, not only to remind art audiences that this was fundamentally a work of art, but also to test how the re-contextualization of the sign-system would generate different kinds of significations.

This methodology finds a different articulation in Dion's project for *The Hartford Courant*: by inviting other artists already invested in analyzing the social and political conditions of the Connecticut context, Dion assumes the role of the *artist as meta-curator*, reframing their commissioned projects in relation to his, and vice-versa. And so this is just as much about an artist organizing the practices of others, as it is about re-framing his own work. It is, harking back to Benjamin, the artist-as-producer, enabling a mode of collaboration with other producers, within a mass media platform. Notably, *The Hartford Courant* apparently did not engage in any form of editorial interference or censorship despite the presence of a number of polemical works, and so the pages of the newspaper became a territory of diverse aesthetic and ideological tendencies, fulfilling the newspaper's central role as a vital organ within the public sphere. Dion's project engages the contextual specificity of the newspaper as a discursive space that might just coax readers into the role of producers by asking them to reflect upon the function of the newspaper as an instrument of communication, and to reconsider the role of art and artist in relation to the public sphere of mass media.

CHAPTER III

Elastic Realities: Rirkrit Tiravanija, Lincoln Tobier, Grennan & Sperandio

Revised version of an essay originally published in *Flash Art*, Summer 1997.

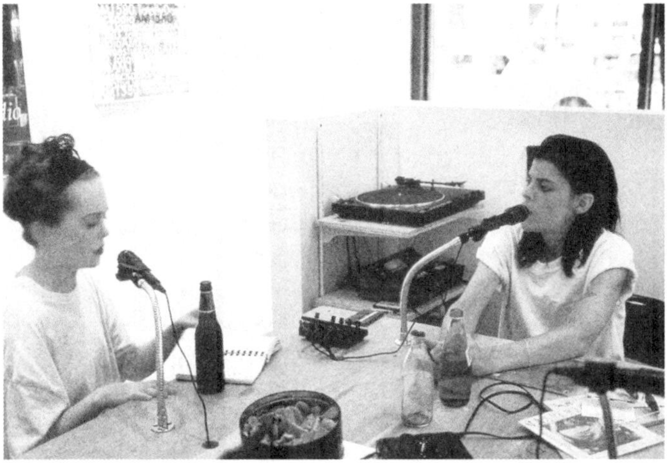

Lincoln Tobier, *Mini-AM*, 1995

When does an organized social event become analogous to an art activity? When the artist—and the context of the artist's activity—endows the social event with an art condition. And what is the art condition? An event, place, or object that is the material manifestation of an artist's definition of what art is, or what it might be. We have become accustomed to converting anything that does not seem, at first, to meet a set of art criteria, into artistic matter.

Artists such as Rirkrit Tiravanija and Lincoln Tobier open up the self-contained artwork, setting up a framework that prepares the ground for the unfolding of some kind of social event or situation. The social activity completes the signifying condition of their respective practices: people eat curries in a gallery, play electric guitars within the context of a museum, or use a mini-AM radio station to broadcast programs within a limited range. This, then, sets into motion a unique kind of theatricality that resembles real life, but actually points back to the real artificiality of the framing device itself. In this conception, the museum is returned to the realm of the mundane, the putative everyday, and in return, certain everyday activities are converted into their aesthetic corollaries. Even in the case of Tobier's radio stations, the inaccessible characteristics of the mass culture apparatus are returned, perhaps more symbolically than materially, to the individual. Of course, that's the irony of Tobier's gesture: a communication system of popular culture such as radio has never really concerned the individual, but rather the cult of individuality that is translated through the magnetism of personality and celebrity. Tiravanija, on the other hand, will construct an environment in which a specific kind of musical or life-activity unfolds, but this will also be understood as a rehearsal for corollary activities that occur outside of the frame of the cultural institution. Tiravanija's practice does not imply that the museum is in any fundamental sense less real than any other cultural context: on the contrary, he sets into motion a folding together of social spaces, and meaning emerges out of that symbolic and material blending of one sphere into another.

Some of today's artists would like to redefine the conditions of artifice, since everyday life appears increasingly more aesthetic than art practice itself. Everywhere, it seems, we want art to penetrate deeper and deeper into reality. Within the various genres that constitute the realm of post-object art today, there has been a general tendency to suggest that a penetration of reality somehow guarantees purchase upon an enhanced authenticity; i.e., an experience of realness that is understood to be not only symbolic but also materially closer in spirit to everyday reality (whatever that may be …). If at the start of the 1990s, certain strategies of institutional critique led to a fetishizing of the museum and its attendant structures and ideologies, such practices eventually exhausted themselves by continuously returning to the same host body (i.e., the cultural institution) for parasitical feeding.

Collaborators Simon Grennan and Christopher Sperandio seek to operate within culture as direct facilitators of other people's imaginations, while also examining the intrinsic artificiality of that very gesture. In recent projects, they have produced comic-book-style publications as sites through which to visually translate received narratives. The evolution of their practice is instructive: in 1993, for example, they joined (labor) forces with unionized workers at a chocolate factory in Chicago to design and produce a new chocolate bar within the context of the *Culture in Action* exhibition; in that same year, for their *Anyone in New York* exhibition at NYU's Grey Art Gallery, Grennan & Sperandio invited university employees to propose whom in New York they would most like to meet, and then proceeded to both arrange and photograph a number of the requested encounters; in 1994, they asked six dentists living in Eastbourne, England, to select their favorite paintings, and then photographed each (with their office assistants) according to the compositional manner of the chosen painting; for a 1995 prison-specific exhibition in Philadelphia, they converted a number of real-life stories of incarceration into a comic book publication entitled *Life in Prison*. In 1996, London's Institute of Contemporary Arts sponsored the project *Cartoon Hits*, wherein the two artists collaborated with 13 ICA members to recreate their life stories in a comic book publication. Garnering the support of Fantagraphics Books (a publisher and distributor of underground comics) for the *Life in Prison* and *Cartoon Hits* books, Grennan & Sperandio have effectively inserted their practice into two distinct streams of distribution and cultural communication: international comic book stores and museum shops!

The conversion of people power into a new kind of public art? While *Fantastic Sh*t* (1996) may not be the first time that Grennan & Sperandio have invited the public to articulate their experiences and imaginations through the agency of an art making process, it does mark the first time that the two have focused upon the phantasmagorical, mythological, mystical, and hallucinatory aspects of everyday life. *Fantastic Sh*t* visualizes the written accounts of a group of people who have claimed to have had experiences of a supernatural kind, the works pictorializing the seminal moment of each putative event. The two artists placed ads in the local newspapers of New York, Glasgow, and Bordeaux (the three linked venue-locations of *Fantastic Sh*t*), inviting written testimonies from any and all. After consulting with as many respondents as possible in order to incorporate their aesthetic recommendations, Grennan & Sperandio initiated the next stage of their collaborative process, and set to work translating the autobiographical narratives into graphic images: silkscreen-on-paper posters designed to be viewed with 3-D glasses. This cleverly provisional team-based method puts a new, good-humored, and mildly ironic spin on a tactic which until recently has been largely in disrepute: a collective, socially-based model of art making that seeks to throw a monkey wrench into our belief in stable authorship, and intelligently challenges the cultural authority that such deep-seated beliefs inevitably, and predictably, reinforce. Grennan & Sperandio bring outsiders into the conceptual stage of the art making process. Their methodology is contingent upon a radically extended collaborative process whereby authorship is fundamentally displaced into—and, to a certain degree, is replaced by—a set of distinct voices. Playing in that symbolic but all-too-real chasm separating the putative art culture from the putative non-art culture, these two artists renegotiate the often estranged relationship between artist and audience, entertainingly transform the public into producers, and suggest that a post-Pop sensibility can also engender unique social transactions and hybrid forms of practice.

The distinction between that which constitutes reality and that which comprises art is merely illusory, yet it is a mirage of difference (philosophical and material) that can be re-invented again and again to such an extent that the illusion itself (i.e., the illusion of the gap between reality and art) seems to disappear. Today, we live according to the rather persuasive illusion that the status, value, and meaning of contemporary art practice have become so unstable that only the most generalizing of social-anthropological distinctions can be offered for our consideration. It is undeniably liberating to acknowledge that art making is as mundane as any other cultural activity, even though it issues forth new meanings and forms through a specialized language.

Art may have the ability to convert the everyday into the extraordinary, or the extraordinary into the banal, it may be able to transform consciousness, yet its palpable role in the transformation of society continues to remain vexingly undetermined.

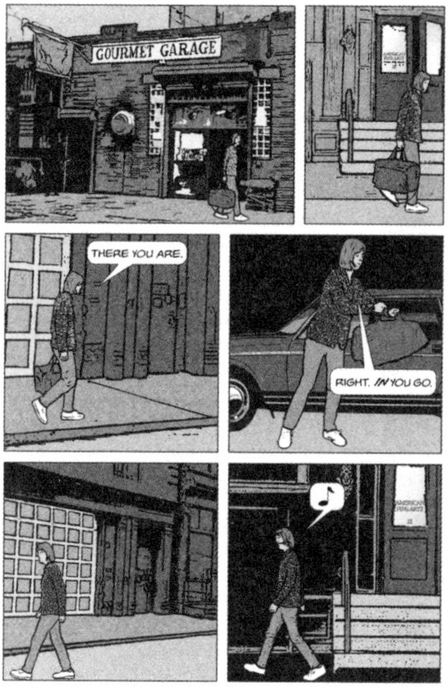

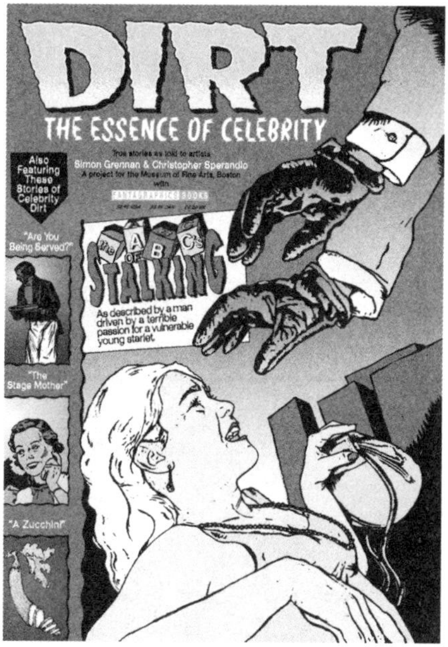

Simon Grennan and Christopher Sperandio, *Cartoon Hits*, 1996 (detail)
Simon Grennan and Christopher Sperandio, Cover of *Dirt*, 1996

Prime Time: At the Nexus of Contemporary Art and Mainstream Television

Revised version of the essay, "Prime Time: 'In the Name of the Place' of Art and Television," originally published in the catalogue of the Mel Chin/GALA Committee exhibition, *In the Name of the Place*, at Grand Arts, Kansas City, Missouri, January 16–March 7, 1998.

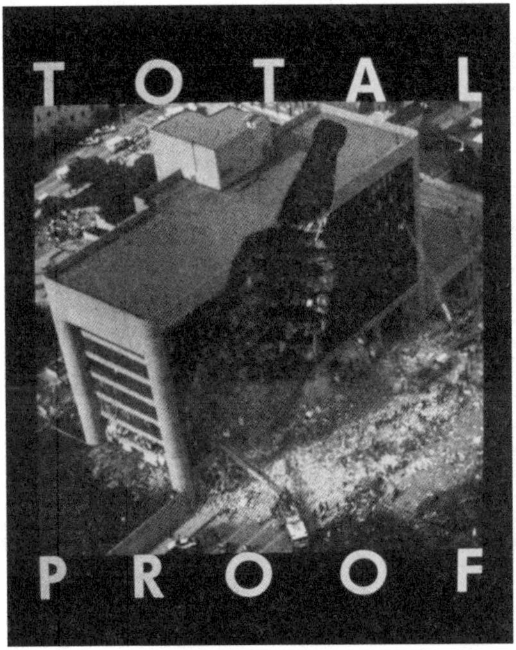

GALA Committee, *Total Proof*, 1997

Bedroom sheets adorned with a pattern of unrolled condoms; a computer-manipulated photograph of the Federal Building in Oklahoma City with the bomb crater reconfigured as a Vodka bottle and framed by the words "Total Proof"; Chinese food take-out bags inscribed with the ideograph for human rights; a brooch designed in the form of a mosquito that is a harbinger of the yellow fever virus; a painting of the bombing of Baghdad; liquor bottles at a bar that double as information-laden objects tracing the complex history of alcohol consumption and related alcohol-culture issues in the United States …

What, you might ask, is being described here? Theatrical set pieces, art objects, or something else? Actually, the aforementioned descriptions refer to hybrid elements that have been appearing, probably unseen to most of us, on various episodes of the prime-time television series, *Melrose Place*. Conceptual art objects camouflaged as props (or is it the other way around?) on the set of *Melrose Place*. Is it possible that art has finally infiltrated mainstream TV, and entered into the cathode-ray tube for worldwide transmission to millions of adoring fans who assiduously follow this controversial program? Is this for real? Well, from a certain perspective, nothing on TV is real, but it is accurate to say that an unprecedented rendezvous of contemporary art practice and contemporary mainstream television has recently occurred: it is called *In the Name of the Place*, a project initiated by Mel Chin. This quickly expanded to become an elaborate collaboration between the artist, students, and faculty from the California Institute of the Arts and the University of Georgia—all of whom collectively constituted The GALA Committee. In a boldly inventive move, Chin—an artist who has developed a substantial reputation for challenging and rethinking parochial notions of public art in the United States so as to engineer new relations between site-specificity, aesthetics, and politics—here recalibrates his long-term involvement with the ecological politics of nature and landscape in relation to another type of space: the wholly public arena of television spectacle. The GALA Committee has sought to create a new model of art that involves the participation of mainstream TV, effectively moving beyond theoretical fantasies of critical media infiltration into an unprecedented framework of cross-cultural and inter media collaboration. Collective art here parallels the fundamentally collaborative nature of television production.

The visual arts and prime-time television rarely, if ever, commingle, leading many people to conclude that the two are not only rather strange bedfellows, but fundamentally at odds with each other. Of course, this is as much an inherited ideological dictum as it is a deeply felt aesthetic proclivity, as the American art world is still struggling to disconnect itself from the thralldom of the hackneyed (and always parochial) high/low dichotomy. As someone who has spent about as much time watching TV as contemplating art, I cannot recall, for instance, one advertisement on prime-time television for an artist or art exhibition. While Public Television has done a number of documentary-style programs on the visual arts (or occasionally presented a William Wegman or Nam June Paik video), it has really never sought to rethink TV as a public space for the commissioning of new kinds of art. With the advent of cable television and a network such as MTV (which briefly aired the forgettable Andy Warhol show in the early 1980s, and more recently paid lip service to contemporary artists by airing something called *Art Breaks* in conjunction with a Whitney Museum Biennial), television really has had no use for art, and art (along with the art world) has generally maintained a rather contemptuous relationship to the tube.

It is a testament to the uniqueness of the GALA Committee's *In the Name of the Place* project that we are willing to reconsider the possibility that prime-time, entertainment-based television such as *Melrose Place*—a show often considered to offer questionable moral instruction to the youth of America—might actually become a site wherein everyday issues such as health, violence, gender, sexuality, violence, environmental conflicts, and other social crises surface in a style that has very little in common with the standard delivery systems of news and infotainment programs. Deftly inserted (and virtually hidden within) certain episodes of the prime-time LA lifestyle show that everyone loves to hate, the art objects-as-props that comprise the *In the Name of the Place* project lay in wait, delivering their sophisticated, yet subliminal, visual and verbal messages to an unsuspecting audience. This strategy reimagines the physical set of the TV show as a framework for the exhibition of artworks—designed artifacts (or, tele-objects) virtually indistinguishable from background props.

The introduction of artworks into the sets of *Melrose Place* (as a mode of televisual site-specificity) was a singular and powerfully idiosyncratic idea in its own right. But what is even more astonishing is that the project garnered the early cooperation of the show's set decorator, Deborah Siegel. At first, Siegel invited the GALA Committee to design a number of adornments for an upcoming episode of *Melrose Place* that would be featured in the bedroom of a doctor known for his sexual adventures, leading to the development and incorporation of the condom-pattern design onto pillowcases and bedsheets (entitled *Safety Sheets*): a new aesthetics generated out of an alternately humorous and earnest reflection upon the increasingly popular—and commercialized—discourse of safe sex. At the early stages of this relatively unofficial cooperation between the GALA Project and Siegel, executive producer Frank South was apparently unaware that these hybrid artifacts were being incorporated into the visual and narrative framework of the show (as were many of the actors), but eventually he was informed, and gave it enthusiastic, official, approval—eventually, he became a GALA Committee member.

The GALA Committee considers the relationship between *In the Name the Place* and *Melrose Place* to be something of an inadvertent coalition between two embattled sites. On the one hand, NEA-supported art institutions (and, by extension, artists) such as The Museum of Contemporary Art in Los Angeles, which commissioned *In the Name of the Place* for the recent group show *Uncommon Sense*, has come under attack by some conservative politicians and religious leaders. On the other hand, *Melrose Plac*e has drawn the ire of ultra-conservative critics who have sought to suggest an analogy between the program's questionable morality about sexual relationships and the supposed pandemic moral decline of the United States. The GALA Committee sees the foolishness and hypocrisy of those who would claim that tax revenue supported vanguard art making and commercially funded rearguard television have become co-conspirators in the subversion of real American values. *In the Name of the Place* forges a temporary, complex alliance between distinct cultural worlds that is at once poignantly real and imaginary. The supposedly superficial narratives of *Melrose Place* are imbedded with layers of coded information that trigger rich cultural and political allegories.

What is especially significant about this cross-cultural collaboration is the extent to which a real working relationship unfolded between the various students, teachers, artists, and academics associated with the GALA Project, as well as the producers, set designers, and scriptwriters for *Melrose Place*. For example, when an episode called for the Samantha character to make a public display of her paintings, the GALA Committee submitted works that depicted famous real-life crime scenes throughout Los Angeles. These crime narratives were then incorporated back into the TV script, so as to generate thematic overlaps.

In the 1997 *Uncommon Sense* exhibition at LA's Geffen Contemporary, the original site of presentation of *In the Name of the Place*, hundreds of the artwork props were displayed in tandem with specially edited video clips of the *Melrose Place* episodes. This included the set of one of the show's primary social hangouts, Shooters Bar. The exhibition design offered an opportunity to locate the discreetly installed objects and embellishments inside the theatrical space of the actual television program. This subtle, mutually reinforcing collaborative interplay between the GALA Committee and the makers of *Melrose Place* would lead to a natural, yet still unexpected, apotheosis: an episode of *Melrose Place* was actually taped inside one of the museum's galleries. This featured the Heather Locklear and Rob Estes characters discussing a Bombing of Baghdad painting (originally commissioned by one of the show's writers from the GALA Committee) as it appears in the *Uncommon Sense* show. The scene was then broadcast on an episode of *Melrose Place* shortly after the MOCA opening, and, appropriately enough, Chin and set decorator Siegel can be seen in the background, bringing full circle this singular fusion of art world and TV world conceptions of visual artifice, fantasy, social narrative, and cultural scrutiny. Here, the spectacle of television is re-staged within the institutional space of a museum, and the context of the art exhibition—itself the product of a collaboration that blurs distinctions between high culture and popular culture—is injected back into the pictorial space of daily television. Art is transmitted through television, television through art, and a remarkably hybrid situation is engendered.

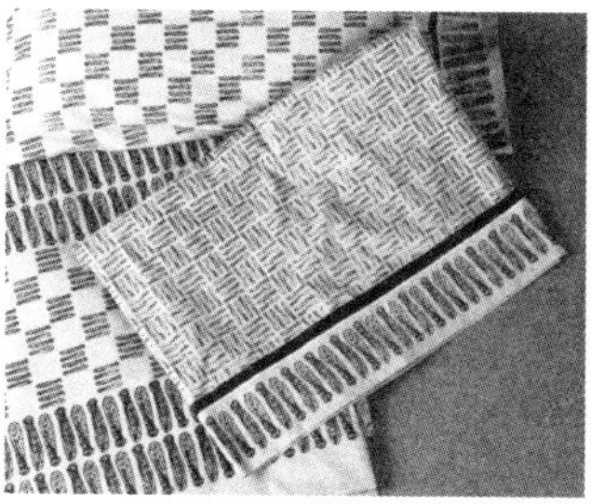

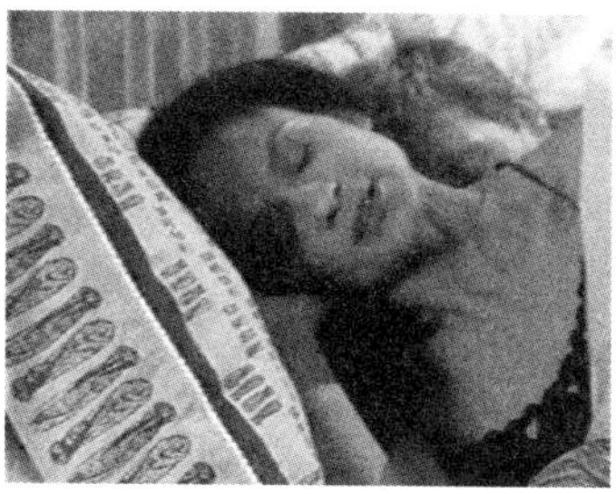

GALA Committee, *Safety Sheets*, 1997

event@rockenschaub.com/inflect/ social mappings/

Revised version of an essay originally published in the catalogue of the Gerwald Rockenschaub exhibition *Funky Minimal*, Kunstverein in Hamburg (April 23–June 13, 1999), and Le Consortium, Dijon (October 23–December 24, 1999), Les presses du réel, 1999.

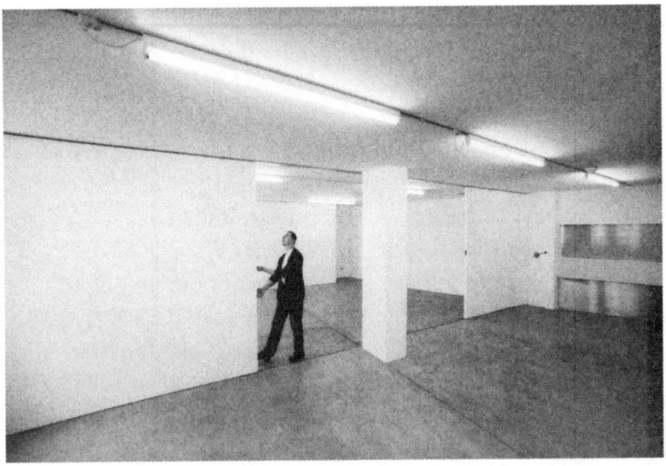

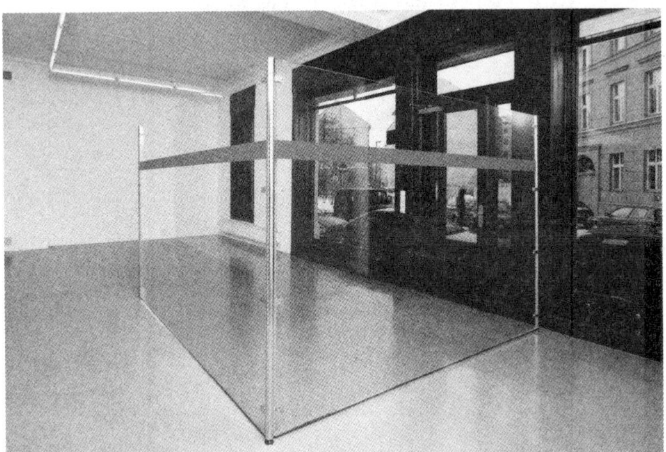

Gerwald Rockenschaub, installation view, EA-Generali Foundation, Vienna, 1991
Gerwald Rockenschaub, installation view, Galerie Mehdi Chouakri, 1998

Gerwald Rockenschaub's visual art language points to notions of what constitutes the event, and how we understand the construction of the social, and social space. Rockenschaub does not produce art with a post-aesthetic aesthetic. Rather, his art language is a highly refined synthesis of architecture, design, painting, sculpture, and installation-oriented production. Inflection is a camouflaged act of intervention. To inflect is to mark a social or spatial territory that has been (already) rationalized. Rockenschaub inflects spaces, locations, and structures. To inflect is to de-territorialize, and to re-territorialize, without declaring war on the context. This requires subterfuge and ironic play. To inflect is also to deflect a set of assumptions about the spatial, social, and cultural characteristics of a situation, of a place. To inflect is to subtly remap.

Take, for example, Gerwald Rockenschaub's *36 acrylic glass plates*, produced on the occasion of his

1989 exhibition at Galerie Paul Maenz in Cologne. A straightforward yet visually ephemeral gesture: overlay the gallery's walls with transparent synthetic sheets. This is an apparently simple procedure, revealing naked walls—just the screws and washers visible as the structural means of attachment. The whiteness of the gallery architecture, recoded as a surface event.

From one perspective, *36 acrylic glass plates* is an ironic variation on the (theoretical) death throes of post-geometric painting, wherein the empty cultural sign of painting is converted into something hybrid: at once pictorial and non-pictorial, physical yet seemingly immaterial. The *pictorialization* of architecture, the *architecturing* of the pictorial frame. The frame-as-frame, the frame-as-picture, and the picture becoming the frame.

Architecture; non-architecture; post-architecture; sculpture and non-sculpture. A form of drawing in space. Transparently present: an absence that unfolds the structural actuality of the context. Rockenschaub's *Dividing curtain made of cellophane*, produced for his 1991 exhibition at the Kunstmuseum Lucerne, continues the artist's process of examining the predetermined structural conditions of a place, and subtly recoding the architecture. The curtain, in this instance, overlays a long museum wall, as if it were a plastic dress or some other article of clothing. In the process, a doorway leading through the wall has been blocked, curtailing the movements of visitors within the space. Yet the public can see through it, into the next room. Tantalizing. The transparent curtain quietly disrupts normative navigations of the museum, while also calling attention to the artificiality of the architectural design. This is a form of theater—i.e., the theatricality of reprogramming space.

Architect and theorist Bernard Tschumi has proposed the notion of architectural "cross-dressing," wherein there is a "cross-programming" of built space. In Rockenschaub's 1991 project for the EA-Generali Foundation in Vienna, the artist provided the audience with an opportunity to transform the architectural conditions of the space (or, the spatial conditions of the architecture): he exposed white "retractable dividing walls" from behind a door, revealing structural elements usually hidden from view. This simple gesture of unpacking, so to speak, the room's infrastructure created the possibility for the viewers themselves to inflect and recode the boundaries of the social space.

That same year, at Galerie Metropol in Vienna, Rockenschaub inserted a new element into the architectural context: the installation of a cordon that functioned as a device to map the boundaries of a section of empty room. Here, the intrinsic social space of the gallery is reframed, a new boundary is established, and the meaning of the gesture is contained within the perception of the territorial boundary itself. A room inside of a space, a space inside of a room, the location as aesthetic framework, an event waiting to unfold. An invented boundary, a real consequence, a situation redefined. A symbolic, yet physical, cut in space.

A Viewing Platform. A Platform for Viewing. Viewing a Platform.

Rockenschaub's *Scaffolding* installation at the Villa Arson in 1992 can be understood as a heavy-metal inflection of modernist space. Viewers walk up a stair-like element on one side of the scaffold, transverse the length of the scaffold (which bisects the width of the gallery), contemplate the empty gallery space, and then return to ground level via another stair-like element. Utilizing an everyday prefab structure that signifies construction (i.e., construction-as-process), Rockenschaub here effectively reframes the context as a situation in process. And therefore, our relationship to place is also in process.

The idea of scaffolding was more extensively elaborated in the artist's contribution to the 45th Biennale of Venice in 1993. In that situation, Rockenschaub designed a catwalk that mapped out the spatial and architectural coordinates of the pavilion's interior space, and allowed visitors to walk from ground-level to window-level, and other in-between elevations. This alternately aggressive and delicate recoding of context functioned to establish a certain kind of theatricality: the scaffold structure as a device that restaged the visitor's relationship to place. The scaffold structure anticipates an event that is about to unfold: the presence of bodies traversing space within an architectural frame.

In 1992, at the Elizabeth Koury Gallery in New York, Rockenschaub installed two black metal frame, red imitation leather seats in front of the gallery windows. Nothing more, nothing less. A room with a view, so to speak. Or, a view with a room. A structure awaiting a presence—the framework of an event yet to unfold. The bench as a symbolic bridge between the space of art and urban space. A viewing platform; a platform for viewing: viewing the platform.

What was once a wall is now an element that invokes the presence of a wall. A door. A peephole in a door, the suggestion of another room, a space beyond, a view through structures. In Rockenschaub's 1993 exhibition at Galerie Metropol in Vienna, the artist constructed an interplay of architectonic spaces and viewing devices: a door with peephole, a tripartite stair unit facing a white wall. Where does one space end, and another begin? How does architectural structure operate to delineate social space? What are the signifying conditions that emerge from the interplay between body, place, and vision?

Perhaps Rockenschaub is suggesting that art is always defined in relation to a set of contextual factors, and that art may also (virtually) disappear into its informing context. Or, conversely, that context may collapse into art. But where then is the art located? And where then might we locate the context? How do we articulate such locations, if not through the application of agreed-upon or previously designated institutional boundaries and definitions? Rockenschaub's inflections continuously map, remap, and occasionally transgress such boundaries.

The inflection of an architectural environment so as to allow the individual to renegotiate the social-institutional space of display: Rockenschaub's series of wooden stair-like units, placed at the (foot of) museum walls, may function as device-platforms that reveal the other side of the boundary. These were installed to offer the public an opportunity to observe, both symbolically and literally, that which exists backstage—specifically, in the 1993 exhibition *Backstage* at the Kunstverein in Hamburg and the Kunstmuseum Lucerne. But what is on the other side of a boundary? Another room, or perhaps that which exists beyond the architectural frame (i.e., the "outside"). Inside-out, outside-in. The simultaneous delineation and folding-together of inside and outside.

What is a fold in space? To fold and unfold: these are terms which the architect Peter Eisenman has borrowed from Gilles Deleuze to characterize the (possible) attributes of contemporary urban space and architecture in relation to the proliferation of media culture. Within a non- or post-Euclidean conception of urban space, continuous modification unfolds, thereby rendering that which is solid ephemeral, and the ephemeral, virtually transparent. The virtuosity of virtual urban territories. Such as the barely visible alteration in space engendered by Rockenschaub's more recent inflatable PVC objects, perhaps? Nearly transparent folds in space, virtual objects, objects of virtuality. Structures for a virtual age. Looking through structure, into another structure. The object as filtering device within social space.

Returning to the year 1994, Rockenschaub used the Secession in Vienna as a platform to mediate between the interior space of the institution, and the external space of the city. *Six chairs (to sit down and look out of the window)* provided the conditions for that precise activity—i.e., the contemplation of the exterior world from the perspective of a constructed place. In the main Secession hall, Rockenschaub presented 34 inkjet prints of views of Vienna—a record of movement through the urban space, perhaps nothing more or nothing less. Here, we moved through—and looked beyond—both literal and symbolic boundaries in order to rethink our assumptions about what constitutes the "frame" of visual culture. From the map of the institution, outward to the mapping of urban space, and back again—an irrefutable, mundane, circularity.

Perhaps Rockenschaub sought to deploy a subjective map through institutional and urban spaces already subjected to the laws of rational organization. Blurring together location and dislocation, Rockenschaub's utilization of computer-assisted photographic imagery as well as video in his 1994 Linz Landesmuseum project suggested an examination of the representation of reality. He injected himself into the city of Linz, and documented a series of normative observations. This was a type of situational aesthetics in which apparently non-aesthetic situations were recoded through gestures of straightforward observation. It is tenable to suggest that Rockenschaub was out to capture his intuitive absorption into the reality that is always in the process of representing itself—as territorialized space—back into the framing apparatus of photography and video.

Form and anti-form: the transparency of objects, the objectivity of transparency. Objects with virtual boundaries: Rockenschaub's inflatable PVC objects flirt with a condition of dematerialization, yet still proclaim a unique quality of presence. These are paradoxical, elegantly absurd objects—at once rigorous and comical, substantial yet playfully inconsequential. Presence as a kind of virtual non-presence. Comprised of four inflatable, transparent PVC structures (and an inflatable picture), Rockenschaub's 1996 exhibition at Galerie Susanna Kulli in St. Gallen was a playful reconsideration of the intrinsic interdependence between object and place. Rockenschaub continued this approach with the ten inflatable PVC objects presented in his 1998 show at Galerie Hauser & Wirth, Zurich. Distributed in an uneven grid throughout the gallery space, these virtually transparent structures flirted with a traditional sculptural monumentality, yet undermined that symbolic authority by virtue of their apparent immaterial materiality. These objects were autonomous, yet somehow also contingent upon the space for completion. Awkwardly precise, weirdly elegant, these are transitory objects assumed an ironic (and iconic) theatricality of permanence.

For Rockenschaub, it might be argued that the art of place addresses the function of context in relation to the making of art. In the end, the place of art (or, the place *for* art) and an art of place become virtually interchangeable as ideas, and perhaps as material practices. At what point does the artfulness of art begin to dissipate? Precisely at the moment when what we have named as art ceases to draw attention to itself as art, precisely at the moment of its disappearance into its frame, its context—i.e., its *place*.

These playfully analytical concerns were evident in Rockenschaub's 1998 show at Galerie Mehdi Chouakri in Berlin. Here, the artist installed two glass plate structures that re-coded the architectonics of the gallery space, and also operated as a kind of meta-pictorial device. In addition, a wide-angle lens was placed on the interior of the front gallery window (facing the street), so that visitors would experience a distortion in the relation between internal social space and the external urban environment.

In a sense, Rockenschaub strips the pictorial conditions of abstraction (both in terms of the codes of painting and sculpture) down to a degree-zero, and injects this emptied lexicon into the architectural conditions of architectonic space. This analytical gesture triggers a recoding of social space through the agency of a transparent structural *intermediary*. The context re-emerges through this condition of transparency enabled by the virtual, quasi-architectural character of the installation. These qualities were indeed echoed by the PVC curtain installed in the second room at Mehdi Chouakri's gallery: a soft, ephemeral element that suggested the poetics of the provisional, assuming the presence of something at once material and immaterial, even as it re-coded the (social) architectonics of that space. And so the space became an event, in the sense that space is always in formation.

Architecture addresses the problem of space by constructing boundaries and borders to circumscribe space; i.e., reshaping space into a navigable, negotiable territory. Rockenschaub's PVC objects—and his other meta-architectural and meta-design works—allow us to understand the site of exhibition as a platform for the construction, unfolding, and dissolving of *space itself*.

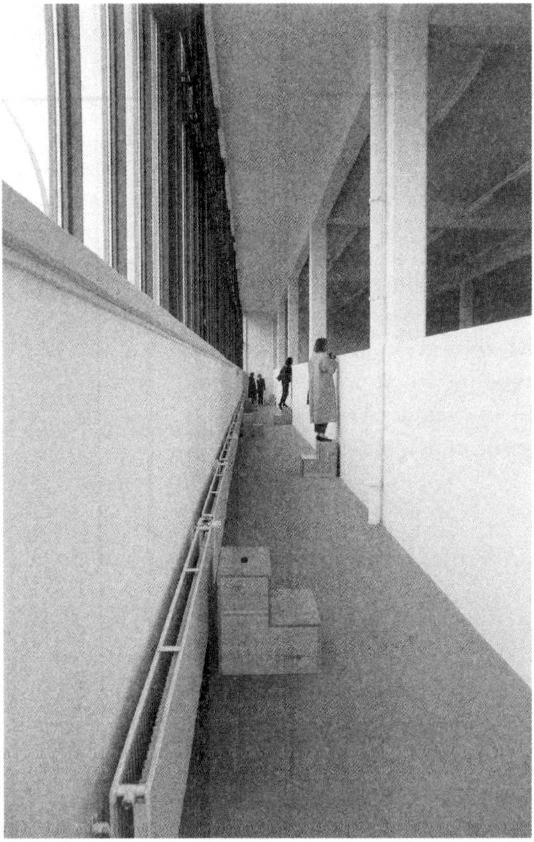

Gerwald Rockenschaub, *Backstage*, installation view, Kunstverein in Hamburg, 1993

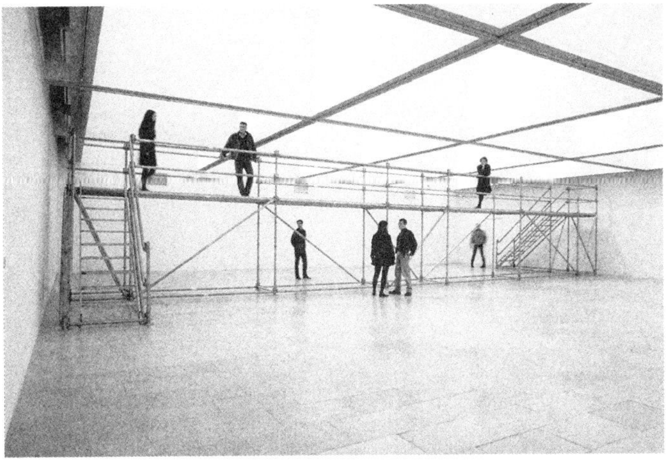

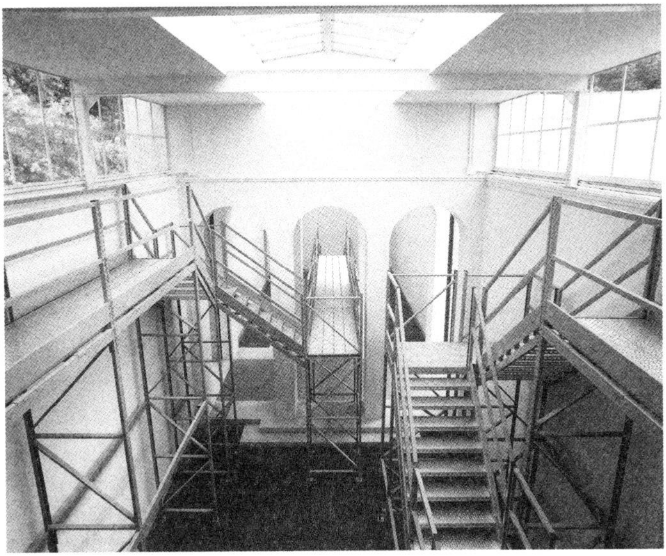

Gerwald Rockenschaub, installation view, Villa Arson, Nice, 1992
Gerwald Rockenschaub, installation view, Austrian Pavilion, 45th Venice Biennale, 1993

The Practice of Cultural Renewal: *Project Row Houses*

Revised version of an article originally published as "The Cultural Practice of Renewal: *Project Row Houses*," in *NU* magazine, no. 1, 2000.

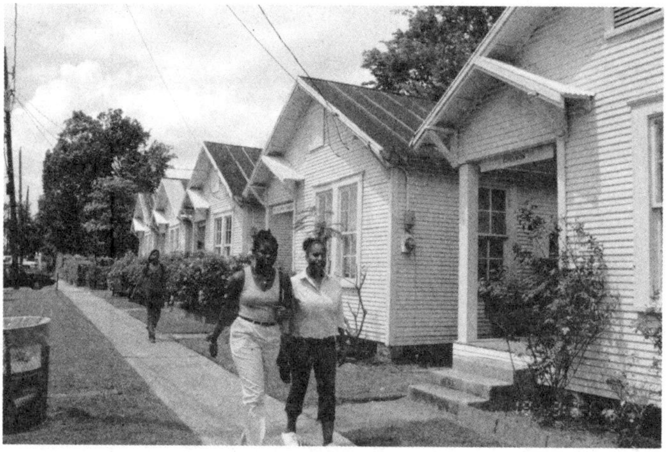

Project Row Houses, Houston, Texas

Far afield from the New York art world, a remarkable situation has unfolded in the small, historically important, economically disenfranchised, and predominantly African-American Third Ward of Houston, Texas. Artist Rick Lowe developed *Project Row Houses* in 1993 as a new form of public art, but with the objective of facilitating the cultural, social, and economic rehabilitation of this neglected neighborhood. Using innovative community-outreach programs, Lowe has sought to enhance the residents' sense of identification with the neighborhood's significant place in the complex social and racial history of Houston. *Project Row Houses* is organized around the nucleus of 22 original shotgun houses that occupy a block and half in a section of the city that emerged during the Civil War as a refuge for blacks escaping pro-slavery states.

Artists' Projects is one of the central elements of Lowe's *Project Row Houses* model: every six months, on a rotating basis, artists from Houston and other places are commissioned to transform the actual row houses. This framework allows the invited artists and guest curators to engage in a unique form of interaction with the local residents during the development and implementation stage of their place-specific works. Conversely, this structure affords the neighborhood residents an opportunity to engage with the visiting artists. *Streetlife*, curated by Jérôme Sans, marks the first time that a European curator has implemented a show for *Project Row Houses;* this gesture reflects Lowe's interest in exploring points of intersection between art considered as an instrument of localized community-based change on the one hand, and art defined in relation to the global discourses of vanguardism on the other. Sans invited local, national, and international artists (Jens Haaning, Joseph Havel, Annette Lawrence, Simon Grennan and Christopher Sperandio, Rirkrit Tiravanija, Nari Ward, and Chen Zhen) to produce new works—with each participant transforming one of the row houses.

Tiravanija, appropriately enough, offered a cooking setup and people from the neighborhood would drop in to sample some of his culinary efforts and, after Rirkrit departed, do their own cooking. In Grennan & Sperandio's *People Around*, the artists invited community residents to visit their row house and make funny faces; the expressions were photographically documented, and subsequently transformed by the artists (utilizing a special computer program) so as to simulate the style of 19th-century woodcuts. Installed on the interior walls of the row houses, these meta-portraits offered the best evidence that community-engaged art making can be at once trenchant and lighthearted. Chen Zhen's *Couldn't Bananas Be Black* was a remarkable, metaphor-rich documentation of research conducted by his brother (who is a leading scientist in China) and his team concerning evidence that the Chinese and other East Asians originated from the African continent. This is a controversial scientific position in Mainland China, and therefore a compelling framework for Zhen to reflect upon his own identity as it comes into contact with this Houston neighborhood and its history.

Lowe sees *Project Row Houses* as an opportunity to trigger new levels of dialogue between the local residents, the broader fabric of Houston, and beyond. As Houston is a dispersed urban territory, with a multitude of economically, culturally, and ethically diverse neighborhoods (some of which are undergoing the requisite, and occasionally startling, processes of gentrification), *Project Row Houses* can also be understood as a political effort to reinvent a new model and practice of urban revitalization in relation to conventional strategies of historical preservation, community services, and education. *Project Row Houses* provides single mothers with housing residencies for a one-year period (to assist them with balancing work, education, and child-rearing); a multimedia center offers local middle-school students an opportunity to gain literacy with photography and other media tools; there is a community garden; and, an African-American festival.

Lowe has also begun to expand the urban reclamation spirit and practice of *Project Row Houses* through the purchase of a nearby block of buildings and land, which will be converted for future community use. In addition, Lowe and his colleagues are working with other American inner-city communities in urban centers such as Los Angeles, Birmingham, and East Saint Louis, so as to promote socially transformative projects that are inspired by the *Project Row Houses* model. Perhaps the time is now right for Lowe to bring his enterprise to New York and shake things up a bit.

Transitory Agencies and Situational Engagements: The Artist as Public Interlocutor?

Revised version of essay published in the book, *inSite_05/[Situational] Public*, inSite_05/Art Practices in the Public Domain, San Diego/Tijuana, 2006.

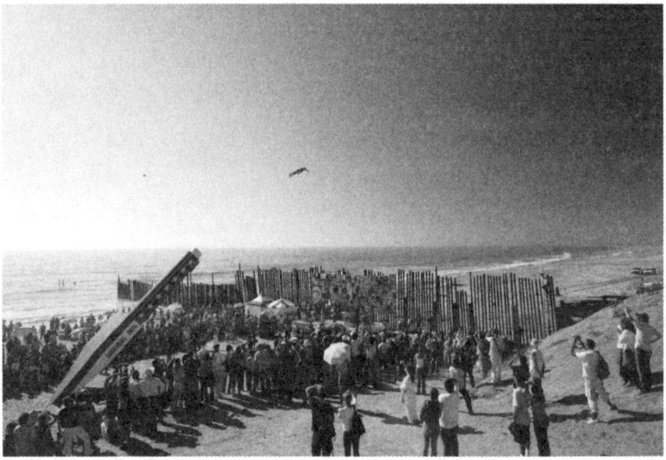

Javier Téllez, *One Flew Over the Void (Bala Perdida)*, 2005

Find a city
Find myself a city to live in …
—Talking Heads, "Cities"[1]

We are concerned with the understanding of how cities and societies change on the basis of collective projects and societal conflicts generated through history.

Our questions address the issue of how and why the creators challenge the dominants …
—Manuel Castells[2]

"WHERE DO I BELONG?" seems to be the question that plagues so many of the discussions that I participate in. As a constant lament it refers to dislocations felt by displaced subjects toward disrupted histories and to shifting and transient national identities.
—Irit Rogoff[3]

What does it mean for artists, today, to "intervene" in public, within public space, in relation to distinct publics? *What is public?* And why should various publics be interested in an exhibition project such as *Interventions*, beyond the relatively insular contingents of cultural intellectuals and producers who have become engaged with the inSite milieu?

> A space is genuinely public, as Kevin Lynch once pointed out, only to the extent that it really is openly accessible and welcoming to members of the community that it serves. It must also allow users considerable freedom of assembly and action. And there must be some kind of public control of its use and its transformation over time.
> —William J. Mitchell[4]

We enter into these ruminations, which are not merely rhetorical, to test out the possible reconstitution of the artist's civic, public role. Yet we also need to be realistic about what and who our various audiences and publics are, while seeking connections to the imaginations of broader constituencies, come what may—particularly if we desire to remobilize our artistic, cultural, and intellectual activities as a force of reconnection (not necessarily reconciliation) with ideologically disparate audiences, publics, and receivers.

Commencing in 1992, the inSite organization in San Diego and Tijuana has functioned as an unprecedented platform for artists and architects to research and develop projects that engage the local, national, and global conditions of the US-Mexico border environs. During those years, inSite was really the only ongoing exhibition event within the United States—or, more precisely, a cooperative binational, transborder event—that was committed to pushing the envelope on models of public art by experimenting with socially based, contextual projects involving a range of novel methods. Just as significantly, inSite continuously retested the public's relationship to art in the public sphere, redefining site-specificity in relation to the economic, cultural, political, and cultural conditions of the various communities and citizens inhabiting the border.

inSite_05's *Interventions* project endeavored to rethink normative notions of public art, site-specificity, community-based cultural production, and the politics of artistic engagement. Although the San Diego-Tijuana border environs has been the primary organizing force of previous incarnations of inSite, it was with this version, entitled *Interventions*, that the border—at least on curatorial-theoretical terms—became an increasingly phantom-like presence: a dematerialized territory of investigation. *Interventions* represented a shift toward a consideration of the conurban environs of greater Tijuana and San Diego as a *liminal* zone of continuous flows and counter-flows. Although previous iterations of inSite had been contingent, to one degree or another, upon a process of research and project development undertaken by artists, architects, and other cultural producers, with inSite functioning as the commissioner of community-based and context-driven projects, it became apparent that the aim of *Interventions* was to amplify *process* itself as a curatorial and artistic methodology—even, in a sense, *the process of process*. And, significantly beyond this, to coax the participating artists to consider the notion of *public as a process*.

> Our belief is that cosmopolitanism and hybridity are the constitutive elements of the post-border condition. If society is understood as a "time-space" fabric upon which the processes of human life are embroidered, then cosmopolitanism and hybridity can be imagined as stretching the dimensions of this fabric into hitherto unforeseen dimensions.
> —Michael Dear and Gustavo Leclerc[5]

Within cities such as New York and San Diego—a condition amplified since 9/11—we understand that public space has become a *readymade* domain: over-regulated, patrolled, increasingly securitized, a placeholder for the eventual arrival, or appearance, of what might be described as public art. Public space, certainly within the US, is normatively defined and identified as an outdoors location (a sidewalk location, a building facade), or an interior space trafficked by numerous pedestrians, that can be made ready to *receive* either preexisting, modifiable, or newly commissioned works of art. In general terms, the megacity has become a platform for the positioning of works within specific urban locations—works which often function as representational signifiers within, and in relation to, the urban environment. Meaning is generated for, and is transmitted in relation to, citizens through encounters with works in the fabric of the city. The encounters constructed for these urban citizens are usually passive in character, although opportunities for more interactive or participatory engagements occasionally arise. The public becomes an audience, perhaps only temporarily, at these encounter-moments, yet is this public-as-audience activated in any substantial way? And, for that matter, where have the spaces for *acts of social impunity* gone? Do the various forms of public art, or even socially responsive practices (constructed as they are through a network of obligatory permissions), constitute an imaginary space of impunity ... perhaps, vicariously, for the citizen?

And what of Tijuana—where questions of space, and of publics, might be more complicated, and less regulated, where there is a peculiar interpenetration of formal and informal economies, habitats, legalities, and identities? How might artists intervene, and collaborate, in this unpredictable context?

> ... the right to the city is not simply about access to what the city contains. The right to the city is a right to change the city, to transform the city, and it has to be also a right that is inherent. By claiming space in public, by creating public space, social groups themselves become public.
> —David Harvey[6]

How do we trace the repercussions—the reverberations—of creative acts upon the fabric of cities, in relation to the imaginations of citizens? How do city-based curatorial initiatives and art projects (whether sponsored by municipalities, private and corporate sources, or synergies between various financial and political supports) function to induce citizens to re-imagine their relationship to lived urban territories? What do we mean by socially responsive practices? What happens when art seems to disappear into the networked flows of social encounters? Or, when cultural production is redistributed into the flows of trans-urban environments—through processes of cooperation, collaboration, negotiation, infiltration, and intervention?

What is this place?
—Edward Soja[7]

The artists and architects who participated in *Interventions* sought to conceptualize and implement unprecedented modes of exploring territorial complexities without offering a *representational fetish* of the border as a literal boundary at once separating and joining two nation-states. This is not to suggest, however, that the border is no longer present to us as a demarcated territory, or that it is completely absent from the considerations (and eventual projects) of the participating artists and architects. The *Interventions* artists took careful steps, on conceptual and practical levels, to avoid littering the border with anything that might be confused with public art objects, opting instead for projects that were either transitory and event-based, such as Javier Téllez's human cannonball performance on the beach at Playas. Or, redistributed into real and imagined social, economic, and cultural networks, such as Mark Bradford's shopping carts deployed within the San Ysidro area as part of the existing *maleteros* system (a network of porters that constitutes an informal economy), Måns Wrange's dissemination of reciprocal good rumors about San Diego and Tijuana through a network of preselected groups of individuals (nodes), and Judi Werthein's distribution of uniquelydesigned sneakers that triggered reflection on the plight of migrants attempting to illegally cross the border from Mexico into the United States.

On the beach in Playas, outside of Tijuana, on a hot August day, bodies melting in the sun, watching a gringo get shot from a canon over the dilapidated yet threatening metal fence that separates Mexican sand from US sand, and a group of psychiatric patients staging their version of a political demonstration. Here, in Téllez's project, *One Flew Over the Void*, the spectacle dissolves into an event, and the event into something more ephemeral—the product of a process that momentarily creates a space of creative impunity, and of ethical inquiry (regarding the nature of Téllez's collaboration with the patients), that is only made possible through a complex network of institutional negotiations and permissions. We all flew over the border on that sundrenched inaugural afternoon, but did we all land in the safety of a net(work) of spectators?

A moment of transaction: exchanging a copy of your house key for a stranger's key, releasing your suspicion just long enough to allow the possibility of someone else to transgress your enclave without permissions. In *Mi Casa, Su Casa*, Paul Ramírez Jonas asked us to reimagine questions of trust and community—and the extent to which the more we securitize the boundaries that putatively separate us from others, whether in terms of official national borders or gated private communities, the more distrust, fear, and suspicion are reproduced in a potentially endless cycle. For those who exchanged the key of their own domicile for the key of another's home, a symbolic act of trust temporarily suspended the cycle of distrust and fear and normative controls were abandoned (perhaps only to return the next morning). Ramírez Jonas presented *Mi Casa, Su Casa* at distinct locations throughout the San Diego and Tijuana environs: the event involved a formal talk on the conceptual development of his project (accompanied by a sequence of images), followed by the artist inviting audience members to consider giving him their house keys. Keys were duplicated immediately on-site, and given to other audience members in exchange for their house keys, and so on and so forth. If one were to engage in this key exchange, you would receive a memento, a gift memorializing this unusual contract in trust, an artifact designed by the artist: a key engraved, on one side, with the representation of two hands overlapping, and on the other, two hands holding keys, suggesting the bond of trust established at that moment between two individuals, involving the sharing of instruments to facilitate mutual transition (mutual trespassing) through portals of privacy in the city, suburbia, and beyond. *Mi Casa, Su Casa* was fundamentally about the regulated conditions of public social space (versus private property, or the ownership of one's space), and how it might be possible to intervene actively in inviting individuals, and by extension, communities, to reconsider their trepidations about the person living next door, across town in another economic enclave—or even on the other side of the border.

Have we reached a point at which art and architectural projects operate on liminal levels—producing critical shadows, rumors, urban mythologies, and silent resistances? Måns Wrange's *The Good Rumor Project* disseminated rumors into the stream of transnational communications and miscommunications about Tijuana and San Diego, as a means of producing unusual linguistic slippages and spillages, and transgressions of stereotypical (rhetorical) representations of urban lives. Language, itself, is a constituent element of public space, a viral agent infiltrating networks of social exchange. During a panel discussion in inSite_05's *Conversations* series, Wrange alluded to the ubiquity of public space. Specifically, that the territories of the white cube gallery or museum space also have public dimensions. Wrange was referring to the interstitial character of social spaces, even within the regulated environments of megacities. Indeed, Wrange's project, *The Good Rumor Project*, to a certain extent alludes to this condition, adapting the discourse and methodology of "rumor theory" to develop focus groups in both San Diego and Tijuana so as to confect a good rumor about each city. Two rumors, apparently circulating through these territories (and perhaps beyond), for nearly a year, with only the participating "nodes" knowing the rumors, and the rest of us perhaps having absorbed the rumors subliminally. Wrange selected one public location for the visual presentation of his project: a promotional video document (produced in the style of a corporate or social-scientific report), discretely displayed on the side of a hotel building in downtown San Diego. Wrange's project actually demanded a very different conception and experience of the public space wherein public art can be instantiated: in this instance, through social communication, like a viral mode of contamination, linked to Wrange's judicious application (and testing) of rumor theory. Beyond research, conceptualization, organization, and implementation, this is where the art is: at those interstitial moments of contact, within the liminal, beyond appearance, seeking another mode of post-representational economy, somehow enunciated through social flows.

Encountering an unusually designed sneaker in a hip, downtown San Diego shop, one observes a modified map of the border between Tijuana and San Diego imprinted inside the shoe. Judi Werthein's *Brinco* is a sneaker designed as a practical navigation system for border-crossers. It is also an index of the globalized relations of labor and production that are ultimately connected to the social, political, and subjective complexities of migration and immigration. This work gains *ambulatory* symbolic power through its status as a *critical design object* camouflaged as a normative product of consumer society ... or is it the other way around? At another location, now in Tijuana, just feet from the dry riverbed that constitutes the border, these same shoes are distributed to migrants endeavoring to cross, illegally, into California territory, perhaps for the first time, or to rejoin their families. What did the migrants make of the sneakers? Will they be empowered through the act of wearing these utilitarian-critical-metaphorical artifacts, or become actors in a transmission of cultural meanings and values beyond their scope of understanding? *Brinco* reached its apex of symbolic distribution and exposure as it penetrated the mainstream media, spurring ideological debates on news outlets such as CNN and Fox News at a time of deepening political divisions regarding immigration and the Mexico-US border—a rare instance of art provoking broader publics to critically reflect on a complex human, political, and economic situation.

A delicate alteration in the established flows of informal economic systems: you might have found yourself just over the border from San Ysidro, within the initial environs of Tijuana, moving through this territory, observing the flow of bodies, goods, transactions, and various economic systems. You might have encountered another kind of "shop" within this strip populated by small entrepreneurial establishments that offer products and services to the pedestrian border-crossers. With *Maleteros*, Mark Bradford effectively negotiated a set of new relationships with people who function as *maleteros* within this zone of informal economies. By modifying a storefront location for the distribution of new shopping carts, and devising a map indicating the multiple nodes and trajectories of economic traffic generated by the *maleteros* (effectively the porters of the border zone), Bradford discretely altered a complex and often invisible system.

A hybrid of economic transactions and social interactions: in a Tijuana shopping mall, on a warm Saturday evening, you might have found yourself selecting the design for a new silk-screened shirt, within the framework of a temporary outdoor clothing shop. What is this establishment?

Is it an entrepreneurial endeavor, a cultural project, or something else? You might have asked related questions encountering the same clothing products within the context of a La Jolla clothing store, such as ... who produced these designs? This is *La Tienda de Ropa* (*The Clothes Shop*), a project by the Tijuana-based Bulbo collective, which has been consistently engaged in the orchestration of events, projects, radio and television shows that respond to the dynamics of youth culture(s) within TJ. For their *Interventions* project, Bulbo developed a complex process of collaboration with individuals from diverse economic and social backgrounds in Tijuana, and worked with them to develop a new line of clothing designs—designs that were arrived at through an indexing, distillation, and translation of observations of particular locations in the city. Bulbo, a localized cultural collective, became temporarily delocalized within the institutional frame of inSite_05, yet their project returned them, in a sense, to local communities.

The Brazilian artist Rubens Mano developed a project entitled *Visible*, which remained, for the most part, *invisible* to many of us who sought to locate it as a materialized phenomenon ... beyond rumor. His project might be emblematic, inadvertently or strategically, of the intriguing contradictions of the *Interventions* exhibition project as a whole: an art intervention within the liminal territories of the transurban region of Tijuana-San Diego that existed only as a social trace. Perhaps Mano wanted his work to disappear from view—a resistance to visibility that also functioned, metaphorically, as a deflection from institutional visibility, or at least symptomatic of an anxiety about institutional affiliation and identification. Was this a strategic disappearance into the liminal social sphere, or a *tactical withdrawal from presence?*

Have we entered the realm of *the work of art in the age of appearances and disappearances*, between visibility and invisibility, resurfacing and de-surfacing at tactical moments of engagement ... or even strategic disengagement?

Taken in its entirety, inSite_05's *Interventions* challenged normative concepts and practices of public art, pushing the envelope in terms of the role of artists as producers of *platforms and situations* that test new interrelationships between artwork, audiences, publics, and constituencies. It asked us to rethink how art might penetrate the social fabrics of life, even disappearing or evaporating into the regulated and unregulated flows of local, regional, and transnational systems: like a rumor, an urban legend or myth, or a whispered possibility. By deploying dematerialized and rematerialized art practices into the contradictory, porous, and hybrid border/post-border environs that simultaneously divide and unite northern Mexico and California (and the United States more broadly), *Interventions* made a strong argument that artists can operate—through modes of social collaboration and participation—as interlocutors capable of navigating fractious social, economic, cultural, and political ecosystems.

In the end, however, we are still confronted with the vexing question of how to connect the dots, so to speak, between artistic interventions, modes of collaborative and participatory practice, the various theoretical discourses that address the border and post-border conditions, and the publics (activated constituencies, passive audiences, etc.) that are generated in these situations. Such interconnections are precarious, unpredictable, difficult to map, and impossible to entirely control in terms of meaning and reception. Yet the inSite_05 *Interventions* exhibition project did effectively reveal the complexity of these interrelationships, helping to shed light on the precariousness of the border—as a material territory, an economic and political construction, and as a contested idea. It also offered a good faith, succinct argument for why it is still worth considering the possibility that—in certain situations, at particular moments, with good networks of local support, and with artists who are willing to continuously and responsively rethink their practices—art can be a useful agent to reactivate the utility of culture.

[1] Talking Heads, "Cities," 1979.

[2] Manuel Castells, *The City and the Grassroots: A Cross-Cultural Theory of Urban Social Movements*, University of California Press, Berkeley 1984.

[3] Irit Rogoff, *Terra Infirma: Geography's Visual Culture*, Routledge, London and New York 2000.

[4] William J. Mitchell, *City of Bits*, MIT Press, Cambridge, Massachusetts 1995.

[5] Michael Dear and Gustavo Leclerc, *Postborder City: Cultural Spaces of Bajalta California*, Routledge, London and New York 2003.

[6] David Harvey, "Dialogue 1: Liminal Zones/ Coursing Flows," *Conversations*, inSite_05, 2004, p. 47

[7] Edward Soja, *Postmodern Geographies: The Reassertion of Space in Critical Social Theory*, Verso, London and New York 1989.

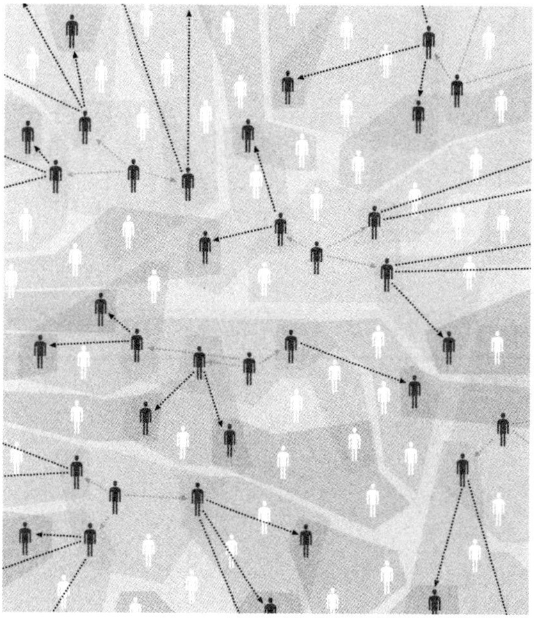

Måns Wrange, *The Good Rumor Project*, 2006–

Rirkrit Tiravanija, *Fear Eats the Soul*

Revised version of a text on Rirkrit Tiravanija's exhibition *Fear Eats the Soul*, at Gavin Brown's Enterprise, New York, March 5–April 23, 2011. Originally published in *Artforum*, May 2011.

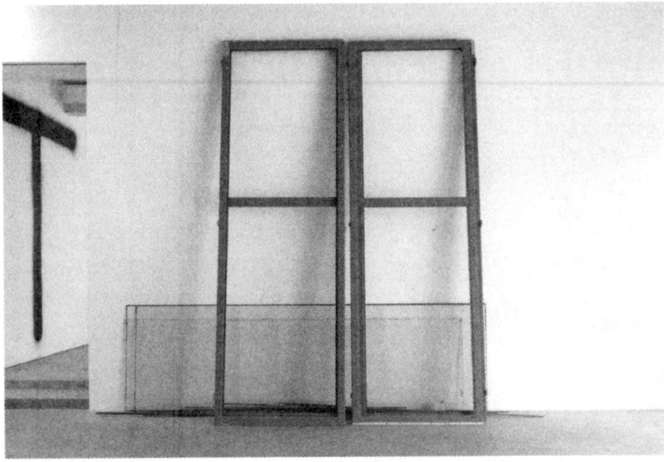

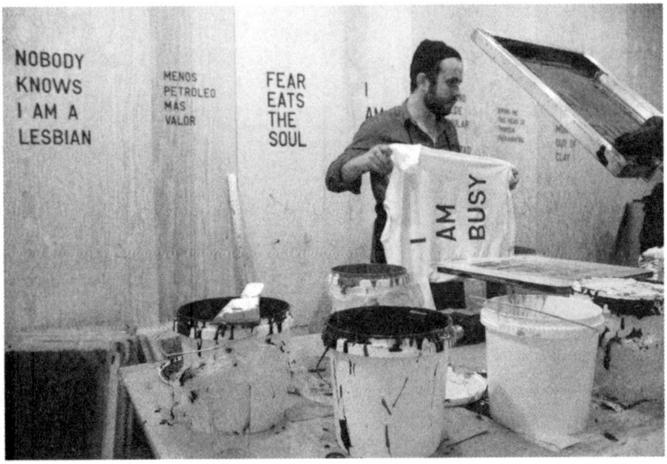

Rirkrit Tiravanija, *untitled 2011 (558 broome st, the future is chrome)*, 2011
Rirkrit Tiravanija, *untitled 2011 (t-shirt, no t-shirt)*, 2011

Rirkrit Tiravanija has always understood, intuitively and intellectually, that a gallery is a social frame, at once quasi-private and quasi-public. Within this space, a diverse range of encounters and frictions connected to rituals of making, displaying, and consuming art are staged. I still recall his exhibition *Untitled, 1992 (Free)*, at the original location of the 303 Gallery in SoHo: structural elements and appurtenances from the back office were displayed in the front of the gallery, and the office was converted into a rudimentary cooking and eating area, with free curries offered daily. On at least one occasion, I participated in this work: a photograph shows Rirkrit and me seated at a table in the gallery, eating lunch together. At the time, this seemed to be a deftly materialized symbolic intervention, playfully utopic and post-utopic, but probably not an attempt to subvert or reinvent the fundamental economics of the commercial art system.

Early on, Tiravanija understood the inherent contradictions and the intrinsic limits of his art—that any actuality or notion of "free" is embedded within a complex matrix. By staging quotidian social processes—cooking, eating, and cleaning up—within the gallery space, he proposed to exchange or substitute (symbolically and materially) an ethos of generosity (i.e., the preparation, distribution, and consumption of food as a catalyst for social gathering) for the normative entrepreneurial codes of a commercial gallery (i.e., a platform for the display and consumption of art as a monetized aesthetic thing), while acknowledging that the conceptual, material, social, and symbolic exchanges that occur inside that frame codify—paradoxically or not—such activities and phenomena within the discursive field of an expanded art condition.

In *Fear Eats the Soul* (the title derived from Rainer Werner Fassbinder's 1974 *Ali: Fear Eats the Soul*), Tiravanija glanced back at—and reconfigured—his own history. The artist created an operational soup kitchen (which he called Soup No Soup) that prepared and distributed soup on Thursdays, Fridays, and Saturdays throughout the duration of the show. Located next to the gallery space proper, it maintained a delicate autonomy. Tiravanija's gesture was characteristically unassuming, humble, and finally, symbolic—i.e., it was either just a place for soup, art, both, or something beyond—and, as with his earlier ad hoc kitchens, he seemed to be asking whether the socio-cultural ritual of eating, framed by the gallery as art, is substantially different than any other experience that one might have in the dense urban environment.

In this spirit, Tiravanija sought to make Brown's space as coextensive with the street as possible. The show's title was prominently spray-painted across various gallery walls in huge, oversize black letters, and one could see it from outside, since the gallery's windows, doorframes, and related utilitarian hardware had been removed; moreover, the space itself was open to the public 24 hours a day, seven days a week (though with a security guard on site). Transformed into a space more or less transparent to the outside world, the gallery welcomed those who might not ordinarily trespass into the white cube. The theme of transparency continued inside, where one encountered a pile of brown earth next to a large industrial steel plate with two machined holes functioning as viewing portals into the excavated part of the gallery below; nearby, leaning against the wall, were tools—shovels, brooms, wooden planks, etc.—apparently used for the site-displacement. This gesture suggested a way to make visible or unpack his process.

Reflecting further upon the codes of his own artistic production, Tiravanija constructed a pair of plywood rooms that replicated the dimensions of Gavin Brown's original diminutive gallery space at 558 Broome Street (1994–1997). One of the rooms contained a remake of artifacts first displayed within the context of a 1994 exhibition that Tiravanija produced and curated there. In this quasi-retrospective look back at his own history, Tiravanija rendered the gallery a platform to reenact recognizable tropes, and to propose new moves. A second plywood room housed a functional T-shirt factory and shop, open the same days and hours as the soup kitchen, where one could purchase T-shirts at $20 dollars a pop, imprinted with playfully activist slogans such as, "the days of this society are numbered," "asians must eat rice," "free china from tibet," "rich bastards beware," and "fear eats the soul." This mini-factory also served as an archive of Tiravanija's previous T-shirt projects, which have always suggested, perhaps ironically, the conflation of everyday fashion, politics, and identity. Overall, this exhibition might be understood as testimony to the enduring limits of the gallery as a platform. Conceptually and organizationally, Tiravanija has, in a sense, already moved beyond this frame, helping to develop a project such as The Land Foundation, initiated in 1998: a piece of land in the rice farming area outside of Chiang Mai, Thailand, that has become a laboratory for rethinking notions of community, sustainable environmental practice, and architecture language, in which forms of artistic collaboration are a key element.

Paul Ramírez Jonas, *The Commons*

Revised version of a text on Paul Ramírez Jonas, *The Commons*, at the Pinacoteca do Estado de São Paulo, Brazil, June 14–September 4, 2011. Originally published in *Artforum*, December 2011.

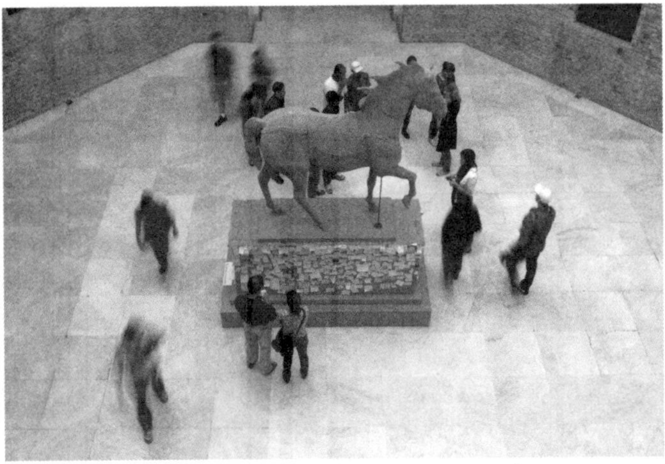

Paul Ramírez Jonas, *The Commons*, 2011

Paul Ramírez Jonas explores how art *becomes public* as it enters various zones of social contact. He typically deploys objects, sculptural installations, and public works so as to amplify the social *contingency* of authorship, and to challenge the already precarious model of the autonomous work of art. For example, his 2005 project for inSite_05, *Mi Casa, Su Casa*, at once analyzed and proposed new ways to think about conditions of private and public space, social exchange, and trust in relation to the San Diego-Tijuana border.

Within the context of the 2008 São Paulo Biennial, Ramírez Jonas produced *Talisman*: upon signing a contract, visitors could exchange a key of their own for a key that would give them access to the Biennial exhibition space after hours. The artist's 2010 Creative Time project, *Key to the City*, offered an opportunity to obtain what is usually reserved for VIPs and dignitaries: an honorific key to the city of

New York. Thousands of the artist-designed keys were distributed, unlocking 24 places throughout the city: this was demotic, participatory practice on a relatively massive social and political scale.

The Commons, 2011, might be described as a kind of participatory sculpture. It was first presented at the Alexander Gray Associates gallery in New York, and subsequently recontextualized within the Octagon project space at the Pinacoteca do Estado de São Paulo. The most direct precursor work for *The Commons* is *Publicar* (which means "to publish" or "to make public"), which the artist produced in 2009 for the seventh Bienal do Mercosul in Brazil. *Publicar* was comprised of a corkboard with pushpins (a plaque surrogate) affixed to the face of a large granite stone; this quasi-functional object operated as an anti-monument that memorialized, so to speak, the active participation of members of the public who used the board to post messages. *The Commons* is likewise fabricated from cork, but it alludes to another kind of monument, an ancient equestrian statue of Marcus Aurelius, the original of which is displayed in the Palazzo Nuovo in Rome; a replica stands outdoors in the Piazza del Campidoglio nearby, and another has been erected at Brown University, which the artist attended as an undergraduate. Ramírez Jonas subtracts the human figure, presenting a riderless horse, subtly inviting public engagement. The cork pedestal with pushpins summons visitors to attach written messages (as with *Publicar*), although in São Paulo other kinds of materials, including, reportedly, money, were also posted; the accumulated items were sent to the artist by the museum after the show closed.

The Pinacoteca was founded in 1905, and it is the oldest art museum in this city. The original building was redesigned by Brazilian architect Paulo Mendes da Rocha in 1993, and the Octagon project space—programmed by the institution's former chief curator, and now its Director, Ivo Mesquita—seems, at least to this writer, to be the architectonic and social core of this institution. High ceilings, natural light, and multiple viewing levels make for a welcoming gathering place, and it was evident that *The Commons* had taken on a new kind of (public) life in this situation. The work's reference to Roman antiquity resonated in a city that still shows the influence of the many Italian immigrants who arrived in the 19th-century. Its questioning of the normative ideological-historical force of traditional civic monuments was amplified by the Pinacoteca's status as the official museum of the state of São Paulo—and by the institution's contextual proximity to an equestrian monument of immense, heroic scale that commemorates the Duque de Caxias (a 19th-century figure) not far from the museum in the old downtown section of the city.

The Commons playfully tested the extent to which museums function as cultural commons; i.e., places of commingled private and public experience and interests. The artist also reminded us that social participation is often governed by (or is contingent upon) institutional permission and artistic *invitation*. By inviting visitors to post messages, Ramírez Jonas endeavored to activate the audiences, constituencies, and cultural tourists that comprise the publics and counterpublics (to invoke Michael Warner's notion) of the museum. When I visited the Pinacoteca, the cork pedestal was brimming with notes, suggesting that visitors had taken advantage of the opportunity to inscribe their thoughts—generating a temporary, mutating, polyvalent constellation of distinct subjectivities and symbolic coauthorship(s).

CHAPTER IV
Convoluted Cities

On Krzysztof Wodiczko's *New York City Tableaux: Tompkins Square*, and the Context of New York's East Village

Revised version of a text on Krzysztof Wodiczko's *New York City Tableaux: Tompkins Square*, Exit Art, New York, September 23–October 28, 1989. Originally published in *Arts Magazine*, January 1990, vol. 64, no. 5, p. 97.

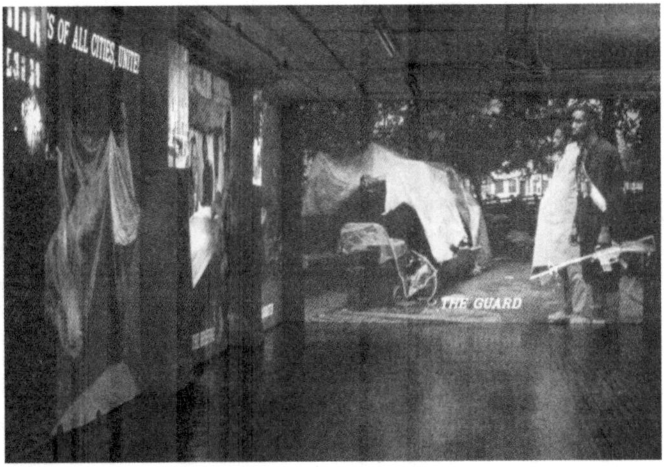

Krzysztof Wodiczko, *New York City Tableaux: Tompkins Square*, 1989, installation view, Exit Art, New York, 1990

In the summer of 1982, while an undergraduate student in college, I lived on East 12th Street, between 1st Avenue and Avenue A. Waves of heat and humidity amplified the uneasy ethos of the neighborhood: police conducted regular drug raids on my block, and throughout the East Village. The northern edge of Tompkins Square Park was nearby, and upon my first visit to the park, I was startled by the large number of homeless people who were utilizing this public place for habitation. It seemed as if the park had become a refuge of last resort.

Tompkins Square Park was a context already marked by a long history of conflict between citizens, communities, and the municipal authorities. A place of conflicting economic, social, and cultural interests, a site of urban and political contestation in which the right to the city, to invoke David Harvey, was repeatedly tested. It is a complex history that cannot be adequately represented here. The park saw its first police riot in 1874, and there were conflicts at various times over the following one hundred years.

Demographically, commencing in the mid-19th-century, the East Village (formerly considered to be part of the Lower East Side) began to attract working class immigrants, first from Germany, and subsequently from Poland, the Ukraine, and other countries. In the 1950s, various Beatniks took up residence in the area; indeed, Allan Ginsberg lived in the building next to mine, and I recall seeing him on the street occasionally. By the 1960s, the area had attracted Hippies and became something of a haven for various countercultures, spawning vanguard art and performance (Warhol organized events with the Velvet Underground), as well as a rock music scene (Bill Graham's Fillmore East). And by the 1970s, the East Village and the Lower East Side (by that point considered to be distinct areas) become central to the development of the East Coast punk rock scene. By the late 1970s, at Club 57, a nightclub located on St. Marks Place, musicians, artists, and performers such as Madonna, Keith Haring, The B-52s, Ann Magnuson, and others came together. I went there a couple of times during my final year of high school in 1979, seduced by the notion of a downtown underground art scene that might offer some form of temporary respite from my dreary lower middle-class home life on Manhattan's Upper West Side—indeed, an escape from the economic, social, and urban precariousness of my childhood neigh-borhood, at the crossroads of Harlem, Spanish Harlem, and Columbia University. After all, can we not think of subculture as, to a certain extent, the embodiment of a desire to escape from the psychological entrapments of one's original family home?

By the time I was living on East 12th Street in 1982, gentrification was slowly creeping into the East Village, inadvertently facilitated by various artists and cultural types, and students such as myself, even though I could barely afford the already low rent. We all contributed to the gradual transformation of the neighborhood, for better or worse, including the galleries that opened in the East Village (Nature Morte, International with Monument, Pat Hearn, etc.) and took logical advantage of the cheap rent and charming storefront spaces—a few eventually migrating to SoHo later in the 1980s (long before the major exodus to Chelsea that commenced in the mid-1990s). In a sense, Brooklyn has become the new East Village for emerging galleries over the past decade. Today, in 2012, one can observe a few new galleries in the East Village, although the main area of expansion has been within the Lower East Side proper, due to the New Museum's magnetic pull on the Bowery.

Back to Tompkins Square Park: on the night of August 6, 1988, the police attempted to enforce a curfew (that was not actually approved in law) to empty the park by 1:00am. According to the "Tompkins Square Park Time Line" compiled by geographer, urban theorist (and gentrification specialist) Neil Smith, and published in Exit Art's catalogue for Krzysztof Wodiczko's 1989 exhibition *New York City Tableaux: Tompkins Square*, approximately 100 protestors (comprised of local residents, activists, students, punks, squatters, the homeless) had gathered in the park to resist the police's attempt to clear out the park. Eventually the park was emptied, but a confrontation between police and protestors on Avenue A (alongside the park) led to a riot. Numerous acts of police brutality were caught on video by a local artist; the tape was distributed to the mainstream media, and helped lead to the indictments of some officers. The park became a battleground in the politics of real-estate development and the ineluctable processes of gentrification, leading people to wonder what kind of city Manhattan would become, whose economic and social interests would be served, and who would become marginalized. Today, large swathes of the East Village have been effectively gentrified (as with most of Manhattan) through the steady erosion of rent control and rent stabilization provisions that helped protect lower-income communities, compounded by the inflation of real estate values. Privatization (the market) won the battle, and Tompkins Square Park was transformed into an agreeable public space, equipped with a dog run. There are still a few pockets in the easternmost regions of Alphabet City that remind one of the good old bad days of the East Village, and some public housing has so far escaped the clutches of privatization. But for the most part, the East Village has become a sanitized, tourist-friendly, stylistic simulation of what it once was.

I first learned of Wodiczko's *Homeless Vehicle* project, the artist's poignant response to New York's homeless crisis of the 1980s, while attending the Whitney Museum's

Independent Study program in 1984–1985. A unique hybridization of public art, socially-activated sculpture, and industrial design, the vehicle was more symbolic than utilitarian—although it was conceptualized and built to provide the disenfranchised with a mobile, utilitarian device. A homeless person could store belongings in it, push it through the city (the wheeled design, to a certain extent, suggested a futuristic shopping cart), and perhaps most significantly of all, use it as a shelter in which to sleep. Only a small number of vehicles were actually produced, and the artist worked with a number of homeless individuals to test the prototype. But Wodiczko's real aim was to remind the city—its citizens, publics, and government officials—that there was an unsolved homeless crisis, that homeless shelters were more dangerous than the streets, and that these marginalized, nomadic individuals mattered as human beings. A few years later, the artist responded to the conflicted urban territory of Tompkins Square Park, and the plight of the homeless in that place.

Wodiczko produced an elaborate slide installation featuring shots of the Tompkins Square Park occupiers (or, temporary residents, if you prefer) interspersed with images of the police actions that took place along the park's periphery. Wodiczko structured the installation along the lines of a mock narrative, unfolding the story of the city within a city (or military camp) established by the home-less within the boundaries of the park. Indeed, the artist deliberately reinforces the idea that a paramilitary occupation is underway; in one image a group of homeless individuals are seated around a table, inspecting some sort of chart (one of the men holds a white M-16 rifle, undoubtedly either a replica or a toy). Beneath this image, the phrase, "The Briefing," appears. In another image, entitled "The Exercise," three men seem to be preparing for a defensive military action against those who would evict them from their adopted home. Wodiczko here re-represents *internal refugees* who have managed to organize themselves (with some help from the Coalition for the Homeless, and other groups) into a self-perpetuating community. It is a community under siege, yet prepared to resist further threats of dispossession.

As an artist and an activist, Wodiczko has committed himself to aiding the empowerment of people who have essentially been deprived of their rights as citizens. Functioning within non-art and art contexts, he has attempted to rethink the segregation of cultural production from direct, unmediated, and pragmatic intervention within the margins of our shared social fabric.

This is not political idealism, but rather a unique form of urban guerrilla *cultural* warfare and resistance; this strategy may help prompt the new mayor of this city to expedite quick and judicious reforms of the shelter system, and increase the availability of low-cost housing.

The Fractious Hybrid State (of Things)

Revised version of an essay originally published in the catalogue of *The Hybrid State* exhibition, Exit Art, New York, November 2–January 25, 1992.

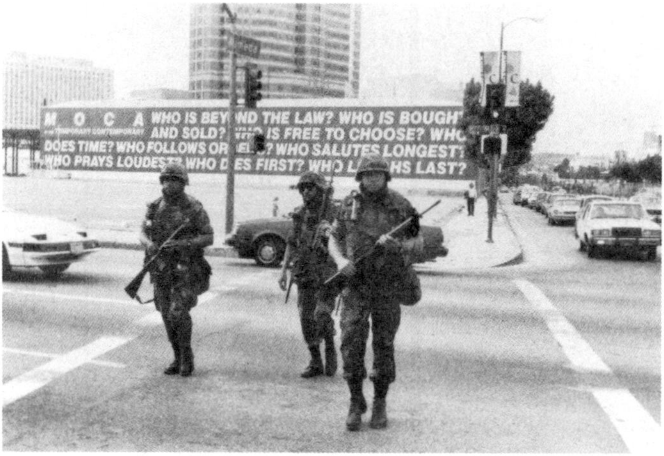

Soldiers from the National Guard cross the street near MOCA Temporary Contemporary at Alameda Street on May 2, 1992 (photograph by Gary Leonard.)

I am in the process of completing an essay on the contradictions of multiculturalism as this notion pertains to contemporary art and visual culture vis-à-vis this country's rather unstable socioeconomic fabric, when it comes to my attention that civil violence has erupted into the streets of the South Central Los Angeles community as a direct response to the not guilty verdict reached in the trial of four white LA police officers accused of using excessive force in the apprehension and arrest of black motorist Rodney King. I turn on the television, and images transmitted live via satellite flood into my domicile. The events unfold, the news coverage is disorganized and reactive: a helicopter hovers above the streets of South Central, sending pictures of an urban topography steadily descending into social unrest and violence. Yet it is immediately clear what is happening: the predominantly black residents of that community have begun to protest against an acquittal which seems to reconfirm their worst fears that the country's judicial system is inherently unjust to African-Americans, that it systematically favors whites. I am angered by a verdict delivered by a mostly white jury in a police brutality trial held in Simi Valley—a Los Angeles suburb with a mere 2% black population. The judicial system has failed in this instance.

The sense of social, economic, cultural, and political disenfranchisement that must be felt by black citizens within a community racked by gang warfare, ubiquitous drug traffic, and black-on-black crime, is difficult to imagine. Following the verdict in the Rodney King trial, that community let loose from years of pent-up frustration regarding the cycle of economic and social decay, disempowerment, and social marginalization. The class and race conflicts that always seem to simmer beneath the surface of this society reached a boiling point; for some, the rage was unmanageable, leading to a micro civil war: angry black youths beating white motorists who had strayed into South Central, angry Korean businessmen organized into a paramilitary organization, firing at looters in defense of their properties. Clearly, the beatings, arson, and lootings were perpetrated by a relatively small contingent of irresponsible, desperate, or criminal elements; ironically, it is reported that the looters comprised a multi-racial coalition (predominantly black, but also Latino and Anglo). A number of the looters were quoted as saying that they needed to feed their families, and took the opportunity. If I had been in a similar situation under similar economic conditions, I might have done the same. After all, isn't the US the land of opportunity?

> The Los Angeles riots were bound to happen.
> The country is always at war over race and class.
> —James Ridgeway, *The Village Voice*, May 12, 1992

The events of South Central—which spread to other parts of Los Angeles, and then to other cities in the US in a much less violent manner—are clear signals of the epidemic social, economic, and cultural disintegration of urban America, exacerbated by economic recession. Everyone is now competing for a smaller piece of a shrinking pie, and low-income populations are excluded. But we are all implicated, regardless of our race, cultural identity, economic status, or social class; it is a question of how we position ourselves in relation to these complexities and contradictions. But perhaps I have fallen victim to the media spectacle of the situation; maybe I am caught up in a mass cultural logic that transforms real social upheaval into a theatrical pro-liferation of televisual abstraction. Maybe my white, liberal identity—itself a hybrid site of ideological, emotional contestation—has been coaxed into amplified self-criticality. Cornel West's 1990 essay, "The New Cultural Politics of Difference," has been useful:

> In the recent past, the dominant cultural identities have been circumscribed by immoral patriarchal, imperial, jingoistic, and xenophobic constraints. The political consequences have been principally a public sphere regulated by and for well-to-do white males in the name of freedom and democracy. The new cultural criticism exposes and explodes the exclusions, blindness, and silence of this past, calling from it radical libertarians and democratic projects that will create a better present and future. The new cultural politics of difference is neither an ahistorical Jacobin program that discards tradition and ushers in new self-righteous authoritarianism nor a guilt-ridden leveling anti-imperialist liberalism that celebrates token pluralism from smooth inclusion. Rather, it acknowledges the uphill struggle of fundamentally transforming highly objectified, rationalized and commodified societies and cultures in the name of individuality and democracy. This means locating the structural causes of unnecessary forms of social misery (without reducing all such human suffering to historical causes), depicting the plight and predicaments of demoralized and depoliticized citizens caught in market-driven cycles of therapeutic release—drugs, alcoholism, consumerism—and projecting alternative visions, analysis, and actions that proceed from particularities and arrive at moral and political connectedness. This connectedness does not signify a homogenous unity or monolithic totality but rather a contingent, fragile coalition building in an effort

> to pursue common radical libertarian and democratic goals that overlap.[1]

As an art critic operating within the territory of a privileged contemporary art culture, how can I hope to articulate a meaningful and persuasive account of the contradictory nature of our hybrid culture? Who constitutes the audience for this text? What are the conditions of its receptions? What type(s) of communications does it establish within and beyond the parameters of the art world? How do we identify those parameters? When I extract a quote from an African-American cultural critic, incorporating it within my discourse, what, if any, are the sociopolitical implications of this act? In the spirit of cultural, racial, ideological, political, and intellectual coalition building, I may be weaving an elaborate intertextuality, but my desire is to reach out beyond the rhetorical enclave of academic discourse, and the institutional and social limitations attached to that language. But reach out to where, and to whom? The streets of South Central LA, or New York's Harlem community? New lines of verbal and visual communication have to be opened through intercultural, interracial, inter-ideological, inter-political, and inter-economic coalitions and dialogue. And we need to demonstrate a fundamental commitment to steer the economic and political systems of this society in more authentically democratic directions.

In his essay "Secular Criticism," the Palestinian-American literary and cultural critic Edward Said called for critics to overcome the pernicious specialization of the insular academic realm (as a literal institutional space, as well as a codified system of theoretical language-formations), and work to recognize the humanistic obligations of the intellectual to operate, "… in that potential space inside civil society, acting on behalf of those alternative acts and alternative intentions whose advancement is a fundamental human obligation."[2] Following Said, I would like to suggest a transformation of the Enlightenment model reinscribed in his text (e.g., "acting on behalf … ") into a differently articulated conception, so that the so-called alternative can empower itself sufficiently so as to act on my behalf, reversing Said's potentially problematic hierarchy of authority. In other words, there must be a way to both conceptualize and actualize new approaches to the problem of cultural authority in this society without recapitulating a neo-enlightenment ideology wherein the benevolent institutional voice of pedagogy offers educational reform and guidance to the underprivileged, or the culturally deprived. Yet today, the prison system in this country has become the school for a disproportionate percentage of young black men; the failure of the public educational system for inner city, low-income youth is pandemic, and is connected to other systematic problems within this nation's institutional, social, and economic infrastructure. The fiction of equal opportunity is made graphically evident at the flash point of reactive urban violence.

Take a good look at today's America: the contradictions and complexities of racial segregation persist, and have become even more firmly entrenched within a seemingly vicious cycle of economic, ideological, educational, and political relations which, in turn, produce wide gulfs between cultural empowerment and disempowerment, representation and non-representation. A recent study published in *The New York Times* once again indicates the almost absurd disparity of economic power between the relatively small percentage of wealthy Americans (who continue to control, proportionally, the majority of capital), and the low-income populations (whose opportunity to improve their economic condition has begun to deteriorate); this is a disparity made even more glaring as fortunes and opportunities also decline for the middle class.

And so what do people mean when they use terms such as "multiculturalism" or "cultural difference" in today's art world? It is abundantly clear that cultural capital remains in the hands of a select, primarily white, network of experts, specialists, connoisseurs, galleries, curators, collectors, artists, writers, etc. The rise of the alternative space in the early 1970s attested to dissatisfactions with so-called mainstream venues, and the emergence of localized, community-based art centers within the city similarly demonstrated a desire for new frameworks of self-representation and self-presentation. Yet such developments have produced a rather paradoxical situation: the virtual segregation of practices by artists of color from other cultural venues that might offer them a greater stake in the art marketplace. The whole rather dead-end issue of mainstream versus alternative, center versus periphery in terms of contemporary visual arts culture suggests a logic of inclusion and exclusion that must be overcome on conceptual and institutional levels, for it is clear that artists within certain ethnic communities beyond the domain of SoHo would like to establish enhanced degrees of cultural-economic autonomy and control.

Yet I am also somewhat uncomfortable with my own motivations as a white art critic attempting to discuss issues of race relations, class, and cultural identity in relation to the contemporary art world, particularly as I have sought to bring into this discussion the recent events in South Central LA vis-à-vis notions of multiculturalism. My discomfort arises from an understanding, however incomplete, of the contradictory and complex nature of my so-called white identity, and the degree to which this hybrid, unstable identity embodies my ambivalent relationship to constructing a discourse on other cultural, racial, and ethnic identities. Michele Wallace has observed:

> Black criticism was blocked from the discussions of Modernism, which are defined as exclusively white by an intricate and insidious cooperation of art galleries, museums, and academic art history, and also blocked from any discussion of "primitivism," which has been colonized beyond recognition in the space of the international and now global museum. At this juncture one is compelled to ask, "is multiculturalism, as it is being institutionally defined, occupying the same space as primitivism in relationship to postmodernism?" For me, a response to such a question would need to include a careful scrutiny of the history of black popular culture and race relations, and account for the sexualization of both, thus defining the perimeters of a new knowledge which I can only name, at this point, as the problem of the visual in Afro-American culture.[3]

Wallace articulates a persuasive depiction of the regulated invisibility of artists and critics of color throughout the dominant narratives of modernist culture, and legitimately questions the recent surge to institutionalize (both within academia and the art world) multiculturalism on the grounds that it is being employed as a term to define a neo-colonialist anthropological exoticization of indigenous racial-cultural differences (a kind of internalized re-objectification). However, I believe that it is inaccurate, if not somehow divisive, to claim that "white males continue to absolutely dominate and control all aspects of postmodern criticism."[4] Doesn't this seem to discount the importance of critics such as Cornel West, bell hooks, and Edward Said—as well as Wallace's own significant impact upon postmodern cultural studies? But who am I to question her assertion?

The dream: to develop the possibility of creating authentic affiliations between distinct conditions of race and gender. West's call for coalition-building in order to identify overlapping libertarian and democratic agendas for whites, blacks, and others, as well as his demand that the new cultural criticism explore different territories and avoid disciplinary and institutional closure or insularity, seem to be essential prerequisites for the struggle to resolve the glaring contradictions and enormous systemic problems facing our hybrid, yet fractious society.

[1] Cornel West, "The New Cultural Politics of Difference," *Out There: Marginalization and Contemporary Cultures*, ed. Russell Ferguson et al., MIT Press and The New Museum of Contemporary Art, Cambridge, Massachusetts and New York 1990, p. 35.

[2] Edward Said, "Secular Criticism," *The World, the Text, and the Critic*, Harvard University Press, Cambridge, Massachusetts 1983, p. 30.

[3] Michelle Wallace, "Modernism, Postmodernism and the Problem of the Visual in Afro-American Culture," *Out There*, p. 47–48.

[4] Ibid., p. 48.

Mesa Vanguardism and SoHo Alterations

Revised version of an article on *Longing and Belonging: From the Faraway Nearby* at SITE Santa Fe, New Mexico (July 14–October 8, 1995), and *Architectures of Display*, New York City (May 20–July 1, 1995), originally published in *Flash Art*, December 1995.

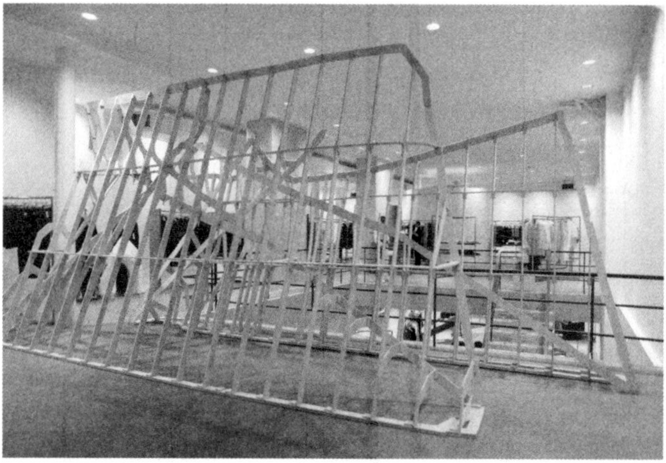

Peter Eisenman and Silvia Kolbowski, *Like the difference between Autumn/Winter '94/'95 and Spring/Summer '95*, 1995

In Bruce W. Ferguson's exhibition *Longing and Belonging: From the Faraway Nearby*—the first international biennial organized by SITE Santa Fe—the question of origins recurred as a central motif within an exhibition that sought to use the context of New Mexico, and Santa Fe in particular, as a framework through which to navigate distinct cultural experiences, social practices, and art languages. Far from Santa Fe, a thoroughly urban, New York-based exhibition project, *Architectures of Display*, organized by Kadambari Baxi, Rosalie Genevro, Laurie Hawkinson, Silvia Kolbowski, Reinhold Martin, and Diane Shamash (presented by The Architectural League of New York and the public art organization Minetta Brook), made an unprecedented effort to use SoHo as a context for various site-specific projects. Miles and cultures apart, and with no direct institutional linkage, these ambitious projects subscribed to variations upon the genre of the context-specific exhibition, yet both came up a bit short.

Santa Fe and Taos constitute a veritable mesa utopia replete with Native American culture and nature-in-the-raw for trust fund beneficiaries, artists and artisans, wandering neo-hippies, affluent tourists, and even a few regular folks who seek the pleasures of the relatively unspoiled high desert. Santa Fe is also an Elysium for people with very deep pockets who long for the luxury of a second home. And who, in their right mind, would not *long to belong* to this unique environment? As an instrument in the service of furthering local cultural development, the exhibition *Longing and Belonging* is the first step in SITE Santa Fe's broader, long-range institutional strategy to attract a more serious international contemporary art audience to the area, and discussions are already under way to plan future projects. Ferguson's show—featuring the work of 31 artists from Brazil, Canada, Cuba, France, Germany, England, Hungary, Japan, Belgium/Mexico, Spain, Uruguay/Sweden, the former Yugoslavia, and the United States—was held at two spaces in Santa Fe: a warehouse that had been ingeniously renovated by architect Richard Gluckman for this inaugural project, and a floor of the Museum of Fine Arts (which houses a permanent collection of works by Georgia O'Keeffe, as well as other artists who have lived and worked in the region). A number of related events were also presented, ranging from an opera by Robert Ashley, a performance by Marina Abramovic, a film by Trinh T. Minh-ha, a symposium, and various community outreach programs.

Although we may have become slightly jaded about site-specific group exhibitions, in which artists are commissioned to produce new works in response to place and context, it is still a relevant curatorial model. *Longing and Belonging,* however, was not a strong example of this approach. Many of the art projects simply did not communicate a persuasive site-specific character. Maybe this had to do with the fact that most of the participants were constrained to make work for museum and museum-type spaces. And it just might be that Ferguson anticipated a situation in which some artists would have difficulties articulating a substantial response to place, assuming that such failures to connect would also contribute significantly to the exhibition's eventual meaning. The title of the show seemed to quietly hint at this dilemma; now, in retrospect, it probably would have been more appropriate to have named the project *Longing to Long to Belong to Santa Fe*.

It also became apparent that certain participants were allowed to take the easy route. Felix González-Torres, Rebecca Horn, and Andres Serrano, for instance, did not really develop unique pieces for the context; slightly modifying extant works does not entirely count. Ferguson included González-Torres' *Untitled (America)* (1994–1995), a work virtually indistinguishable from a piece that was part of the artist's recent early-career retrospective at the Guggenheim. In New York, the suspended necklaces—comprised of bare-bulbs and electrical cords—transformed one of the museum's rooms into an eerily elegant, mundanely sacred place. In *Longing and Belonging*, Ferguson (with the consent of the artist) broke the work up into two parts: some elements dangled from the ceiling on the second floor of the Museum of Fine Art's pueblo-style structure, the installation visible from both the street and within the building; a larger constellation hung awkwardly from the ceiling of the warehouse space's front area, situated opposite Anish Kapoor's *Oblivion #1, #2, #3*, three truly mediocre limestone boulder-like pieces from 1994. These González-Torres' works are elegantly dilapidated, yet in Santa Fe they seemed to be profoundly lost, insecure about the spaces they were asked to occupy. On the other hand, I was quite fond of contributions by Belgian/Mexican artist Francis Alÿs. His synthesis of magic realism and Latina-inflected kitsch culture—*In the Palm of Your Hand* (a large mural), and *Mexico D.F.* (a modified snow globe)—both from 1995, offered humorous, fantastical, and poignant reflections upon the paradoxical architectural and social conditions of Mexican society.

It seems that Ferguson was counting on the mainly non-native participants to develop strong projects based upon their outsider interactions with the local environment. Regrettably, tepid is the word that comes to mind in characterizing many of the artists' place-oriented efforts. For example, in a nod toward vernacular furniture style, Jenny Holzer designed a new set of wooden text-laden benches from the *Lustmord* series, which were installed in the Museum of Fine Art's quaint courtyard. Her gesture, however, was altogether too gentle for this context. From a quite different ideological perspective, Canadian Rebecca Belmore's installation, *New Wilderness* (1995)—a moralizing tribute to the unfortunate predicament of Native Americans who are forced to sell their kitschy wares to Anglo tourists—played blatantly upon an already abundant White Guilt, tugging at our proverbial heartstrings. And though there was something genuinely provocative about both Marina Abramovic's 1995 *Knife Ladder*—comprised of a ladder, with rungs made from knifes, extending up to a small, glowing rectilinear cavity in the wall—and Lorna Simpson's 1995 installation *Suspended*—a grouping of images, laser-transferred onto felt rectangles, from colloquially romantic 19th-century prints featuring pictures of personal and social violence and disasters (such as a suicide and a train wreck), placed across from a magnet suspended above verbal descriptions of the same scenes—I was hard-pressed to locate any persuasive connections to New Mexico or Santa Fe in these works. The pieces that actually came closest to stirring things up in a thoughtful way were Canadian Gerald McMaster's indirectly conceptual, quasi-documentary, video-in-the-round representation of the annual all-nations gathering of Indian peoples entitled *Pow(er)wow* (1995), as well as Carlos Capelan's *Naming Songs* (1995), a visually explosive installation that was designed as a critical allegory regarding how anthropological and archaeological modes of exhibition-construction attempt to represent native cultures. Capelan, born in Uruguay and currently living in Sweden, used vitrines, wall drawings, a Jimmie Durham text entitled "A Certain Lack of Coherence," and other textual elements to assemble an absurdist ethnographic museum of imaginary artifacts.

The subtitle of Ferguson's exhibition, *From the Faraway Nearby*, refers to an expression that Georgia O'Keeffe—the consummate progenitor insider/outsider artist—used on her correspondence; this is a sentiment that seems rather prescient in relation to our era of instantaneous and simultaneous access, communications, and interactions. And what of the artists in *Longing and Belonging*—did they long for a faraway that could be transformed into the nearby through institutionalized rituals of cultural contact? And what does it mean for art to belong somewhere? When an artist from

Eastern Europe, for instance, is asked to produce something for an eventual destination in a place such as Santa Fe, New Mexico, does this form of projection engender creative, critical reflections on these disparate cultural locations? Or does this suggest an opportunistic interest by institutions to engineer counterfeit border crossings within a global system of geographic, cultural, political, ideological, economic, and aesthetic relations?

Ultimately, Ferguson's effort seemed rather tame compared with the curatorial framework of *Architectures of Display*, in which teams of artists and architects were invited to collaborate on developing and implementing site-specific projects in the SoHo district of Manhattan, focusing upon how structures and ideologies of architectural display constitute zones of commerce. Given that the past five years have seen a boom in the number of boutiques, restaurants, and other entrepreneurial establishments in a neighborhood until recently dominated by art galleries, the time was ripe for these sites of commerce to be critically addressed. The participants, along with their respective sites of engagement, included Renée Green and Laura Kurgan (Portico Home), Peter Eisenman and Silvia Kolbowski (Comme des Garçons), Group Material and Merrill Elam (Duggal), Tom Burr and Toshiko Mori (Hot & Crusty), and Krzysztof Wodiczko, Sulan Kolatan, and William MacDonald (Angelika Film Center). Green and Kurgan's project, *Browsing*, established a tenuous linkage between the actual consumer space of Portico Home and the real-time interactivity of the Internet's World Wide Web's zone of abstracted communication. In Wodiczko and his collaborators' project *Lobbying for Bit Parts*, video surveillance was set up at various points within the Angelika Film Center on Houston Street (film theaters, lobby, sidewalk), and fragments of these videos were then patched into the real-time interactivity of the Web network. Here was an inventive attempt to use the Internet as a connective tissue to make new ties between the actual social space of the movie theater and the virtual world-space of computer networks, giving individuals the ability to directly sample (and re-combine) images from a menu of daily narratives.

The persuasive collaborative installation of architect Eisenman and artist Kolbowski at Comme des Garçons (entitled, *Like the Difference Between Autumn/Winter '94/'95 and*

Spring/ Summer '95), offered the best evidence for the need to organize more exhibition projects that engage the social spaces of everyday consumer culture. Employing computer morphing technology, Eisenman and Kolbowski fused together two designs of a clothing item representing the '94 and '95 seasons, and then used the resultant mutant shape as the basis for a skeletal, wooden architecture—a kind of virtual wall that consumers and exhibition visitors alike passed through while entering the store. In addition, a video superimposing runway shows of recent Comme des Garçons fashion collections ('94 and '95) was presented near the front of the store as a visual hook for prospective browsers. And from the street, the membrane-like quality of the temporary wall seemed designed to echo the transparency of the shop's front window, allowing desirous pedestrians to gaze, uninterrupted, into the spare, neo-modernist interior of this still-hip establishment. Staging an unobtrusive and stylish critical infiltration, Eisenman and Kolbowski's ingenious project responded to a milieu of fashion and commerce by allowing it, in effect, to prosper.

Whether any of the interventions in *Architectures of Display* actually compelled people to reflect more critically upon their relationship to urban place, or their libidinal involvement with shopping or movie going is, of course, quite unclear. What many of the projects did make evident, however, was the extent to which negotiation and compromise are central components of the unstable social contract that emerge whenever artists—even in conjunction with the sanctioning presence of architects, who are more accustomed to these situations—attempt to work in non-art commercial sites. After all, the interests of artists and business owners often do not converge. But whereas *Architectures of Display* at least endeavored to test how artists and architects can negotiate quotidian spaces of commerce and social interaction (thereby making somewhat transparent the complexities of such initiatives), the initial iteration of the SITE Santa Fe biennial largely came across as a gallery or museum show transposed from the cosmopolitan center to the periphery—in other words, a missed opportunity for the participating artists to *belong* to the site.

Communication City

Revised version of essay published in the catalogue of *Transfert: Art in Urban Space*, Biel-Bienne, Switzerland, June 17–August 31, 2000.

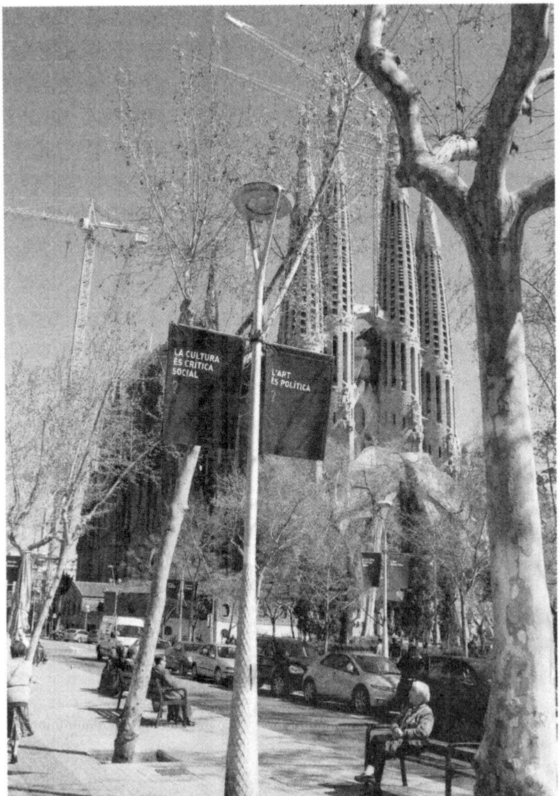

Alfredo Jaar project near Antoni Gaudi's La Sagrada Familia, Barcelona, March 16, 2009.

Every person is a city and every city is a person. Each city is an abstract and material embodiment of its citizens. Every city—regardless of its global location, or social, political, and economic conditions—is a multidimensional complex of paradoxical elements, wherein heterogeneity and homogeneity coexist in a continuous state of tension. Cities have the capacity to incorporate everything into their dense fabrics; cities at once trigger and absorb transformative social exchanges. Interlaced rhythms of stasis and motion are characteristics of every urban context. The city is an amalgam of public space, private space, the social, the antisocial, politics, religion, culture, health, sickness, wealth, poverty, law, criminality, sex, abstinence, birth, death, dirt, electricity, communication systems, fauna, flora, transportation systems (both private and public forms), diverse architectures, and much, much more.

Urbanist Henri Lefebvre understood the city to be an arena for the "encounter between differences," a space which produces social relations and is produced by social relations. Lefebvre suggests that we tend to think about the contemporary urban environment in contradictory terms: as both an abstract space modeled upon hierarchical orderings (e.g., center, periphery) that may reinforce dominant economic relations, and as a space of ruptures, disjunctions, flux, and "pulverizations" (Lefebvre's term). Against the will to homogenize urban space (and therefore urban experience) according to the logic of advanced capitalism, social subjects—i.e., individuals—attempt to articulate distinct uses of that space, employing imagination as a device to reinvent their negotiations of urban order.

To a certain extent, the development of the genre of the city-based art exhibition during the 20th-century is related to a broader issue. Namely, the effort to open up the relative autonomy of art, to redistribute the practice, language, and ideologies of art making back into the fabric of so-called everyday life. Taking art out of its specialized containers—i.e., the studio, the gallery, the museum, the private collection—and returning it to the so-called ordinary precincts of life: e.g., the street. In other words, injecting art into non-specialized domains, while also suggesting the possibility of reinventing the relationship between culture and public. In one sense, this reflects a more recent (i.e., late 20th-century) preoccupation with reinjecting the insulated activity of the art world back into the mainstream of society.

With the emergence of industrialized urban centers in Europe during the mid- and late 19th-century, and the attendant bourgeois self-consciousness of belonging to a new model of social organization (articulated with vivid, poetic resonance in the writings of Baudelaire, and later in Breton's metaphoric meanderings through Paris, and still later with Debord's Situationist writings), the stage was set for the notion of the city as a context for the unfolding of aesthetic experiences. This would become a defining—if not paradigmatic—conceit of the 20th-century. The city as muse. A new urban sublime, exemplified by those artists, poets, and architects, and other cultural producers who used the social energy of the city as fuel for experimentation and innovation.

The longstanding desire (or fantasy) to locate a space of cultural production that is not encumbered or burdened by the art system is paradoxical. Today, with the emergence of a fully globalized art world of interconnected urban centers, this desire is often expressed in relation to the space of the city. There is an effort to recolonize public city space as a platform for specialized art making activities, so that artists are given an opportunity to respond directly to the everyday urban environment. The city as cultural laboratory? The city as adjusted readymade?

There have been adventurous platforms for the development of art in public space, such as Mary Jane Jacob's well-known 1993 exhibition, *Culture in Action*, in Chicago, the New York-based *Architectures of Display* in 1995, and inSite97. One could argue that the utilization of city space as an environment for the development of art exhibitions has also been an effort, fundamentally, to expand and rethink the interrelationship between art production and the broader cultural-social realm. This is a symbolic (and, to an extent, material) re-purposing of the city for art activities. Yet we also understand that the utilization of city space as a platform for artist's projects and group exhibitions is related to the desire to develop new interconnections between site-specific art and cultural tourism. Prominent examples include the most recent Istanbul Biennial (wherein the exhibition was dispersed into various nodes of the city), as well as the ongoing Münster Sculpture Project (where the city has always played the role of a platform or stage).

Fundamentally, the city space exhibition should endeavor to reinvent relationships between production and reception, between art and audience, between consumer and producer. The development of exhibitions that are interdependent upon the architectural spaces and infrastructures of a city reveals a desire to introduce new models of curating that will, in turn, suggest new possibilities for art making. In other words, an urban-based curatorial framework invariably seeks to compel artists to rethink the conventions of their own respective practices in relation to the multiple material and imaginary trajectories of the city.

Yet a number of important questions persist. Is anything really reinvented in these circumstances? Or does the city-based exhibition merely provide an expanded institutional venue for the artist: i.e., the redistribution of the site of the museum into various other urban spaces? If the city becomes a stage for art making, does this transform the fundamental relationship between artist, artwork, and the public? The organization of an exhibition in city space is an opportunity for these questions to be publicly discussed by all those who inhabit that particular urban environment—not only art specialists, but people from all types of professions, economic backgrounds, cultural and ethnic affiliations, tastes, desires, and ideological proclivities. An open, inclusive public discourse regarding the function and meaning of urban-based exhibitions will serve, hopefully, to precipitate new lines of communication across the symbolic and actual boundaries of disciplinary specialization.

Beyond the concrete territory of the actual city, the Internet and the web are being used to explore new types of virtual urban and meta-urban environments, facilitated by interactive modes of communication. The interrelationship between the off-line world of the city and the on-line world of the web is now one of most important areas of exploration, requiring us to rethink traditional modes of organizing our locations and identities in relation to the body, the community, the city, the nation, time and space, and the globe. We live in a world wherein older types of mapmaking are no longer entirely reliable, wherein distinctions—on the level of theory and lived experience—are increasingly difficult to maintain between the material off-line world and the immaterial on-line world. Each time we enter the Internet, and build things on the web, we are at once located in a rational spatio-temporal dimension (at the computer terminal), yet simultaneously delivered into an ephemeral arena of continuous flows that resists classical explanation.

If I live in a city, and I am plugged-into the Internet, I am located and dislocated, plugged-out, somewhere and nowhere—all at the same time. Of course, it is paradoxical. I am in a constant state of being in between locations.

In a sense, the actual space of the city is being dispersed into the virtual terrain of the web, and vice-versa. The web can be theorized as a composite of multiple theoretical cities, organized according to the new interlaced dynamics of community and communication. And, with the advent of new wireless web technology, the mobile phone is becoming a portable Internet device that will facilitate all modes of on-line interface. Everything is being connected to everything else. So, the question is no longer where you are physically located, but rather, whether (and how) you are connected.

Invoking the visionary work of the British group Archigram, our cities are not only plugged-in, but urban centers have also become constellations of people-driven wireless interfaces. Actual cities (and suburban environs) may still be the locus of commerce, culture, and information, yet the web has become a free-floating nexus between all virtual cities, towns, businesses, institutions, and individuals. Internet technology has amplified exchanges of commerce, information, and culture within the urban environment. In other words, cities are now plugged-out, facilitating new interchanges (on symbolic and literal levels) with suburban and rural territories. It is not only a question of what unfolds within the actual space of a particular city, but more significantly, how that local urban environment interacts with a multiplicity of other local environments around the globe via the Internet and web.

A Strangely *New* New York: From Viewing Platform At WTC/Ground Zero to Prada Epicenter Store

Revised version of an essay originally published in *Flash Art*, March/April 2002.

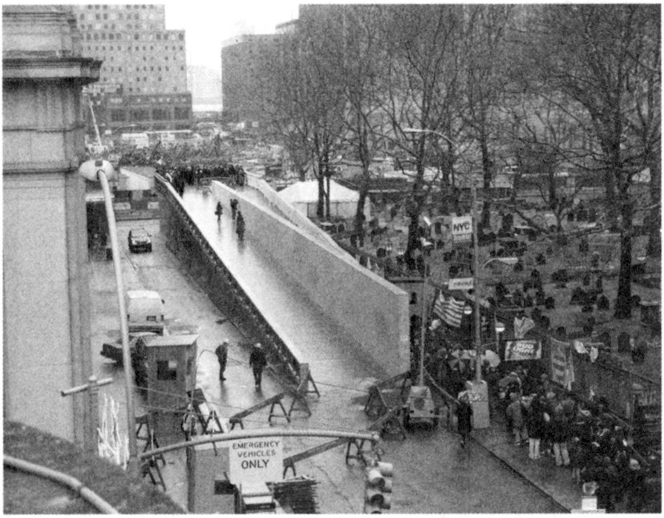

World Trade Center Temporary Viewing Platform, New York, 2001

It is late January, and more than four months have elapsed since September 11. Life in New York City remains subtly transfigured. In this urban environment I imagine a conjunction, a context-based linkage, between two distinct places in downtown Manhattan. One is located near the corner of Broadway and Fulton Street in the Financial District, the other at the corner of Broadway and Prince Street in SoHo. In early January 2002 I visited the new Viewing Platform constructed at the site of the destroyed World Trade Center (a.k.a., Ground Zero). Later, on the walk home northward up Broadway, curiosity led me into the new Prada "epicenter" store in SoHo (formally the downtown Guggenheim). By coincidence, the Prada store had opened in mid-December and the Viewing Platform went public on December 30.

The Viewing Platform represents a collaboration between architect and designer David Rockwell, corporate architect Kevin Kennon, and the architectural team of Diller + Scofidio. It is not exactly a memorial, but instead, a humble temporary structure that offers the public an opportunity to witness, firsthand, the reality of Ground Zero: the palpable aftermath of the WTC disaster. The Platform has already become a locus for an entirely unprecedented form of cultural tourism (echoing the unprecedented events of 9/11), where people seek visceral connection with the actual place. Beyond the proliferation of media representations of Ground Zero, the platform facilitates tangible commemoration, individual and collective acts of witness, and perhaps a more enduring kind of solace. Yet this is an unsettling place to visit; one experiences substantial internal conflict. Standing on this proscenium onto a ruin, overlooking a mass grave, it was unclear if I really belonged there.

The Prada store is conceived and designed by Rem Koolhaas/OMA. It is, fundamentally, an elaborate space of consumerism, a project conceived to rethink the spatial and visual terms of a boutique—and, of course, an attempt to trigger the libidinal shopping desires of Prada clientele. The store has already become a locus for consumer-based cultural tourism, an architectural attraction (or spectacle?) in its own right. From a certain perspective, both the Prada store and the Viewing Platform can be understood as presentational stages. Koolhaas has staged a theatrical, extravagant meditation on consumer culture in order to re-present (i.e., repackage) the Prada image. Various theories regarding shopping are promulgated by Koolhaas/OMA in the recently published Prada book, *Project for Prada Part 1*. A central notion involves the creation of various "epicenter" Prada stores (New York, Beverly Hills, San Francisco), representing a shift from the conventional model of a stable flagship into a newly evolving model of mutable, unpredictable environments for shopping. If "space is a marketing tool," as the book suggests, Koolhaas would like to create shopping spaces that will be responsive (synergistically) to the evolution of Prada designs, and emblematic of the intersection of fashion and other cultural practices. The designers of the Viewing Platform, on the other hand, have created a modest, temporary, functional, and deliberately unspectacular stage-like structure that compels quiet reverie. People visit the Viewing Platform to heal their psychological wounds, to find emotional closure, or to partake, vicariously (as cultural tourists) in the trauma embodied by this site.

The Prada store is not only a venue for shopping (hypothetical and actual), it is also a place in which to reflect upon various rituals of shopping (i.e., shopping as subject matter). The question, of course, is whether the entertaining, quirky, technologically clever, over-the-top, and somewhat self-indulgent Koolhaas design will help sales. Koolhaas would like us to become more self-conscious about the voyeuristic aspects of consumerism; he wants to redefine the boutique as both event and entertainment, and shopping as a performance. But will the potential high-end shopper be seduced or mystified? A prior decoding of the store's topography is recommended for the serious consumer. Entering from the street, I was a bit startled by the fragmented flower wallpaper covering the north wall, a design motif that might be a self-conscious attempt at decorative tackiness. (Apparently, the wallpaper motif will change every few months, in line with the concept of a partially mutable interior space.) I discovered a large cylindrical glass elevator, which also incorporates a display of exotic Prada wares. The Prada store is an enormous circus of presentational devices for shoes, handbags, suits, dresses, knickknacks, and other merchandise, at once brilliantly orchestrated, yet strangely disconcerting.

We are continuously and conspicuously reminded that everything is on display (including ourselves), that we have entered a theater of metaphorical interchange, a sequence of literal and symbolic platforms or stages upon which to view articles of clothing, shoes, accessories, and other elegant merchandise. These qualities are exemplified by a large concave structure that Koolhaas refers to as the "Wave." This is a kind of internal stadium comprised of two ramps: one features rows of seating (with an extensive shoe display), while the other is reminiscent of a skateboard ramp, and is covered with something called zebrawood. The "Wave" area was conceptualized by Koolhaas as a multiuse space. It is a built-in platform that unfolds, converting the area into a stage for cultural events (apparently to be programmed by the Prada Foundation). After experiencing this platform area of the store, my thoughts started drifting back to the Viewing Platform, and I began to imagine odd overlaps of social function and architectural program between these two places. Beyond the extensive mirrored surfaces and the translucent polycarbonate walls of the Prada context, the shopper will discover a wired environment: video monitors hang amongst the racks of suits and dresses, showing images of fashion clips and other phenomena. Movable, perforated metal cages hang from the ceiling above the Wave area, clothes entrapped in a manner suggestive of strip clubs (Las Vegas anyone?). The dressing rooms are equipped with glass partitions that transition from transparent to opaque with the touch of a button, allowing you to be displayed for your shopping partner, lover, or even a voyeuristic stranger. A hybrid video-mirror apparatus records your movements, allowing you access to other corporeal perspectives. There are also screens that provide information to locate clothing color, size, and collection styles. Here Koolhaas achieves an eroticized interplay of private and public, utilizing technology to fuse body and fashion. Waiting rooms are equipped with video screens that transmit images of sexy fashion shows, and information on Prada's global network. Yes, Prada would like you to actually buy a $3,500 dollar handbag while navigating these zones, but the delirious intermix of architecture, interior design, and interactive multimedia may frustrate the shopping process.

To access the Viewing Platform, you first must be issued a free ticket at the South Street Seaport (a primary tourist area), which is about a 10-minute walk from Ground Zero. You then return to the corner of Fulton and Broadway, wait in line, and eventually proceed up a simple wood plank ramp, reaching an elevated platform located on the northeast side of Ground Zero. On architectural terms, the Viewing Platform succeeds because it does not compete with Ground Zero; it is humble and provisional, in harmony with the surrounding transitional urban landscape. Handwritten messages from visitors are inscribed all over the raw wood surfaces, revealing the fundamentally social character of the place. It is an in-progress site of public inscription, participation, and reflection. The view from the Platform reveals that Ground Zero has become an immense construction site, a landscape of heavy machinery and endless labor. Because of the efficient cleanup and recovery process, very little evidence remains of the WTC ruins. People are quietly reverent, speaking in hushed tones; cameras click and camcorders whir.

Some argue that the extravagance and opulence of the 24,000-square-foot Prada store, rumored to cost $40 million dollars, is inappropriate for a more somber post-9/11 New York. Others contend that it is the perfect antidote, that it offers sophisticated entertainment (as compared with the undifferentiated visual excess of Time Square). The Koolhaas store *is* an architectural confection, at once alluring and slightly distasteful in its hyper-postmodern excess. However, beyond bankrolling architectural experimentation, Prada ultimately wants upper-end consumers to fetishize and purchase merchandise (and not only to applaud Koolhaas). Time will tell if the Koolhaas/Prada synergy is financially viable, and whether other planned "epicenter" stores in Beverly Hills and San Francisco will be completed. Much of this depends upon somewhat unpredictable economic factors.

Regarding the appropriateness of the Viewing Platform, this is an issue—moral, ethical, and spiritual—that each of us has to reflect upon. Many people—on regional, national, and global levels—want to, and will, make pilgrimages to Ground Zero. The Platform does help to regulate the flow of visitors through lower Manhattan, even though its existence, paradoxically, may attract more people. At the same time, no one wants to be perceived as linking the Viewing Platform to a broader marketing campaign to revitalize New York's tourist economy; this would be distasteful. (And what of the family members who lost loved ones in 9/11: how do we gauge their various perspectives?) New Yorkers are concerned, legitimately, about escalating voyeurism and spectacle, particularly since bodies are still being unearthed from the site. At the same time, given that live and recorded images of Ground Zero have been on television continuously for months, and that the site exists for most people as pure media event, the Viewing Platform does, at the very least, create the opportunity for another kind of experience. This is all a preamble, of course, to the public debates that will heat up regarding the actual redevelopment of the WTC site, and the design of a permanent memorial.

2012 Postscript: The 9/11 Memorial, designed by architect Michael Arad (the winner of the 2003 international design competition) with landscape architecture firm Peter Walker and Partners, opened to the public on September 12, 2011. The Rem Koolhaas-designed Prada store in New York City remains open for business. And the new One World Trade Center building—designed by David M. Childs of Skidmore, Owings & Merrill—is under construction (as of June 2012 it had risen to 104 floors), and will apparently become the tallest skyscraper in the United States; there will be still other office towers built as part of the WTC master plan. The One WTC tower already lords over the increasingly congested urban environment of my Tribeca neighborhood—a beacon of hope and progress for some, a less palatable element of the cityscape to others. All we can hope for is that history, in this place, does not repeat itself.

Marjetica Potrč, *Future Talk Now: The Great Republic of New Orleans*

Revised version of a text on Marjetica Potrč, *Future Talk Now: The Great Republic of New Orleans*, at Max Protetch Gallery, New York, January 12–February 9, 2008. Originally published in *Artforum*, April 2008.

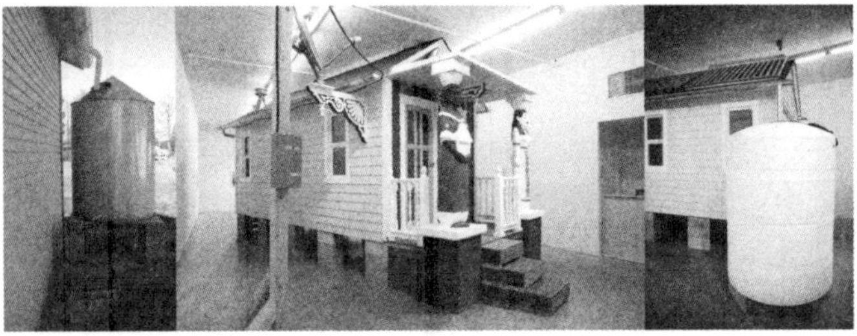

Marjetica Potrč, *New Orleans: Shotgun House with Rainwater-Harvesting Tank*, 2008

It is an irony that should be lost on no one: Ljubljana-based artist Marjetica Potrč, best known for her community-driven interventions in local urban and rural areas within the developing world, has recently turned her attentions to a US city: New Orleans. *Future Talk Now: The Great Republic of New Orleans*, Potrč's third exhibition at Max Protetch Gallery, is the result of the artist's recent engagement with this traumatized place. Potrč continues to engender a deft fusion of architectural and sculptural language to propose unusual solutions for communities in the midst of economic and ecological crisis, or in the grip of deep poverty.

A past Fellow at the Vera List Center for Art and Politics in New York, she has engaged in extensive research about the Big Easy, and took part in *Something from Nothing*, a group exhibition of site-specific projects organized by the Contemporary Art Center of New Orleans in 2008. While there will always be debates about whether art can be an effective instrument for just and fair urban redevelopment, an artist such as Potrč invariably seeks to establish sustainable localized community partnerships as a precondition for engagement. In other words, she is the antithesis of a parachute artist.

Here, Potrč used the commercial gallery context as a hub, or transmission site, for her utilitarian remixing of indigenous codes of habitation to create tool sets for survival that also propose an imaginative eco-activism. Amplifying local architectural vernacular, she presented a vividly colored, "sculptural" case study of a New Orleans shotgun house front and center. Two caryatids (one seeming to represent a black woman, the other a Caucasian woman) support the structure. For Potrč, apparently, these figures allude symbolically to the role of citizens in the reconstruction of their homes. The purple, red, and yellow shotgun shack is equipped with a satellite dish and a rainwater gathering apparatus, reflecting the environmentally committed, do-it-yourself approach of some New Orleans residents.

Water is the key ingredient here, the element that binds the city's natural, cultural, social, and economic tributaries. Potrč alludes to the interdependence of water and community through a sequence of subtly altered topographical photographs of wetland areas, each paired with one of her visionary drawings. The photos effectively register the sinking territories of the region, but it is in the drawings that the artist achieves a hallucinatory poetic effect. Amidst her fluidly drawn and slyly humorous microcosms, Potrč injects phrases such as "Cluster=Community," "Citizens Grow Democracy," "Communities Make Sense, Not the Megalopolis," and "Small-scale economy! Acre, Amazonia: Florestania is our citizenship!" The latter references the "Xapuri: Rural School" that she developed during a residency in that Northwest Brazilian state, a highlight of the 27th São Paulo Biennial in 2006. The exhibition also featured a quasi-documentary video, "Future Talk: The Great Republic of New Orleans," showing the New Orleans wetlands with a textual overlay that offers a poignant narrative suggesting the empowered voice of a citizenry avowing to reconstruct for themselves, on their own terms, using bottom-up methods and indigenous resources: "We are the ones who build the city."

Michael Cataldi and Nils Norman, *The University of Trash*

Revised version of a text on Michael Cataldi and Nils Norman, *The University of Trash*, at SculptureCenter, New York, May 10–August 3, 2009. Originally published in *Artforum*, September 2009.

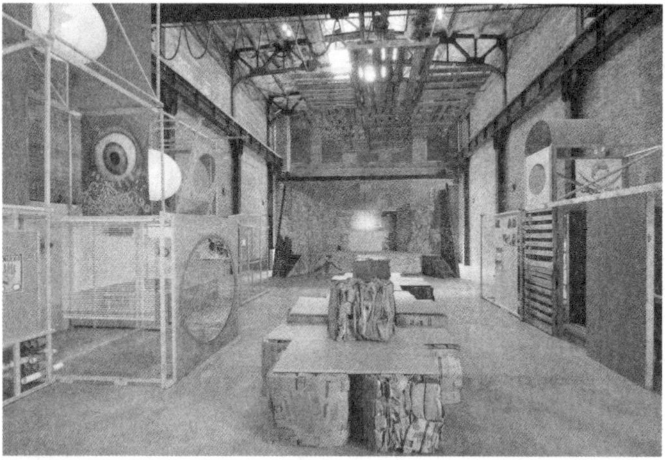

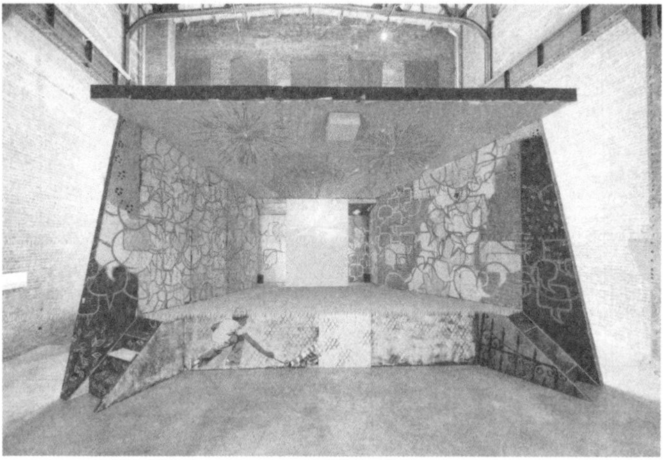

Michael Cataldi and Nils Norman, *The University of Trash*, installation view, SculptureCenter, New York, 2009
Michael Cataldi and Nils Norman, *The Tompkins Square Park Band Shell and JustSeeds Mural*, 2009

Envisaged as a site of alternative pedagogy, *The University of Trash*, 2009, was a collaborative project that took place over three months. Organized by New York-based artist Michael Cataldi and British artist-activist Nils Norman, it posited DIY design and urban social activism (e.g., squatting) as factors influencing the emergence—and, increasingly, the adoption as policy—of progressive urban and environmental politics. Against the backdrop of gentrification, Cataldi and Norman invoked a countercultural ethos in an effort to offer an authentically public (i.e., free and open) educational framework for tactical, community-responsive engagements with contemporary urbanity.

An old red ambulance parked at one end of SculptureCenter's outdoor courtyard served as a radio transmitter—a contribution to the project by artist Max Goldfarb—broadcasting events organized on-site by groups such as the radio-based art collaborative neuroTransmitter, and the Center for Urban Pedagogy, a Brooklyn nonprofit focusing on citywide educational projects. Within SculptureCenter's main space, meanwhile, the environment suggested an interpenetration of formal and informal, reductive and chaotic elements.

Casual, open-ended networks of deconstructed rooms (often fabricated from recycled materials) were replete with leaflets, videos, and other informational materials about alternatively minded grassroots organizations and events. Along with some graffiti-like tags and mural-like imagery on the walls, there was a large blackboard for notes, which was, on the day I visited, a palimpsest of mainly undecipherable writings. Nearby, a number of calendars were available for people to propose courses and events for what was dubbed "The Free Skool." Throughout the duration of their temporary subaltern university, the artists also programmed a series of workshops and discussions. *The University of Trash* thus sought to function as an assembly of collectives and alternative educational initiatives, but it was unclear—at least to this writer—whether there was a substantial response from the public.

Several events were staged in a recreation of the original Tompkins Square Park band shell (removed when the park was renovated in 1991), here adorned with a mural by the Just Seeds/Visual Resistance Artists' Cooperative. This structure strategically invoked the historical tensions surrounding urban development, gentrification, homelessness, and affordable housing that have often coalesced around Tompkins Square Park, notably during the 1988 riots that followed the city's attempt to clear the park of homeless people. In the center of the exhibition space a number of compressed geometric agglomerations of paper and cardboard formed a series of stacked "Living Cubes" developed by "The Skool of Refuse and Appropriation," a project involving students from the alternative high school program City-as-School. The students took their cue from John Hennessey and Victor Papanek's 1972 book *Nomadic Furniture: D.I.Y. Projects that are Lightweight and Light on the Environment*, which has historically provided a blueprint for strategies of transitory urban emplacement. Serving as a catalyst for the designing of temporary functional spaces, recycling here became the emblem of a struggle to reclaim disused—and misused—urban space. In a kind of dilapidated or deconstructed squatter-like office area across from this, "House Magic: Bureau of Foreign Correspondence," was installed—referred to in the press release as "a working research office dedicated to squatted social center movements throughout Europe, containing images, documents, and videos collected by Alan Moore and members of ABC No Rio visual arts collective in New York."

The University of Trash set out to test counter-hegemonic educational processes and activate new kinds of social participation, as well as to function as a platform for a broader ideological defense of what social theorist and critical geographer David Harvey has called the "right to the city" (discussed elsewhere in this book). Yet this playful and somewhat anarchic environment also revealed the undeniable ambiguities and complexities of socially collaborative, bottom-up working processes, and encapsulating some unavoidable contradictions: for all its forsaking of the hierarchies of art in the service of multiple collaborators and participants, *The University of Trash* was ultimately signed—and culturally codified—by the co-authorship of Cataldi and Norman. Furthermore, by utilizing SculptureCenter as a temporary base of operations, the project reaffirmed the normative function of the art institution as a nexus of post-Enlightenment knowledge production and authority, even though the artists were arguing for a radically *decentralized* politics of collaborative, participatory power.

Exiting SculptureCenter, I observed a new glassy condo building that had gone up next to this art institution, with the following recession-era advert: "premiere condos—stimulus pricing from $350,000." For years, gentrification has been slowly creeping into this Long Island City neighborhood, and art spaces such as SculptureCenter (and even more significantly, MoMA P.S. 1, just a few blocks away) have become *cultural attractors* that spur processes of urban development—for better and for worse. So while Cataldi and Norman's experimental university-as-art project offered examples of activist tool sets that have been deployed to intervene in the city's contested spaces (where housing and real estate are at stake), the effectiveness of these strategies and tactics to counter the interests of unrestrained free-market capitalism remains unclear.

CHAPTER V
The (Un)De-definition of Art

Donald Judd (vis-à-vis Wollheim and Baudrillard)

Revised version of an article on the 1986 Donald Judd exhibition at Paula Cooper Gallery, originally published in *Arts Magazine*, December 1986.

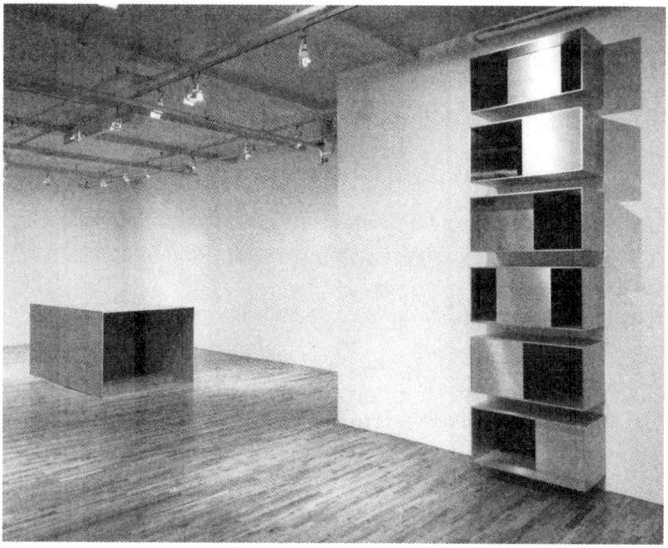

Donald Judd, installation view, Paula Cooper Gallery, New York, 1986

In 1986, Donald Judd appears to be offering not much more than a neatly (even luxuriously) packaged assortment of tired formal conventions. Judd's longstanding adherence to his own rigorously systematic program of Minimalist language—in which normative codes of both painting and sculpture were challenged—is admirable. Yet what was once considered to be a difficult, even radical, vanguard aesthetic, by the 1980s seems to have been all too easily assimilated into the sanitized spaces of high modernist architecture (i.e., the corporate lobby). Perhaps this should not come as a surprise, since Judd's language always alluded to the materials and infrastructures of the postindustrial age, and in certain respects was tailor-made for the sleek modernism of urban environments.

Judd, however, does have an uncanny ability to reconstitute his important contributions of the 1960s and the 1970s in the present moment, somehow managing to endlessly reproduce the aura of his art historical significance. Perhaps his work remains seductive for some because he has constructed an idiom that functions in spite of its seemingly dogmatic ideological posture towards a contemporary visual arts culture that has become increasingly pluralist and heterogeneous—a context wherein aesthetic orthodoxies seem passé (for better or for worse).

Judd's exhibition of recent work, regrettably, has something of a design showroom atmosphere about it, with various models to choose from. His unswerving logic of serial production—which functions as the meta-signature of the artist—remains compelling. Yet even Judd's reductive language needs occasional spicing up and doctoring, and color serves this purpose. Although Judd has occasionally employed color throughout his career, it now seems to be used merely as a device to hold the viewer's already diminished attention; this has the perhaps unintended consequence of increasing the decorative qualities, and preciousness, of the objects. Maybe this has always been the case, yet it seems more amplified now. And so, if in the 1960s Judd's work seemed a brilliantly articulated retort to American and European postwar sculpture, today his work seems to have become peculiarly emblematic of the homogenizing forces of mass culture, wherein art has become part of the overall landscape of commodities.

In his 1965 essay, "Minimal Art," philosopher Richard Wollheim endeavored to define Minimalism by analyzing it in relation to the tradition of 19th-century aesthetics. According to Wollheim, what distinguished the Minimalist art object from other art was that the former sought to deny its aesthetic autonomy for the sake of a radical "undifferentiation" from everyday objects in the world—whereas other forms of art relied upon this condition of autonomy for legitimation. In other words, the Minimalist object did not call attention to itself as something possessing the uniquely defining characteristics of the traditional art object. So if traditional art immediately and naturally differentiated itself as an autonomous thing from the world of mundane objects, Minimalism sought to change this relation, in order to conjugate itself as part of the everyday world (but, one assumes, in a different way than Duchamp's readymades,

Pop art, etc.). Wollheim, though, failed to account for the extent to which the Minimalist artists (along with a number of committed dealers, curators, and critics in the United States and Europe) participated in the construction of an increasingly viable contemporary art market for their art in the 1970s, revealing the extent to which these practices became increasingly comfortable within the space of art commerce—not as everyday objects, but as artworks, of course. Alas, certain modes of philosophical discourse are not up to the task of contending with the realities of economic systems of exchange. If anything, Judd is now making everyday artworks.

It can be argued that the central paradigm initially identified by Wollheim (among others) as the most radical feature of orthodox Minimalism—i.e., the claim of achieving a homological relationship with everyday objects and the structures of industrial society—has become just an expression of assimilation into the mechanisms of serial production for the art market. Art and its economic markets always interpenetrate, yet it is questionable to suggest that Judd's practice evinces a critical relationship to these conditions. However, his reductively abstract language is not entirely self-referential or tautological: it does signify integration into the organizational logics of industrial society. In the essay "Gesture and Signature" from his 1972 book *For a Critique of the Political Economy of the Sign*, Jean Baudrillard eloquently locates this particular logic:

> ... in systematizing itself according to a formal constraint, in constituting itself according to a play of successive differences, that the work of art offers itself of its own initiative as immediately integratable in a global system that conjugates it like any other object or group of objects. In this sense, modern works have indeed become everyday objects: although laden with cultural connotations, they pose no problems to the environment.

Perhaps this is a suitable epitaph for Judd's recent sculptures, which seem to pose very few problems indeed.

Interview with General Idea, Conducted in Los Angeles and New York, 1991

General Idea was comprised of AA Bronson, Felix Partz, and Jorge Zontal.
An excerpted version of an interview originally published in *The Journal of Contemporary Art* (New York), vol. 4, 1991.

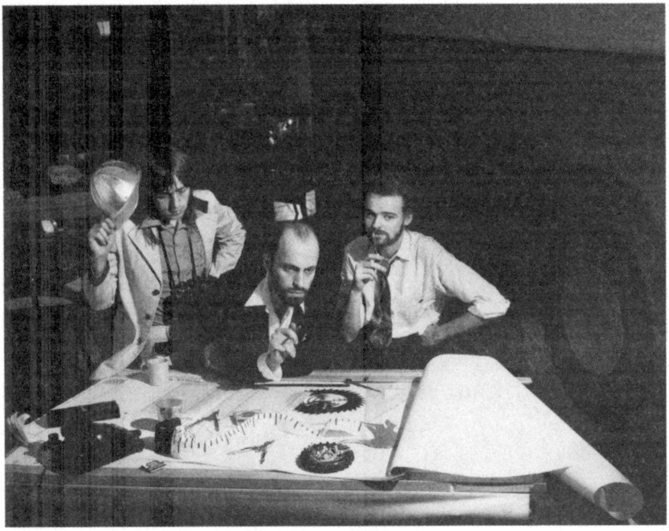

Rodney Werden, *Portrait of General Idea*, 1974

JOSHUA DECTER How does General Idea address the distinction between working in one particular cultural realm, for instance, the gallery or museum, as opposed to another domain, such as the street?

AA BRONSON We consider all the various types of activities that we are involved in as art. For many years we never bothered to distinguish between the gallery and other situations because, in fact, we never utilized the gallery situation all that much early on. A General Idea text from the mid-1970s refers to the gallery's relationship to art being very much like the garage's relationship to the car: we use the gallery to tinker with and repair the work, but the real function of our art is out on the road, in a way—it's within the current of the culture.

JD And so, by entering as cultural producers into this current, your work is necessarily participating, as sign or image, in the larger visual and verbal sign system that constitutes the contemporary languages of culture, politics, ideology, etc.

AA If you look back to our earlier projects, such as when we brought out *File* magazine in 1972, we saw this as a sort of parasitic art project. By using the format of *Life* magazine, we could occupy territories staked out by that mainstream magazine. *File* could be placed in the newsstands and, because of its visual familiarity, it could pass through a general distribution system and be picked up by people who would not ordinarily be exposed to this type of work. This was a type of parasitic process. But with the AIDS projects that's somewhat less evident.

JD Yet it is certainly parasitic of a signature work by Robert Indiana ...

AA And also because it uses available distribution and communication systems—it hooks into them and the image is carried through these systems.

FELIX PARTZ It's intended to proliferate itself.

AA It's intended to get out of our own control.

JD Do you sense that it has gotten out of your control, and if so, how?

AA Yes, and quite purposefully in some ways. For example, we designed a variation on the AIDS logo for the German AIDS Foundation, and they use that logo any way they want. They have incorporated it into lottery tickets, posters, and so on and so forth. So there is a whole national production of this image over which we have no control.

JD But don't you retain copyright control?

FP Yes, but we gave them permission ...

AA ... to do whatever they want with it, on the condition that they not alter it. It's not presented as an artwork, even though a credit appears for General Idea—it's used as a logo. With this work we have cooperated with anyone who has approached us to use the logo; for instance, a hospital used it for public awareness programs and television has used it as a background motif on the set of a discussion. It has been used on the covers of magazines—*Ontario Dentist*—things like that! I suppose we have ultimate legal control if we want to make use of that, but essentially we don't.

JD In terms of the so-called institutional parameters of art production and display, do you undertake to undermine, transgress, or puncture the supposed boundaries that exist between your function as artists and the capacities or roles of noncultural producers; in other words, to engender a productive breakdown of disciplinary segregation so as to allow for the dissemination of usually marginalized or repressed images, signs, messages, etc.?

FP I don't think that we distinguish that much between the gallery or museum context and the newsstand; I think we see them as similar contexts, even though a lot of the work over the past ten years has been museum or gallery related. We were never anti-gallery or anti-museum. We never saw that it was more compromising to be in a museum than it was to be next to *Fortune* magazine on the newsstand. Maybe it is that the punctures or the transgressions function at those points where the context doesn't exist anymore.

JD In other words, the boundaries or parameters show themselves at those points where there is a puncture, a transgression …

FP Right. Moving back and forth between contexts, bringing things out of one and into another. Also, we once did a work for something called "The Room of the Unknown Function," a generalized term that we were using for the museum, which was also intended to investigate what the function of the museum actually was. What purpose did it serve? What exactly are these spaces for? On the simplest of levels, the gallery or museum is comprised of white walls that allow for a display; they isolate things to see—as in a showroom.

JD To one extent or another, the museum, the gallery, and the newsstand function as public sites of display.

FP Yes. They say that people are intimidated to go into a museum, but people are also intimidated to go into the Valentino boutique on Rodeo Drive, though most people are not intimidated about entering a supermarket. And there are of course galleries that people are intimidated about going into—so there are many different manifestations of the psychological and social reaction to the public and private domain.

JD And do you consider factors of context and audience reception as important components of General Idea's process?

AA Well, in a way. When we were first working together in Toronto there was no real audience. And we were quite aware of trying to assemble an audience out of existing audiences for other types of material—for instance, a music audience, rock-and-roll audience, design audience, architecture audience, trendy audience. We were quite conscious of attempting to pull together all those audiences in order to key into a diverse public. In the late 1970s we became aware of the museum audience; at that point in history museums began to change character, particularly in terms of attendance. We began to realize that the museum was becoming another form of mass media, so we added the museum audience to our repertoire. It was the time of the first real blockbuster exhibitions, and it became clear that the museums were beginning to market themselves in a very new way.

FP But also the entire art scene began to move into becoming a popular consumable item. When the money arrived and the stars began to be made, as we could see in the magazines, it became a part of popular culture.

JD So it's almost as if the entire cultural milieu of the so-called art world began to market itself.

FP Yes, and so it became just another aspect of popular culture. Instead of looking at rock-and-roll, we simply looked back at the art world itself to see how it operated, what were its conventions—and how did one transgress, how did one present, what was the audience, what were their expectations, what were the excesses ...

JD Do you consider the *Miss General Idea Pavilion* to be an allegory of those conditions of contemporary culture that you have just described?

AA Yes, we have this fake structure within which we see the pavilion. There are five elements to that structure: "General Idea" as representing the artist; *The Miss General Idea Pageant* which we think of as the process of creation; *Miss General Idea* as the artwork itself; *The Miss General Idea Pavilion*, which is clearly the museum or the gallery; and what we call "Frame of Reference," which is essentially the audience and the mass media, as in *File* magazine. So we can assemble all our work within that structure and recreate the art world, and the world of media that surrounds it, within the structure of our own work. This structure began to build itself between 1970 and 1971 and was quite evident by 1975. We have, to some extent, stepped away from that structure over the past five years or so.

JD In what way?

AA Work such as the AIDS project, although it operates in the same way as all the Pavilion and Pageant projects did, and uses what we learned in those earlier projects, doesn't really incorporate itself into that structure; the AIDS projects constitute a parallel structure.

JD In terms of General Idea's working method, does one person produce one type of work while someone else makes another type of work—or are there no actual rules that dictate the approach to production?

FP There are similar situations, but there are a variety of them. Sometimes one person will physically carry out the idea of another person; sometimes one of us will work out an idea to a certain point and then another one of us will take that process over. Or sometimes it's just a matter of having a fabricator make something for us. Because a lot of the work is based on the elaboration of existing projects, it doesn't ultimately seem that important who is doing exactly what. For example, the AIDS project began as one painting and then became elaborated into new forms and everyone had different involvements at different stages. A lot of the projects are like that. We look around and try to find something, like the AIDS logo, that has the potential to be expanded into multiple projects, but it is a quite intuitive process. Like the poodles …

JD How were the poodles arrived at?

FP Well, all I can say is that it was some sort of intuitive thing—an idea and image that had the possibility of considerable proliferation, a lot of potential meanings, and graphic potential. We felt that it could be manipulated into many different forms.

AA We first used the poodle around 1981 and, in a way, the poodle is a mass media image. There is a whole history of poodle imagery, but it had been rejected from the language of contemporary culture at the time that we first used it, except as a kitschy thing. We came to it as a rejected image that nevertheless had many meanings already attached to it; like the "French poodle," the fag hairdresser poodle, and it also happens to be a hunting dog.

FP I think, in a lot of cases, these things are brought out and then they're test-marketed. We first produce something and then decide what to do with it, and this does not always mean that there will be a positive reaction. With the poodle, one thing that became immediately obvious was that many interpretations were provoked: some people saw it as an old ladies' dog, and others as the brassy tart, and then there are the gay connotations. We like to produce such ambiguities. And the AIDS project is similar in that some people are aware of the history of the LOVE logo while others are not. There are some who are familiar with the LOVE logo but are not aware that it was an artwork by the artist Robert Indiana. For others it just means what it states: AIDS. But what are the multiple meanings of AIDS itself? When we place an AIDS poster in the context of the street, it's hard to know what the spectrum of reactions is—it ranges from ripping the posters down to taking them home as collectibles.

JD But in the AIDS project, you are appropriating an already commodified or reified emblem, the Robert Indiana LOVE logo, and then transforming and transvaluing that relatively familiar image.

AA We're particularly interested in that aspect because all of the prior commodification to which you refer occurred without the participation of Indiana himself—the fact is that the consumer world picked up the image and turned it into a million products without his permission, without him making any money from it. This situation is interesting to us. Another aspect was that it seemed to carry two meanings in particular: one was the sexual revolution and free love, the other one was brotherly love. In relation to AIDS, these two notions are uncomfortable bedfellows. A lot of people have criticized us because the AIDS posters are not didactic, that there is no message on them ...

JD Criticized for their ambiguity?

AA Yes, that they don't indicate what their message is. But this is to a large extent what interests us, because it actually has the effect of bringing more issues to the surface. People seem to project their own agendas onto the image and assume that the meaning of the work is correspondent to what makes them uncomfortable. One possible interpretation, a rather negative one, is that love leads to AIDS; another interpretation, this one more positive, is that AIDS brings out love in the community. Hopefully the second interpretation will be more often heard.

JD You have managed to develop an image and sign that has multiple symbolic meanings, yet has been distributed widely. Does the AIDS logo have a deliberately incomplete informational dimension that is designed to challenge normative channels of social communication?

AA We want to make the word AIDS normal. AIDS is sort of playing the part that cancer did in the 1960s. By keeping the word visible, it has a normalizing effect that will hopefully play a part in normalizing people's relationship to the disease—to make it something that can be dealt with as a disease rather than a set of moral or ethical issues.

FP It is just like an advertising campaign, like seeing a repetition of billboard advertising imagery. It's not the individual billboard that sells: it's in the repetition of the product image. The image becomes entrenched in the mind, so when you walk into the supermarket you have been prepared to want a particular product.

AA They create a familiarity.

FP And part of it is just a visibility campaign because so many people don't want to deal with AIDS. On this level there really is no difference between the street and the gallery context since there is equal resistance about dealing with the issue in both contexts. By putting the logo in the format of painting, it allows for an entry into the gallery domain as a series of painting-sized billboards, simply occupying space.

AA There have been galleries that have refused to show it.

JD For what reasons?

AA Oh well, there's always a reason, such as, "They've already seen so much ... "

FP Or, "We've already done our AIDS show ... " So we're doing a series that is more subtle, that won't be so aggressive!

AA Yeah, we're doing our black on black Reinhardt series.

JD With the same AIDS logo?

AA Yes. Specifically for gallery situations.

JD If the AIDS project is in part informed by the language of advertising, then in some way it must, by logical extension, be selling something—or at least generating a desire for a product.

AA Well, the public service announcement is another form of advertising and it has different effects, but it operates on the same principles. I guess the AIDS project would be more akin to this approach.

FP It is also territorial in some way, almost like the graffiti tag. It's here, over there, and so on.

JD So it's almost as if you are mapping out a territory with transformed but familiar cultural signs.

AA We placed the AIDS posters in the New York subway system so they would pass through every geographic and ethnic barrier within the urban context.

FP Many of our projects have occurred in transportation systems: railways, subways, buses, even stamps—all the things that pass through the bloodstream of culture and the social.

JD This allows for the widest possible dissemination of the ambiguous sign ...

AA But it also allows for it to pass through borders that would otherwise be obstacles.

JD In what sense?

AA Well, in the sense that in New York City, for example, if you do something in SoHo, certainly the audience in Harlem will most likely not see it. Our projects are aimed at more types of audiences than conventional art production would normally reach.

JD Do you think that the AIDS logo is accessible to that wide, heterogeneous audience that you would like to address?

AA It's quite interesting to what extent people know that

the AIDS logo could also be a LOVE logo or even read it as actually saying love if they look at it quickly. Some people in various countries also seem to have associated it with a 1960s aesthetic.

FP When the AIDS logo first appeared, people in the art world immediately connected it to the appropriation and commodification aesthetic that was dominant in the mid-1980s. But now, with the 1960s revival going on, it has begun to take on different connotations and associations. In particular the kids respond to it because it seems to reflect this general recuperation of the 1960s styles and images. We like the possibility of a more pop culture oriented reading.

JD On the other hand, I find that the heraldic poodle images have a much more hermetic character to their symbolic condition.

AA That's true. But one quality of the images that we like working with is the possibility that different audiences can read the same image on different levels. I think the case of the AIDS images is unusual in that almost any audience can read it at more or less the same level. But in the case of the *Fucking Poodles*, the image can be read in a rather large number of ways, and many different levels of meaning can be brought out according to one's background and context. The same can be said of the *Fin de Siècle* piece with the seals that was shown at Koury Wingate Gallery. It's amazing how many people, even people who know us, did not catch on to the simple fact that there were three seals!

JD And this seems to correspond clearly to the triadic configurations of the poodle images …

FP There's three of everything … in the heraldic series, they're almost all threes.

JD But do the *Fucking Poodles* and the *Fin de Siècle* pieces, for instance, maintain a relationship to the practice of self-portraiture, since they clearly reflect the triadic structure of General Idea itself?

AA Yes, they are sort of self-portraits.

FP Well, some of the poodle images are distinctly self-portraits. You can actually pick out who's who. The Three Graces.

JD What is the nature of the three-person collaborative structure?

AA You get a particular kind of collaboration out of two people and a quite different form of collaboration out of three. I doubt we would have survived this long as a group if we had been four or five. I think three …

FP … is more than enough.

AA It seems to be a very stable structure.

FP Some of the original usages of self-portrayal, I think, were very superficial on one level, like a marketing technique, because when we were starting off we had purposefully confused who was General Idea. And then at some point we determined that this strategy was working against us because nobody knew who we were—there was always a mass of confusion. So those early self-portrayals became a clarification campaign about who we were. There was a growing interest from the outside concerning how we worked in collaboration, so we did various photo pieces that sometimes became formalized into self-portraits in the threesome structure. This has permeated much of our work.

AA In the *Fin de Siècle* work this notion of self-portraiture was articulated in a very subtle way by asking the taxidermist to give each seal individual characteristics. They are quite different from one another if you look closely.

JD There seemed to be a plethora of contradictory interpretations associated with that piece, ranging from abject confusion or bewilderment to more didactic political readings. The work's radical ambiguity of meaning or symbolism was quite provocative, and engendered a destabilizing of certain conventional notions of how so-called political practice should produce meaning.

AA But obviously now within the art world there are so many different levels of social, political, or theoretical meaning around which artworks are being constructed. We structure our work so it becomes difficult to determine specific, one-dimensional readings—the more meanings, the better, from our point of view.

The Theatrics of Dissemination: A General Idea Model

Revised version of an essay published in the catalogue for General Idea's *Fin De Siècle*, Wurttembergischer Kunstverein Stuttgart, Centre d'Art Santa Mònica, Kunstverein in Hamburg, The Power Plant in Toronto, Wexner Center for the Arts in Columbus, and the San Francisco Museum of Modern Art, 1992–1994.

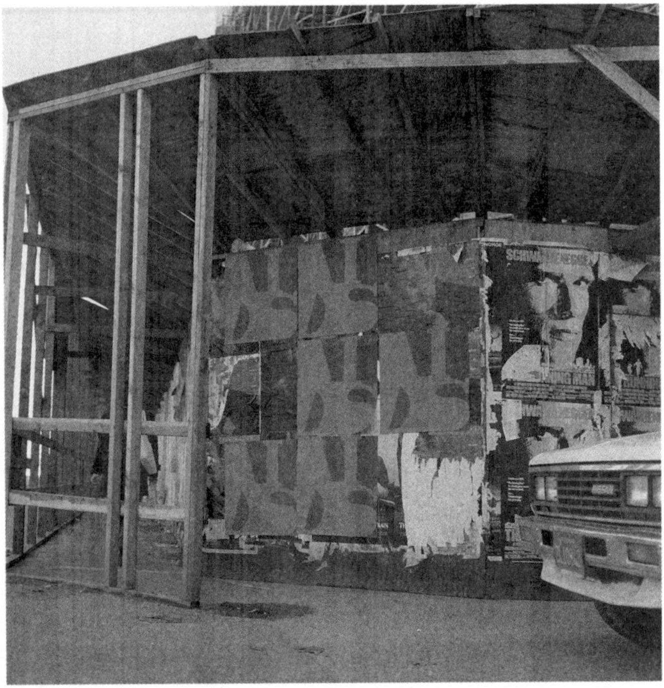

General Idea, *AIDS* (poster project), San Francisco, 1988

In 1968, AA Bronson, Jorge Zontal, and Felix Partz reinvented themselves as General Idea, and commenced producing films, videos, performances, and photographs (among other less easily categorized events and situations) in order to inhabit a fictional construct. Producing and reproducing themselves in the image of whom they desired to be—as if engaged in the ultimate makeover—General Idea represented themselves as figures of a faux popular culture: they courted fame, fortune, and glamour. As veritable children of Andy Warhol, General Idea orchestrated their own version of a subcultural milieu during the late 1960s and early to mid-1970s so as to invent a framing structure for their new identities and offer a metaphorical and literal stage upon which to perform their cultural activities.

During this early period, General Idea attracted players from the worlds of art, theater, film, and music to participate in the construction of a diverse subculture—a grand theatrical illusion of artistic persona. Yet, what clearly distinguishes the General Idea model from that of Warhol is the extent to which the former had, from the outset, established a self-consciously fake structure within which to produce a quasi-parodic mimicry of the art world's aspiration to the status of popular culture. By the early 1970s, Warhol had already begun to achieve the rather unique status of an artist from the vanguard subculture who had managed to rise to the level of a pop-culture star. This was a status that Warhol had actively sought out, and his art operated as the key apparatus through which to redefine himself as a celebrity; he had transformed himself into the *court* portrait artist for the rich and famous, yet he still managed to retain a cutting-edge, vanguard mystique. In a sense, General Idea had come to recognize the potential of operating in that newly articulated, yet highly ambiguous territory in between the domain of an insular art vanguard and the seemingly capacious realm of popular culture. They began to appropriate—or assume a parasitic relationship to—models of behavior and language derived from popular culture in order to cultivate pre-existing systems of entertainment into which they might inject their fictive, invented identities. The construction of this type of hybrid context and language (sharing borders with traditionally antithetical realms) permitted transgressions, deviances, subversions—all those things conventionally discouraged or prohibited under the auspices of sanctioned, official mass culture.

General Idea's development of *The 1984 Miss General Idea Pageant* (performed in various ways from 1970 to 1978), and the subsequent *The 1984 Miss General Idea Pavilion*, functioned as elaborate framing structures referencing popular entertainment. In other words, the beauty pageant and pavilion as public spectacles of commerce. General Idea sought to construct visual and performance languages that would suggest a kind of ambiguously ironic, coyly tongue-in-cheek version of aspects of pop culture, a virtually absurdist rendition which was as complicit as it was critical. They attempted to infiltrate the material and behavioral manifestations of this value system so as to simultaneously participate with—and contaminate—the norm. General Idea developed an elaborate masquerade for their quasi-fictional induction into (pseudo)stardom: they orchestrated an elaborate and persuasive publicity machine to sell their fictive images to the public. They devised various modes of (self) dissemination—for instance, publicity shots of their various masks of identity, or a video documenting the orchestrated and programmed cheers of an audience (*Towards an Audience Vocabulary*, 1978).

General Idea appropriates mainstream forms in which to deposit or insinuate ambiguous, unstable signs that generate the potential of multiple readings—a counter to the overdetermined systems of representation employed by mass culture. They explore the question of audience in the era of an expanding popular culture, producing allegories (and burlesques) of the way in which film and television, in particular, operate as arenas of seduction—apparatuses of entertainment that construct particular types of audience reception. General Idea dismantles the popular mythologies of art and artist by parodying these conventions, enacting this parody through the masquerade that life is art, and art is life. For them, it has always been a question of locating the most opportune mechanism through which to enter this general current of cultural signs (the connective tissue of social communication), injecting this stream with a proliferation of unstable signs. In a sense, *The 1984 Miss General Idea Pavilion* became that hypothetical archive under whose auspices the fictional language codes of General Idea (as concept and practice) were catalogued—the inauguration of a fictive, imaginary space within which General Idea were the curators of their own unique self-representations, their theatrical masks. Yet at the close of the 1970s, this imaginary architectural edifice—*The 1984 Miss General Idea Pavilion*—was destroyed. General Idea had begun to stage the demise of their own fictive self-representation. Ironically, this catastrophe only engendered a process of partial reconstruction: the creation of a false archaeological inventory comprised of the remains of *The 1984 Miss General Idea Pavilion*. Evocative of the self-referential museum frameworks of Duchamp and Broodthaers, General Idea developed a sophisticated ensemble of related visual language codes and formations that were designed to represent the artifactual residuals of this destroyed fiction—a process which engendered, paradoxically, a new inventory of aesthetic constructs. One fiction merely replaced another.

During the early and mid-1980s, there emerged what can be described as General Idea's post-apocalyptic codes of self-portraiture—mediated through the proliferation of fragments salvaged from the ruin of the pavilion. Endowed with titles such as *Pink Poodle Fragment* or *Black Poodle Fragment*, these objects assumed the guise of ancient artifacts from a dead civilization that deified poodles—judging, at least, by the (false) evidence! The poodles became the new mascots for General Idea—an iconography rich with kitsch implications, and ambiguous yet charmingly vulgar sexual and gender connotations. It is a figurative language through which the members of General Idea vicariously signal their general, collective fantasy. In some of these faux fragments, three poodles are depicted engaged in sex acts, assuming a wide range of positions that suggest the erotic sophistication of the anthropomorphic order. The anthropomorphized canines gracefully, if somewhat mechanically, demonstrate an encyclopedic variety of triadic fucking postures—a suggestive, scandalous pictorial proxy for the mechano-balletic union of General Idea's hypothetical sex-play. Perhaps an allegory of the collaborative dynamics of art making?

In the 1980s, General Idea responded to the art world's resurgent fascination with painting—e.g., German and Italian brands of so-called Neo-Expressionism, and the American brand of Neo-Geo. They strategically produced a coy, critical emulation of these conditions by manufacturing their own version of Painting. To facilitate this endeavor, they appropriated identifiable attributes of certain stylistic codes of the period. For example, the *Mondo Cane Kama Sutra* paintings from 1984, which feature one yellow, one orange, and one pink poodle engaged in spectacular acts of humping, seem to exploit Neo-Geo. These *ménage à trois* emblems index the insular nature of General Idea's language codes and operate in relation to predetermined codes, suggesting a parasitic connection to the host body of both mass and high culture.

The AIDS Project, begun in 1987, is exemplary of General Idea's working method and language. In that year, the AIDS logo first appeared, based upon the appropriation of the color scheme and design of Robert Indiana's famous and ubiquitously disseminated LOVE emblem. General Idea used their unique AIDS logo for projects within the boundaries of art institutions and galleries, as well as the more public context of the street in the form of posters. Although each territory constructs a different type of public reception, the context of the high-culture venue demands a familiarity with a more specialized mode of visual language, and immediately establishes a different mode of communication from that encountered in the street; or does it? General Idea anticipated different types of public reception by selecting the appropriate visual constructs for each context: the paradigm of painting for the museum or gallery, and the poster for the street. The substitution of AIDS for LOVE—in and of itself has multiple political and cultural implications. By injecting this linguistic term—in actuality, a medical acronym for Acquired Immune Deficiency Syndrome, a condition that had already reached epidemic proportions in the late 1980s—into a preestablished iconography connoting the fusion of high art and mass culture into an ubiquitous emblem (i.e., LOVE), General Idea facilitates a system of dissemination that can feed into any context. To use the metaphor of viral proliferation, General Idea sought to *infect* a mass-culture emblem with new linguistic and symbolic meaning, enabling a distribution of this sign throughout the body of the social. Yet the question remained as to whether this sign had a fixed meaning, or whether it was unstable, capable of producing multiple meanings. General Idea were interested in enhancing the ambiguous condition of this sign-as-image/image-as-sign; that is, they sought to catalyze an interplay of didacticism and abstraction, information and visual pleasure, pedagogy and distracted contemplation, agitprop and entertainment. Furthermore, they attempted to naturalize this emblem within the already densely packed field of cultural signs, yet still allow the distinct qualities of the AIDS emblem to seep into the public's visual field of reception. AIDS posters have been seen in the streets and subways of New York, Berlin and San Francisco. The AIDS logo has been used to create a stamp edition for *Parkett magazine*, to produce paintings displayed in galleries and museums globally, and as public sculpture. Entering the broader public sphere, General Idea has generated a complex yet accessible mode of communication regarding a health crisis that still requires our attention.

Andrea Zittel, *Prototypes*

Revised version of a text on Andrea Zittel at Andrea Rosen Gallery, New York, March 4–April 8, 1995. Originally published in *Artforum*, Summer 1995.

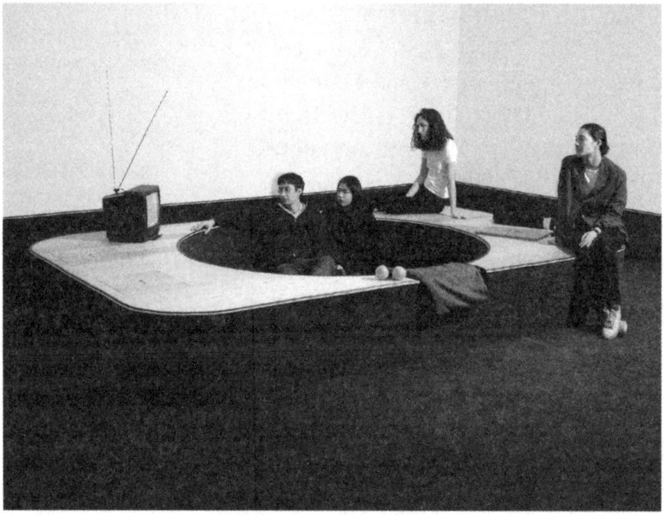

Andrea Zittel, *Prototype for A to Z Pit Bed*, 1995

Andrea Zittel just wants to make our lives a little bit more livable, and she seems determined to find a workable confluence of art, design, and architecture that will lead the way towards enhanced domestic experiences. To that end, she has established an "administrative services" business. Under the auspices of her company A–Z, Zittel both manufactures and tests utilitarian art objects—or "prototypes" as she prefers to call them—within the comforts of her own domicile, regularly inviting friends over to sample the goods. In a sense, all of her artworks are hypothetical objects of utility. Or is it the other way around?

Recently, the artist published a catalogue that offers examples of the various "selected sleeping arrangements" that are available for purchase, a booklet that serves as a visual and conceptual guide for this show, as well as concurrent projects at the Whitney Biennial and the Rooseum in Sweden. It even includes an enthusiastic letter—a veritable testimonial—to Zittel from a satisfied customer. This is a most fetching personalized gesture of self-promotion, one which reinforces our impression that Zittel's humanistic optimism and sober nostalgia do not appear to be riddled with our period's requisite doubt, regardless of how much more comfortable we might feel if it were.

Her *Prototype for A to Z Pit Bed* (1995) could almost be 21st-century IKEA, and that is a bit how it feels, too. This low, wooden structure (rectangular with curved corners) measures 12 feet in length and 8 feet wide, its edgings covered with the same deep-purple carpeting upon which it sits. A circular pit opens up at the center of the structure, allowing viewers (or, rather, participants) to engage in activities such as watching television, sleeping, or just sitting around chatting it up with friends. At the foot of this *Prototype*, two adjacent yet virtually hidden compartments hold optional sleeping materials. Formally, the piece—i.e., environment—brings together the codes of Minimalism with 1960s-style modern Swedish furniture design for that groovy, understated hot-tub look. In the back gallery, Zittel's *Prototypes for A to Z Platform Beds* (1995)—variously-sized, circular pancake beds on wheels upholstered in attractive red/black and pale green/black geometric combos—lie about the place like bedroom props from a James Bond movie, beckoning us to do anything but sleep on them!

It may well be that Zittel occasionally daydreams of those bygone laboratory environments of the Bauhaus, de Stijl, or the Constructivists, where and when it was still a righteous thing to consider the systematic mingling of distinct kinds of artistic labor as socially progressive, transformative, and unifying. In 1922, for example, Alexei Gan—in his tract entitled *Constructivism*—could write:

> the end has come to pure and applied art. A time of social expediency has begun. An object of only utilitarian significance will be introduced in a form acceptable to all.

And, in the following year, Walter Gropius would propose his central philosophy in *The Theory and Organization of the Bauhaus*:

> The guiding principle of the Bauhaus has therefore the idea of creating a new unity through the welding together of many "arts" and movements: a unity having its basis in Man himself and significant only as a living organism.

Today, in retrospect, our general cynicism is perhaps more than a little justified when we recognize that the failure of those movements to abolish the hierarchical and ideological separations between art activities and life activities under the name of supposedly transgressive cross-media cultural production set the stage, paradoxically, for the reinforcement of those very institutional divisions within modern European and American society. As history demonstrates, the already tenuous coupling of rank idealism and a systematic pragmatism usually demanded subscription to a collective politics that could—and would—prove to be just as coercive as emancipatory.

While I do not mean to suggest that Zittel is lamenting the loss of all those historical moments filled with (false?) revolutionary promise, it nevertheless seems fairly certain that she expects her work to perform a kind of social or socializing function that will compel us to rethink how we might fashion new bridges between art and the so-called everyday. Yet Zittel's pursuit of an integrative language that is more than symbolically useable has the effect of reminding us of art's ineluctable divorce from practical concerns. And it is precisely at the center of this conceptual gap that we will find the exquisite irony of her project. The old model of utopianism that promised a new and improved tomorrow has been replaced by a phantasmal utopianism that promises a new and improved today; speaking in what might be described as the *future present* tense, Zittel offers a model of what things might look like if our today was less about a possible tomorrow than about a probable today. In the meantime, we might as well just lounge around.

Stephen Prina and Mike Kelley in Discussion with Joshua Decter

An excerpted version of a 1996 discussion with Mike Kelley and Stephen Prina that took place in Los Angeles. Originally published in the exhibition catalogue of *a/drift*, Center for Curatorial Studies Museum, Bard College, October 20, 1996–January 5, 1997.

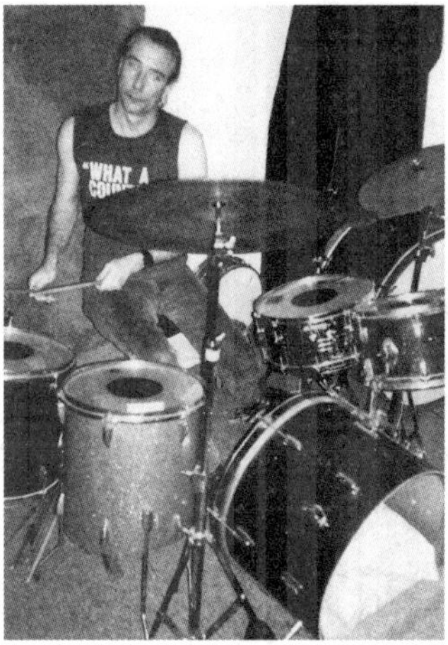

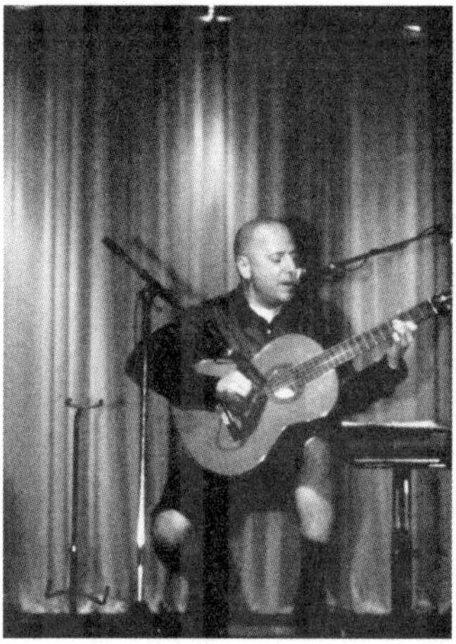

Mike Kelley (early 1990s)
Stephen Prina (*Sonic Dan*, SO 36, Berlin 1996)

MIKE KELLEY It seems that one place to start is perhaps to talk about the aesthetic politics of music. And then we have a place to begin talking about cultural history. What do you think?

JOSHUA DECTER What do you mean exactly by the term "aesthetic politics"?

MK For me, music wasn't ever about fun—it was always about cultural production. And that's from—first of all—being in church, and then sexual politics, politics in general, and eventually about aesthetic discourse. I was not interested in pop music as something prepackaged for my pleasure, or something merely about relaxation.

JD So, the basis for you is not entertainment culture per se, but something prior to that?

MK Well, my entrance into art was through the counterculture, and my entrance to the counterculture was through progressive rock. Rock was not supposed to be populist, but rather designed to be a negative aesthetic, a counter-aesthetic. And so for me, as a young person, there was no difference between music that did that job and art which did that job. It was the same. And it was only the fact that Americans were predisposed to music that prevented them from liking art that was done in a similar way. This was just a cultural problem in America.

JD Predisposed because rock became an entertainment industry—a sphere that excluded art culture?

MK Predisposed because people were generally more inclined toward music as a form, and so the entertainment industry could peddle it more successfully. If you wanted to peddle Jackson Pollock, for example, you had to hide its meaning—hide it inside of linoleum design!

JD But you also evoked the church as a kind of negative example ...

MK I was just saying that from the very start of my life, music was considered something important, not something that went on in the background. It meant something, as in church music. People would argue about the aesthetics of church music.

STEPHEN PRINA I'm smiling at this point because, well, you can also look at church music as a kind of industry. I didn't learn guitar first and foremost because of certain rock models; that wasn't the real facilitator. Sister Mary Lucille was the facilitator because she needed a guitar army for her folk mass. And so she enlisted certain people for that purpose, including myself ...

MK I have an almost opposite story. I didn't have much love for pop music when I was a kid, and I went to Catholic School. There was a nun who was trying to teach us about the American musical heritage and was playing us Leadbelly records, which I hated. I was surrounded by pop music, and I just didn't care one way or another about it.

JD Steve, you indicated that there was some sort of preoccupation with the idea of the rock guitarist?

SP I was at a crossroads. I was interested in the model of the rock guitarist, but I found myself in elementary school and the facilitator of my introduction to guitar was quite different. My relationship to pop music was always conflicted: as Mike suggested, there's always the condition of pleasure and entertainment in pop music, but these were not the most significant points of impact for me. I first played in a folk mass army, but then quickly joined a rock-and-roll band in the ninth grade. I went through a variety of bands and then gave up on rock-and-roll for a while; I became more involved with jazz and free jazz, noise experiments by people like Captain Beefheart or Frank Zappa.

MK When I attended public high school, I had already become entrenched with the idea that I had no ability, and therefore had no interest in learning. It was too late, anyway. So I hooked up with rock people; I was already a fanatic because of my interest in psychedelic music, which was the first music that I considered to be truly my music. I understood this music, where it was coming from, its eclecticism. I think psychedelic music is postmodern, if you want to use that expression. It's like garbage can music: you throw everything together. But since I believed that I didn't have the musical aptitude to play an instrument, I became a roadie.

JD Did you arrive at the psychedelic genre, so to speak, outside of the sphere of drug culture in general?

MK Oh no, it was all one thing. One was part of the other. To choose that type of music—which was contrary to everything that was on radio, or so-called normal music—was basically to raise your freak flag and proclaim, "I'm abnormal."

SP But in terms of the issue of crossover culture, this was never a problem or issue for me, because the idea of overlaps in cultural interest was just something that came naturally when I was younger. I had simultaneous interests in art, music, and cultural politics, but they weren't categorized as separable things. It was later that I discovered that I would be subjected to that kind of categorization. Here's a good example: when I arrived at art school, I found out that there was a tradition of brute music, or music that wasn't based on music theory; in a sense, this is what produced Destroy All Monsters, along with aspects of the Stooges, the Velvet Underground, Captain Beefheart, and bands like this, who were experimental. And then I discovered composers such as John Cage and Stockhausen, who were doing non-notational scores. You didn't have to know how to read music to perform these scores.

JD I think both of you are suggesting that certain gestures in music production are intrinsically understood as being "different" from what one hears on radio, distinct from sanctioned institutional models. I'm interested in this kind of symbolic entry, which articulates a distinction from a set of norms. This, itself, has become a familiar countercultural process.

SP There are other assumptions or presuppositions which are disturbing, for example, what music is a more direct mode of expression, that you can't analyze music because it's about emotions, or that it isn't as highly mediated as other cultural forms. I could never understand these sorts of arguments, because music is as highly mediated as any other kind of cultural material.

MK There is a difference for the recipient: people do perceive music as being less mediated. When I used to talk with Kim Gordon she said, "You can't have a crush on a painting, but you can have a crush on music." The way I understood this had to do with a popular kind of perception: you can hum a song to yourself over and over again. I responded to Kim by saying, "Well, I experience a completely opposite effect; there are certain images that I think about all the time." But I did realize what she meant in terms of mass culture, and it made me sad.

JD Sad?

MK Well, it made me sad that something that seemed to attract a lot of people's attention was based on the mistaken impression that it wasn't considered. And that's the appeal of music: it doesn't need to be thought about; it's innate, natural, and intuitive.

SP Or, that thinking about music too much is somehow unnatural.

MK The huge split between the worlds of art and popular culture was furthered by the Pop artists. Warhol, for example, wanted art to function like a pop song; art was to be recognizable, like a catchy tune. And so Pop art was to operate on the terms of pop music, and all other visual art would continue to remain ambiguous to people.

JD And what of the relationship of counterculture to popular culture?

MK Well, many of the things that used to signify countercultural activities are now so very culturally entrenched. It's that simple.

JD So now we have an immediate conversion from subcultural material to general cultural material.

MK Well, the historical countercultural materials have become part of our folk art. They have been passed down by so many gestures that anyone can produce this kind of cultural material—anyone knows how to make a Velvet Underground song, since three generations of kids have already done it.

SP It's not so much about quick appropriation, but it's more like a slow folding over time. Kids today don't need to think about how to make a Velvet Underground sound! It's become intuitive.

JD The Factory is always an important phenomenon in this sort of discussion. The Factory was a kind of matrix for the sort of symbolic and material cultural intersections that we're addressing here. To use the metaphor of folding that Stephen introduced, I think it is appropriate in relation to the Factory situation, particularly if we understand it as a place where there were significant transgressions of already institutionalized disciplinary segregations …

MK I don't know. I've always understood the Factory as a situation in which the high-mindedness of art was dispensed with, as if to say that art was as much a part of capitalism as any other cultural product.

SP Yes, but it is more like a kind of realism—a reflection that seemed to state, "This is really the way it is, and so this is a realist image."

MK Modernists have been coopting the world forever.

SP That's what realism is, though: it's a construction designed to respond to that which is, and so it was an explicit rendering of the way in which Warhol and his cohorts thought culture was produced and distributed. In this sense, there was nothing transgressive about the Factory.

MK I think it was only transgressive in a milieu such as New York City, where there was already a major culture industry built upon the maintenance of difference and division between practices …

JD I'm suggesting that Warhol understood this, and that they understood themselves to be somehow transgressive. They cultivated this posture, and marketed themselves as such. The Factory was a site that exteriorized a model of cultural interface and offered this model for public consumption. Today this model of cultural interface is already built into the practices of younger musicians and artists, and the public eats it up.

MK An interface between what and what? There's no high and low anymore—what is the nature of this interface? There is no interfacing today.

JD Well, distinctions between high and low still exist, whether we like it or not. I certainly don't like it on a conceptual level, but these two figures still float around …

MK I'd have to be convinced of this. I don't know what the signifiers for high and low are at this point.

JD Perhaps this is also a semantic issue, and how certain phrases are used in a particular context …

SP Well, it's not only a semantic question, but also a deeper separation between aesthetics and politics. I suppose that's what you were suggesting, Mike, when you said earlier that there was no fundamental separation between visual art culture and music culture in your youth; that there wasn't a separation between countercultural politics and the way you would work as a musician, artist, writer, whatever.

MK Also, it's important to remember that once you stand outside of your particular cultural community where all the terms are established, you learn that these things may mean something very different in another context.

JD In both of your cases, you've performed as musicians, or performers, so you have entered into the symbolic and material economy of club cultures.

MK Yes, I think this is where Steve and I have somewhat different positions. Since I've known him, Steve has incorporated his musical works into his production in general. This ended for me when I stopped doing performances, which were very structural works. Since that point, music has become more recreational for me, something akin to doing sports. I would make no claim for its artistic worth. And that's the difference between Steve and myself, perhaps. To me it's experimental, and maybe I can learn things from it. But unlike my earlier production when I was doing art performance, I used sound in a way that had particular meanings—it was meant to be art. Now it's not.

SP My thought is that we do many things as productive agents in culture now. And as was stated earlier, much of this has to do with context. I recall Peter Nagy saying at one point, "Well, of course, we're going to show in galleries, we're educated in the system to do that, and we can have access to that because of our pedigree and our credentials. We can decide to exercise this pedigree or not." So it becomes a question of venue and the context in which you exercise certain kinds of ideas: either in a gallery or a museum. I make music. And that means that it can happen either in a concert hall, in a recorded situation, in a festival, in a rock club—it can happen all over the place. I'm an educator, too, so I work with artists who are practitioners in an educational context—but then I also teach film classes in that context. And so there are many different ways in which one can be productive at any given moment, and you realize that they're all operating in slightly different contexts, and that you're addressing different kinds of audiences at distinct moments—and with somewhat different ways of speaking.

MK For the most part, the younger audiences that see what I do in clubs have not experienced this type of situation before. Or, if they have, it probably signifies something countercultural to them; for me, it doesn't.

SP When I make pop music, I draw upon all of my resources to make decisions. I suppose I do consider the music to be a part of my art production, but I don't refer to it as art music, per se.

MK I'm attempting to find a way to think about my interest in sound and performance as a kind of art practice again. But many of my assumptions are so historically rooted at this point that unless it's nostalgic, it can't be art. The older you get, the harder it becomes. When I first started doing performance, I didn't know exactly where I was going, but it ended up in an art sound that was quite complex—it meant something in an art context, on ideological and other levels. And then I reached a point where it didn't make sense any more.

SP And it's not so much that you can figure out the next historical imperative to seize. You have an assessment of what you've done, what is possible at the moment, and then you make an attempt. But in terms of popular culture, I've always taken pop music very seriously because you have to account for its reception: how it connects with so many people, how the synthetic spectacle operates. I would think that there's still a way to make popular music with a kind of critical investment.

MK I think so too, but it would have to avoid the kind of ironic superiority that seems to be so prevalent in today's situation. We're in a contradictory period, in which people soak in the popular culture because it's there and then articulate a privileged, superior relationship to that same material. And this is why it so difficult to work in popular forms. Often what we get is the production of nostalgia for a known time of resistance: tropes of resistance return, the music doesn't operate politically.

JD So you're suggesting that these recycled music idioms do not carry a kind of political charge or a social detonation …

MK It can, if it's framed in a particular way, but not in and of itself—not when the form itself is no longer shocking.

The Dance Floor in the Gallery: Piotr Uklanski's *Untitled (Dance Floor)*

Revised version of text on Piotr Uklanski's *Untitled (Dance Floor)* at Gavin Brown's Enterprise, 1996. Originally published in *Artforum*, April 1997, p. 95.

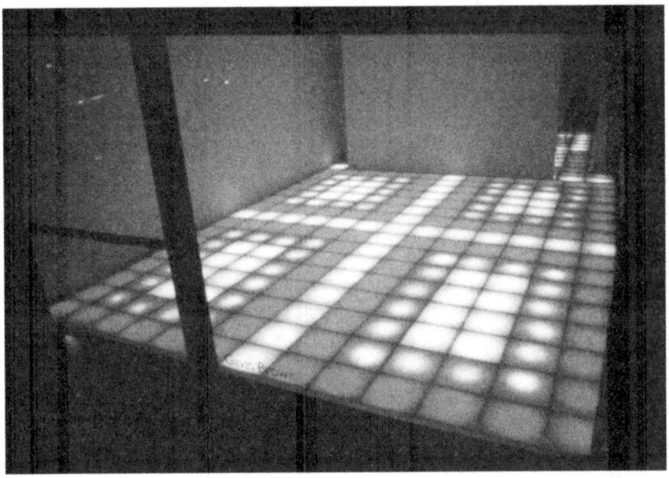

Piotr Uklanski, *Untitled (Dance Floor)*, 1996

By installing a dance floor in Gavin Brown's gallery, Piotr Uklanski staged a tongue-in-cheek transformation of this space, invoking a 1970s-era milieu just a few hustle (or boogie) steps away from that archetypal discotheque set in the *Saturday Night Fever* movie. With an economy of formal means, the raised structure—made from Plexiglas and colored lightbulbs—was designed to also function as a temporary substitute for the gallery's existing floors. The grid of multicolored lights had been programmed to flash in synch with the beats and rhythms of the songs, suggesting an automated DJ system. For some reason, the mid-1990s have witnessed a certain amount of nostalgia for the halcyon days of 1970s disco culture: actor John Travolta has made a triumphant comeback; music group The Bee Gees were recently honored by the American Music Awards as International Artists of the Year; KC and the Sunshine Band's

"That's the Way I Like It" has resurfaced as a jingle for a Burger King television commercial; and more than a few fashion designers have resurrected leotards and synthetic fabrics evocative of 20 years ago. Wisely, however, Uklanski sought to defuse this nostalgia bomb, at least to a certain extent: rather than inundating visitors with a hit list of period-specific disco music, various musical genres drift through the space, including Techno.

The aesthetics of Uklanski's luminous, dance floor-as-installation suggested a meeting place between a pre-fab Pop culture ethos (this was not a readymade dance floor, even though it simulated this condition), and a somewhat irreverent referencing of historical codes of Modernist geometric abstraction, aspects of Minimalism (imagine Dan Flavin designing a dance floor), and perhaps even a nod to the California Light and Space artists. It was a clever, witty spin on the typically sober results of site-specific strategies. By covering both the public area of the gallery space, as well as the quasi-private office area, Uklanski engineered a transformation that proposed a kind of equivalence, challenging spatial hierarchies and territorial divisions. Uklanski's gesture might suggest a type of social sculpture, wherein an environment or platform is constructed for the audience, for viewers, so that they become, in a sense, central to the artwork. So, after eating curry or practicing electric guitar within the environs of a Rirkrit Tiravanija project, why not go dancing in—or rather on—a Uklanski? Were we meant to lose ourselves in the hypnotic pulsing colors of the dance floor? It would seem, that yes, feel-good aesthetics was certainly part of the desired effect here. And, after visiting the gallery, it occurred to me that the party atmosphere would have been enhanced by the presence of a cluster of Warhol's silver, helium-filled balloons—floating just beneath the gallery's ceiling.

Coincidentally, shortly after Uklanski's project was de-installed from Gavin Brown's gallery, a specially commissioned Dan Flavin light sculpture went up in the windows of Calvin Klein's new store on Manhattan's Upper East Side. It seemed that a rather perversely appropriate convergence had occurred, somehow connecting the Uklanski and the Flavin. In Flavin's case, his context-specific effort within a space of commerce and fashion only reaffirmed Minimalism's descent into a corporate-ready aesthetic. In Uklanski's case, his dance floor appeared to flaunt the sad condition that Minimalism now finds itself in, by reanimating a Minimalist idiom through the filter of Studio 54 aesthetics. Oddly enough though, at least from my reading, Flavin's project succeeded (if inadvertently) as merely an inspired ornamentation for shopping; i.e., perhaps the light sculptures could no longer be considered art … but rather interior design in the context of a shop. Whereas Uklanski sought to playfully provoke a situation in which the question was no longer whether the dance floor was art (it was, of course, a sculptural installation), but if it was designed to function primarily as a framing device—or catalyst—for socializing and partying. Perhaps this is all to be expected when it seems that, as we approach the end of the millennium, art's greatest aspiration is to inhabit the glorious superficiality of entertainment and fashion culture.

The Sailboat in the Museum: Jorge Pardo's *Untitled*

Revised version of a text on Jorge Pardo's *Untitled* (1997), at the Museum of Contemporary Art, Chicago, January 25–March 13, 1997. Originally published in *Artforum*, Summer 1997.

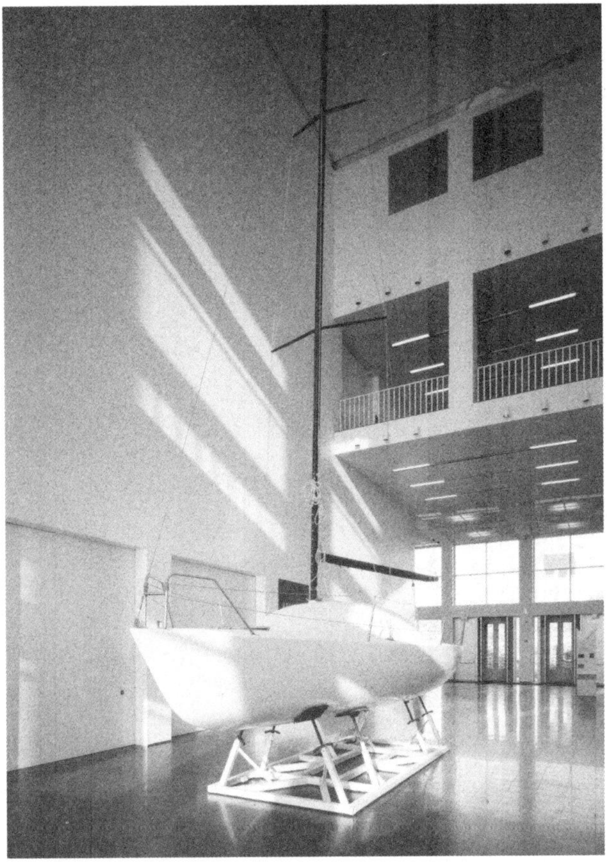

Jorge Pardo, *Untitled*, 1997

Had you visited the new MCA building in Chicago within the past few months, you would have stumbled upon a gorgeous white sailboat placed in dry dock within the museum's dramatic four-story atrium. Appearances, however, are nowadays somewhat deceiving, particularly in a time when art often camouflages itself as something else so as to become art. A sailboat is art is a sailboat.

The main element of Jorge Pardo's exhibition project, *Untitled* (1997) is both more and less than what it appears to be, or may be in actuality. It is, to a certain extent, an adjusted readymade: a racing boat (the Santa Cruz 27, originally created by famous designer Bill Lee), or more precisely the shell of a Santa Cruz 27, the interior of which has been only nominally modified, obliquely reflecting Pardo's interest in the architectural design of Rudolph Schindler's 1922 home. The other component of Pardo's project is a series of displays (installed in a separate, upstairs gallery space) that change on a weekly basis over a nearly three-month duration. The second week, for example, featured a Martin Puryear sculpture from the MCA's collection, along with a Frank Gehry dining set. In the following week, Pardo displayed artworks made by his young nephews, including hilarious yet artful renditions of the *Beavis and Butt-Head* cartoon characters. This MCA exhibition is somewhat mirrored by a project underway for the Museum of Contemporary Art in Los Angeles. Pardo is constructing a house in the Mount Washington neighborhood of LA, in which he will install works from MOCA's collection on a rotating basis.

So many things to recontextualize within the museum—but so little time. Artists often remind us that the putative real world is just an inexhaustible reservoir of stuff waiting to be appropriated. It is no wonder that we still look to R. Mutt's legendary urinal as the archetype of all adjusted readymades, and as one of the most inspired acts of irreverent vanguard aesthetic transfiguration. Indeed, some of today's most intriguing art, like Pardo's, inevitably evokes Duchamp—the great patriarch who received God's found-object law on the mountaintop, and led us to the promised land where everyday artifacts were conjugated as elements of an expanded art language and vehicles of theorization. It is therefore perhaps not so ironic that Pardo's 26-foot-long sailboat shares with the urinal one important characteristic: not only that each object left behind its utilitarian existence for a new life as aesthetic material (Pardo's water craft can be sailed, yet it is difficult to piss into an upside-down toilet), but more significantly that both are white. This may seem an irrelevant coincidence, yet it suggests that the visual condition of whiteness itself may be a signifier for conceptual activity: whiteness as a filtering system, a bridging device, across or through which other ideas, associations, and sensations may travel. Understood on these terms, the iconic urinal is not merely a new breed of sculptural thought-object, but is also a discourse on the complexities of gender and sexuality. Likewise, Pardo's iconic sailboat is more than a resplendent high-design (adjusted) readymade: it assumes the condition of a tabula rasa, a blank writing tablet upon which is inscribed—and through which are symbolically filtered—the artist's series of weekly presentations. Conversely, we are invited to contemplate these changeable displays as analogs to the boat: rendering the ordinary aesthetic, weeks four and seven featured a variety of adhesives (e.g., Band-Aids) collected in the Chicago area, elegantly displayed upon white, floor-hugging, pedestal-like units. In relation to Pardo's furniture-inflected installations and candy-like lamps, these sticky works exude a provisional quality that is at once naive and refined.

Propped upon a skeletal cradle, the black mast reaches toward a skylight recessed in the ethereal ceiling. The sailboat has been oriented in the direction of Lake Michigan, located just a few blocks away from the museum and viewable through a series of glass partitions from the fourth-floor gallery (overlooking the atrium space). Pardo engineers a stable formal marriage between the austere white neo-modernism of the Josef Paul Kleihues-designed museum space and the craft's immaculate, refined contours, yet shrewdly insinuates an undercurrent of doubt within the situation: why, after all, is there a sailboat parked in the middle of a museum?

CHAPTER V

Negotiating Convivial Dispersals

Revised version of essay published in the exhibition catalogue of *Waves In Particles Out* at the CCA: Centre for Contemporary Arts, Glasgow, Scotland, October 24–December 5, 1997.

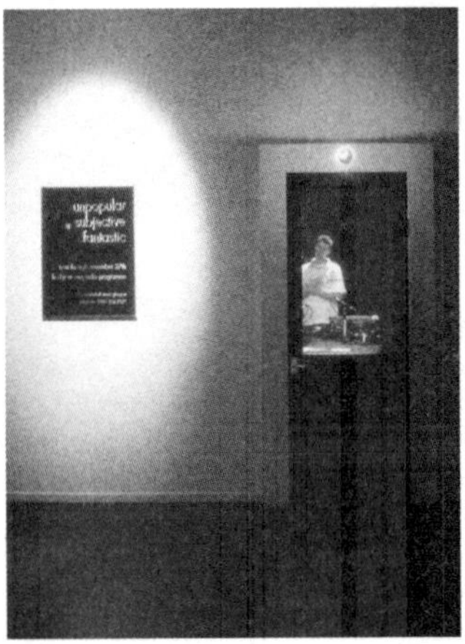

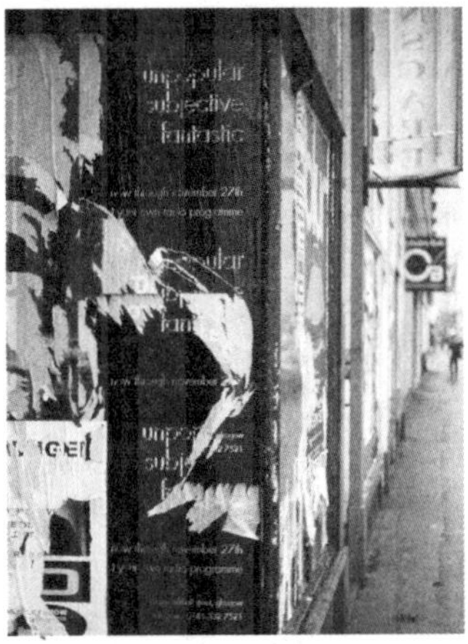

Lincoln Tobier, *Unpopular Subjective Fantastic*, 1997
Lincoln Tobier, *Unpopular Subjective Fantastic*, 1997 (street view with posters)

Certain artists endeavor to redistribute the conceptual and material processes of art making into what is perceived as the territory of social everydayness; by everydayness, I mean the interpenetration of art activity and life activity that becomes ritualized through art practice as yet another dimension of daily social existence. These processes are understood to be co-extensive with an aesthetic that defines itself as post-aesthetic.

Yet, we may no longer worry about this apparently contradictory logic, this lovely circularity. Long live the moribund avant-garde—i.e., the avant-garde of Fluxus, Happenings and event-based art—with its claims of exploding expertise, or replacing expertise with a dilettante experimentalism that celebrates freedom and access. Artists such as Lincoln Tobier (who utilizes radio as an instrument of flexible and accessible communication for alienated publics) and Henrik Hakansson (who develops frame works of inter-species discourse that transgress normative disciplinary and biological borders) have injected irony, doubt, and reflexive humor into their respective practices so as to question the utopianist or social-scientific ideologies that have traditionally been attached to participatory and institutional critique strategies—such as Allan Kaprow's Happenings, Hans Haacke's sociopolitical interrogations of cultural contradiction, or Michael Asher's museological dislocations.

Where is the Rauschenbergian gap between art and life? What does it look like? Tobier is endeavoring to open up the self-contained structure or language of art to a public that is fundamentally alienated from specialized culture: constructed social situations set into motion the signifying conditions of his art practice. With Tobier's limited-range radio stations (which have been produced in Los Angeles, Paris, New York, and now Glasgow), the public has an opportunity to access a relatively old-fashioned communication system as a way to *perform* (i.e., broadcast) themselves into an extended social space—out and into the airwaves. Irony is built into Tobier's strategy: his putative opening-up of mass media signals the relatively circumscribed range of artistic transmission.

When does an organized social event become analogous to an art activity? When the artist—and the context of the artist's activity—endows the social event with an art condition. Artists such as Tobier, Hakansson, Jonnie Wilkes, and Piotr Uklanski map their distinctive relations to this notion. In a sense, they reinforce the idea that art making is more than a materialized conceptual activity—it is also a form of social activity that occurs in relation to shared cultural languages and rituals.

Recombinant culture suggests a loose, mobile, fluid, fugitive organization of distinct social, institutional, linguistic, and visual particles that spin around, inflect, and alter each other. Today's material, symbolic, ideological, and psychological cross-pollinations are generated across distinct systems, and build upon each other like organic architectures—expending and contracting, reshaping, mutating, producing hybrid languages and a welcome confusion of categories, functions, values, and protocols. In a maneuver that subtly reverses the strategy of remaking a non-art event inside the institutional context of art, Jonnie Wilkes—in collaboration with other DJ's and recording artists from the Glasgow electronic music scene—will set up a recording studio in the city under the name Voder Show. For Wilkes, the studio is not to be understood as the product of a conceptual process, but rather as a real situation that happens to coincide with an art exhibition. What results might be understood as a deliberately inadvertent parallel between the framework of the recording studio and the framework of the art institution, which means that a new social relation (both symbolic and actual) unfolds in-between the distinct subcultural worlds of music and art.

All of art's gestures toward similitude with so-called *reality* make sense only as metaphor, symbolism, or allegory. Take, for example, Hakansson's wonderfully fantastic scenarios involving both literal and metaphorical conjunctions between the communication systems of insects, amphibians, and humans. In Hakansson's world, crickets are enlisted as rock stars to play their natural sounds in venues around the globe, and frogs are invited to mix their throaty calls with the aural environment of trance-music. This is the stuff of wild imagination: impossibly possible cross-species socializations that are charmingly irrational, suggestive of children's fairy tales spun through the filter of youth subculture. With this lively interface between the discipline of zoology and the ritualized entertainments of club music or the pop concert, Hakansson invents an alternately utopian and dystopic social space that aligns laboratory methodology with the sublime absurdities of dreaming.

Hakansson, Tobier, Wilkes, and Uklanski may want to redefine the condition of artifice in such a way that everyday life appears increasingly more aesthetic than art practice itself. Within the various genres that constitute the realm of post-object and post-studio art today, there has been a general tendency to suggest that a penetration of reality somehow guarantees authenticity—i.e., an experience of realness that is understood to be not only symbolically but also materially closer in spirit to quotidian reality. Occasionally, as with Uklanski's pulsating dance floor, a vernacular structure that signifies a specific cultural ritual of social interaction and leisure is replicated (i.e., remade) within the context of the gallery or the museum. In this humorous recontextualizing of a seminal icon from the era of disco culture within the present context, Uklanski smartly plays into the more generalized nostalgic recuperation of American-style 1970s culture, while also using an architectonic-sculptural installation as the literal support structure for a social event. A continuous dance party in the museum? With the lights flashing to the beats and rhythms of music selected by artist and audience, there really is no choice but to get up and boogie the day and night away: here, the participatory logic is fundamental, and contagious in the extreme.

Yet what happens after all the social events have been staged, and all the transmissions sent—when the music stops, the lights are dimmed, the domesticated crickets and frogs returned to their indigenous habitats, and the radio stations cease broadcasting? What then, after life-activity has caught up with art-activity, and art-activity with life-activity? Implosion, explosion, or exhaustion? Or perhaps, just television.

The Bonvicini Factor

Revised version of an essay originally published in the catalogue of Monica Bonvicini's exhibition, *Scream and Shake*, at MAGASIN – Centre National d'Art Contemporain, Grenoble, June 3–September 2, 2001, p. 10–16. The exhibition traveled to P.S. 1 Contemporary Art Center, New York, and Kunst-Werke, Berlin.

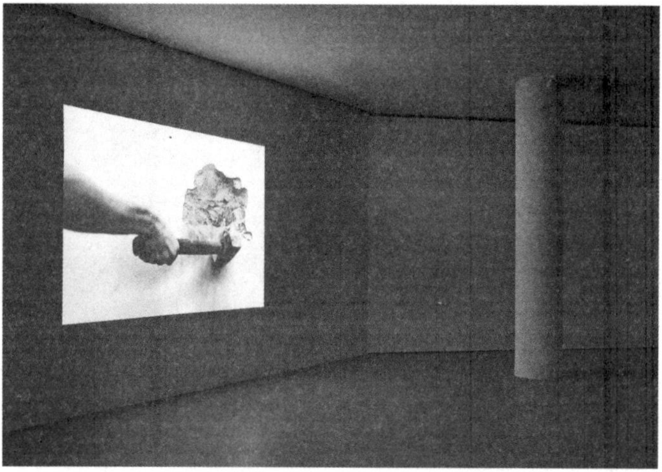

Monica Bonvicini, *Hammering Out (an old argument)*, 1998

What do you want from art today? This is the sort of question that rattles around inside my brain on almost a daily basis. Do I want from art what I cannot get from anything else in life? Sometimes, I still would like art to challenge all forms of authority. This may just be an old-fashioned desire. My confession for today: I just want to be fucked-up by art, in the most positive sense of that expression.

I would like art to tear down the walls of protocol, to explode conventionality, to hammer down the walls of institutional malaise, to make lots of trouble, to give me more than sufficient pleasure, to make me think differently. Art should aspire to be as extreme as possible, whatever its methodology or language. This is not asking too much, is it? In a sense, perhaps, I would like vanguard art to fulfill its basic, conventional societal function: to satisfy those needs (intellectual, sexual, political, etc.) that cannot be gratified elsewhere in my daily life. If art can no longer provide these symbolic—and ephemeral—satisfactions, I no longer have time for it. If art is merely pleasant entertainment, or an academic folly, life is too short for such frivolities. One can find more than enough distraction and frivolousness in popular culture, but art's job is still distinct from television, movies, and fashion magazines, even though such distinctions are sometimes blurred.

Monica Bonvicini's work is smartly irreverent. Perhaps, art is one of the few things that still may have the potential to be genuinely irreverent today. By genuine irreverence I mean gestures that are not swiftly recuperated in the name of sheer entertainment value, or nullified by their commodity status. Bonvicini conveys, through the artifice of art's language, a playful disbelief in institutional structures, and how sexual hegemonies are transmitted through built space.

It is apparent that Bonvicini would like to resist the tremendous pressure exerted upon artists to produce commodifiable things—i.e., merely baubles of the creative process. Of course, nothing really escapes the commodity status in our hyper-consumer culture, not even sex and death. But, there are strategies that artists can use to at least articulate dissent. In Bonvicini's case, process-oriented and performance-inflected strategies characterize many of her videos, installations, and other hybrid productions. For Bonvicini, every act of material transformation is also an opportunity for ideological, social, and political intervention.

For example, *Plastered* (1998) is an architecturally specific work that undergoes continuous alteration—in fact, deterioration—over the duration of its presentation in a space. When visitors walk upon the layer of plaster that has been installed over the space's actual floor, Bonvicini's false floor is crushed by the weight of bodies. The interplay between construction and destruction, between structural integrity and structural entropy, pervades much of Bonvicini's work. In a sense, meaning is suspended between these two states, or mutually interdependent conditions. *Plastered* is fundamentally a process-oriented work that relies upon the presence of the audience to trigger material transformations; it is as if the audience becomes integral to the eventual formal constitution of the work—as if the audience were performing the deconstruction of the work.

Bonvicini's work investigates the inherent aesthetic-political significations of architectural language, tearing away at superficial order to reveal something irrational, disordered, corporeal, entropic, erotic, sexualized—desublimated from beneath the surface.

In the video *Hammering Out (an Old Argument)* (1998), we observe what may be a woman's hands using a hammer to smash an area of a wall, exposing the underlying bricks. The video suggests that once you have broken through the initial layer, you encounter yet another layer. Perhaps this is a way of suggesting that all art is in some way an act of conceptual repetition, even as artists repeatedly endeavor to tear down the walls of history. Bonvicini acknowledges this paradox throughout her various works.

On certain occasions, every once in a while, a work of art takes you by surprise, arrests you for a moment, makes you think differently for a few days, even gets you off. Bonvicini's *Wallfuckin'* (1995) had this startling effect on me, which is why it is the primary focus of this text. Bonvicini has come up with one of the best titles ever for an artwork, and this is no small accomplishment; the title *Wallfuckin'* is both direct and ambiguous, frank and mysterious—just like the work itself. And yes, I derived pleasure from watching a video of a woman holding onto the edge of a wall, rubbing her body and—in particular—her sexual parts, against the architecture. I am not ashamed to admit that, as a heterosexual male, this did hold some erotic and libidinal appeal for me. The video created a force field of sexual energy that any viewer would appreciate—regardless of gender, sexual orientation, or politics.

Is the woman in Bonvicini's video engaged in a unique, customized ritual of self-arousal? If this is an act of masturbation, is it designed (or destined) only for herself, or also for an audience? Is it the exteriorization of an intimate process of self-pleasuring? Or, is she marking her territory, suggesting a process of recoding the neutral, generic architectural edifice? In other words, endowing a space that might be considered as gender-neutral (but which is, at least in historical terms, associated with the male gender) with the codes of female physicality and sexuality? And there is a related issue: the significance of the architectural enclosure in which the video monitor is located. Bonvicini has placed it on the floor, surrounded by an unfinished drywall structure. We might ask what the relationship is between the literal architectural walls, and the wall that we see in the video? Are we meant to imagine that Bonvicini shot the video within the space that we are actually occupying? The suggestion of this possibility is sufficient to provoke another level of psychological engagement from the viewer. Symbolically, perhaps, we can imagine ourselves performing this sexual dance in—and on—the architecture. As in Bonvicini's *I Believe in the Skin of Things as in that of Women* (1999), we are invited to consider the skin of the architecture as a corporeal surrogate, a material that connotes the material presence of the body. As that work suggests, architecture has generally been coded in terms of male sexuality—in particular, the hard-edge Euclidean geometries of high modernism, and reductive Minimalism.

In *Wallfuckin'*, the woman's identity is not revealed to us; her head and face are withheld from the field of vision. Bodily abstraction, and objectification, pervade. Perhaps this is a deliberate, albeit ironic, gesture to keep the woman's face outside the frame, deferring our ability—and impulse—to seek a certain kind of identification. In other words, a strategy designed to defer a certain level of gratification and symbolic possession. This could be read as a critique of how women's sexuality has been traditionally objectified within popular culture, and a push back against those who regard women as willing victims of a male gaze that fetishizes their bodies.

In the *Wallfuckin'* installation, the codified system of desiring gazes is short-circuited. We are not allowed to complete a process of identification with the individual. This suggests that the viewer has the opportunity to imagine projecting him- or herself *into the place* of that woman. There is a dialogical relationship between the depicted interior space of the video on the one hand, and how we occupy the literal space of the architecture on the other. The video dwells within its own platform, which functions as a stage set and framing device. A related dynamic is generated in Bonvicini's *Hausfrau Swinging* (1997), in which a woman—her face masked by a house-like form—performs a sequence of movements in front of an architectural structure. As in *Wallfuckin'*, the video monitor is displayed on the floor directly in front of what appears to be the identical architectural structure. This effectively produces visual and spatial tautology.

It is tenable to suggest that Bonvicini's relationship to rigid structures (formal, architectural, and ideological) that have historically been gendered as male—and her reflection on the female body as a site of sexual and political contestation—might be informed by certain precursors. Bonvicini seems to have an indirect kinship—attitudinal, if not methodological—with Lynda Benglis, whose postminimalist works from the early 1970s played with the language of orthodox Minimalism. This was especially evident in her notorious 1974 advertisement in *Artforum* magazine, where Benglis appeared naked (with sunglasses), straddling a huge dildo. Funny and provocative, the ad was a targeted critique of the apparently masculinist tendencies of the high (male) priest of Minimalism, Robert Morris. Benglis' ad responded to a poster Morris had made for his 1974 show at Castelli-Sonnabend Gallery. In it, a shirtless Morris (grease accentuating his muscled upper torso) is adorned only with a spiky metal collar around his neck, a heavy chain draped over his body, dark sunglasses, and a German WW2 helmet on his head (Benglis and Morris were apparently lovers at the time).

In *Wallfuckin'* it remains unclear if it is Bonvicini herself who is featured in the video. I think not, but it is really of minor importance, although there are undoubtedly viewers who may have a benign curiosity, or a prurient preoccupation, in identifying the young naked woman who appears to be engaged in an autoerotic act with the architecture. By frustrating our ability to identify, Bonvicini illuminates how desire operates. There is also something within *Wallfuckin'* that is reminiscent of the profane spirit of Vito Acconci's works from the 1970s. Of course, Acconci often made explicit reference to his own body, which functioned as the artist's reflexive site for many a memorable ritualistic intervention. Yet, something compels me to imagine a transhistorical interconnection between Acconci's *Seedbed* and Bonvicini's *Wallfuckin'*.

Art is fundamentally paradoxical: it may have the capacity to provoke us to think critically about our lives, it may allow us to question certain dominant constructions of power, gender, and sexuality. However, art operates within a relatively insular—and insulated—system that sometimes reproduces those same problematic constructions of power, gender and sexuality. This is a difficult contradiction to accept. Bonvicini has developed her own cleverly profane approach to the ways in which power and authority are constructed; her work is at once intellectual and sensual, clinical yet sexy. Whether or not we label Bonvicini as a feminist or activist artist is really not the key issue. The real question is whether Bonvicini's anti-establishment spirit will continue to resist—at least on symbolic terms—an art world preoccupied with commerce and power. Hopefully, she will continue hammering away. Because that is what I still want from art and artists today.

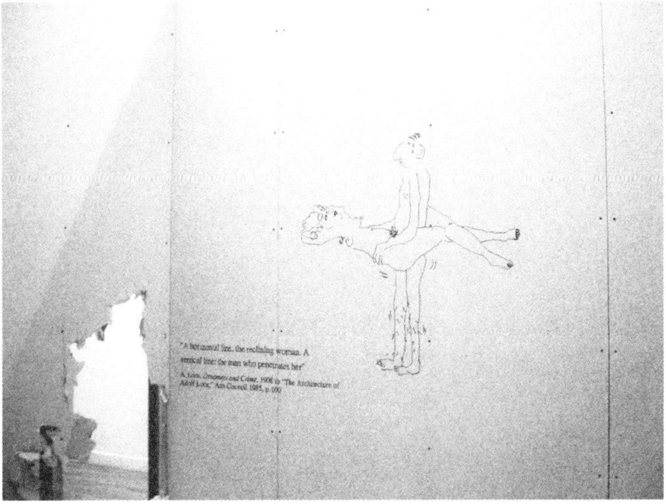

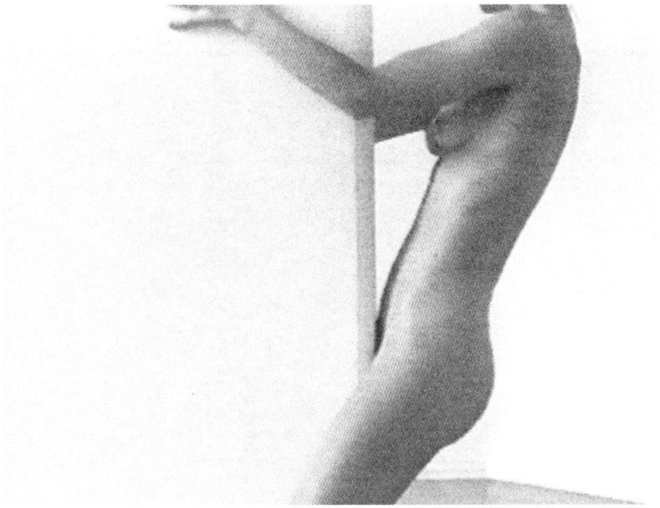

Monica Bonvicini, *I Believe in the Skin of Things as in that of Women*, 1999
Monica Bonvicini, *Wallfuckin'*, 1995

CHAPTER VI
What Do We Want from Exhibitions?

The Desire for documenta

Revised version of an essay originally published in special edition of *Texte zur Kunst* on documenta IX in 1992 (Winter 1992).

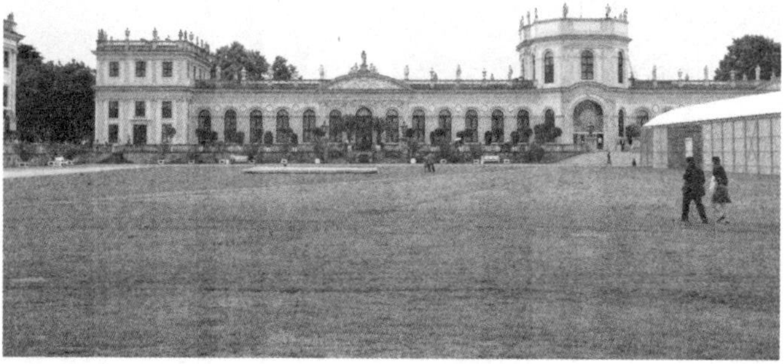

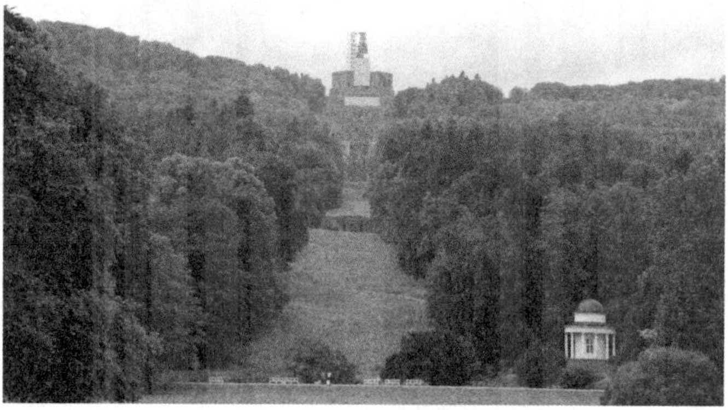

The grounds of documenta XII, Kassel, June 2007

Utilizing Isabelle Graw and Stefan Germer's concept statement for this event (entitled "documenta as Anachronistic Event") as a springboard for some critical reflections, I was initially struck by their suggestion that the art critics and art historians (among other cultural producers) who were invited to deliver speeches today should be, and I quote, "willing to take their socially assigned role as experts literally." While I endorse their strategic attempt to pose a critical intervention at documenta through the virtual circumvention of that institution's logic of incorporation (i.e., the refusal to conduct a structured public dialogue with documenta's organizers, and so to some extent avoiding complicity with an officially sanctioned institutional collaboration), I am less comfortable with the notion that it is necessary to reinforce the socially defined role or task of our so-called expertise as a prerequisite for examining the political, cultural, ideological, social, artistic, and economic implications of the type of large-scale international exhibition epitomized by documenta.

Indeed, such an investment in the language and practice of disciplinary expertise or specialization, particularly in the realm of art history and art criticism, may serve to reproduce the very same relations of power that facilitate the authority of certain dominant cultural institutions and international exhibition platforms (like documenta, the Whitney Museum's Biennial, The Carnegie International, et al.). To understand critique as a method of developing a framework for the dialogical analysis of specific cultural practices, situations, or symptoms (as opposed to mere negation), we must take care not to inadvertently reconfirm the questionable authority granted to us as cultural experts or academic specialists, since this is the same logic of authority exercised by the very individuals and institutions that we seek to not only critically deconstruct, but also to challenge. Although many of us have been supposedly trained (as art historians, artists, philosophers, sociologists, cultural critics, etc.) to assume the social role of expert, and are therefore inevitably implicated in a desire for some form of institutional legitimation (the university post, an editorial position, as obvious examples), it is our intellectual obligation to contest not only the pernicious segregation of disciplinary categories and functions that occurs when critiques of the museum or exhibition are restricted to so-called experts and specialists within the field, but also to invent newlanguages and practices which can defy the hegemony of intellectual specialization. We must undermine the tautological insularity of a revisionist art critical and historical methodology which claims to analyze cultural institutions and production in terms of a wider framework of political, economic, and ideological relations, but invariably spirals back into the circularity of a discipline-specific discourse and protocol.

The methods we use as critics and historians may be as anachronistic or obsolete as the curatorial-organizational model used in documenta. Let us reflect critically upon our individual agendas and investments in the type of critical intervention occurring today in Kassel—what do we find?

Let us reflect upon our desire to construct ourselves as critical outsiders, all the while engaging in a sophisticated insiders' game.

Today's large-scale international shows continue to play upon the art world's desire for figures of authority to locate, organize, and provide representations of what they deem to be important or provocative contemporary art. Like any proposed representation of cultural production, a narrative is constructed so as to legitimate curatorial selections, arguments; a fiction is materialized in the form of a specific organization and display of objects or practices within (or outside of) the museum—as (self)appointed cultural experts, we participate in the construction of this grand fiction, simply by following established disciplinary protocols of institutional critique. So, in response to one of the questions proposed by Isabelle and Stefan ("Who is defining the canon of contemporary art?"), I would suggest that, on a rather obvious level, this "canon" is constructed and maintained through certain laws of consensus or contracts of agreement (among artists, critics, art historians, curators, dealers, collectors, et al.) that regulate it as a collective fiction. The perpetual revision and rewriting of art historical narratives (whether due to new research materials, or shifts in methodology) is emblematic of a continuous struggle among experts in the field to produce (or reproduce) their authority.

A fictional construct that claims purchase on truth, vanguard visual art culture promises what it cannot deliver: exemption from the rational laws and protocol of society. documenta has institutionalized these cultural contradictions.

Today, in Kassel, we are performing the almost obligatory, if not anachronistic, ritual of critiquing an institutional logic that we desire to condemn—and are condemned to desire. Without wanting to sound unduly cynical, we might not be posing a critical intervention in Kassel if documenta IX had accommodated the specific artistic, cultural, and ideological-political interests of the organizers of today's event—many of which this writer does happen to concur with. And, finding agreement with Edward Said, I would reiterate that criticism must never relinquish its "suspicion of totalizing concepts … its discontent with reified objects … its impatience with guilds, special interests, imperialized fiefdoms, and orthodox habits of mind … "

Back to Babel: *Project Unité*, Firminy

Revised version of an essay (co-authored with Olivier Zahm) originally published in *Artforum*, November 1993.

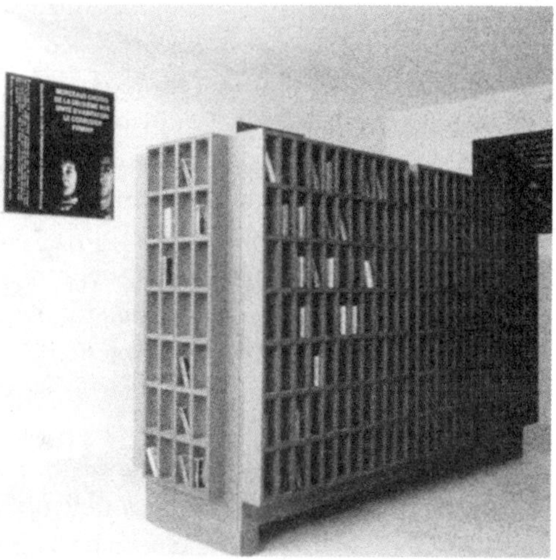

Clegg & Guttmann, *The Open Music Library*, 1993

Le Corbusier's *Unité d'Habitation*, a monumental block of low-income apartments awkwardly wedged into the hills surrounding the small city of Firminy in France, may once have functioned as a beacon of hope; now it bears witness to a return of the repressed—capitalism in crisis haunting the house of high Modernism. Completed in 1967 as part of a larger complex including a youth center, a stadium, and a church, the building was intended as a visionary response to the economic disenfranchisement caused by rapid industrialization. Continuing recession, however, has sharply reduced the local population, and many of those who remain prefer individual residences. Today the *Unité* stands half empty.

French curator Yves Aupetitallot selected the Corbusier building for his project precisely because of its symbolic complexity—its status as both a monument of France's greatest modern architect and a model for the reinvention of urban communal living. He envisioned the site as a catalyst for European and American artists, designers, and architects to establish a temporary society, a microcosm (paralleling the micro-society of the inhabitants) in which they would reexamine preconceptions about the broader cultural meaning of their practices.

Project Unité was not the only exhibition in Europe in 1993 animated by a desire to reinvent relations between art, culture, politics, and society. For the most recent incarnation of Sonsbeek, the international sculpture show in Arnhem, Holland, the American curator Valerie Smith chose artists who rejected traditional public art approaches, and encouraged them to rethink their methodologies in relation to actual social environments. In doing so, she advanced the idea that art, released from its institutional cage—though still tethered to an institutional leash—can at least be an agent of social commentary, if not transformation. But Aupetitallot's show constituted a considerably more radical attempt to escape institutional limits into the extrinsic social domain, by replacing the art institution with a functioning community—one that already symbolized, within a *living monument* to an unfulfilled utopian pragmatics, a grand, if flawed, integration of art, architecture, design, national culture, economic, politics, and the social. In effect, the participants were asked to assume the role of inhabitants and to reflect upon collective living within the machinery of Corbusier's social architecture. Each apartment became a symbolic space for cultural exploration as well as surrogate studio or gallery, while the building as a whole was transformed from a residence into a laboratory (re: Bauhaus) that doubles as a readymade museum.

Participants were invited to begin researching both the town and the building more than a year before the opening of the project; the results of their investigations and their dialogue with Aupetitallot helped shape the final form of the project. Much of this developmental work has been documented in a continuing series of newsletters and catalogues that underscore Aupetitallot's understanding of the project as an ongoing process as well as finished exhibition *product.*

But how then were we to evaluate the works themselves? According to what criteria? In practical terms, the structure of the exhibition was somewhat conventional. Each participant was allotted an apartment on one floor of the building's empty north wing, and the projects were restricted to that area. As viewers, we were necessarily compelled to scrutinize the floor where the projects were located as a kind of autonomous, privileged site, and our relationship to the other residential part of the building remained peripheral. We moved through the row of apartments as if negotiating gallery rooms in a cultural space, and so were forced, ultimately, to confront each project as a distinct work, even though our criteria of evaluation had to take into account the unique contextual circumstances. The restriction, moreover, of the projects to one floor created a subtle but troubling feeling that this part of the complex was divorced from the occupied wing. It seemed as if the territorial divide between the cultural expert and the resident population had inadvertently generated a climate of alienation in which the experts, engaged in social analysis or subjective rumination, expected the residents to be cooperative—if estranged—witnesses (or accomplices) in the probing of their environment by outsiders. Not that Aupetitallot sought to produce such a logic of segregation; on the contrary, his apparent goal was to compel the participants to reflect upon these problems and if possible to engage the residents in a dialogue about them. And by evoking the utopia of Corbusier, he hoped to galvanize both the residents and the Firminy community in general to reconsider the values entrenched in Corbu's design ideology. But if Aupetitallot believed that the visitors and residents could somehow work collectively to develop a new type of intercultural engagement, the decision to limit projects to one floor seriously comprised this agenda, reinforcing the very us/them logic he sought to avoid.

The artists responded to the situation in diverse ways: some offered a revisionist institutional critique that examined the literal architectural and social conditions of the place, while others employed allegory and metaphor to articulate a relationship to the site. Swiss artist Christian Philipp Müller addressed himself to the very real problem of noise control, both in the thin-walled apartments and throughout the building, by hiring experts to record the sound levels. He then framed the graphic representations of the technician's tests and displayed them as surrogate artworks in his apartment, which was curtained with soundproofing material. Müller's sophisticated and witty examination revealed that Corbusier's desire to reinvent traditional notions of privacy by largely ignoring the psychological impact of the sound environment had been experienced by the residents as a crucial design flaw, if not an act of outright sadism visited upon them from the grave.

The relationship between the space of the exhibition and the space of the inhabitants was also taken up by a number of other participants, with varying degrees of effectiveness. American artist Renée Green lived in one of the vacant apartments for a week, using it as a monastic retreat in which to read books and reflect upon her new surroundings. The traces of Green's presence, indicated by various everyday artifacts as well as by video and audiotapes, marked the site-specificity of her lived engagement. By reproducing the conditions of what it might be like to inhabit an apartment, Green offered a kind of documentary fiction, a model of subjective experience that reflected the peculiar distance between the artist (as cultural tourist, masquerader, and infiltrating critic) and this unfamiliar environment. Austrian artist Heimo Zobernig transformed an apartment into a public café, cleverly offering a functional response to the question of what constitutes the difference between public and private space within quasi-collective living conditions. On the lighter side, American Jim Isermann covered an apartment's walls with his trademark moderne designs, evoking the pop flip side of sober high Modernism.

Ironically, very few of the participants directly engaged the residents in their projects. Exceptions included German artist Regina Möller, who, together with the children of some of the residents, created dollhouses as reflections upon Corbusier's concept of the apartment as a playful pedagogical space, and Clegg & Guttmann, whose *Firminy Music Library* was one of the strongest contributions. The pair asked residents to lend selections from their music collections, which were then taped and stored in a cabinet designed as a miniature of the Corbusier building—each tape placed in a slot corresponding to the location of the apartment from which it came. Although the names of the residents did not appear on the cassettes, their individuality emerged, through the agency of musical taste, against the backdrop of an environment defined by inexorable regularity. In a maneuver somewhat related to Clegg & Guttmann's project, the Italian team of Premiata Ditta examined the *Unité* as an organic community by creating a map that indicated the social relationships between residents in the building. Residents were given the opportunity to present photos of their own apartments, allowing us limited knowledge of their response to the predetermined architectural conditions. Sadly, their distinct personalities were only given visual form through the documentation of interior design decisions, and so remained on the level of abstraction, a condition that somehow reinforced the more pernicious effects of their environment.

In the realm of allegory and metaphor, there were collaborative projects by Mark Dion and Art Orienté Objet (a visionary look into the future of the building's ecosystem; a hypothesis that the only nature that could occupy Corbusier's model would be nature in a state of entropic decline; an apocalyptic landscape of Modernist decay and death), and by Dominique Gonzalez-Foerster and Anne Frémy (a critique of Corbusier's ethnocentric bias expressed through a reinterpretation of Jean Giraudoux's *Suzanne and the Pacific*, itself a rewriting of *Robinson Crusoe*, wherein civilization is reconstructed according to the logic of a grand unifying program that drowns cultural identity). French artist Philippe Parreno presented an idiosyncratic film about cultural masquerade, in which an art historian living in the Corbusier *Habitation* researches—or rehearses—a book on Modern art by impersonating famous artists, replacing the artists'voices with those of contemporary pop culture figures.

Although Aupetitallot included the work of architects, designers, video makers, and even painters (whose work ironically ended up being represented in the form of posters) in an attempt to challenge traditional divisions of cultural production, their presence, in contrast to that of installation artists, seemed mere tokenism. French designer Olivier Vedrine, by creating a reception area, commented upon the notion of a total design system (inspired by Corbusier's model of social architecture), and the *Unité* jacket designs by ABR Stuttgart—lab suits for a brave new future of administered fashion statements—provided only fleeting comic relief.

Without question, this was one of the more challenging exhibition projects to be mounted in many years, yet one could not help feeling that some of its shortcomings could have been readily avoided. For example, why were there no *collaborations* between the participating artists, architects, and designers? Such interactions could have broken down disciplinary boundaries—a process that might have been expected in such a context. Ultimately, however, relations of cultural authority and power remained largely unmolested, and it was business and art as usual: the itinerant group of cultural experts moved on to other projects, and the residents, perhaps somewhat enlightened by the transient encounter, were left behind to enjoy the privilege of living in an unquestionably depressing environment with only a dilapidated cultural pride for consolation.

On the Proliferation of Curatorial Programs, Biennials, and Institutional Bureaucracies

Revised version of a statement originally published in *Men in Black: Handbook of Curatorial Practice*, Künstlerhaus Bethanien, Berlin (Revolver Press, Frankfurt, 2004).

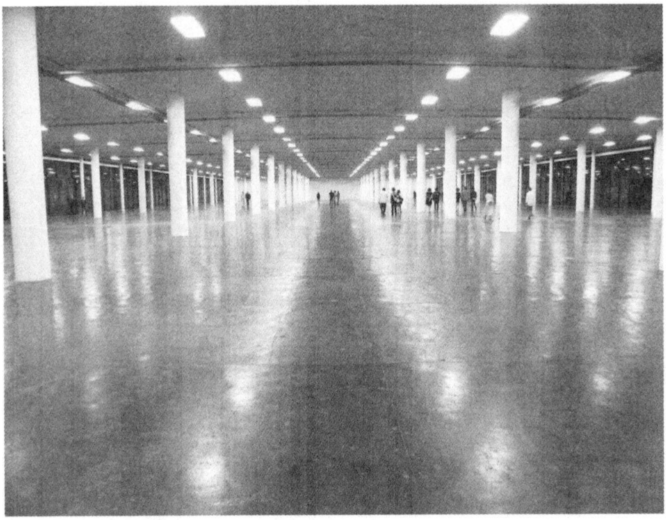

The second floor of Oscar Niemeyer's Bienal pavilion, during the 28th edition of the São Paulo Bienal, October 29, 2008

Although the mediation and distribution of art is never more significant than the production of art, the question of what constitutes art, per se, undergoes continuous redefinition and reevaluation. What curators do is related to some form of cultural production, whether we refer to it as cultural mediation, interpretation, distribution, or interlocution. Clearly, the languages, methods, and strategies of exhibition organization can be more or less "creative," conventional, challenging, bureaucratic, self-critical, non-critical (among other possible traits); what matters, however, is the constitution of subjectivity and inventiveness without the arrogance of authorial power. But do curators' programs function as engines of curatorial innovation, or do such programs actually encourage a certain kind of herd mentality in relation to curatorial protocol? I remain unsure.

An interesting yet annoying dual trend has emerged: it appears that as biennials proliferate in more and more cities in order to generate cultural tourism, the creation of curatorial programs has become a growth industry within academia and in non-academic contexts. Everyone wants to get in on the act of cultivating the next talent pool of cultural arbiters and mediators. As the product of one such program (the Whitney Museum ISP Program in the mid-1980s), I am well aware of the allure, strengths, and weaknesses of these contexts. I organized a major exhibition at the Center for Curatorial Studies Museum at Bard in the mid-1990s, taught curatorial students at CCS Bard, and recently designed a new graduate program at USC in Los Angeles to rethink the framework of an academic curatorial program in relation to the public sphere, and public space issues. Yet, a pragmatic question always returns: after we have prepared these ambitious graduate students to enter the ranks of professional curators, writers, and organizers, what kind of job opportunities will actually exist for them (beyond the art gallery context)? And, will those students saddled with loan debt (at least in the US context) be in an adequately solvent financial position to develop their own spaces or institutions?

If curating has become a more interesting and diversified field of activity over the past few years (a rather arguable assertion), is this evidence of the success of curatorial programs—or, in spite of such programs? It is difficult to say, I think. In some curators' programs, professional networking is generally privileged over critical thinking, and an uninteresting form of dilettantism gains ground over self-critical experimentation. In certain circumstances, it is no longer possible to maintain a laboratory or think-tank environment in which methods and frameworks are deeply investigated. In other words, many programs appear to operate according to an ideology of the vocational: that professionalization and managerial expertise should be the final result of curatorial programs. Should this be the desired result? And, on the other hand, do we really just want to produce the next generation of nomadic, international curator-luminaries?

I have, however, been asked by the editors to respond directly to two questions:

> Is the current "Guggenheim-ization" of the art scene threatening the freedom of curatorial practice? And do you identify a gap between European and US curatorial attitudes?

In response to the first, I do not believe that the art scene is being subject to "Guggenheim-ization" per se; and might we also deploy the phrase "Tate-ization" for instance? And, furthermore, since when was curatorial practice truly "free"? Are we not all beholden to this or that set of interests, to this or that constituency, regardless of how independent or autonomous we imagine ourselves to be? The art culture, as a whole, has been shifting toward what might be described as a bureaucratic ethos, and this is a discouraging tendency. At least in the US, small, medium-sized, and large cultural institutions are under increasing financial pressures, due to economic recession, among other factors. These institutions will argue that they have no choice but to develop programming that is somehow more populist, more accessible, educationally responsible, yet also entertaining (as in middlebrow blockbuster provocation, replete with scandalous or naughty artists), in an attempt to bridge the gap between specialized and lay audiences. Such institutions claim they are forced to make more conservative choices, even though most contemporary artists, curators, and arts administrators in the US tend to resist conservative ideologies. Paradoxically, the values of the art market are largely based on fiscal conservatism, and around and around we go, particularly in an age of ubiquitous art fairs.

Regarding the second question about curatorial attitudes: yes, we can always find a gap in attitudes. In some situations it is widening, while in others it is narrowing. My concern, on more global terms, is that a curatorial ethos of *when attitudes become forms* has been diminished into *when attitudes become markets*. I suppose we are all responsible for this state of affairs, to one extent or another.

Biennial in Your Brain: California Might Not Be (T)here With 2012 (Post)Postscript

Revised version of an essay originally published in the catalogue of the 2008 California Biennial, Orange County Museum of Art, October 26, 2008–March 15, 2009.

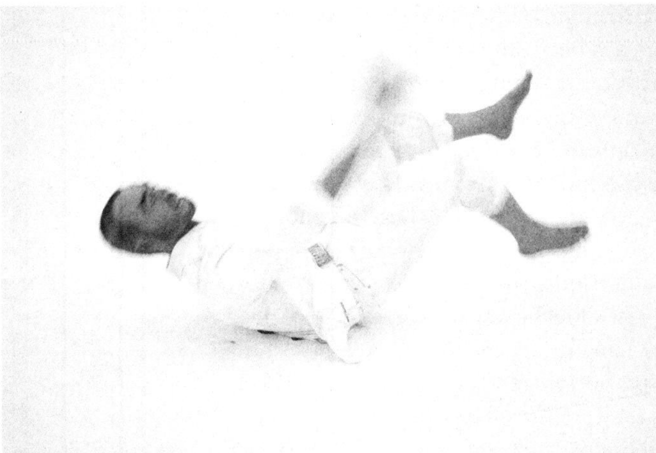

Daniel Joseph Martinez, *Call Me Ishmael: The Fully Enlightened Earth Radiates Disaster Triumphant*, 2006

Do we need another biennial?
And where is California located, anyway?
On the freeways between LA and San Diego?
The underpasses of San Francisco?
The subdivisions of the Inland Empire?
The gated communities of Orange County?
The working-class neighborhoods of East LA?
Joshua Tree?
San Ysidro?
LAX?
SFO?
La Jolla?
Watts?
Venice Beach?
Hollywood?
San Bernardino?
Napa?
Will this California Biennial provide the cultural navigation that I so dearly seek in Los Angeles?
Will it function as a CPS (Cultural Positioning System), supplementing my GPS?

The California Biennial covers a lot of territory—
the State of California.
Does this not seem a bit anachronistic?

If we inhabit the role of (putative) free agents within territories of neoliberal capital in order to release the energies latent within culture, where exactly are we located? And if location, considered at once materially and metaphorically, is up for grabs, so to speak, why is it necessary to rely upon the geopolitical contours of statehood to determine the parameters of an exhibition? I'm sure that the museum has posed this kind of question to itself and to others. This is not the first California Biennial, and it probably will not be the last, but why not just produce a general biennial that happens to be organized by the Orange County Museum of Art and that is inclusive of art from anywhere in the nation, or from anywhere in the world for that matter? California is a global state, embodying attributes of a globalized cultural economy: would it not be more compelling to generate an interpenetration, every two years, between practices from the West Coast and other global regions and territories?

I'm just asking …

Much has been written about the disorientations of life within globalization, pertaining to identity, geopolitics, sexuality, cultural production, and just about every category of existence. It is no longer we *think therefore we are*; now we *travel and therefore we are* able to inhabit various identities, various selves. We are most like ourselves when we are no longer ourselves, perhaps. Life, it seems, has become one big biennial or, with somewhat diminished expectations, an art fair of the everyday. I do not wish to re-mystify the commonplace rituals of business or touristic travel from station to station. Only to propose that the operating code of the contemporary art world is generated in the psychological, physical, political, economic, and cultural currents of endless (privileged) mobility, wherein we experience an interpenetration of place and displacement. This is an expression of a broader global macroeconomic phenomenonin which both labor and capital have become steadily delocalized.

And what of the supposed flattening of economies in the post-Fordist, NAFTA world of increasingly transnational and cross-integrated economic and, by extension, social flows? Has the biennial become part of a pan-global cultural services industry that is becoming undifferentiated from expositions of capital-laced cultural production? Life and work in the contemporary arts have been relatively flattened for some time, with denizens shuttling to and fro, back and forth, from one urban node to another, generating an increasingly complex web of social, intellectual, and business relations that reveal a distinct matrix of interconnections among localized cultural conditions, resilient and eroding nation-state boundaries, trans-regional interplays, and interstitial frictions and liaisons, all set into motion within a global matrix that can be conceptualized on nebulously poetic terms or as a highly calibrated engine of ever-evolving processes and relations that require us to restage our assumptions about what constitutes relevant art practice and relevant exhibition models in the today of tomorrow. Know what I mean?

And so one might imagine the California Biennial occurring in some other state, in some other country, in some far-flung time zone, in a remote location, simply as an idea of an elsewhere California. The California Biennial in Shanghai, in New York, in Istanbul, or in Berlin; the California Biennial along the Pacific coast of Mexico, the California Biennial as an idea had by someone who never knew that the California Biennial existed. The California Biennial in a supermarket, in a closet, on an airplane, on the subway, in your bed, or up in the air. Or, for that matter, bring all the other global biennials to California in the form of franchises within a strip-mall context, in a dramatic gesture of neoliberal reabsorption or re-assimilation. However, the world is not actually flat—it is more like a sphere of overlapping rhizomic networks, perhaps analogous to the complex artistic, cultural, political, ethnic, and geologic enclaves of California, that in turn, echo various global territories.

Does it matter anymore whether a biennial actually happens, since it might be considered a cultural fiction anyway? A fiction in the sense that the reality of any biennial is the result of a complex evolution that is historically and ideologically constructed and determined, interconnected with the histories of the museum and the development of institutions of public culture (even with the proviso that every institution of public culture also contains its dialectic opposite, which is to say privatized culture). Any biennial is a construction that has staying power principally as a means of sustaining the heritage of place and tradition and the possibilities of expanded cultural capital (entrepreneurialism) and art tourism. It is about the building and/or rebuilding of a city as a cosmopolitan center (or decentered place) for the production, promotion, and display of art practices—whether this is in Cairo, Berlin, Ljubljana, Tijuana, New York, Dakar, Sharjah, or São Paulo.

Of course other models exist: the five-year plan of documenta, or the ten-year plan of Skulptur Projekte Münster. It is interesting to reread Münster through its own history—as a kind of accrual of public art projects within the space of that small city, or large town, over the past 30 years. Should a city or institution in California adopt a Münster-like model of periodic exhibition making that engages specifically with the broader public sphere of the urban and the suburban?

Since 1996, Manifesta has rethought aspects of the traditional biennial model by redistributing cultural capital to different cities within the Euro area, thereby reactivating the local, national, and trans-nation-state characteristics of distinct urban places under the rubric of a European biennial infrastructure. However, much in the same way as other biennials, Manifesta has accumulated sufficient cultural, political, and perhaps economic power to function as a driver that mobilizes hundreds of thousands of people (specialists, cultural tourists, local citizens, and others) to make pilgrimages to their exhibitions. Biennials generate temporary (constructed) zones of public-space experience, transitory moments of social interface that produce the real fiction of collective cultural experience. Is this what the California Biennial desires?

Biennials seek to compel belief in the power of art and culture to harness the capital and energies of multiple creative agents, and yet we may grow frustrated with how to ground these temporary, ritualized displays of cultural practices into sustainable engagements. And this does not even begin to account for the proliferation of art fairs ... which is not the purview of this rumination, thank goodness, although it has become apparent to all that a troubling but entirely predictable inter-substitution has been under way for some years: an invasion-of-the-body-snatchers syndrome, wherein the biennial appears on the surface to resemble a biennial but actually has the soul of an art fair and, conversely, an art fair for all intents and purposes looks like an art fair but has the soul of a biennial.

Is the notion and practice of a regional (or state-based) biennial an anachronism or an opportunity ripe with the potential to launch an examination of the codes of biennials and related exhibition platforms? Is it still tenable to deploy the recuperated modernist terms of vanguardism to suggest that a biennial, state-based or otherwise, can be experimental in character? Of course, if the desire is to constitute something experimental or just innovative, in terms of curatorial methodologies and art practices, we would want this to be a transformative experience—that is, transformative of our understanding of a place, or a constellation of locations that together might be deemed to constitute a state, such as California.

And what of the regional? Where exactly is the regional located? Does the notion of the regional pertain to the geographic markers of a territorial region (e.g., a state, such as California), or are we talking about a state of mind, an ethos, a predilection for things that occupy a zone of social or ideological familiarity, that suggest a common code or shared values? Perhaps it is best to think globally within a regional field of action and then hope that folks in other places and situations take notice of what is happening in the place(s) one is endeavoring to activate.

How does an entire state become embedded within a biennial and, conversely, a biennial within a state?

A place called California might exist, but not where one imagines it to be.

The California Biennial might similarly exist, but not where we expect to find it.

Postscript

This text was written in the following cities, although not necessarily in this order: Paris, New York, Los Angeles, and São Paulo. The California Biennial, as an idea, trespassed through these places.

2012 Post-Postscript

Made in LA, the first edition of the Los Angeles Biennial, opened in June 2012, organized by The Hammer Museum in collaboration with LAXART. If one insists upon establishing more biennials, I suppose it is better to reduce the focus to a large urban environment such as Los Angeles, rather than attempting to offer a macro-perspective on something as ungainly as an entire state (i.e., California). By definition, a Los Angeles Biennial reproduces the tired, localized logic of LA-based boosterism that runs all the way back to the 19th-century (and has been effectively critiqued by the likes of Norman Klein and Mike Davis), and so this is not a particularly interesting model (just as MoMA P.S. 1's series of *Greater New York* exhibitions reproduces the tired, localized legacy of NY boosterism). Of course, Los Angeles (just like New York) is the name given to an urban situation that is a constellation of micro-localities, and so it might make just as much sense to have the Hollywood Biennial, or the Silverlake Biennial, or the East LA Biennial. But when I learned that there would be a weekend event called The Venice Beach Biennial (a coy reference to the Venice Biennial in Italy), in which artists would be presenting work and site-specific projects outdoors on the Venice Beach Boardwalk, an anxiety emerged: contemporary art aspires to a condition of cultural hyper-ubiquity, an *everywhereness*, that seeks to convert every place into an art venue. Enough already, perhaps?

Art and the Cultural Contradictions of Urban Regeneration, Social Justice, and Sustainability: Transforma Projects and Prospect.1 in Post-Katrina New Orleans

Revised version of an essay originally published in *Afterall Journal*, #22, Autumn–Winter 2009.

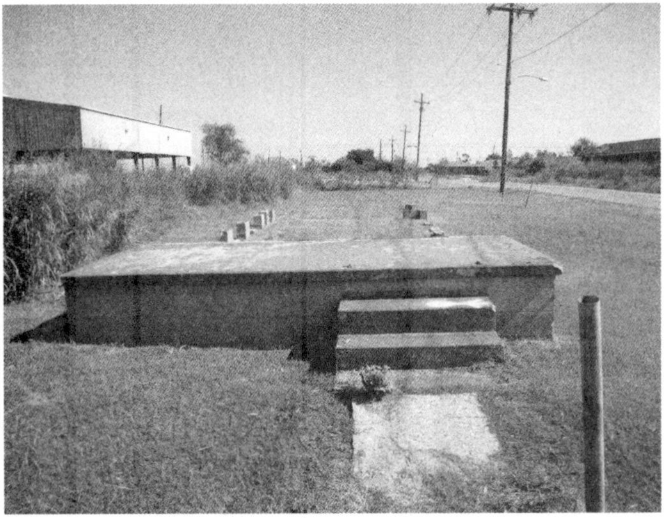

Remains of a house in the Lower Ninth Ward, New Orleans, October 31, 2008

Preamble: A Flood of Questions

What is at stake when artists, architects, curators, organizers, and other cultural producers facilitate bricks-and-mortar change on the ground in cities, with citizens, communities and institutions? How do we test the interrelationship between the practices of artists and urban policy makers? What is the metric that we might use to determine effectiveness? And what do we mean by effectiveness—the putatively emancipatory outcome generated by some kind of new situational knowledge? Or is it a question of generating ambiguity, *per se*, as a means of problematizing hegemonic political, economic, and cultural formations?

Is it conceivable to imagine that the cultural and intellectual capital of artistic labor can generate sustained—and sustainable—responses to urban crises that would offer palpable functionality (or applicability) for people's lives—contra to the useful uselessness of the aesthetic condition that is supposedly ennobling of mind and spirit, or generative of disinterestedness as a prerequisite for absorption and contemplation? It is perhaps just a question of recalibrating our criteria or, at the very least, how we communicate to others our experience of a specific work within a particular situation, so that criteria remain sufficiently fluid and tactical? What does it mean to encounter a work of art in the midst of economic and social ruination?

This essay seeks to raise such questions in relation to a new biennial (Prospect.1), and a new cultural initiative (Transforma Projects). These two projects were developed for New Orleans after the Hurricane Katrina disaster, which in 2005 flooded 80 per cent of the city and killed nearly 2,000 people. Both Prospect.1 and Transforma Projects seek to engage in the regeneration, rebuilding, and revitalization of that city's cultural, economic, and social life. The two organizations are distinct from each other on ideological and organizational terms. Prospect.1 represents itself as the first international biennial in New Orleans (i.e. event-oriented), with official support from local and state government and major art-world benefactors, with a more conventional "top-down" hierarchical curatorial and exhibition process. Transforma Projects sees itself as a grassroots cultural initiative, involving "bottom-up" socially participatory processes (i.e. rethinking normative institutional hierarchies). Transforma's mandate is to generate and deploy art projects to spur rebuilding within the city's economically and socially disenfranchised communities (such as the neighborhood of the Lower Ninth Ward). Yet major art foundations support Transforma as well.

There have always been debates within the contemporary art context in the US (and to a certain extent in Europe) about what constitutes "public practice," "community-based practice," and "cultural-activist practice." At times, this becomes a debate about who has the right to articulate the interests of a community and whether so-called outsiders can legitimately work with a particular community; this may ultimately be a question of cultivating trust, one of the most complex challenges facing artists who seek to work with, or in relation to, citizens and their life-spaces. Transforma Projects seems to want to function organizationally as a long-term incubator of bottom-up art initiatives. Prospect.1 is currently functioning as a biennial exhibition of art, designed to periodically bring international artists and their works into contact with the local artists, institutions, communities, and cultural milieus of New Orleans. It is important to keep in mind, however, that Prospect.1 and Transforma Projects are not mutually exclusive models.

Bayou-Urbanity: Trespassing in the Lower Ninth

What ultimately made the biggest impact during my visit to New Orleans in late October/early November 2008 was the few hours I spent walking—or, as it seemed then, trespassing—through the Lower Ninth. It was a ghosted neighborhood, barely inhabited, and rarely visited. We are all interlopers here, in this aftermath of governmental neglect, looking for signs of life, the remains of community. A landscape of malicious neglect, burned into the mind. At one street corner, a skeleton of a house. Is the owner living elsewhere in New Orleans, or in a neighboring state, still maintaining the lot for the possibility of a future rebuild? All that remains is a foundation, in this place of non-places. What does it mean to trespass upon someone's property, into the remains of their home, as if visiting an archaeological site? This is the archaeology of disaster. What is art doing in this situation? And what am I doing in this place?

One of the most eloquent analysts of post-Katrina urban environment in New Orleans is sociologist and Tulane University professor Kevin Fox Gotham, who has published extensively on the subject. In an article cowritten with Miriam Greenberg of the University of California–Santa Cruz, titled "From 9/11 to 8/29: Post-Disaster Recovery and Rebuilding in New York and New Orleans," the authors argue that urban recovery in New Orleans, as in New York, is a market-driven phenomenon "aggravating inequalities and impeding community recovery efforts." They write that, "Such inequity will likely continue unless there is a significant shift in the priorities and oversight of post-disaster recovery efforts, and in the aims and measures of urban revitalization more broadly."[1] Will the current recession trigger a fundamental rethinking of the social and economic politics of urban redevelopment, or merely induce a pause?

Biennial as Urban Cultural Capital?

One of the central issues behind the linking of contemporary art initiatives to processes of urban revitalization has it roots in Enlightenment thinking: faith in the beneficent effects of art upon publics, not to mention the creation of publics *for* art. The notion of an increasingly democratized realm of culture—in which various forms of art are displayed for the growing publics of cities—is predicated upon various forms of financial support. With the increased privatization of public space (and the role of public art in these processes), the line between public culture and privatized culture is increasingly blurred—a condition which is amplified when there are public-private partnerships. Longstanding episodic large-scale, nation-state and municipally-based exhibition projects such as documenta, Skulptur Projekte Münster, the Venice Biennale, the São Paulo Bienal, the Whitney Biennial, the Istanbul Biennial, the Carnegie International, and other variants demonstrate the continued attraction, and drawing power, of international expositions in relation to the growth of contemporary art-oriented tourism, which may function as an incubator for broader economic growth within cities and nations. Within the United States, we have seen the emergence of "cultural enterprise zones" for urban redevelopment schemes; this can lead to gentrification, wherein communities are fragmented by predatory economics, and unregulated real-estate markets and other manifestations of unfair social policies lead to a wider gap between the working poor and the US upper-middle class.

The operating code of the contemporary art world is generated in the psychological, physical, political, economic, and cultural interpenetrations of places within the global space—*placelessness*—of capital. Biennials and other periodic exhibitions attempt to instrumentalize art as cultural capital to reinscribe the power of place—the remaking of a city as a cosmopolitan center for the production, promotion, and display of art practices, whether this is in Berlin, New York, Venice, Sharjah ... or New Orleans. One of the side effects of biennials and other periodic exhibitions is the mobilization of thousands—sometimes hundreds of thousands—of people into making pilgrimages to these events and situations. These events generate temporary, constructed zones of public-space experience—transitory moments of social interface that produce the fiction of collective cultural experience. We depend on the power of art to harness the energies of multiple creative agents, and yet we often seem unable to connect the dots between the biennial as a ritualized festival model, and the biennial as facilitator of sustained (and sustainable) engagements with place—beyond the assumption (neoliberal or otherwise) that any large-scale art event will bring some economic benefit to a city.

On the Prospect.1 website we read:

> Prospect.1 New Orleans [P.1], the largest biennial of international art ever organized in the United States … has been conceived in the tradition of the great international biennials, and showcases new artistic practices as well as an array of programs benefiting the local community. Over the course of its 11-week run, Prospect.1 New Orleans will draw international media attention, creative energy, and new economic activity to the city of New Orleans.[2]

(Notably, significant financial support for Prospect.1 came from a network of major art benefactors that included both private art foundations and individuals.[3])

So how do we evaluate the role and effectiveness of an international art biennial in the midst of complex social, economic, and infrastructural conditions? Whose interests were served by Prospect.1? Did the biennial indirectly and inadvertently echo aspects of disaster-tourism—at least to the extent that a component of the exhibition was staged within the context of the Lower Ninth? And if so, could this not be understood as a potentially beneficial type of cultural intervention that might help to generate the symbolic, ideological, and political pressures (since art can really only facilitate symbolic "effects" … or perhaps merely the "affects" of social transformation …) for economic and social justice?

Although many of the artworks featured in Prospect.1 (pre-existing, or specially produced for the occasion) were displayed conventionally at institutional sites such as the Old US Mint, the Contemporary Arts Center, and The New Orleans Museum of Art, curator Dan Cameron did commission a number of works specifically for the context of the Lower Ninth. Among these, Mark Bradford's attracted considerable local and national attention, since it was the most spectacular: a 22- by 64-foot-long ark-like construction, *Mithra* (2008) was assembled in Los Angeles from plywood barricade fencing recycled from local construction sites, disassembled and placed into containers, and shipped to New Orleans, where it was then reassembled in an empty lot on the corner of Caffin Avenue and N. Miro street. It is a clever piece of pop culture-inflected protest (fragments of posters advertising events and DVDs, including a glowering face of Denzel Washington) that also alludes to the Old Testament. In scaling-up his method of using collage-oriented procedures to transform found materials, Bradford effectively amplified his aesthetic language for this context. The artist's decision to display the actual shipping container is humorous yet poignant, reinforcing our understanding that this ark arrived much too late to evacuate the residents of the Lower Ninth. Ultimately, *Mithra* functions as an allegory of its own powerlessness as a work of art in the face of such environmental devastation. Other notable efforts included Nari Ward's eccentric multimedia installation inside the flood-ravaged Battle Ground Baptist Church at 2441 Flood Street (yes, *Flood* Street), and Paul Villinski's mobile *Emergency Response Studio* (2008), which I encountered at the site of the Global Green Project, an environmental non-profit, on an empty lot on Andry Street (but which moved around to other sites throughout Prospect.I's duration, including the New Orleans Museum of Art and Loyola University).

A number of art projects in Prospect.1 incorporated means of redistributing not only symbolic cultural capital, but actual money back into the local community. For *Sarah's House* (2008), Wangechi Mutu created a series of prints to benefit the owner (Sarah Lastie) of a now-empty lot on the corner of Caffin Avenue and Chartres Street in the Lower Ninth Ward where the artist has sited her project. Due to contractor fraud, Ms. Lastie lost the money that she earmarked to rebuild her house that had been swept away by the floodwaters of hurricane Katrina. Mutu's work is a ghost-like echo of this disappeared edifice: a site-specific sculpture in the form of the infrastructural frame of a shotgun house (a characteristic style of working-class residences found in

New Orleans). Mutu adorned this skeletal architecture with lights, set it on a black platform, and placed a single chair in the middle of the structure, creating a subtly theatrical effect that was at once celebratory and mournful.

The Danish art group SUPERFLEX developed a project titled *When the Levees Broke We Bought Our House* (2008), which was comprised of a framed black-and-white photograph featuring a house (family members seated outdoors in the front yard) in what appears to be a suburban context, with the following descriptive text:

> This Danish family bought their house in the aftermath of Hurricane Katrina. Katrina caused a drop in the interest rates in Denmark, enabling the family to afford the house. This photograph has the price of $20,000; equivalent to the amount the family saved buying their house. When sold, the money will be spent on constrution materials to be used by families in the Lower 9th Ward, New Orleans.

The photograph and text were hung in an empty warehouse-like space in the Lower Ninth Ward, the dimensions of which corresponded to those of a typical New Orleans home in the Lower Ninth, alluding to the potential conversion of the project into something with restorative use-value for citizens within this particular community (contingent upon whether the photograph is actually sold). On conceptual terms the project required some decoding, especially in relation to the claimed causal interrelationship between Hurricane Katrina and interest rates in Denmark.[4]

While it is apparent that SUPERFLEX researched the interconnectivities of local and global economic systems, and desired to return the capital (both real and fictitious from the sale of this photograph to families within the Lower Ninth, it remains unclear as to whether this model could be sustainable in terms of the long-term rebuilding needs of this section of New Orleans, or whether it was a well-intentioned symbolic gesture that might have a delayed social impact.

Thai artist Navin Rawanchaikul (in collaboration with Tyler Russell) organized *Narvin's Party* (2008), an actual funeral parade (qua art event) for the late Marvin Kimball.

The banjo player for the Preservation Hall Jazz Band, Kimball died in March 2006 in Charleston, South Carolina, where he had been evacuated to just before Katrina struck. Kimball's subsequent funeral in New Orleans was not considered sufficient by the community, so Rawanchaikul and Russell facilitated a proper jazz funeral that traveled through sections of the city, ending at the Jazz Preservation Hall, and providing Kimball and his family the funeral procession that he deserved. Rawanchaikul also commissioned billboard painters in Thailand to make a number of paintings commemorating Kimball, which were carried through the streets and then eventually given to Kimball's family. I witnessed the start of this art event-as-funeral procession, obtained one of the freely distributed *Narvin's Party* T-shirts, but then was whisked away by some friends who had heard of something "more real": a (i.e. non-art) funeral parade for another New Orleans resident that was about to start in an adjacent neighborhood. The idea was that we would have a more authentic experience of New Orleans by seeking out the "real" funeral procession, rather than participating in an artist-generated version. We eventually located the other funeral event, and walked through the city with people we did not know, but who welcomed us anyway. Perhaps this kind of encounter between strangers within the flow of everyday life is what constitutes authentic social experience, in distinction from other kinds of real/unreal experience generated through a socially participatory art event? But who is to say which one was *more* real?

Perhaps the most important achievement of Prospect.1 was to help bring outsiders to New Orleans so as to witness the social, economic, and infrastructural aftermath of a natural and political disaster. Is this, however, enough to justify the existence of the biennial—or the possibility of its future?

Into the Grassroots Trenches

Transforma Projects is a New Orleans-based project developed by both non-local and local artists and organizers: Rick Lowe (based in Houston), Sam Durant (based in Los Angeles), art consultant Jessica Cusick (based in Santa Monica), and New Orleans-based organizer Jess Garza. Here is an excerpt from the project's mission statement:

> Transforma Projects New Orleans seeks to unite creative thinking with the physical and social needs of our city. Our goal is to highlight and imbed the arts into the decision-making processes that affect all neighborhoods and communities. Some strategies for accomplishing this are: actively engaging and giving voice to local artists and art communities. Infusing preexisting local cultural projects with new ideas and resources. Creating projects that partner local communities with national and international artists. Providing resources to artistic vehicles that fundamentally impact a community (such as residencies, long-term and short-term projects and cultural preservation) in the following areas: Housing, Education, etc.[5]

Transforma Projects might be understood as an initiative purpose-built to provide a cultural infrastructure for New Orleans by promoting the idea of artists (and art) as potential facilitators of urban regeneration, and working with communities and citizens to influence actual civic policies. The project aims to develop a cultural platform that the people of New Orleans will take symbolic and pragmatic ownership of, thereby creating a dependable umbrella organization for locally generated projects that benefit communities as directly as possible. One of the central components it administers is the application-based Creative Recovery Mini-Grant Program, which "supports work that exists at the intersection of art, social justice and recovery in New Orleans," and "… fuels the recovery by supporting the vibrant activity that occurs on the ground."[6]

Grant amounts range from $500 to $2,500, and to date, three rounds have been awarded. The funded projects are diverse and operate at different scales and levels of complexity, including: St. Claude Avenue Sankofa Sustainable Marketplace, a community-building initiative featuring utilitarian artworks, horticultural arts, and music performances in the Lower Ninth Ward; *New World Wailing Wall*, a sculptural installation sited on the vacant lot of a former family home; 7th Ward Artist Residency; Open Window Project, a news and culture website developed by youth in collaboration with media professionals; and "How to Rebuild a City:

Field Guide from a Work in Progress," a community-based initiative that will document how artists, writers, activists, and other citizens from various backgrounds have contributed to the reconstruction of New Orleans.

One might even consider that Transforma Projects functions in a manner akin to a cultural NGO (channeling funding from major art foundations directly into local cultural projects)—and perhaps appropriately so, in the economically and environmentally challenged site of New Orleans. It seems that Lowe and Durant's strategy has been to downplay the possible perception of Transforma Projects as an "art project" *per se*, and instead embed it, grassroots style, as a self-organized entity with deepening interconnections with the social and environmental textures of those sections of New Orleans that require support. This still depends upon the assumption that cultural projects have the power to generate sufficient cultural capital to raise other levels of support for these communities: for instance, persuading the local government to participate in the rebuilding of various infrastructures (educational, environmental, architectural, etc.).

Though Transforma Projects has sought to avoid being pigeonholed as an art-world phenomenon, part of its funding does come from key art foundations such as The Andy Warhol Foundation for the Visual Arts, the National Endowment for the Arts, the Joan Mitchell Foundation (not to mention larger foundations such as the Annenberg and the Ford). This reflects the degree to which the higher-profile protagonists of the project (Lowe and Durant) were able to leverage their cultural capital for the sake of Transforma Projects in a rather ethical way. Lowe is best known for Project Row Houses in Houston, founded in 1993, which represents a significant rethinking of models of community-based art practice. In that situation, Lowe essentially built a local cultural organization to help trigger urban redevelopment in an economically marginalized part of Houston. This required an understanding of art world funding sources (e.g., foundations), as well as a navigation of local municipal politics. So it seems that on financial terms, the only effective way to embed an art initiative within a distinct local community—at least for Transforma Projects in New Orleans—is to take seed money from foundations that are principally based in New York or on the East Coast. The capital (abstract and literal) that flows through these systems and the cultural partnerships across diverse geographies and social groups is essential to start initiatives that, perhaps, one day might become a self-sustaining economic model.

Future NOLA?

Urban redevelopment is a tricky process, and New Orleans is a testament to these complexities; one always has to determine whether development is in the service of economic justice or bottom-line motives—and, furthermore, what role art plays in these processes.

If one of the goals of Prospect.1 was to promote cultural tourism and, by extension, to spur urban renewal, it would be necessary to do comprehensive surveys (empirical, statistical, sociological, anthropological, psychological) to determine the impact of the biennial upon the city's economy and its people. Yet it was possible, if only to a limited extent, to observe the conversion, the *transvaluation,* of art into cultural capital, and then into the capital of cultural tourism—and to consider the ethical, economic, social, and other implications of this process as it unfolded through the streets of New Orleans. Did the biennial serve the public interest in this situation? The citizens of New Orleans will undoubtedly be asking themselves this question for some time.

Transforma Projects has the potential to become a locally networked cultural service provider in New Orleans. It will only be sustainable, however, for as long as it needs to be sustained, based upon the desires and needs of the community it is meant to serve. Transforma Projects will need to be agile, and duly responsive to a changing city. Prospect.1—even if it is remade every two years with a new set of contextually driven art commissions—is less flexible, because it has identified itself, institutionally, as a formalized biennial. Prospect.1 was distributed through a range of locations and sites throughout the city, suggesting an effort to become integral to the cultural life of the city, representative of a positive step toward sustainability.

The question is not whether New Orleans (or other parts of the United States that are experiencing significant budgetary, infrastructural, and social challenges) should be rebuilt to benefit citizens and communities, but it is rather how to ensure equal and equitable urban development. Rebuilding does not have to lead to profit-driven corporate redevelopment schemes, and therefore to the most pernicious kinds of gentrification. For decades, there has been widespread economic and social inequity in New Orleans, and so just rebuilding, *per se*, is not sufficient. The real issue is how local communities can assert more control in the reshaping of their places of habitation—in relation to local and state governments (and related public institutions), and in relation to private developers. The realities of these issues are complex, and it is difficult to evaluate the impact of art and culture in terms of urban redevelopment.

Will residents ever return to the Lower Ninth? Can the community be reconstituted? If smart, good-faith efforts to rebuild the Lower Ninth into a zone of sustainable, affordable housing—through initiatives such as URBANbuild, a program of the Tulane School of Architecture and the Tulane City Center, or even the Brad Pitt-initiated Make It Right Foundation—inadvertently pave the way for eventual corporate redevelopment and gentrification, it will have been a waste.[7]

Meanwhile, to get a sense of just how confusing and dysfunctional the situation continues to be in the official recovery efforts nearly four years after Katrina, take a look at a *New York Times* article from May 7, 2009, titled "Leaving the Trailers: Ready or Not, Katrina Victims Lose Temporary Housing."[8] It will make you bristle with frustration about the continued apparent ineptitude of FEMA (the Federal Emergency Management Agency). No wonder, then, that many former residents of the Lower Ninth are still reluctant to return. Will the more empowered citizens and communities within New Orleans join in a sustainable partnership with the disenfranchised of the city (and the displaced residents who together constitute a kind of internal economic and social diaspora within the United States) to not simply reconstitute some aspect of what has been lost, but actually establish economic and social justice?

And how do we evaluate the impact of Prospect.1 upon the various micro-economies of New Orleans (not merely on the macro-level)—particularly in relation to those communities experiencing economic and social crisis? Did Prospect.1 merely function as a preamble to the neoliberal redevelopment of these undeveloped precincts? Which citizens, communities, and economies benefited the most from the biennial—and who wants it to become a sustainable event in the city? Do local artists, art spaces, galleries, and museums desire a sustained international biennial? And then we must also ask whether a more below the radar, grassroots-oriented cultural project such as Transforma Projects suggests a paradigmatic shift toward post-symbolic, socially transformative processes. And how would we measure these social outcomes?

Just as Paul Chan's project *Waiting for Godot in New Orleans* (2007, co-produced by Creative Time and The Classical Theatre of Harlem) could be read, at least partially, as an allegory of the citizens of the Lower Ninth and Gentilly neighborhoods' endless waiting for federal government help in the aftermath of Katrina, an optimistic reading of efforts such as Prospect.1 and Transforma is that each emerged because it was no longer possible to wait for others to marshal the cultural capital of art in an effort to respond to a municipal crisis. And, though I experienced some discomfort participating in a form of cultural tourism within this context, my visit did provide an opportunity to witness, first hand, the conditions of the Lower Ninth Ward. It is unbelievable and inexcusable that this could be a part of the United States in the 21st century. And so the flood of contradictions, and questions, surges on.

Postscript, 2012

Following Prospect.1 in 2008, the second edition of the New Orleans biennial, Prospect.2, took place from October 2011 through January 2012. The third installment, Prospect.3, is scheduled to open in the fall of 2014.

Transforma ended its operations in 2010.

[1] Kevin Fox Gotham and Miriam Greenberg, "From 9/11 to 8/29: Post-Disaster Recovery and Rebuilding in New York and New Orleans," *Social Forces*, no. 87, December 2008, page 1056

[2] http://www.prospectneworleans.org (accessed August 2013).

[3] Sponsors included Toby Devan Lewis, Peter Lewis, The Getty Foundation, The Andy Warhol Foundation for the Visual Arts, Agnes Gund, Bloomberg, Metabolic Studio (under the auspices of Lauren Bon and the Annenberg Foundation), and governmental institutions such as the State of Louisiana (Department of Culture, Recreation & Tourism).

[4] A member of SUPERFLEX explained in an interview that this was as an attempt to reference certain (abstract and invisible) globalized economic conditions in terms of real-estate markets. See "Economic Sur-Realities: A Conversation with Bjørnstjerne Christiansen of SUPERFLEX," art:21 blog, June 2, 2009, available at http://blog.art21.org/?s=Economic+Sur-Realities%3A+A+Conversation+with+Bj%C3%B8rnstjerne+Christiansen+of+SUPERFLEX (last accessed August 2013).

[5] http://www.prospectneworleans.org (accessed August 13, 2013).

[6] Cited from website, as above.

[7] For more information on these initiatives, please visit their respective websites, http://www.tulaneurbanbuild.com and http://www.makeitrightnola.org (both last accessed April 2013).

[8] http://www.nytimes.com/2009/05/08/us/08trailer.html?pagewanted=all&_r=0 (last accessed August 2013).

(Questioning) Serbia: Frequently Asked Questions

Revised version of text on *Serbia: Frequently Asked Questions*, Austrian Cultural Forum, New York, September 23, 2010–January 11, 2011. Originally published in *Artforum*, February 2011.

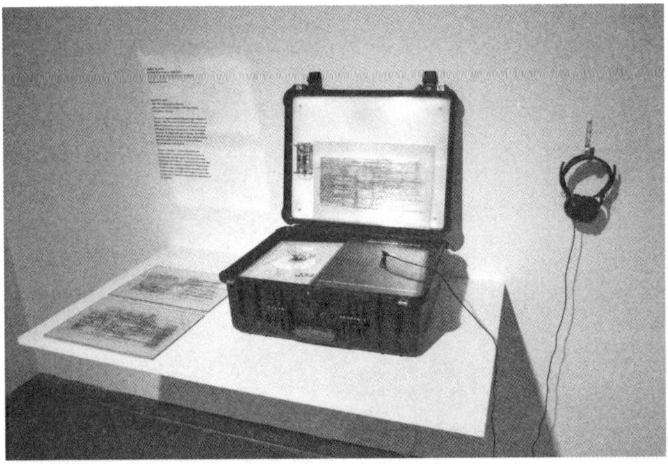

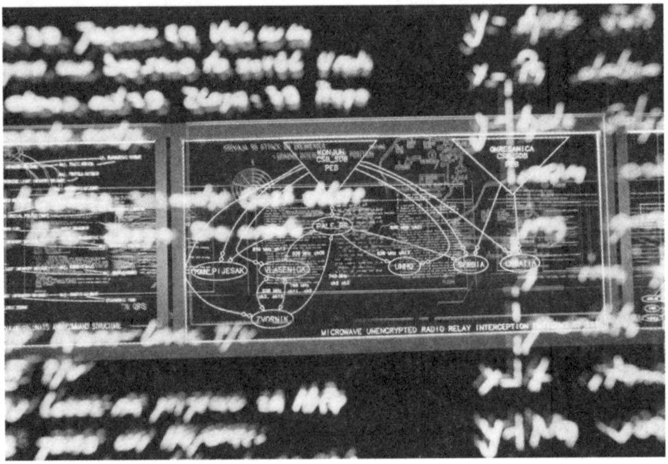

Marko Peljhan, *TERRITORY 1995 Evidence*, 2006–2010
Marko Peljhan, *TERRITORY 1995*, 2006–2011

Yugoslavia's disintegration commenced in 1991 with the secession of various republics, triggering an ethno-religious civil war among Orthodox Serbs, Catholic Croats, and Muslim Bosnians. Much of the conflict centered on Bosnia-Herzegovnia, and, for many in the West, the genocidal campaign against Bosnian Muslims—orchestrated by the Milosevic-led Bosnian Serb ultra-nationalist army and paramilitary—came to typify the egregious violence of the war. Aware of this legacy, the curators of *Serbia: Frequently Asked Questions*—organized by the Austrian Cultural Forum New York and the Museum of Contemporary Art Belgrade, and featuring artists from several nations in the region—hope to counter the "stereotyping" of Serbians as "intolerant and nationalistic people" by presenting work that engages critically with the history and contemporary traces of this conflict, and in various ways interrogates the volatile psychological, social, ethnic, and religious entanglements that can lead to a nationalism gone awry.

Perhaps the most unnerving work in this show is Belgrade-based Zoran Todorovic's *Warmth*, originally on view in the Serbian Pavilion at the 2009 Venice Biennale. Considerably scaled down for its presentation here, the work consisted of wooden dollies stacked with dark gray felt blankets made from human hair; a number of small monitors played videos of the cutting of the hair at hairdressers and military barracks and the processes of manufacturing the fabric. Though the felt itself is an artifact of comfort and survival, Todorovic evokes an insidious biopolitics: the extremes of social instrumentalization by which the body is converted to "bare life," to borrow Giorgio Agamben's term. One can experience the work as an allegory of the reemergence of the concentration camp apparatus during the Balkan wars, and imagine it in relation to Agamben's notion of the fundamental, paradoxical interpenetration of the sovereignty of the body and that of the nation-state.

Other works here consider the body as a site of identity mediation, including Serbian Milica Tomic's video *One day, instead of night, a burst of machine-gun fire will flash, if light cannot come otherwise* (2009), and Albanian Anri Sala's *Naturamystic (tomahawk #2)* (2002). The former portrays the artist, holding a Kalashnikov rifle in one hand and a plastic supermarket bag in the other, walking to places in Belgrade where armed resistance to the Nazis took place, while the latter depicts a man from Belgrade vocally simulating the sound of NATO missiles flying through the sky. In Czech Stefanos Tsivopoulos' two-channel *The Interview part A* and *The Interview part B* (both 2007), one screen featured testimony by a Serbian soldier who committed atrocities during the Bosnian war, while the other depicted an actor repeating the same testimonial. It is up to the viewer to determine which is the actual soldier, or whether such distinctions are pertinent in relation to the transmission of the *facts* of the narrative itself, which takes on particular resonance in relation to how the evidence of war crimes is reconstructed. And Austrian Marko Lulic has produced an intriguingly enigmatic, experimental dance video—*Jasenovac* (2010)—that somehow corporealizes a 1966 modernist monument commemorating the Serbs, Jews, and Roma who perished in a notorious World War II-era extermination camp in Jasenovac, Croatia.

The difficulty of cutting through the fog of war to reconstruct the (historical) facts on the ground takes on particular urgency with Slovenian Marko Peljhan's *Territory 1995 Evidence* (2006–2010). Based upon fastidious research into the military, legal, and technological conditions of the Srebrenica massacre, Peljhan's project is comprised of 12 palimpsest-like plates (featuring a layered agglomeration of information) and audio elements (including intercepts of the military's communications used as evidence during the genocide tribunals) that together generate a complex analytical re-mapping of communications, command, and control networks used by the Bosnian Serbian military and paramilitaries leading up to the tragedy.

Still, a number of important questions remain. Is Serbia—an independent republic since 2006 and a candidate for EU membership—recuperated in the global consciousness? Did it ever need to be? And does the artistic *culturalization* of its past only serve to ameliorate, or merely sublimate, the traumas of the Balkan war? Art, as demonstrated in this show, is an aporia that allegorizes its own indeterminate relationship to the real, and therefore cannot provide answers. Yet it is possible to imagine that society still needs artists to produce work that questions how readily man's violence against man has become institutionalized at the level of the nation-state.

CHAPTER VII

On the Curatorial Road

Don't Look Now

Revised version of *Don't Look Now* exhibition catalogue essay, Thread Waxing Space, New York, January 22–February 26, 1994.

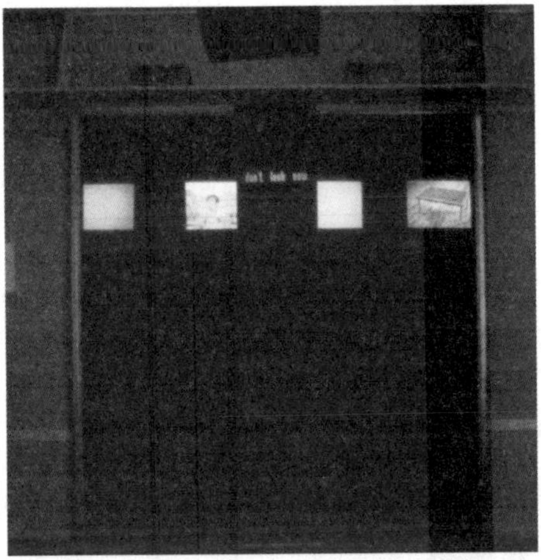

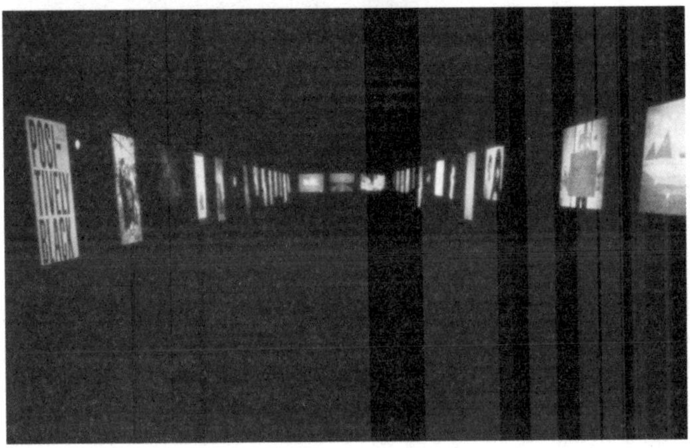

Don't Look Now, installation views, Thread Waxing Space, New York, January 22–February 26, 1994

The dream of identity: to be oneself, and to have this self be recognized by others …
—Roland Barthes

The title of this exhibition was appropriated from Nicolas Roeg's 1973 film, *Don't Look Now*, a psychological or *psychic* thriller set in Venice starring Donald Sutherland and Julie Christie. In the opening sequence of the film, we observe Sutherland—playing an American architect named John Baxter—contemplating a 35 mm slide image of the interior of an old Venetian church that he has been hired to restore. The image reveals a red-hooded figure in the foreground, and as Baxter peers into the pictorial space, blood appears to flow out of that mysterious individual. A moment later, his young daughter, who happens to be dressed in a red raincoat, drowns in the pond near their home.

The slide, therefore, becomes a kind of premonitory device,

setting into motion a series of tragic events which are either accidental, or predestined (depending upon one's worldview). The slide also provides an opportunity for Baxter to glimpse—as representation—his own identity and possible future destiny—an identity, and future, which he continues to glimpse throughout the film, but which he cannot accept. Haunted by visions of what he believes is his dead daughter, Baxter is finally unable to see, and is murdered by the red-hooded figure—who turns out not to be the ghost of his deceased daughter, but a dwarf serial killer plaguing the streets of Venice.

Sixty-eight artists, architects, musicians, filmmakers, writers, and curators—from the US, Canada, and Europe—were invited to consider the notion of identity (psychological, sexual, social, ideological, aesthetic, etc.) as a visual and symbolic projection into the public realm, and to produce a work in the form of a single 35 mm slide in response to this conceptual framework. The resultant 68 distinct, static slide-works were continuously projected onto individual screens, housed within a darkened, quasi-theatrical spatial environment comprised of an architectural corridor. The overall effect suggested a meta-frieze of glowing images in the age of post-mechanical reproduction—anticipating the transition from analogue to digital culture.

Don't look now, or you may discern the images offered in this exhibition. Everything here speaks of mediation, a re-processed world. A world is as actual or as counterfeit as you want it to be. The viewer is invited to read a sequence of pictures, to find meaning in what might appear at first to be inscrutable. For some, the accumulation of images may suggest a narrative, thematic, or even poetic dimension; for others, it may seem to be an arbitrary collation of visual signs. Any logic, or order, will be the product of the viewer's perceptual engagement—and a desire, perhaps, to impose meanings, a story, or subject. Instead, the exhibition may only lead to other questions.

What happens in that space, that gap, between what we believe distinguishes the imaginary from the real? Where is that putative space located? Aren't we always substituting one imaginary for another, and by naming it, it becomes a signpost for the real? Is this exhibition not comprised of the (invented) signs of others? How is one's otherness, one's putative identity, projected to … others? Maybe this projection is at once a naming and an un-naming (of identity).

Where does the supposed reality reside: inside and/or outside the images? Or in that space between the (projected) image and the (projected gaze) of the viewer?

Is there a narrative that you, the viewer, continue to seek? What is that story you wish to enter, and to understand? Perhaps this is just a sequence of unrelated images, with no narrative, subject, or theme to decode.

We sign ourselves into the world, we stylize our entry into the social, but what is the culture's signature? Are we always speaking through others, inhabiting something beyond our own horizon of experience that, then, vicariously, becomes part of our experiential life? Can we inhabit someone else's history?

Don't look now, or you might just see your surrogate, your projection. We desire the image to be a projection of who we are. We may deploy images to suggest a means of projecting what/who we are, for others, for receivers, to engage in a process of identification. But this is not necessarily our identity.

Maybe, the (projected) image is merely a kind of passport: something used for the purpose of identification, an instrument of identity.

Participants

Hilton Als, Judith Barry & Ken Saylor, Ashley Bickerton, Douglas Blau, Henry Bond, Sarah Charlesworth, Mark Dion, Orshi Drozdik, Jeanne Dunning, Jimmie Durham, Kate Ericson & Mel Ziegler, Daniel Faust, Peter Fischli & David Weiss, Andrea Fraser, Aki Fujiyoshi, General Idea, Liam Gillick, Robert Gober, Dominique Gonzalez-Foerster, Felix González-Torres, Dan Graham, Renée Green, Federico Guzmán, Fariba Hajamadi, Peter Halley, David Hammons, Ronald Jones, Ilya Kabakov, Tom Kalin, On Kawara, Mike Kelley, Jon Kessler, Martin Kippenberger, Jutta Koether, Sean Landers, Glenn Ligon, Ken Lum, J Mascis, Marlene McCarty & Christine Vachon, John Miller, Matt Mullican, Paul Myoda, Philippe Parreno, Theresa Pendlebury, Raymond Pettibon, Michelangelo Pistoletto, Lari Pittman, Stephen Prina, David Reed, Jason Rhoades, David Robbins, Alexis Rockman,

Andrei Roiter, Allen Ruppersberg, Julia Scher, Annabelle Selldorf, Lorna Simpson, Sonic Youth/Kim Gordon, Haim Steinbach, Jessica Stockholder, Sam Taylor-Wood, Lynne Tillman, Rirkrit Tiravanija, Rosemarie Trockel, Lawrence Weiner, Fred Wilson, Andrea Zittel, Heimo Zobernig.

Screen

Revised version of curatorial statement, *Screen*, Friedrich Petzel Gallery, January 19–February 24, 1996.

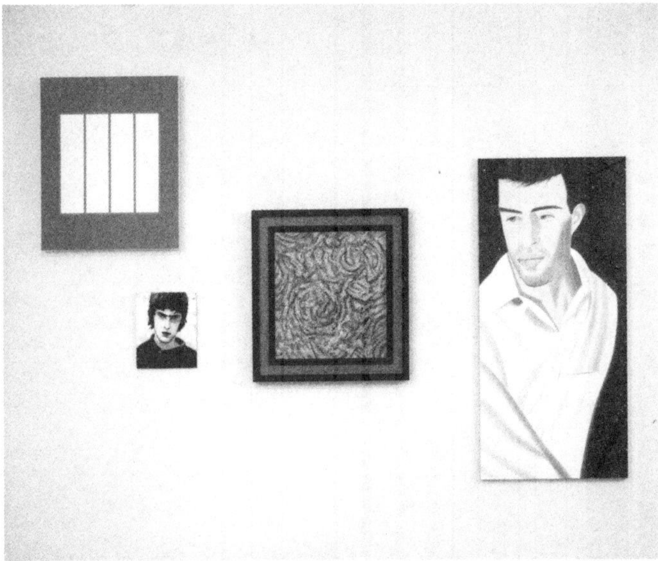

Screen, installation view, Friedrich Petzel Gallery, January 19–February 24, 1996
From left to right: Peter Halley, Elizabeth Peyton, Richard Artschwager, Alex Katz

Painting on Television, Television on Painting. An Exhibition Inside of a Show Inside of an Exhibition

Screen: it is all there to be seen. A painting show. A painting show on television. Television in a gallery. Different velocities of seeing. In life, as in art, things rub up against one another, and there is as much discord as flirtation. Contradictions abound, and linkages are proposed. Where, for instance, does the abstract or representational space of television end, and the abstract or representational space of painting begin? In the realm of video, perhaps.

Why do we watch television? For distraction and absorption. Why do we look at paintings? For absorption and distraction. And, of course, for pleasure—the alternately rarefied and banal pleasures afforded by these distinct languages.

Today, it is possible to consider painting to be as much about distraction as television, and television to be as much about absorption as painting. Yet it is the notion of a third condition that is most intriguing: an intermediary territory between the more discrete experiences that painting yields, and the more collective experiences contrived by television. What are the worlds created by painting and television? Painting is a *screen* that transmits. Television is a *screen* that transmits. Television is a visual field that absorbs. Painting is a visual field that absorbs. Television is all around us; it is a kind of social tissue. Painting removes itself partially from the discursive flow, yet it is also a form of social communication.

Television projects itself into and through the texture of everyday life. Painting is projected into the texture of everyday life, and creates a pause. Painting lays a trap for our looks, and our gaze is either laid into or laid upon the screen that is the canvas. Television reaches out to touch our look, our gaze, and we reach out to caress its immaterially material, ubiquitous glow.

Screen is a rhetorical gesture: a doubling of the exhibition inside the site of the exhibition. Prior to the opening, I worked with a photographer to shoot the installation according to a specific design, and the resultant photographic images were then digitized. These digitized pictures became the building blocks for a videotape that I edited on an AVID system. The video reconstructs the installation, offering another way of seeing the painting show, in relation to television. The video is played on two television monitors within the gallery space. A third monitor offers regular television programming, with a remote control and a TV Guide for selection possibilities and to enhance general viewing pleasure. A limited-edition video catalogue of the exhibition is available. A web specific project related to *Screen* that I developed is on view concurrently with the exhibition at äda 'web < http://www.adaweb.com/influx/decter/screen.html >.

> When everything that was directly lived had moved away into a representation, there was no real life, yet no other life seemed real.
> —Greil Marcus

Television has always been an aggregate of bodies, institutions, and transmissions in continual transformation.
—Jonathan Crary

The one thing to say about art and life is that art is art and life is life, that art is not life and that life is not art.
—Ad Reinhardt

Participants

Richard Artschwager, John Currin, Nicole Eisenman, Gaylen Gerber, Peter Halley, Mary Heilmann, Peter Hopkins, Alex Katz, Byron Kim, Jutta Koether, Bill Komoski, Udomsak Krisanamis, Jonathan Lasker, Glenn Ligon, Allan McCollum, John Miller, Laura Owens, Jorge Pardo, Elizabeth Peyton, Lari Pittman, Sigmar Polke, Richard Prince, Gerhard Richter, Matthew Ritchie, Alexis Rockman, Gary Simmons, Rudolf Stingel, Philip Taaffe, Luc Tuymans, Chris Wilder, Sue Williams, Christopher Wool.

Cathode Ray Clinic #1

Revised version of curatorial statement, *Cathode Ray Clinic #1*, Apex Art, New York, May 16–June 16, 1996.

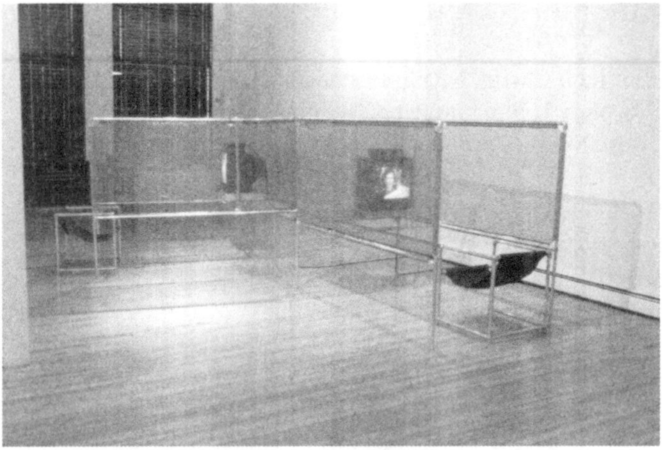

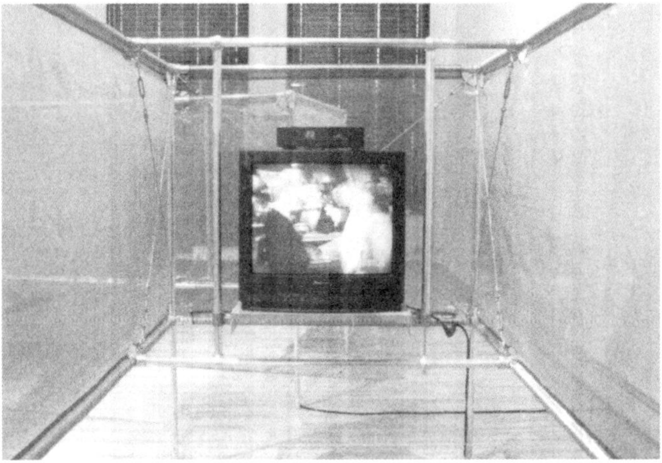

Cathode Ray Clinic #1, installation views, Apex Art, New York, May 16–June 16, 1996

Cathode Ray Clinic #1 constructs a theoretical therapeutic context wherein TV functions as a prescribed remedy for our media oversaturation. It builds an experience that gives us what we want from television, while evoking how TV works upon our desires, and our reception of information.

Crisis Scenario: Imagine the World without Television.

What would your life be like? Who would you be? How would things look? No more Saturday morning cartoons, MTV, Dan Rather, Home Shopping Network, football, The World Series, late-night stripper shows, *I Dream of Jeannie* re-runs, cereal commercials, *Star Trek*, Bill Moyers, *Seinfeld*, Public Access, BET, Court TV, *The Simpsons*, The Weather Channel, CNN, David Letterman, or whatever else turns you on.

Suddenly, it will all have been turned off; we would have been turned off.

Television would become a strictly contraband drug, as our already entrenched mass addiction, the great tube habit, clamored for satisfaction.

Remedy

Cathode Ray Clinic #1 is a therapeutic context wherein TV is prescribed to cure the addiction that television has itself triggered. No longer an over-the-counter drug, regulated exposure to TV now becomes the only prescribed remedy for the debilitating effects of chronic media withdrawal. Feed the deprived mind, and then deprive the fed mind, until the addiction is overcome or transposed. As you eat TV, TV will eat itself, eating you!

Cathode Ray Clinic #1 is not only a framing device for television viewing, but also a diagnostic tool that has all the answers. Comprised of two TV viewing structures, and a multimedia computer/television workstation, *CRC #1* is conceived as a site where you can absorb the energies of the media, and engage in the endlessly disjunctive narratives of communication and information that television naturally offers. Squeeze the remote, and watch the tube until you're satisfied. There are no prohibitions in *CRC #1*, just more freedom than you know what to do with.

CRC #1 brings back the pleasure, bathing you in the ethereal glow of the cathode ray. Here is the therapeutic answer to your TV-deficiency problem. When you are aching for some channel surfing, *CRC #1* will provide you with a sufficient dose. And, as a souvenir, you can take away a TV screenshot of your choice, a picture of a picture—an artifact of the multimedia computer-television experience.

a/drift

Revised version of the essay in the *a/drift* exhibition catalogue, Center for Curatorial Studies Museum, Bard College, October 20, 1996–January 5, 1997.

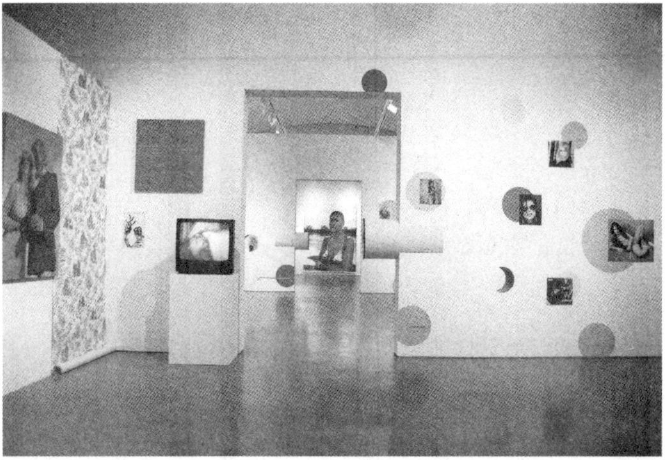

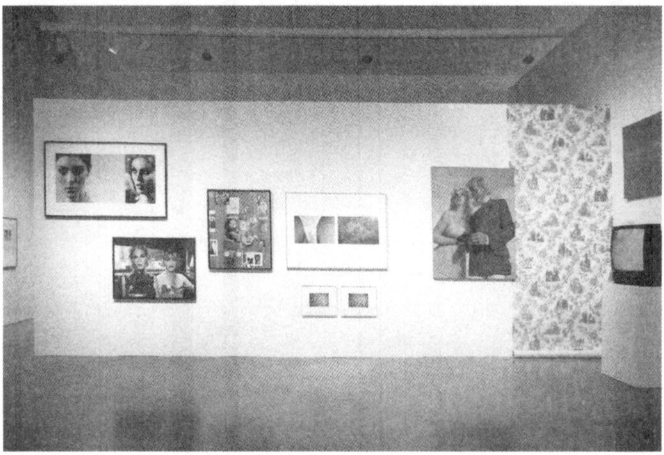

a/drift, installation view, Center for Curatorial Studies, Bard College, Annandale-on-Hudson, New York, October 20, 1996–January 5, 1997

{every thing speaks through every other thing}

a/drift is a multidimensional topography of correspondences—
a grammar and syntax of exhibition practice that celebrates the imaginary reality of our social artifices. Narrative and metaphorical possibilities are enacted through an interplay of artworks, exhibition design graphics, icons, and artifacts drawn from various parts of culture. In this allegory of youth subcultures, apathy and affirmation, nihilism and blank social critique, identities slip back and forth across gender, racial and social boundaries, linked to the meanings generated by the installation of artworks and other cultural materials within the exhibition space. In this way, the exhibition combines an intuitive, non-didactic cultural anthropology with the visual poetics of display and composition.

The museum is an alternately *real and artificial* social environment.

Which is to say that it is a theatrical place, one that can be used both to invent and explore relationships between artworks and everything else in the immediate vicinity—elements that might be named non-art. In a/drift, the museum is acknowledged to be a stage-like framework wherein persuasive fictions are created in order to make visible the links between art making and other forms of cultural representation such as advertising, music, and fashion. The exhibition looks at the symbolic systems of youth cultures as they drift through distinct territories of the social, often directed by the virtually libidinal forces of commercial imperative that transform alternative life-styles into stylized marketing campaigns for jeans, under-wear, and cologne.

a/drift might be understood as a kind of meta-exhibition, to the extent that it is comprised of eight relatively autonomous zones that interrelate fluidly: "Elasticity"; "Where Is the Identity?"; "A Lovely Entropy"; "TV Heads"; "Almost Dumb, Distracted, and Apathetic Enough"; "Lifestyles of the ... "; "From Reticence to Smart Anger, Nihilism to Hope and Back Again"; "Carnal Matters." In tandem with an exhibition/graphic design that was developed to materialize ideas and sensations of porousness, overlap, and drifting, the show celebrates its own fictive condition. Inspired by methods of sampling at the heart of hip-hop music, the exhibition reappropriates artworks and fragments of the general culture and then weaves these together; the exhibition becomes a panorama of conjunctions.

Here, the metaphor of drifting has been used on a number of different, but intrinsically related, levels: as a way to suggest that drifting and drift can be understood as rhetorical figures for how distinct forms and languages pass through each other within the culture, how everything filters through everything else. This is a way to move beyond the exhausted binary opposition of high and low, to understand that culture dwells within society as a thoroughly porous constellation of practices, languages, discourses. The trope of drifting also allows for reflection upon the various manifestations of youth culture-driven representations that have influenced American culture since the 1960s. *a/drift* is fundamentally about framing the continuous cross-pollinations of visual imagination that can be identified in the gap between art making and cinema, television, fashion, and other cultural languages.

{recombinant culture}

Recombinant culture suggests a loose, mobile, fluid, fugitive organization of distinct social, institutional, linguistic, and visual particles that spin around, inflect, and alter each other. Today's material, symbolic, ideological, and psychological cross-pollinations occur within distinct representational or sign systems that build upon each other like organic architectures—expanding and contracting, reshaping, mutating, producing hybrid languages. Mere binaries are extinct. An aphorism for recombinant culture: everything furtive eventually makes itself available for visual articulation, then drifts away into an as-yet untranslatable hybridity.

{art, life, museums, real artifice}

Adrift. A drift. a/drift.

The assertion of equivalence between the space of the museum and other everyday social spaces—e.g., restaurants, shopping malls, or cinemas—is as untenable as the familiar argument that art's greatest aspiration during the latter part of the 20th-century has been to become literally indistinguishable from everything else in life. All of art's gestures toward identity or similitude in relation to reality have been forceful only as articulations contingent upon metaphor, symbolism, or allegory. Likewise, this exhibition can only and ever be understood as an allegorical and symbolic project, one that seeks to articulate possible relations of influence between artists and their environments.

To fill up the museum with an admixture of artworks and other cultural artifacts, and then to argue that we are no longer in a position—intellectually, spiritually, or ideologically—to make distinctions between these things as they circulate through various social institutions would be, at best, tenuous. It is always the distinctions that must be recognized and understood. To construct an environment in which these sorts of cultural, aesthetic, and semiotic lines can be illuminated is one of the central desires of this exhibition project.

Of course, this curatorial gesture exploits the already artificial environment of the museum. The museum has the potential to reveal the artificiality—i.e., the constructedness—of reality conceived as an ever-evolving, often conflicting, network of language formations. As a symbolic construction, *a/drift* suggests that the museum is a place where culture can be made and studied under specific conditions; this involves allowing fragments of external culture to infiltrate the museum.

{art drifts from one condition to the next ... }

Art has always drifted from one condition to the next, from one use to another, from one set of definitions to the next, from one language to the next. Neither merely a fetishizing of reality, nor a poetics contingent upon the production of reality effects, a trend has emerged toward the development of an interior reality that desires to be materially and conceptually indistinguishable from a shared, social experience of reality. But perhaps it is the other way around. Art consumes anything that would deny its right to exist, legitimizing itself by making everything else seem a simulacrum of art. Life imitates art, and meanwhile art drifts into the life-condition.

Anticipating a cultural ethos predominant for many of us today, Vladimir Tatlin remarked in 1924: "Research into everyday life as a certain form of material culture." But reversing this maxim suggests an equally pertinent idea: research into material culture as a certain form of everyday life.

Art, as we know by now, is perhaps the most chameleon-like of cultural activities: it seems to become what it emulates. And the chameleon-like nature of art is contagious: any material that is used to make art becomes, both conceptually and materially, art. Anything that does not seem, at first, to meet a set of art criteria can be converted, formally and ideationally, into artistic matter. Art feels quite comfortable wearing borrowed clothing in order to assume any sort of identity, and it travels on occasion with a passport bearing a false name, allowing vicarious entry into the artifice of the everyday and the ordinary. Art can recycle itself into anything, and anything can be recycled as art.

{closing at the start: the exhibition-as-fantasy}

The drifting of various materials into the site of the museum, a depositing of cultural residues, the blending of visual signs: the exhibition as a platform for an economy of symbolic interplays, a theatrics of display and composition, an amplification of the situational artificiality. Constructing a moment of visual culture, then disassembling it.

a/drift inverts the so-called rhizomatic exhibition structure, where the museum or gallery is used merely as a filtering system through which the viewer is directed back to *the putative reality of the real world* in order to encounter a network of dispersed/displaced artists' projects in various external places. This rhizomatic structure promises a marriage of art and the everyday that is repeatedly frustrated, since art wants nothing more from reality than for it to submit to transformative gestures, and reality wants nothing more from art than for it to celebrate its artifice.

a/drift constructs an imaginary arena of reality within a context—the museum—that only understands reality to be a fiction. Rather than dispersing art into the world, the contents of the world are poured into the container of the institution, and the museum becomes its own reality—and that is precisely where the fantasy begins.

Participants

Catherine Opie, Vito Acconci, Cindy Sherman, Renée Green, David Cronenberg, Billy Name, Sam Durant, Simon Grennan & Christopher Sperandio, Doug Aitken, Nan Goldin, Vanessa Beecroft, Adrian Piper, Sam Samore, Dawoud Bey, Cady Noland, Laurie Simmons, Lyle Ashton Harris, Larry Clark, Dana Hoey, Georgina Starr, Nayland Blake, General Idea, Bruce Nauman, Wolfgang Tillmans, Inez van Lamsweerde, Henry Bond, Mark Morrisroe, Elizabeth Peyton, Chris Burden, Sharon Lockhart, Douglas Blau, John Currin, Damien Hirst, Sue Williams, Tamara Fites, Lincoln Tobier, Coco Fusco & Paula Heredia, Jeff Wall, Nicole Eisenman, Collier Schorr, Thomas Ruff, Rirkrit Tiravanija, Karen Kilimnik, Ken Lum, Mike Kelley, Andy Warhol, Daniel Oates, Sean Landers, Jeff Koons, Jack Pierson, Paul McCarthy, Glenn Ligon, John Miller, Gillian Wearing, Spike Jonze, Alex Katz,

John Lindell, Sigmar Polke, Piero Manzoni, Gerwald Rockenschaub, Lari Pittman, Beat Streuli, Meyer Vaisman, Gary Simmons, Claes Oldenburg, Jennifer Silitch, Felix González-Torres, Raymond Pettibon, Mariko Mori, Stephen Shore, Hirsch Perlman, Jutta Koether, David Robbins, Richard Prince, Stephen Prina, Jason Rhoades, Franz Ackermann, Noritoshi Hirakawa, Charles Long, Steven Parrino, Martin Kippenberger, AC2K (the artist formerly known as Art Club 2000), Robert Longo, Miltos Manetas, Mark Borthwick, Serge Comte, Bernard Joisten, Maurizio Cattelan, Laetitia Bénat, Vidya & Jean Michel, and Anders Edstrom.

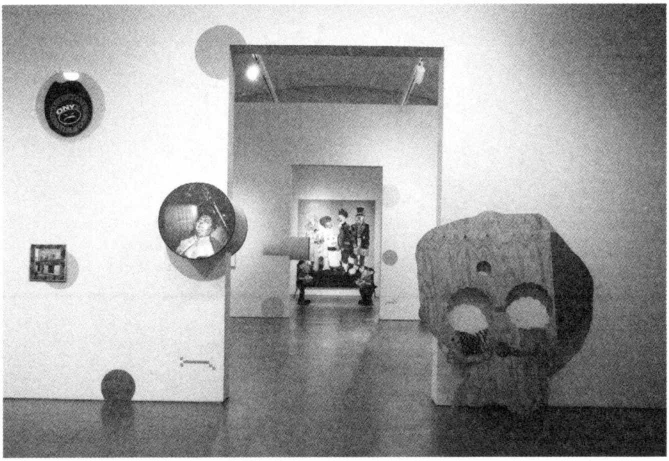

a/drift, installation view, Center for Curatorial Studies, Bard College, Annandale-on-Hudson, New York, October 20, 1996–January 5, 1997

Transmute

Revised version of essay in the brochure of *Transmute*, Museum of Contemporary Art, Chicago, August 21–November 7, 1999.

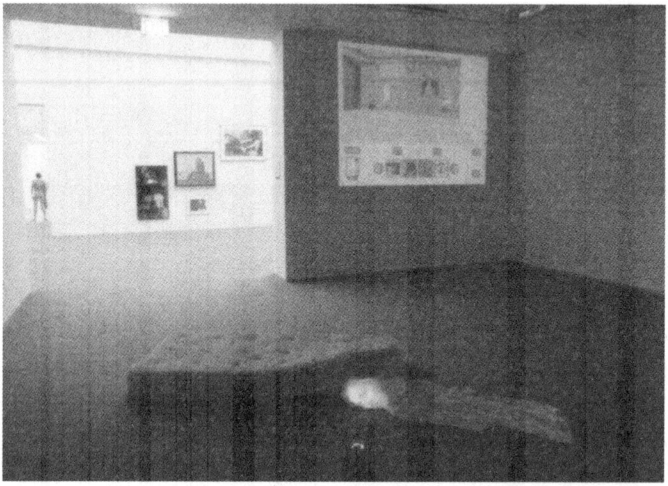

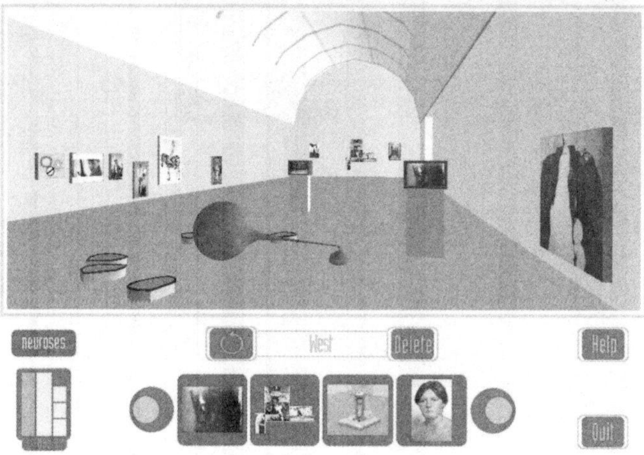

Transmute, installation view, Museum of Contemporary Art, Chicago, August 21–November 7, 1999
Transmute, screen shot of "Virtual Curator" interactive program, Museum of Contemporary Art, Chicago, August 21–November 7, 1999

Upon the invitation of the Museum of Contemporary Art in Chicago, I developed an interpretive reinstallation of works from the MCA's collection, challenging the museum's normative approach to historical chronology and thematic organization. During this process, I conceived and codeveloped (in collaboration with a programmer and web designer) virtual curator and virtual artist interfaces for the public to reinvent the exhibition within virtual space, utilizing on-site interactive computer kiosks, and a web-based extension.

How do curators of contemporary art negotiate the relationship between audience and museum collection? And what is the role of technology in the mediation between artworks and viewers? Can museums use technology to redefine, in significant ways, the public's experience—facilitating transformative moments of engagement, participation, and interpretation?

In *Transmute*, I have endeavored to address these questions by developing an interactive exhibition that enables museum visitors to use artworks from the MCA Collection to explore conceptual and visual interconnections. *Transmute* brings these works together in the museum's galleries and as simulations on computer terminals, thereby giving visitors an opportunity to explore roles as *virtual curators* and *virtual artists*. The interactive portion of the exhibition is also accessible on the MCA website.

The character of an art museum is expressed through its collection, which is assembled by its director, curators, and trustees, and embodies an institution's cultural identity. Museum collections, while often presented as stable, are actually in a state of continual transformation. Most collections, whether ancient or contemporary, reflect a complex negotiation (and consolidation) of diverse artworks and aesthetic tendencies, as well as sometimes contradictory attitudes toward society. Curators select artworks for exhibitions to amplify specific concepts and themes, which is in effect a transformative process for the audience. In this exhibition, technology is deployed to generate new connections between works from the MCA Collection, and to change the audience's relation to the museum and the curator's role. In *Transmute*, visitors may become virtual curators, arranging their own version of the exhibition within a simulated environment of the museum space. Using a touchscreen monitor, visitors can select a work of art, move it within the virtual museum space, and redesign the exhibition. In addition, one computer screen is projected on the wall, providing visitors with an opportunity to virtually navigate in a cinematic context. Visitors may also choose from a selection of works from outside the MCA Collection by contemporary artists who were invited to participate in the virtual component of the show. These artists include Liam Gillick, Grennan & Sperandio, Fariba Hajamadi, Noritoshi Hirakawa, LOT/EK Architecture, Miltos Manetas, John Miller and Richard Hoeck, Gerwald Rockenschaub, Sam Samore, Julia Scher, and Måns Wrange. In the virtual artist component of *Transmute*, visitors will see a reproduction of John Baldessari's *Fish and Ram* (1988), a work from the MCA Collection. In *Fish and Ram*, the artist arranged six photographs appropriated from mainstream sources.

Using computers (within the museum galleries), viewers can recombine these photographs—as well as a selection of images submitted by members of the public in response to Baldessari's work—in many variations. By incorporating their own ideas and visual tastes into the framework of Baldessari's work, visitors become virtual artists, reinventing *Fish and Ram*.

Participants

Vito Acconci, John Baldessari, Matthew Barney, Chris Burden, John Coplans, John De Andrea, Jeanne Dunning, General Idea, Gilbert & George, Mona Hatoum, Gary Hill, Jim Isermann, Mike Kelley, Jeff Koons, Barbara Kruger, Charles Long, Rene Magritte, Iñigo Manglano-Ovalle, Bruce Nauman, Claes Oldenburg, Tony Oursler, Jorge Pardo, Jack Pierson, Richard Prince, Mel Ramos, Allen Ruppersberg, Ed Ruscha, Andres Serrano, Jim Shaw, Cindy Sherman, Laurie Simmons, Lorna Simpson, Franz West, Liam Gillick, Simon Grennan & Christopher Sperandio, Fariba Hajamadi, Noritoshi Hirakawa, LOT/EK, Miltos Manetas, John Miller and Richard Hoeck, Gerwald Rockenschaub, Sam Samore, Julia Scher, and Måns Wrange.

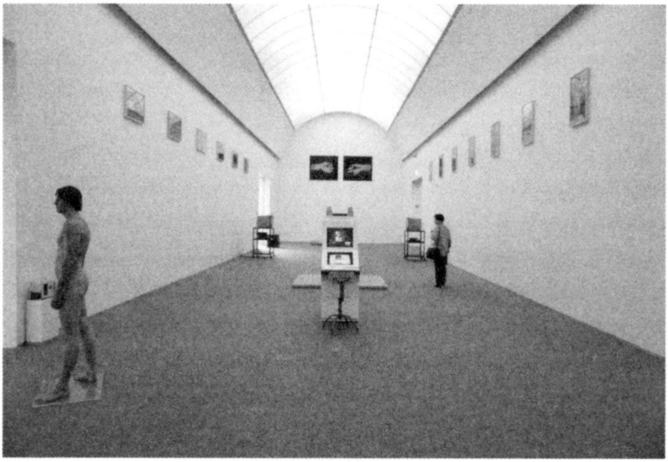

Transmute, installation view, Museum of Contemporary Art, Chicago, August 21–November 7, 1999

Tele[visions]

Revised version of essay in *Tele[visions]* exhibition catalogue, Kunsthalle Vienna, October 18, 2001–January 6, 2002. (A German-language translation was published in the catalogue.)

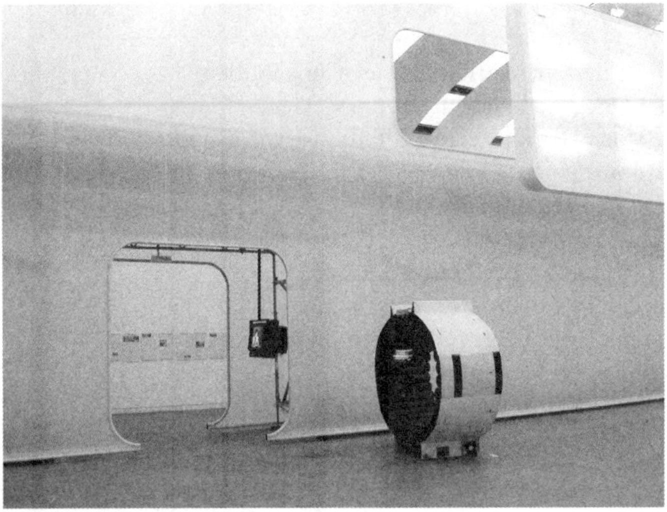

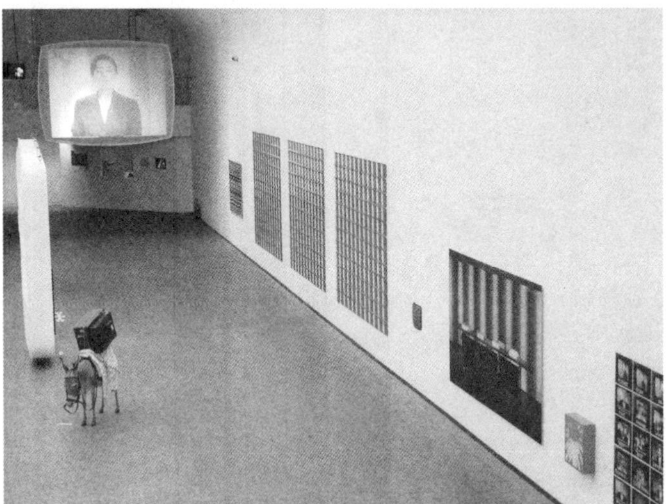

Tele[visions], installation views, Kunsthalle Vienna, October 18, 2011–January 6, 2012

Why, at this historical juncture, develop a show on the topic of television? In a sense, it is akin to organizing an exhibition on any other genre of life: food, sex, entertainment, sleep, death, animals, etc. Of course, television touches all of these aspects of life, and more; television, in one way or another, whether we like it or not, touches *everything*. As we enter the new century, it is a propitious moment to look back at the impact of television, and to reevaluate its relationship to art making. Now is not the time to relegate television to the dustbin of history. For some, television has become an almost obsolete and exhausted issue, displaced by a fixation upon the Internet and related technologies. Yet TV will be a part of any technological future, on both theoretical and practical terms. An exhibition about art and television may also suggest ways of thinking about the transformation of television *as* a technology.

Tele[visions] is fundamentally an exhibition about how artists look at television. It is not an exhibition about every aspect of television, and it does not seek to reference a comprehensive, global television culture. *Tele[visions]* is not an exercise in cultural studies, nor an academic gesture of interdisciplinary analysis. The show declines to recapitulate the well-trodden argument about the influence of generic entertainment culture on art making, since this is beyond the obvious. *Tele[visions]* does not propose a counter-hegemonic, revisionist history of television-influenced art practices. This exhibition suggests that the expansive culture of television has generated a reservoir of imaginary narratives that people regularly use to negotiate or map aspects of their identities and lifestyles. From this perspective, television is understood to function not only as a primary delivery system for information and entertainment (or its synthesis, infotainment), but also as a conduit for manifold representational codes.

Tele[visions] seeks to offer a rather straightforward, almost transparent, curatorial approach: the audience is invited to rethink art through the filter of television, and vice-versa. It is a subjective reconsideration of how artists have absorbed, embraced, critically challenged—and occasionally reinvented—our experience and understanding of television over the past three decades. The show is comprised of painting, photography, sculpture, installation, single-channel video, multi-channel video, drawings, prints, books, and other materials. The artworks here reveal the presence of television in a variety of ways: from the literal (i.e., iconographic) referencing of the ubiquitous television-as-object to more indirect allusions regarding the atmospherics of TV-permeated life. Some participants deliver a critique of television's sociopolitical operations, while others prefer to ambivalently index television's aesthetic effects and affects.

In "The Museum of Accidents," I say at the end of the article that television is the actual museum. In the beginning, I say a museum of accidents is needed, and the reader imagines a building with accidents inside. But at the end, I say, no, this museum already exists, it's television.

> —Paul Virilio, from "Cyberwar, God, and Television: Interview with Paul Virilio," by Louise K. Wilson, October 1994

Everyone Is a Television Expert

With few exceptions, most people are fluent, in one way or another, with television. Everyone, in a sense, is a television expert, since TV is perhaps the most populist cultural language we have invented. Television victimizes us, and yet it is our salvation. It has become our second nature, and we always know how, when, and where to plug into it.

> You never forget how to use TV because you never have to learn how. Like any other relationship, it seems you just sort of "get along" with this chatty appliance; you "do" it, it "does" you. We "do" TV by letting its juices flow. Not flesh-and-blood juices, of course, but continuously acrid signals, impulses that flow from its artificial circuitry to our own. Like humans, television is sensitive to our touch. We flick a knob on its chassis and it performs for us.
> —Barbara Kruger, "TV Guides," September 1989, in *Remote Control: Power, Cultures, and the World of Appearance*

Television is the static of our lives, it is the material and symbolic representation of the distraction that we crave as a respite from labor, from family, and from emotions. Television has consumed family, sex, romance, sports, reading, and many other life experiences, effectively infiltrating all of these activities to the point where we have begun to reproduce, in our daily lives, the character of TV relations. Television is a mediator, and a relational medium.

Couch Potato Theory

At once worshipped and demonized, a catalyst of absorption and distraction, apathy and engagement, TV is a cultural force that just will not go away. After more than 50 years, television still triggers debate, assuming the perennial role of the scapegoat for the supposed dumbing-down of society, or the erosion of morality. Material yet intangible, dumb and brilliant,

TV is actually a complex delivery system of multiplying and frequently contradictory value systems. TV delivers alternately global and localized discourses that promote the universal rituals of (transnational) consumerism, while also consolidating the indigenous social/political mores of nations. Television has occasioned the symbolic collapse of distinctions between private and public space within an interconnected world of simulations.

Many years ago, media guru Marshall McLuhan claimed that "We Become What We Behold." This became a mantra for many theorists and academicians, as well as for practitioners involved with early video-based technologies. But this notion also generated controversy, particularly among those who rejected the techno-organic argument that television is a technological extension of our bodies. We *may* become what we behold, as television takes hold of our eyes, minds, and imaginations, but we are also cognizant that we are being absorbed, on corporeal and perceptual levels, into media.

Who, among us, has not been a couch potato at one point in their lives? No one is exempt: not even members of the intellectual elite. If you think about it, the couch potato is able to speculate about his or her condition, and such conjectural activity does little to dissuade him or her from passively absorbing television emissions on the living room sofa. For some, even, the passivity of being a couch potato creates the opportunity to enter into a state of disinterested contemplation—which is the adequate prerequisite to any kind of critical activity. Passive TV absorption can be converted thereby into critical TV absorption, which allows most people the opportunity to scrutinize, with expertise, what they are watching. All TV viewers, in other words, can develop a reflexive, critical relationship to television, and become TV *critics*. So, do we really need academics and specialists explaining television to the rest of us? From a certain populist perspective, many folks are already critical viewers of media culture. They understand that television, for example, began as an experiment with technology, gradually became a mass medium, injected itself into our domestic space, transformed our domestic space, and then extended itself—historically, ideologically, socially—through our bodies, to become a tactile, material, thing. Yet, at the same time, television is a control mechanism for consumption.

> TV, by virtue of its mere presence, is a social control in itself.
> —Jean Baudrillard

Television, Work, Leisure, Convergence

Today, ironically, there may still be more debates about the usefulness or uselessness of television than there are about the relevance of the Internet. The former, TV, is still dismissed, by some, as a "boob tube" or "idiot box" that merely offers rank commercialism, worthless entertainment, and promotes degraded cultural values. The latter, the Internet, is often considered an indispensable communication, informational, and educational tool, even though it has become, ironically, increasingly congested with pop-ups, cookies, and porn.

> I will characterize the material basis of television as a current of simultaneous event reception.
> —Stanley Cavell

It used to be that cinema was the primary instrument of visual/narrative entertainment in popular culture, and then it was displaced by television. Cinema was actually folded into the space of television, with the advent of home video. If television became our principle respite from work, our apparatus for distraction, information and entertainment, the introduction of computers (and the Internet) into domestic space has complicated matters—even as it has revolutionized access. Complications arise as more and more people are discovering that leisure time and work time have converged. It is now possible to fold virtually all activities, experiences, forms, and representations into the space of the computer. And, with the rapid development of mobile communication/phone devices, access to everything—including TV transmissions—will be virtually anywhere, all the time. TV will be patched into our brains, for better or worse. There *does* seem to be a desire, as expressed in these recent technological innovations and business models, to converge television, the Internet, the web, and mobility—emblematic of the ethos to create an interpenetration of work and leisure. This fusion is not necessarily a good thing.

The Art Factor

There are many who argue, with some legitimacy, that television is no longer an available context for the development of innovative art practices, if it ever was. Of course, corporations do not see a viable business model in relation to contemporary art, and governments with cultural programs have been known to be skeptical. Even public television, in the United States, has largely divested itself of producing experimental TV. So, what are the possibilities of artists working on—or, inside of—television in the future? Today, many people in the cultural community have inaugurated the Internet as the new, open, under-regulated context for artistic experimentation, often comparing it to the over-regulated, hyper-commercialized territory of TV. But is such optimism about the Internet—and negativity about TV—actually warranted? Because it is still relatively inexpensive for artists to set up websites (i.e., their own private art showcases), access to broader circuits of communication is possible. But a more important question arises: what are artists doing with that access? Of course, it is difficult to imagine that, in the foreseeable future, artists will have the economic or political clout to establish viable TV channels (commercial, experimental, or hybrid), but with the ongoing evolution of TV-Internet convergence, hopefully new possibilities can be tested by artists, and even cultural institutions. Of course, much depends upon the evolution of economic models, and the ongoing tension, or perhaps irreconcilable differences between, media experimentation, and media commerce.

Life Without Television?

Television is ultimately our choice, and our responsibility: watch it, do not watch it, but it will not disappear from the scene. TV will continue to mutate, to frustrate us, and to seduce us. The *televisual* will always permeate our lives … until it ceases to exist (not likely in our lifetime). It will remain a locus for the invention and projection of our imaginary lives, the filtering of our histories and identities. TV will persist as an engine for consumerism, at once democratic and anti-democratic. TV will always embody the best and worst of any society, because it is an expression of us. Right now, at this very moment, a baby is being born, a person is dying, and someone is watching TV. Constant, endless television ...

Participants

Participants: Maike Abetz/Oliver Drescher, Vito Acconci, Ant Farm, Apsolutno, Art Club 2000, Michel Auder, John Baldessari, Martin Beck, Mark Bennett, Ashley Bickerton, Dara Birnbaum, Dike Blair, Candice Breitz, Chris Burden, Miguel Calderon, Sophie Calle, Maurizio Cattelan, Sarah Charlesworth, Larry Clark, Hans-Christian Dany & Christoph Schäfer, Thomas Demand, Jessica Diamond, Jan Dibbets, do-Foundation, Peter Dombrowe, Tracy Emin, Harun Farocki, GALA Committee, General Idea, Nan Goldin, Paul Graham, Grennan and Sperandio, Keith Haring, Astrid Herrmann, Christine Hill, Jonathan Horowitz, Jim Isermann, Sanja Ivekovic, Christian Jankowski, Martin Kippenberger, Alexander Kluge, Barbara Kruger, Sean Landers, Louise Lawler, LOT/EK, Miltos Manetas, Dorit Margreiter, Allan McCollum, John Miller, Antonio Muntadas, Tony Oursler, Nam June Paik, Paper Tiger Television, Philippe Parreno, Zhang Peili, Raymond Pettibon, Daniel Pflumm, Richard Prince, David Reeb, Tobias Rehberger, Pipilotti Rist, Gerwald Rockenschaub, Ursula Rogg, Julian Rosefeldt, Martha Rosler, Christoph Schlingensief, Ilene Segalove, Richard Serra, David Shrigley, Laurie Simmons, Michael Smith & Joshua White, Doron Solomons, Wolfgang Staehle, Haim Steinbach, Szuper Gallery, TVTV, Van Gogh T.V., Klaus vom Bruch, Carrie Mae Weems, William Wegman, Olav Westphalen, Måns Wrange, Joseph Zehrer.

Dark Places: A Phantasmagoria of Simultaneous, Multiple, Looped Curatorial Scripts

Revised version of essay in *Dark Places* exhibition catalogue, Santa Monica Museum of Art, January 21–April 22, 2006.

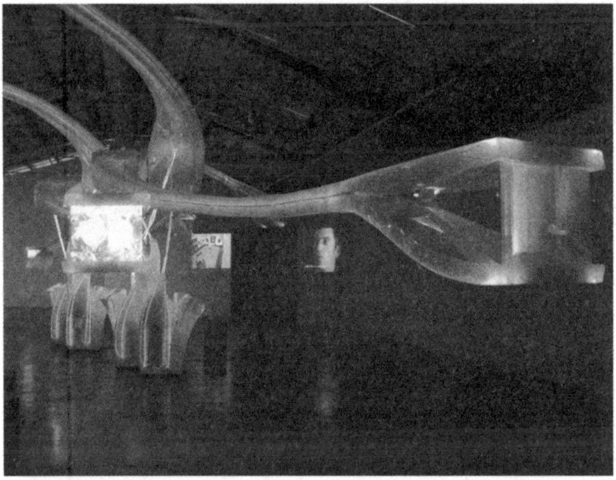

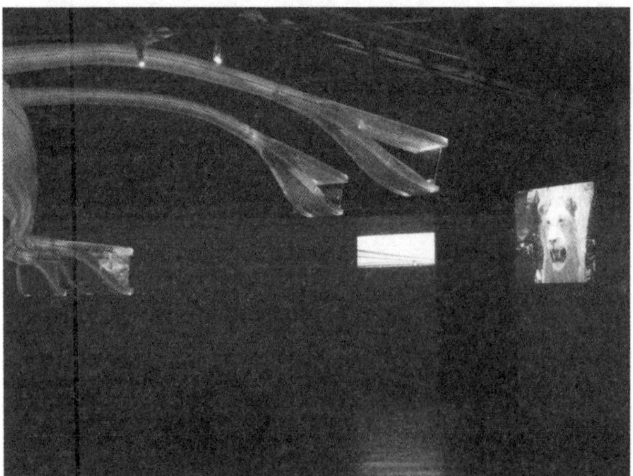

Dark Places, installation views, Santa Monica Museum of Art, January 21–April 22, 2006

Is it possible for a group show to function as a critical allegory of the conventions of the group exhibition itself? In certain respects, *Dark Places* developed out of my 1994 exhibition, *Don't Look Now*. The earlier exhibition was comprised of artworks in the form of 35 mm slides, each projected onto its own screen within a constructed architectural environment. Testing a new kind of exhibition design—i.e., a specific format/display system—was key for the *Don't Look Now* exhibition, as it is for *Dark Places*.

Rather than developing a conventional issue-oriented or thematic group show, *Dark Places* endeavors to reanimate relationships between art, architecture, and media/technological design in order to generate an imaginary, *noir* urban environment inside the frame of the museum context. This is a theatrical scenario in which the artificial and real blur together in an ecstatic mosaic of still and moving images, and multiple narratives and counter-narratives. It seeks to explore interconnections between social space and architecture, the possibility that psychological conditions are scripted into the fabric of our physical environment, and to reconsider how we navigate through urban (and other) territories—on bodily, perceptual, political, psychological, ideological, and aesthetic levels. The exhibition endeavors to consider the ways in which modern and post-modern neuroses and pathologies are generated at the intersection point between social trauma and built space. How bodies, minds, and the built environment (architecture, infrastructure such as streets, etc.), as well as the imaginary overlay of narratives from popular culture (cinema and television, particularly), are always in a state of interpenetration.

Dark Places embodies a desire to engineer a very different kind of group exhibition experience for viewers, and represents a fundamental challenge to normative curatorial methods. Artworks are presented in digital form; the digitized images are entered into a database, and flowed through various monitors housed within the architectural structure. The exhibition's translucent, modular plastic architectural design establishes an unprecedented way of presenting visual materials, and is designed to function within a darkened space. This display system is laced with a network of fiber optics that is subtly responsive to the activity of visitors at the workstations.

The 75 participating artists and architects have produced new works, or modified extant materials. The show, on one level, is a mechanism through which to deliver an inventory of digitized artworks and architectural projects, with eight distinct curatorial scripts functioning as interpretive sequences. Each of the eight sequences/scripts is looped and projected within (and out of) a designated display unit; the display units transmit these sequences, simultaneously, throughout the day, generating visual and aural interpenetrations within the space. Each unique sequence/script of works has been organized according to a variety of curatorial criteria: subject, visual attributes, conceptual frameworks, and other factors.

Dark Places suggests that the real is nothing more than an agglomeration of images and representations (of imagined realities); the exhibition seeks to reanimate the negotiation of the real and the imaginary.

Imagine yourself entering a darkened space, encountering multiple images and videos projected from a translucent architecture structure, a simultaneity of visual elements, sequenced, circulating, looping, interpenetrating.

... walking into the scenario, the staged environment, of an exhibition, one is only capable of perceiving the situation as a constellation of visual articulations, a continuous flow of visual signs ... and then you look more closely ... and you see the integrity of individual works ... of unique positions and voices ...

... an imaginary social space ...

The possibility of experiencing the exhibition as an interplay of micro-exhibitions ... an interweaving of curatorial scripts and distinct durations, to be reassembled by the visitor at distinct moments of viewing.

... the project suggests a rhizomatic system ... akin to a visual hypertext, in which viewers/readers can move fluidly from one narrative location to another, generating their own correspondences ...

A continuous circulation of related and unrelated practices, correspondences and tensions ....

A space reanimated by an ephemeral, glowing armature, by the cycling of pictures, videos, films, digitized paintings, architectures, and other visual elements that allude to a range of atmospheric conditions within urban experience and media cultures.

No beginning, middle, or end, just immersion within a space inflected by an interlacing of projected artworks and architectural projects ... a network of correspondences, relationships, frictions, harmonies, and contradictions delivered for the audience to navigate through, and to negotiate with ....

Experience the curatorial scripts as a kind of visualized intertextual map (at once rational and irrational) of diverse artistic and architectural practices that allude to enigmatic conditions—real and/or imagined—of the urban, strange domesticity, the penetration of media representations into social space ...

An intermingling of psychological territories ... death, beauty, despair, hope, humor, which inflect, or rescript, our navigations of built space ...

A phantasmagoria of aligned, unaligned, related, and contested visions of urban situations on the brink of transformation, identities on the edge of formation and deformation, places at once recognizable and then de-familiarized, the pleasure of interpenetrating ambiguities and certainties, rational analysis and self-indulgent pleasure, diverse styles and voices.

Participants

Acconci Studio, Franz Ackermann, Francis Alÿs, Michael Ashkin, Jaime Avila Ferrer, Dennis Balk, Matthew Barney, Judith Barry, Thomas Bayrle, Julie Becker, Douglas Blau, Monica Bonvicini, Daniel Bozhkov, Mark Bradford, Troy Brauntuch, Candice Breitz, François Bucher, Sophie Calle, Eduardo Consuegra, Jordan Crandall, Teddy Cruz, Jonas Dahlberg, Stephen Dean, Anne Deleporte, Diller + Scofidio, Sam Durant, Anna Gaskell, Douglas Gordon, gruppo A12, Fariba Hajamadi, Pablo Helguera, Noritoshi Hirakawa, Julian Hoeber, Emily Jacir, Christian Jankowski, Vincent Johnson, Mitchell Kane, Joachim Koester, Glenn Ligon, Dorit Margreiter, Fiorenza Menini, John Miller, Muntadas, Paul Myoda, Yoshua Okon, Catherine Opie, Lucy Orta, Hirsch Perlman, Raymond Pettibon, Richard Phillips, Richard Prince, Raqs Media Collective, Miguel Rio Branco, Alexis Rockman, Julian Rosefeldt, Aura Rosenberg, Peter Rostovsky, Sam Samore, Paige Sarlin, Julia Scher, Gregor Schneider, Allan Sekula, Andres Serrano, Nedko Solakov, Doron Solomons, Wolfgang Staehle, Javier Tellez, Anton Vidokle, Eyal Weizman/Nadav Harel, James Welling, Wim Wenders, Judi Werthein, Charlie White, Måns Wrange, Jody Zellen, Heimo Zobernig.

List of Illustrations

p. 6
Rirkrit Tiravanija, *Untitled* (free), 1992
Installation view at 303 Gallery, New York
Courtesy of the artist and Gavin Brown's enterprise

p. 36
Michael Asher, *Untitled*, 1988. Installation dimensions variable
Courtesy of the artist and Artists Space

p. 42
Silvia Kolbowski, *Enlarged from the Catalogue: The United States of America*, 1988 (view of plan element of the installation).
Courtesy of the artist

p. 46
Judith Barry, exhibition design as artist contribution to the exhibition *Damaged Goods: Desire and the Economy of the Object*, New Museum, New York, June 21–August 10, 1986.
Courtesy of the artist

p. 52
Andrea Fraser, *Museum Highlights: A Gallery Talk*, 1989. Performance.
Courtesy of the artist. Photo: Kelly & Massa Photography

p. 58
Louise Lawler, *Pollock and Tureen, Arranged by Mr. and Mrs. Burton Tremaine, Connecticut*, 1984. Silver dye bleach print. 28 × 39 in (71.1 × 99.1 cm)

p. 67
Mark Dion and Jason Simon, *Artful History: A Restoration Comedy*, 1987. Film, sound, color. Duration: 28 min. Courtesy of the artists

p. 68
Daniel Buren, *To Transform*, situated works, John Weber Gallery, New York, November–December 1991 (detail). © D.B.-ADAGP Paris

p. 72
Renée Green, *Import/Export Funk Office*, 1992. Installation Dimensions variable. Courtesy of the artist and Free Agen Media

p. 78
Installation view (Renée Green, Julia Scher), *Kontext Kunst*, Neue Galerie Graz, Künstlerhaus, Graz, 1993. Photo: J. Koinegg

p. 85
Julia Scher, *Warning Sign*, 1995. High gloss paint printed onto bulletproof glass. Edition of 4. Production by Massimo De Carlo.
Photo: Julia Scher

p. 86
Fred Wilson, *Guarded View*, 1991. Installation view of *Black Male: Representations of Masculinity in Contemporary American Art*, Whitney Museum of American Art, New York, November 10, 1994–March 5, 1995. © Fred Wilson, courtesy of The Whitney Museum of American Art. Photo: Geoffrey Clements

Glenn Ligon, *Cocaine (Pimps)*, 1993. Oilstick, synthetic polymer, and graphite on linen. 32 × 32 in. Collection of The Whitney Museum of American Art; promised gift of Emily Fisher Landau. Courtesy of the artist

p. 96
Stephen Prina, *Dom-Hotel, Zimmer 101, Köln, 1994*, 1994. Installation view, American Fine Arts, Co., New York, October 22–November 19, 1994. Courtesy of the artist

p. 100
Heimo Zobernig, installation view, Wiener Secession, Vienna, 1995. Photo Archive Heimo Zobernig

p. 108
Peter Halley, *Two Cells with Circulating Conduit*, 1986. Acrylic, Day-Glo acrylic, and Roll-a-tex on canvas. 64 × 104 in.
Courtesy of Peter Halley Studio

p. 114
The Occupy Wall Street scene, Zuccotti Park in Lower Manhattan, October 17, 2011. Photo: Joshua Decter

p. 126
The Ren & Stimpy Show, Nickelodeon Animation Studios

p. 133
Beavis and Butt-Head, MTV Networks (Viacom)

p. 134, 137
Liam Gillick, *The State itself Becomes a Super Whatnot*, installation view, Casey Kaplan, New York, 2008, installation view.
Photo: Cary Whittier

p. 138
Superflex, *Flooded McDonald's*, 2008. Video, color, sound.
Courtesy SUPERFLEX and Peter Blum Gallery, New York

p. 142
Emily Jacir, *Lydda Airport* 2007–2009. Single-channel video animation. Duration: 5 min. 21 sec. Photo: Jason Mandella

p. 145
Emily Jacir, *stazione (Arsenale)*, 2009. Digital C-print on aluminum. 18 1/4 × 23 3/4 in (46.4 × 60.3 cm). Courtesy of the artist and Alexander and Bonin, New York

p. 146
Yael Bartana, *Kings of the Hill*, 2005. © MoMA PS1

p. 153
Yael Bartana, *Trembling Time*, 2001. © MoMA PS1

p. 154
A Jeff Koons balloon flower sculpture in front of the Spielbank Berlin Casino on Marlene-Dietrich-Platz, Berlin, June 18, 2008.
Photo: Joshua Decter

p. 160
Alfredo Jaar, *The Sound of Silence*, 2006. Installation view, Galerie Lelong, New York, 2009. © Alfredo Jaar. Courtesy Galerie Lelong, New York

p. 164
Sam Durant, *Dead Labor Day*, 2010. Installation view, Paula Cooper Gallery, New York, 2010. © Sam Durant. Courtesy Paula Cooper Gallery, New York

p. 168
Jill Magid, *A Reasonable Man in a Box*, 2010. Installation view, Whitney Museum of American Art, New York, 2010. Courtesy of Sheldan C. Collins

p. 172
Pawel Althamer, *sciezka (pfad)*, 2007. Skulptur Projekte Münster, 2007. Courtesy the artist and neugerriemschneider, Berlin; Foksal Gallery Foundation, Warsaw. Photo: Joshua Decter

p. 178
Harun Farocki, *Serious Games I: Watson is Down* (2010), from *Serious Games (I-IV)*, 2010. Video, color, sound.
Duration: 8 min. Courtesy of the artist and Greene Naftali, New York

p. 288
Rodney Werden, *Portrait of General Idea*, 1974, Gelatin silver print: 39.8 × 50.2 cm. Collection General Idea, Toronto/New York

p. 302
General Idea, *AIDS* (poster project), San Francisco, 1988

p. 308
Andrea Zittel, *Prototype for A to Z Pit Bed*, 1995. Wood, carpet, foam. 18 × 96 × 144 in (45.7 × 243.8 × 365.8 cm). ARG# ZA1995–003. © Andrea Zittel. Courtesy of Andrea Rosen Gallery, New York. Photo: Peter Muscato

p. 312
left: Mike Kelley (early 1990s)
right: Stephen Prina (*Sonic Dan*, SO 36, Berlin 1996). Courtesy of the artist and Friedrich Petzel Gallery, New York

p. 322
Piotr Uklanski, *Untitled (Dance Floor)*, 1996. Installation view, Gavin Brown's Enterprise, New York, October 1996

p. 326
Jorge Pardo, *Untitled*, 1997. 456 × 330 × 72 in (1158.2 × 838.2 × 182.9 cm). Installation view, Museum of Contemporary Art, Chicago

p. 330
left: Lincoln Tobier, *Unpopular Subjective Fantastic*, 1997. Mixed media and FM radio transmission. Dimensions variable. Exhibition view, C.C.A., Glasgow. Courtesy of the artist.
right: Lincoln Tobier, *Unpopular Subjective Fantastic*, 1997. Mixed media and FM radio transmission. Dimensions variable. Street view with posters, Glasgow. Courtesy of the artist

p. 336
Monica Bonvicini, *Hammering Out (an old argument)*, 1998. Video color projection, sound, amplifier, 2 speakers. Duration: 18 min. 45 sec. Installation view, *MORE IS MORE*, Centre of Contemporary Art Znaki Czasu in Torun, Torun, Poland. Photo: Wojciech Olech

p. 342
Monica Bonvicini, *I Believe in the Skin of Things as in that of Women*, 1999. Drywall panels, aluminium studs, wood panels, graphite. Approx. 7 m × 4 m × 2.5 m. Installation view, *Monica Bonvicini. Scream & Shake*, Magasin, Grenoble, June 03–September 02, 2001. Photo: Monica Bonvicini

Monica Bonvicini, *Wallfuckin'*, 1995/96, 30 min, b/w video, monitor, wood panels, drywall panels, aluminum studs, bricks, plaster, white paint, door. 250 × 310 × 330 cm
Courtesy of the artist

p. 346
Photographs of the grounds of documenta XII, Kassel, June 2007. Photos: Joshua Decter

p. 350
Clegg & Guttmann, *The Open Music Library*, 1993. Installation comprised of a cabinet (approx. 250cm × 175cm × 60cm), five photographs of the covers of the CDs (each photograph approx. 60cm × 60cm), and a small listening station with a tape recorder with headphones. *Project Unité*, Firminy. Courtesy of the artists and Galerie Christian Nagel, Cologne

p. 358
The second floor of Oscar Niemeyer's Bienal pavilion, during the 28th edition of the Sao Paulo Bienal, October 29, 2008. Photo: Joshua Decter

p. 362
Daniel Joseph Martinez, *Call Me Ishmael: The Fully Enlightened Earth Radiates Disaster Triumphant*, 2006. Mixed-media installation with silicon over fiberglass skeleton and computer-controlled pneumatics. Dimensions variable. Installation view, United States Pavilion, Tenth Cairo Biennial, Cairo Museum of Art. Courtesy of the artist and Roberts & Tilton, Culver City

p. 370
Remains of a house in the Lower Ninth Ward, New Orleans, October 31, 2008. Photo: Joshua Decter

p. 386
Marko Peljhan, *TERRITORY 1995 Evidence*, 2006–2010. Documents, sound reconstruction, transparencies. Dimensions variable. Installation view, *Serbia: Frequently Asked Questions*, Austrian Cultural Forum, New York, September 23, 2010–January 11, 2011. Courtesy of the artist. Photo: David Plakke

Marko Peljhan, *TERRITORY 1995*, 2006–2011. Installation. Dimensions variable. Installation view, Van Abbemuseum Eindhoven (with the Territory 1995 archive), April 2–August 9, 2011. Collection Van Abbemuseum, purchased with the support of Stichting Promotors. Courtesy of the artist. Photo: Miha Bratina

p. 392
Don't Look Now, installation views, Thread Waxing Space, New York, January 22–February 26, 1994. Photo: John Berens.

p. 398
Screen, installation view, Friedrich Petzel Gallery, January 19–February 24, 1996. Courtesy of Friedrich Petzel Gallery, New York

p. 402
Cathode Ray Clinic #1, installation views, Apex Art, New York, May 16–June 16, 1996. Photo courtesy of apexart, New York

p. 406, 413
a/drift, installation views, Center for Curatorial Studies, Bard College, Annandale-on-Hudson, New York, October 20, 1996–January 5, 1997. Courtesy of the Center for Curatorial Studies, Bard College. Photos: Joshua Decter

p. 414
Transmute, installation view, Museum of Contemporary Art, Chicago, August 21–November 7, 1999. Courtesy of the Museum of Contemporary Art, Chicago. Photo: Joshua Decter.

Transmute, screen shot of "Virtual Curator" interactive program, Museum of Contemporary Art, Chicago, August 21–November 7, 1999. Courtesy of the Museum of Contemporary Art, Chicago

p. 417
Transmute, installation view, Museum of Contemporary Art, Chicago, August 21–November 7, 1999. Courtesy of the Museum of Contemporary Art, Chicago. Photo: Joshua Decter

p. 418
Tele[visions], installation views, Kunsthalle Vienna, October 18, 2011–January 6, 2012. Courtesy of the Kunsthalle Vienna. Photos: Joshua Decter

p. 426
Dark Places, installation views, Santa Monica Museum of Art, January 21–April 22, 2006. Courtesy of the Santa Monica Museum of Art. Photos: Joshua Decter

About the Author

Joshua Decter is a New York-based writer, art critic, curator, theorist, educator, editor, and organizer.

He has curated exhibitions for a wide range of museums, alternative spaces, and galleries, and his critical writings and essays have been published extensively for more than 25 years.

Decter has taught at the Center for Curatorial Studies at Bard College, The School of Visual Arts in New York, The School of the Art Institute of Chicago, New York University, UCLA, Art Center College of Design in Pasadena, and Bennington College. From 2007 to 2011 Decter was the Director of the Master of Public Art Studies Program at the University of Southern California's Roski School of Fine Arts in Los Angeles, where he designed and founded a new graduate program, MA Art and Curatorial Practices in the Public Sphere.

Decter has lectured internationally, participated in numerous symposia, and organized various conferences, including *Critical Forums: The Organization of Oppositionality & Practices: The Problem of Divisions of Cultural Labor*, co-sponsored by the New Museum and The Drawing Center in New York in 1992; *Transgressions Within the White Cube: Re-Considering Inter-Relationships Between Site, Object, Installation, Identity, and the Socio-Political* at the School of Visual Arts, New York, in 1992; *Strange Days Are Here: Painting into Media Culture Toward Painting, and Beyond*, at the School of Visual Arts, New York in 1996; *The Architecture of Display: New Approaches to Exhibition Design* at the Santa Monica Museum of Art, 2006; *The Question of the City*, Museumsquartier, Vienna Art Week, 2006; *The Situational Drive: Complexities of Public Sphere Engagement*, co-sponsored by inSite, Creative Time, and The Cooper Union, New York, in 2007; and *Participation and Friction: Rethinking Art and Architecture as Public Culture (Architecture, Design Art: Strategies for Survival* & *Art and Architecture in the Public Sphere of Cities*) at the University of Southern California in Los Angeles, in 2009.

Acknowledgments and Thanks

Thanks to all of the artists, galleries, museums, institutions, and magazines that have provided images and/or text copyright permissions for this book.

To the following for their support, collaboration, critical feedback, professional collegiality, and friendship at different points over the past 30 years: Vito Acconci, Doug Aitken, Rhea Anastas, Suzanne Anker, Bill Arning, Sara Arrhenius, Jan Avgikos, Martim Avillez, Dennis Balk, Jack Bankowsky, Judith Barry, Norton Batkin, Ute Meta Bauer, Carol Becker, Maurice Berger, Douglas Blau, Tim Blum, Francesco Bonami, Gregg Bordowitz, Mark Bradford, Benjamin Buchloh, Ron Clark, Papo Colo, Paula Cooper, Osvaldo Sánchez Crespo, Carmen Cuenca, Arthur Danto, Colin de Land, Roger Denson, Chris Dercon, David Diao, Mark Dion, Tom Eccles, David Erdman, Charles Esche, Lauri Firstenberg, Emi Fontana, Andrea Fraser, Gaylen Gerber, General Idea, Jeff Gibson, Sheila Glaser, Thelma Golden, Felix González-Torres, Jay Gorney, Michelle Grabner, Tim Griffin, Christopher Grimes, Melissa Gronlund, Fariba Hajamadi, Pat Hearn, Alanna Heiss, Richard Hertz, Laura Hoffmann, Michael Ned Holte, Jeanette Ingberman, Paul Ramírez Jonas, Mitchell Kane, Norman Klein, Helena Kontova, Bettina Korek, Vasif Kortun, Heather Felty Kouris, Michael Krichman, Sean Landers, Knight Landesman, Pablo Lafuente, Sharon Lockhart, Elsa Longhauser, Elizabeth Lovins, Gabriele Mackert, Richard Martin, Gerald Matt, Allan McCollum, Lisa Melandri, Ivo Mesquita, Karen Moss, Paul Myoda, Peter Nagy, John Peter Nilsson, Peter Norton, Tim Nye, Klaus Ottmann, Jorge Pardo, Anne Pasternak, Chris Perry, Friedrich Petzel, David Platzker, Jeff Poe, Steven Rand, Robert R. Riley, David Robbins, Alexis Rockman, Andrea Rosen, Sam Samore, Irving Sandler, Magda Sawon, Ken Saylor, Elizabeth Schambelan, Julia Scher, Peter Schjeldahl, Barry Schwabsky, Alex Scrimgeour, Amy Sillman, Bennett Simpson, Roberta Smith, Tom Solomon, Christopher Sperandio, Carol Stakenas, Haim Steinbach, Nahum Tevet, Nato Thompson, Sidney Tillim, Rirkrit Tiravanija, Mascha Veech-Kosmatschof, Stuart Veech, Anton Vidokle, Oliver Wasow, Benjamin Weil, Charlie White, Lloyd Wise, Krzysztof Wodiczko, Denys Zacharopoulos, Olivier Zahm, John Zinsser, Andrea Zittel.

Apologies to anyone I have inadvertently overlooked.

My appreciation to Lionel Bovier for believing in the possibility of this book.

Affection for my half-sister Naomi and my nieces and nephews. My half-sister Rachel is forever in my heart.

I am grateful to John Miller for his editorial astuteness throughout the formation of this book, as well as his friendship and support since the early 1990s.

This book would not have been possible without the love and support of Lilian Tone and Olivia Costa.

Finally, this publication is dedicated to my late parents, Paula and Moshe, who sacrificed so that I might have a chance in the world.

Imprint

Edited by John Miller

EDITORIAL COORDINATION AND COPY-EDITING
Clare Manchester

DESIGN CONCEPT
Gavillet & Rust, Geneva

DESIGN
Rémi Brandon, Vera Kaspar

TYPEFACE
Genath (www.optimo.ch)

PRINT AND BINDING
Présence Graphique, Monts (Indre-et-Loire)

PUBLISHED BY
JRP|Ringier
Limmatstrasse 270
CH–8005 Zurich
T +41 43 311 27 50
E info@jrp-ringier.com
www.jrp-ringier.com

IN CO-EDITION WITH
Les presses du réel
35, rue Colson
F–21000 Dijon
T +33 3 80 30 75 23
E info@lespressesdureel.com
www.lespressesdureel.com

ISBN 978-3-03764-195-8 (JRP|Ringier)
ISBN 978-2-84066-621-9 (Les presses du réel)

Distribution

JRP|Ringier publications are available internationally at selected bookstores and from the following distribution partners:

GERMANY AND AUSTRIA
Vice Versa Distribution GmbH, Immanuelkirchstrasse 12, D-10405 Berlin, info@vice-versa-distribution.com, www.vice-versa-distribution.com

FRANCE
Les presses du réel, 35 rue Colson, F-21000 Dijon, info@lespressesdureel.com, www.lespressesdureel.com

SWITZERLAND
AVA Verlagsauslieferung AG, Centralweg 16, CH-8910 Affoltern a.A., verlagsservice@ava.ch, www.ava.ch

UK AND OTHER EUROPEAN COUNTRIES
Cornerhouse Publications, 70 Oxford Street, UK-Manchester M1 5NH, publications@cornerhouse.org, www.cornerhouse.org/books

USA, CANADA, ASIA, AND AUSTRALIA
ARTBOOK|D.A.P., 155 Sixth Avenue, 2nd Floor, USA-New York, NY 10013, dap@dapinc.com, www.artbook.com

For a list of our partner bookshops or for any general questions, please contact JRP|Ringier directly at info@jrp-ringier.com, or visit our homepage www.jrp-ringier.com for further information about our program.

Documents Series 13:
Joshua Decter
Art Is a Problem

This book is the thirteenth volume in the "Documents" series, dedicated to critics' writings.

The series is directed by Lionel Bovier and Xavier Douroux.

Also available

DOCUMENTS SERIES (IN ENGLISH)

John Baldessari, *More Than You Wanted to Know About John Baldessari*
ISBN 978-3-03764-192-7 (JRP|Ringier) [*Vol. 1*]
ISBN 978-3-03764-256-6 (JRP|Ringier) [*Vol. 2*]

Raymond Bellour, *Between-the-Images*
ISBN 978-3-03764-144-6 (JRP|Ringier)
ISBN 978-2-84066-513-7 (Les presses du réel)

Joshua Decter, *Art Is a Problem*
ISBN 978-3-03764-195-8 (JRP|Ringier)
ISBN 978-2-84066-621-9 (Les presses du réel)

Gabriele Detterer & Maurizio Nannucci, *Artist-Run Spaces*
ISBN 978-3-03764-191-0 (JRP|Ringier)
ISBN 978-2-84066-512-0 (Les presses du réel)

Dorothea von Hantelmann, *How to Do Things with Art*
ISBN 978-3-03764-104-0 (JRP|Ringier)
ISBN 978-2-84066-361-4 (Les presses du réel)

Christian Höller, *Time Action Vision*
ISBN 978-3-03764-124-8 (JRP|Ringier)
ISBN 978-2-84066-396-6 (Les presses du réel)

Hans Ulrich Obrist, *A Brief History of Curating*
ISBN 978-3-905829-55-6 (JRP|Ringier)
ISBN 978-2-84066-287-7 (Les presses du réel)

Chantal Pontbriand, *Parachute: The Anthology* [*Vol. 1*]
ISBN 978-3-03764-196-5 (JRP|Ringier)
ISBN 978-2-84066-575-5 (Les presses du réel)

Igor Zabel, *Contemporary Art Theory*
ISBN 978-3-03764-238-2 (JRP|Ringier)
ISBN 978-2-84066-573-1 (Les presses du réel)